LAW, SOCIETY AND POLITICAL CULTURE IN LATE MEDIEVAL AND REFORMATION GERMANY

Manchester University Press

Manchester Medieval Sources Series

Series editors Jonathan Lyon, Sarah Davis-Secord and Simon MacLean

This series provides translations of key sources that are directly usable in students' own work, with accessible and contextual introductions and helpful annotations throughout. The books meet a growing need amongst students and teachers by providing texts central to medieval studies courses and focus upon the diverse cultural, social and political conditions that affected the functioning of all levels of society. The series welcomes a range of sources from across Europe and the Mediterranean. Volumes can be comprised of one or two longer narrative works or collections of shorter texts, including documents. Proposals for new volumes should be accompanied by sample introductory material and examples of annotated translation.

To buy or to find out more about the books currently available in this series, please go to: https://manchesteruniversitypress.co.uk/series/manchester-medieval-sources/

Medieval Sources *online*

Complementing the printed editions of the Medieval Sources series, Manchester University Press has developed a web-based learning resource which is now available on a yearly subscription basis.

Medieval Sources *online* brings quality history source material to the desktops of students and teachers and allows them open and unrestricted access throughout the entire college or university campus. Designed to be fully integrated with academic courses, this is a one-stop answer for many medieval history students, academics and researchers keeping thousands of pages of source material 'in print' over the Internet for research and teaching.

For further information and subscription prices, see *https://manchesteruniversitypress.co.uk/manchester-medieval-sources-online/*

LAW, SOCIETY AND POLITICAL CULTURE IN LATE MEDIEVAL AND REFORMATION GERMANY

Selected sources translated and edited by Duncan Hardy

MANCHESTER UNIVERSITY PRESS

Copyright © Duncan Hardy 2025

The right of Duncan Hardy to be identified as the author of this work has been asserted by them in accordance with the Copyright, Designs and Patents Act 1988.

Published by Manchester University Press
Oxford Road, Manchester, M13 9PL

www.manchesteruniversitypress.co.uk

British Library Cataloguing-in-Publication Data
A catalogue record for this book is available from the British Library

ISBN 978 1 5261 6587 9 hardback
ISBN 978 1 5261 6589 3 paperback

First published 2025

The publisher has no responsibility for the persistence or accuracy of URLs for any external or third-party internet websites referred to in this book, and does not guarantee that any content on such websites is, or will remain, accurate or appropriate.

EU authorised representative for GPSR:
Easy Access System Europe, Mustamäe tee 50, 10621 Tallinn, Estonia
gpsr.requests@easproject.com

Typeset
by Cheshire Typesetting Ltd, Cuddington, Cheshire

TABLE OF CONTENTS

Preface and editorial principles	x
Maps	xiii
List of romano-german kings and emperors (1273–1564)	xv
Introduction	1

I: The imperial monarchy in theory and practice

1. The 'Two Swords Theory' in the *Swabian Mirror* (thirteenth–fifteenth centuries) — 29
2. The origins of the Holy Roman Empire and its transfer to the Germans in the *Nuremberg Chronicle* (1493) — 31
3. The procedure for electing a monarch in Peter of Andlau's *Little Book about the Imperial Monarchy* (1460) — 34
4. A chronicle account of Emperor Charles IV's peace-keeping approach (late fourteenth century) — 37
5. The deposition of King Wenceslas (1400) — 38
6. King Sigismund's staging of royal authority in Ulrich Richental's chronicle (1417) — 44
7. A letter of Emperor Frederick III requesting troops from the imperial cities (1475) — 48
8. King Maximilian I's exhortations to an imperial diet in Constance (1507) — 51
9. An electoral contract between the electors and King Charles V (1519) — 55

II: Assemblies and ordinances to the mid-fifteenth century

10. Aeneas Silvius Piccolomini's observations about German diets in a letter to Juan Carvajal (1444) — 68

11. King Wenceslas summons Strasbourg's envoys to a diet in Nuremberg (1383) — 70
12. The electors summon Strasbourg's envoys to a diet in Nuremberg (1422) — 72
13. Emperor Frederick III summons the imperial princes to a diet in Regensburg (1454) — 74
14. The 'Golden Bull' (1356) — 76
15. The imperial land-peace and alliance issued at a diet in Eger (1389) — 98
16. A planned levy at a diet in Nuremberg for the war against the Hussites (1422) — 107
17. A peace-ordinance promulgated at a diet in Frankfurt (the 'Royal Reformation') (1442) — 116

III: Conflict, compromise and constitutional change at the imperial diets, 1467–1555

18. An urban envoy reports on the negotiating process at an imperial diet (1487) — 132
19. Maximilian I summons the estates to an imperial diet in Augsburg (1509) — 139
20. Peace-ordinances promulgated at imperial diets in Nuremberg, Regensburg and Frankfurt (1467–86) — 142
21. A peace-ordinance promulgated at an imperial diet in Worms (the 'Perpetual Public Peace') (1495) — 148
22. An ordinance promulgated at an imperial diet in Worms establishing the new imperial cameral court (1495) — 155
23. A treaty for 'the administration of peace and justice' promulgated at an imperial diet in Worms (1495) — 168
24. An ordinance to create an imperial governing council promulgated at an imperial diet in Augsburg (1500) — 173
25. An ordinance to expand the imperial circles promulgated at an imperial diet in Trier and Cologne (1512) — 187
26. A peace-ordinance promulgated at an imperial diet in Worms (1521) — 190

TABLE OF CONTENTS

27. The recess of an imperial diet in Speyer (1526)	193
28. The full protestation of the evangelical estates at an imperial diet in Speyer (1529)	199
29. A peace agreement and recess between Emperor Charles V and the evangelical estates (1532)	207
30. The imperial recess from an imperial diet in Augsburg (the 'Peace of Augsburg') (1555)	212

IV: Imagining political and religious reform

31. King Sigismund calls for the reformation of the Church and Empire in a summons to an assembly (1417)	229
32. *The Reformation of Emperor Sigismund* (1439)	231
33. The proposals of an archbishop of Trier for reforming the Holy Roman Empire (1452)	241
34. *The Little Book of One Hundred Chapters with Forty Statutes* (c. 1490–1510)	250
35. Martin Luther, *To the Christian Nobility of the German Nation Concerning the Improvement of the Christian Estate* (1520)	256
36. The 'grievances of the German nation' at an imperial diet in Speyer (1526)	262

V: Alliances and associations

37. An alliance and land-peace in Swabia (1356)	273
38. The eternal alliance of Zurich, Lucerne, Uri, Schwyz and Unterwalden (1351)	277
39. An alliance of the six German electors (1424)	281
40. An alliance of Hanseatic cities (1443)	284
41. The first treaty of the Swabian League (1487)	288
42. An association of the prelates, knighthood and towns of the duchy of Mecklenburg (1523)	293
43. The founding treaty of the Schmalkaldic League (1531)	296

TABLE OF CONTENTS

VI: Feuding, warfare and arbitration

44. The feud-declaration of Wolf of Wunnenstein against Strasbourg (1395) — 305
45. The feud-declaration of Count Ulrich V of Württemberg against Esslingen (1449) — 306
46. The arbitrated settlement of the 'Margravial War' (1450) — 308
47. The arbitrated settlement of the war between Abbess Hedwig of Quedlinburg and Bishop Gebhard of Halberstadt (1477) — 313
48. The imperial condemnation of Götz of Berlichingen and his allies for violating the public peace (1512) — 316
49. A letter of safe-conduct to arbitrational proceedings at an imperial diet in Augsburg (1555) — 318

VII: Law, gendered rules and social discipline

50. The *Swabian Mirror* on feudal law and the fluidity and entanglement of lordship for men, women and clerics (thirteenth–fifteenth centuries) — 327
51. Three prisoners' commitments to the lords of Henneberg in exchange for their release (1401) — 331
52. Fragmented and entangled properties and jurisdictions in the Black Forest (1427) — 332
53. 'Unwritten' customary law and peasant agency in the village of Wagenschwend (1435) — 334
54. A land-ordinance for Thuringia issued by a duke of Saxony and the Thuringian nobility and towns (1446) — 336
55. An ordinance for the policing of prostitutes in Strasbourg (1471) — 341
56. Nuremberg's *Reformation of Statutes and Laws* and the oath for the city's Jews (1484) — 343
57. Compensating for sexual violence in a land-ordinance for Baden (1495) — 347
58. Sumptuary laws in an imperial recess (1500) — 348

TABLE OF CONTENTS

59. The preamble to the first Empire-wide criminal code (1532) — 351
60. Incorporating the imperial public peace into the *Bavarian Land-Ordinance* (1553) — 352

Glossary — 353
Bibliography — 358
Index — 365

PREFACE AND EDITORIAL PRINCIPLES

This book aims to fill a specific gap: the near-total lack of sources in English translation from the late medieval Holy Roman Empire. Between the mid-fourteenth and mid-sixteenth centuries, the German-speaking lands of the Empire were the stage for some of the most significant developments in Europe, from ecclesiastical councils that mooted sweeping reforms, to the rise of the Habsburg dynasty to continental pre-eminence and the early stages of the movements that historians now call 'the Reformation(s)'. These developments are all the more fascinating because they unfolded within political and social structures that sometimes differed substantially from those in the Western European kingdoms and polities held up as normative in most historiography, and especially in the textbook literature for general audiences. While the sixty sources that follow can only provide a selective and partial picture of political and social life across two centuries of German history, I hope that they offer enough of a window into this region's unique facets and dynamics to help end the status of late medieval Europe east of the Rhine and north of the Alps as a *terra incognita* for Anglophone readers.

The translations in this book are a mixture of extracts and texts in their entirety. In the latter case, my aim has been to enable readers to understand key passages in the context of the entire source. This is especially important for those legal and political texts that were hugely significant in the history of the Empire, such as major ordinances promulgated at the imperial diets, yet – as is true of almost all the sources in this book – have never been translated into English before. There is, however, a balance to be struck between providing these sources in their entirety and keeping this sourcebook within a reasonable length. In some cases, I have opted to paraphrase some sections while translating the most influential or revealing passages in full. All paraphrased or abridged passages are indicated by square brackets. I have also used square brackets to provide biographical details about the historical figures mentioned in the documents and to provide chapter and verse references for Biblical quotations and allusions. The numbering of articles and sub-sections in many of the sources follows that in the cited edition of the text in its original language. (Most of the sources themselves – whether they were written by a scribe on parchment or paper or, in a few cases, printed – do not include this numbering.) All people's names are given in the original German (but with regularised modern German spelling, where applicable), except in the cases of those kings and emperors whose names have well established English versions. Likewise, place names are given in modern German, unless they are widely known by a different name in English (e.g. Nuremberg). Wherever possible, I have sought an English equivalent to context-specific German terms. For unusual or ambiguous terms, I have included explanations in footnotes or included the word(s) in the Glossary. Its entries provide the German vocabulary to which the English terms equate.

I should acknowledge that the translations that follow are those of a historian, not a linguist or literary scholar. In other words, while I hope that my familiarity with the history and evidentiary record of the late medieval German lands has enabled precise, well-contextualised translations that hew closely to the original meanings of the texts, they may well lack the elegance that a scholar more attuned to their aesthetic qualities could provide. These are mostly legal texts, so – as with legal writing in any period – their language is jargon-ridden and repetitive, often aiming for forcefulness and exhaustivity over beauty or subtlety, though they certainly contain their share of rhetorically rich and ideologically charged passages. The sources' penchant for interminable sentences, which frequently reiterate the same lightly reformulated ideas several times, and embed endless qualifications within subordinate clauses, does not lend itself to sharp and stylish translation. Still, I hope that the extracts that follow will at least convey the cadence and rhythm of Middle High, Middle Low and Early New High German legal and political writing, offering a taste of the discomfiting yet instructive experience of reading the texts in their original languages. Needless to say, specialists in the field will want to look at the original sources to discover the nuances, uncertainties and potential alternative readings of the texts for themselves.

All historical research is to some extent a collaborative exercise, undertaken with the help of a community of fellow scholars, past and present, but this is especially true of translating and editing sources. One cannot simply skip past challenging passages, but must always be extending one's familiarity with even the most obscure facets of the languages and societies under study to discern the most plausible, context-specific meanings of a text. For this, the expertise of others is invaluable. I warmly thank all the historians, linguists, archivists and librarians – more than I can name here – who provided insights into difficult concepts and passages, in person or on social media. Several anonymous peer reviewers offered very useful feedback in the early and late stages of this book's creation. In particular, two reviewers kindly went through large sections of the complete manuscript in the course of 2024 and provided extensive and valuable comments that have helped me to avoid some embarrassing errors. I am also very grateful to Alexandra Kaar and Oren Margolis for generously reading and commenting on some of my translations. Jonathan Lyon and Len Scales have offered encouragement and support for this project at every stage of its development. Finally, I gratefully acknowledge the help and encouragement of Meredith Carroll, Siobhán Poole and Laura Swift at Manchester University Press. The responsibility for any remaining errors and infelicities in the translations that follow lies entirely with me.

MAPS

Map 1 Major principalities and customary regions of the Holy Roman Empire *c.* 1350–1550. Borders are not shown owing to constant shifts, enclaves and overlapping jurisdictions.

Keys:

Customary regions (based on historical identities, culture and language, but not politically unified)

Temporal principalities (ruled by a dynasty and princely government, but sub-divided among multiple dynastic branches for some or all of this period)

Spiritual principalities (ruled by a bishop or abbot)

• Seats of princely government

MAPS

Map 2 Major free and imperial cities of the Holy Roman Empire c. 1350–1550.

LIST OF ROMANO-GERMAN KINGS AND EMPERORS (1273–1564)

Key
(A) = disputed election (sometimes called an 'anti-king')
(H) = from the family that we now call the 'Habsburgs'
(L) = from the family that we now call the 'Luxemburgs'
(W) = from the family that we now call the 'Wittelsbachs'

Rudolf I (elected and crowned king 1273, died 1291) (H)

Adolf I (elected and crowned king 1292, deposed 1298, died 1298)

Albert I (elected and crowned king 1298, died 1308) (H)

Henry VII (elected 1308, crowned king 1309, crowned emperor 1312, died 1313) (L)

Frederick 'the Fair' (elected and crowned king 1314, died 1330) (H) (A)

Ludwig IV 'the Bavarian' (elected and crowned king 1314, crowned emperor 1328, died 1347) (W)

Charles IV (elected and crowned king 1346, re-crowned king 1349, crowned emperor 1355, died 1378) (L)

Günther of Schwarzburg (elected and crowned king 1349, died 1349) (A)

Wenceslas (elected and crowned king 1376, deposed 1400, died 1419) (L)

Rupert I (elected and crowned king 1400, died 1410) (W) (A)

Jobst of Moravia (elected 1410, never crowned, died 1411) (L) (A)

Sigismund (minority candidate 1410, elected 1411, crowned king 1414, crowned emperor 1433, died 1437) (L)

Albert II (elected 1438, never crowned, died 1439) (H)

LIST OF ROMANO-GERMAN KINGS AND EMPERORS

Frederick III (elected 1440, crowned king 1442, crowned emperor 1452, died 1493) (H)

Maximilian I (elected and crowned king 1486, proclaimed emperor 1508, died 1519) (H)

Charles V (elected 1519, crowned king 1520, crowned emperor 1530, abdicated 1556, died 1558) (H)

Ferdinand I (elected and crowned king 1531, proclaimed emperor 1556, died 1564) (H)

INTRODUCTION

Until quite recently, there was very little coverage of medieval and early modern Germany in the English language. In 1894 the historian Ernest Henderson lamented: 'And yet what do the ordinary English or American readers know of the medieval German Empire, or, to give it the full title it enjoyed when in its prime, of the Holy Roman Empire of the German nation?'[1] Half a century later the situation had not improved. As he put the finishing touches to his classic work on the origins of modern Germany in the waning years of the Second World War, Geoffrey Barraclough highlighted pre-modern German history as a 'gap' that 'remained to be filled' for Anglophone readers.[2] As late as 1986, it was still justifiable to observe that 'most English-speaking scholars have ignored German scholarship' of the Middle Ages.[3]

Happily, the picture has changed rapidly in the early twenty-first century. Many more scholars in British and North American universities have engaged with medieval and early modern German topics, producing both cutting-edge research and accessible overviews.[4] To this flourishing Anglophone secondary literature can be added a growing body of translated primary sources, although these relate mostly to the early and high medieval periods, or else to the religious and social upheavals of the sixteenth and seventeenth centuries.[5] In particular, there are virtually no translations of the abundant primary sources stemming from the late medieval Romano-German kings' and emperors' activities and the growth of legal and governmental institutions at all levels (especially at the emerging representative assemblies known as the imperial diets),

---

1 Henderson, *History of Germany*, p. viii.
2 Barraclough, *Origins of Modern Germany*, p. x.
3 Freed, 'Reflections', p. 554.
4 See, for example, Scales, *German Identity*; Whaley, *Germany*; Wilson, *Holy Roman Empire*; Stollberg-Rilinger, *Holy Roman Empire*.
5 See, for example, Warner (ed./trans.), *Ottonian Germany*; Lyon (ed./trans.), *Noble Society*; Scott and Scribner (eds/trans.), *German Peasants' War*; Wilson (ed./trans), *Thirty Years War*.

not to mention the social and cultural effects of this institutionalisation. Even for the early sixteenth century, which is well covered from a religious perspective through numerous English editions of the German and Swiss reformers' writings, there are few translations of the sources pertaining to the momentous changes then afoot in the Holy Roman Empire's political institutions. In short, even the most essential primary sources related to German legal, political and social history between the mid-fourteenth and mid-sixteenth centuries have remained largely inaccessible to English readers. The purpose of this book is to rectify that situation.

The surviving evidence from late medieval Germany is not only worth studying for its own sake. The entity known as the Holy Roman Empire was of central importance to European history. Studying its political and legal culture can help expand and modify interpretations of the continent in this period that have all too often been skewed by a disproportionate focus on Western Europe. The Empire's notional borders extended from what is now northern Italy to Denmark, and from eastern France and Belgium to Poland and Hungary, wholly or partially encompassing some fifteen modern-day European countries. The noble houses whose members competed to secure the Romano-German crown in the fourteenth, fifteenth and sixteenth centuries – most notably the Luxemburgs and the Habsburgs – were among the most prominent dynasties in Europe, with titles and influence that extended far beyond the Holy Roman Empire's German-speaking core. Commercial routes along the Rhine and Danube rivers and their tributaries, as well as the North Sea and Baltic littorals, produced clusters of some of the wealthiest and most politically ambitious cities north of the Alps. The many secular and ecclesiastical principalities and lordships in the German lands also enjoyed substantial autonomy. Together with the cities, German princes and lords were able to demand an increasingly formal role in decision-making in concert with the monarchy, most obviously at the emerging representative institutions known as the 'imperial diets' (*Reichstage*) by the end of the fifteenth century, endowing the Holy Roman Empire with a uniquely decentralised and multilateral political and legal order. Many of this period's most significant conflicts were also fought in the lands of the Empire, from the 'Town War' of the 1380s, through the Hussite Wars (*c.* 1420–34) and the Burgundian Wars (1474–77), to the Schmalkaldic War (1546–47). Finally, the

INTRODUCTION

Empire's peculiar political landscape ensured that the many religious controversies of this era played out with particular ferocity in the German lands – from the Papal Schism (1378–1417), through the general councils of Constance (1414–18) and Basel (1431–49) and the accompanying struggles between conciliarists and papalists, to the emergence of evangelical reform movements pioneered by the likes of Martin Luther.

The sources in this book shed light on all of these developments, and many others. Its first priority is to offer the reader access to a selection of key sources relating to the monarchs and institutions of the Holy Roman Empire between the reigns of Charles IV (1346–78) and Charles V (1519–56). Section I showcases popular theories about royal authority and the passage of the Roman imperial title to the Germans, as well as highlighting the behaviours and obligations of the most prominent kings and emperors of this period. In a decentralised realm like the Empire, monarchs were only one part of the political system, as a matter of pragmatism and increasingly also in the developing imperial laws and institutions. Sections II and III therefore highlight how the monarchs acted in concert with the most prominent political actors among the German princes and other 'members' or 'estates' of the Empire to manage imperial administration and change its governmental framework. This took place at assemblies, which were increasingly known as diets (*Tage*) and then imperial diets (*Reichstage*), and at which legislative ordinances were promulgated with increasing frequency as the late medieval period wore on. The ongoing resort to collective treaties and ordinances at imperial diets continued into the sixteenth century, even after the estates were divided between Catholics and adherents of the new evangelical confessions. All of the major ordinances of the Holy Roman Empire between 1356 and 1555 can be found in translation in this book, including the critical 'reformist' legislation promulgated around the year 1495. From a long-term perspective, these two centuries saw extensive political change, although it mostly unfolded gradually and with significant compromise among all involved. The recurrent crises facing the German lands prompted some learned commentators to envision more urgent or radical changes, sometimes articulated in terms of a 'reformation' of the Empire and the Church. Excerpts of their arguments and ideas can be found in section IV.

This 'upper layer' of government in the Holy Roman Empire, consisting of the assemblies, laws and institutions that pertained to the polity in its entirety, was only a small part of a much larger and more complex political landscape. The elites who assembled at the diets each had their own power bases, some much larger and more consolidated than others. Beside the princes, lords and cities who answered only to the monarch and participated in the diets was a broader array of somewhat less independent nobles and towns in the localities. All of these political actors had both horizontal and vertical ties to one another and their subjects. In the Holy Roman Empire, horizontal relationships were often more formalised than in other realms, and section V contains a variety of sources that demonstrate the ways in which German political elites regulated their interactions through treaties and contracts. The late medieval period saw frequent low-level feuding as well, and occasionally larger-scale armed conflicts, which tended to find resolution through nearby parties mediating and organising formal arbitrational summits. These dynamics are illustrated in section VI. The individual units within the Empire – towns, principalities, bishoprics, noble lordships and, ultimately, villages – formed the main administrative framework at the local level and tended to become more consolidated over time (although this varied dramatically between different German regions). A sense of the gradual codification of customary law, judicial procedures and methods of delineating jurisdiction at local and regional levels, as well as how these processes intersected with the overarching imperial framework, is conveyed in the sources of section VII. The agencies behind this codification and consolidation also sought to regulate aspects of everyday life, such as normative behaviour for men and women of various different statuses and public religious morality, and some of the legislative sources in this section reflect these aspirations.

Each section of this book begins with an introduction that provides the reader with background information on the topics that link together its selection of primary sources, placing them in historical context and summarising relevant historiographical debates. First, however, the concepts and scope of 'the Holy Roman Empire' and 'Germany' require a little more exploration – in terms of how late medieval and early modern people understood them, and how modern historians have debated the most plausible and accurate interpretations of German-speaking Central Europe. We will also examine the nature of the surviving evidence that enables historians to study the German lands of the Empire, and from which the sources in this book have been selected.

Defining and debating the 'Holy Roman Empire' and 'Germany'

The entity that had come to be known as the Holy Roman Empire in the time period covered by this book traced its origins to the Frankish empire of Charlemagne (r. 768–814). At the outset of Charlemagne's reign, the title of 'Roman emperor' had disappeared from Western Europe for several centuries, although the rulers of the Eastern Roman/Byzantine Empire continued to use it. In 800 Charlemagne resurrected the imperial title in a coronation in Rome, with the collaboration of the pope, and each subsequent senior Frankish ruler styled himself *imperator augustus*. The Frankish empire split into multiple realms in the course of the ninth century, and in the tenth it was a Saxon noble family, known to us as the Ottonians, which perpetuated the imperial title in the West. The Ottonians and their successors in the eleventh to early thirteenth centuries, the Salian and Staufer dynasties, ruled an 'empire' in which most inhabitants spoke German dialects, centred on modern-day Germany, Switzerland, Austria and parts of Belgium and the Netherlands. It also included French- and Italian-speaking regions, in areas of the former kingdoms of Burgundy and Italy, as well as the emerging Czech kingdom of Bohemia. However, the enemies of the Salian and Staufer monarchs – including, frequently, the popes, with whom they struggled for supremacy over parts of Italy and over authority within the Church hierarchy – could plausibly diminish their imperial claims by labelling them as a mere 'king of the Germans' (*rex Teutonicorum* or *rex Alemannorum*). The intertwined 'Roman' and 'German' identities of the polity forged by the Ottonians and their successors are the basis for modern historians' neologism 'Romano-German' (*römisch-deutsch*) as an adjective for this nebulous realm and its monarchy. In the course of the twelfth century, learned members of the imperial court and chancery began to employ the concept of a 'holy emperor' and 'holy empire'. This terminology ultimately stemmed from Byzantium. The entourage of Frederick I 'Barbarossa' (r. 1152–90) encountered and adopted it through that monarch's frequent contacts with clerics in Italy.

By the mid-thirteenth century, 'Holy Empire', 'Roman Empire' and 'Holy Roman Empire' (*sacrum Romanum imperium*, *heiliges römisches Reich*) were all in common usage in both Latin and the vernacular to describe the political entity ruled by the Staufer monarchs.[6]

Alongside the crystallisation of this nomenclature, more fundamental transformations were underway within the imperial polity. In the tenth to twelfth centuries, the Romano-German monarchs presided over a relatively centralised royal administration (compared to the contemporary situation in France, for instance) and sought to project a highly exalted and sacralised image of themselves. While dukes, counts, bishops and other nobles enjoyed substantial autonomy in some respects, these elites were beholden to the monarch in many areas of political life. This dynamic changed considerably during the thirteenth and fourteenth centuries. Already under the last major Staufer emperor, Frederick II (r. 1212–50), the leading princes obtained more formal recognition of their authority within their localities and as custodians of judicial administration and peace-keeping in the core German regions of the Empire.[7] A political crisis following the extinction of the Staufer in 1254 and a twenty-year 'Interregnum' (characterised by weak monarchical candidates with only partial support) further cemented the agency of the princes and other prominent title-holding nobles and communes in imperial government.

In particular, it became a matter of established custom that a select group of electors (*electores*, *Kurfürsten*) should choose each new monarch. Even after the partial stabilisation of royal administration by Rudolf I (r. 1273–91), a count of Habsburg elevated to the throne by the electors, the elective principle remained intact. Subsequent generations of electors would assert it throughout the late Middle Ages and into the early modern period. They chose each new 'king of the Romans' (*rex Romanorum*, *römischer König*) and oversaw his coronation, conventionally in Aachen, Charlemagne's old seat of government. Some but not all kings went on to acquire the title of emperor (*imperator*, *Kaiser*) through coronation by a pope, usually in Rome. Until the longer and more stable reign of Ludwig IV 'the Bavarian' (1314–47) the electors

6 Sulovsky, '*Sacrum imperium*'.
7 See Arnold, *Princes and Territories*.

arguably dominated political events, selecting one minor count or duke after another, resulting in frequent civil wars between rival candidates in the decades around 1300. In parallel with these turbulent events in electoral high politics, this period also saw more profound structural shifts in the political landscape. The thirteenth and fourteenth centuries witnessed the rapid proliferation of free and imperial cities answerable only to the monarchy. At the local level, structures of lordship became more fragmented and complex, as feudal tenure and other flexible methods of ownership of lands, revenues and judicial powers enabled the transfer, disaggregation and recombination of properties and jurisdictions within networks of nobles, clerics and burghers.[8]

Thus, by the period beginning in the mid-fourteenth century, the Holy Roman Empire was a highly decentralised and multipolar political entity. Its monarchy was still symbolically central, as it underpinned much of the conceptual apparatus that animated the Empire: the king or emperor was the bearer of the Roman imperial office, the head of the hierarchy of fief-grantors (*Heerschildordnung*) and the ultimate fount of law and justice, from whom many regalian rights (from criminal jurisdiction to coin minting) were notionally delegated. Possibilities remained for monarchs to direct and intervene in the Empire, despite their dwindling public resources and increasing reliance on personal and hereditary power (*Hausmacht*) [4, 6–8].[9] In practice, however, and increasingly in legal theory too, a cast of other political elites claimed a stake in imperial governance at the highest levels. We have just seen that the electors self-consciously adopted this role in the post-Staufer decades. Their power to elevate a new king of the Romans by majority election was formalised in the 1338 Declaration of Rhens, which rejected any requirement for papal approval of the electoral outcome, and in the 1356 Golden Bull [14]. The latter compendium of laws codified the procedures for election and the status and obligations of the seven electors: the archbishops of Mainz, Trier and Cologne, the Count Palatine of the Rhine, the duke of Saxony, the margrave of Brandenburg and the king of Bohemia. They would remain major protagonists in German politics throughout and beyond the period covered by this book.

---

8 On changing structures of lordship, see Rösener, 'Die Grundherrschaft'.
9 Isenmann, 'König oder Monarch?'.

The electors were just one exclusive group within a much larger body of dukes, margraves, landgraves and prelates claiming the status of 'prince' (*princeps*, *Fürst*), most of whom presided over substantial power bases of their own. In the case of the ninety or so archbishops, bishops, abbots and abbesses who answered directly to the crown throughout the late medieval and early modern periods, these power bases were often relatively stable, albeit subject to disputes with cathedral chapters, split episcopal elections and vicious power struggles with major urban centres. A smaller and more fluctuant number of secular, dynastic principalities also dominated the political landscape. These were more vulnerable to partition, conquest and familial extinction, but also typically much larger and wealthier than episcopal and monastic lordships. Less influential, but nonetheless significant, especially as contributors of troops and ad hoc taxes or loans to imperial initiatives, were counts, lords and barons (*[Frei-]herren*), and free and imperial cities that were *reichsunmittelbar* ('imperially immediate', i.e. subject to the crown and *Reich* without intermediate lords).[10] Princes, the upper nobility and city councils employed an array of petty nobles as retainers, squires or military servitors. Alongside an increasing number of educated administrators, the lower and middling nobility also frequently served as officers or representatives of more powerful rulers. In regions such as Franconia, the knighthood collectively defended its imperially immediate status even as its members sought employment with nearby princes.[11]

What of the rest of society – people who were neither imperially immediate authorities, nor members of the noble, urban patrician or university-trained elite that served those authorities? As elsewhere in pre-modern Europe, the majority of people were peasants of some kind. In the surviving sources from the fourteenth to sixteenth centuries, the mass of rural inhabitants tended to be categorised broadly as 'subjects', 'subordinates' or 'residents' (*Untertanen, Hintersassen, Einwohner*), who – in principle – had little political or legal agency. Yet these sweeping terms encompassed an array of often quite stratified groups, whose status and ability to shape their own lives and situations varied widely across

---

10 For a recent collection of essays in English on these themes, see Loud and Schenk (eds), *The Origins*.
11 Schneider, *Spätmittelalterlicher deutscher Niederadel*.

INTRODUCTION

Germany's diverse topographical and seigneurial landscapes. Male tenant farmers with representation in their village communes (the group sometimes, though not always, denoted by the word *Bauern*) experienced quite different social, economic and legal circumstances from those men and women who were serfs or bondspeople (*Leibeigene*), and even serfdom took divergent forms in different regions.[12] Particularly in southern and western Germany, assertive rural communes had room for manoeuvre within institutionalising but perennially fragmented lordly and princely regimes to negotiate favourable seigneurial and judicial customs for themselves [53]. The 'Peasants' War' of 1524–26 [36] was only the most extreme demonstration of the self-conscious social identities and political and legal aspirations that village and small-town residents could adopt, often under the widely shared label of 'the common man' (*der gemeine Mann*).[13]

Readers have probably noticed by now that most of the protagonists in the political and social world of the Holy Roman Empire appear to have been male. This would not be an inaccurate impression. Certainly, the office of king or emperor of the Romans was only ever held by men (owing to its elective, rather than hereditary, principle of succession). Territorial administrations and the imperial diets were mostly male spaces, although princely and noble women often wielded at least informal influence on the government of their husbands' and sons' patrimonies.[14] (Also, the Golden Bull [14] briefly acknowledges the ceremonial roles played by empresses and queens of the Romans at imperial gatherings, which must have entailed much more expansive influence behind the scenes.) Political and social interactions were encased in a masculine-coded economy of honour, which can be witnessed at its most explicit in the feud-declarations of noblemen [44–45].[15] Where women are mentioned in imperial, territorial or urban legislation in this period, it is often with reference to social discipline; for example, through sumptuary laws that sought to ban extravagant clothing (for people of both genders) [58] or the regulation of brothels and the sex workers who inhabited them [55]. In short,

12 Scott, *Society and Economy*, pp. 48–55, 166–97.
13 Blickle, *From the Communal Revolution*.
14 On female participation in government, see Rückert, Thaller and Oschema (eds), *Starke Frauen?* with further references.
15 On masculine honour and the feud, see Zmora, *The Feud*.

this was a patriarchal world. Yet, as research in the field of medieval women's and gender history has repeatedly shown, resourceful women could find ways to assert their agency and shape their life options in specific contexts, even in the face of oppressive attitudes and institutions.[16] Even the normative sources for feudal law had to allow for the possibility that a high-status woman might hold lands, revenues or jurisdictions in one form or another, if notionally on behalf of other family members [50]. Abbesses could exercise formal seigneurial and political powers even more freely, since some convents were imperially immediate, making possible careers like that of Abbess Hedwig of Quedlinburg (1458–1511), who engaged in the same practices and dynamics of arbitration and warfare as her male princely counterparts [47].

In the two centuries encompassed by this book, the role of the governing elites in the Holy Roman Empire became gradually more formalised and institutionalised. In the course of the fifteenth century the concept of the 'Empire' expanded not only to mean a vague universal authority and a more defined area within Europe under the rule of the Romano-German monarchy, but also to refer to the collection of princes, nobles and cities who labelled themselves as imperial 'members' (*membra/latera, Glieder*) and, later on, 'estates' (*status/ordines, Stände*) that embodied the Holy Roman Empire and the German lands or nation within it. The identification of the *Reich* with its leading members was driven by the emergence of pan-imperial institutions at their behest: diets and collective peace-ordinances and treaties in the fourteenth and fifteenth centuries [10–21]; and an imperial cameral court and co-ordinated districts or circles, among other innovations, between 1495 and the mid-sixteenth century [21–26, 30].[17] Although the product of extensive political wrangling and compromise between the estates and monarchs, and within different factions among the princes and cities, this iterative framework of interlocking laws and institutions created at the imperial level proved durable. This was in large part because it was not created by fiat 'top-down', as modern compendia of German constitutional documents risk implying, but developed organically from the political culture of diverse localities, borrowing concepts from and delegating powers

---

16 Bennett and Karras, 'Women, Gender, and Medieval Historians'.
17 See Schubert, *König und Reich*; Moraw, *Von offener Verfassung*.

to a regional apparatus of urban and princely jurisdictions and peace-keeping leagues that consolidated in parallel with the Holy Roman Empire's multilateral framework [37, 41, 60].[18]

This imperial framework was severely tested in the 1520s to 1550s by the Reformation, as a substantial minority of princes and cities embraced evangelical teachings and rejected the claims of the monarchs and estates to be able to regulate religious affairs [28]. Its flexibility and resilience is attested by the way in which, for all their intractable religious differences, the estates eventually found ways to apply the functions and logic of the diets and peace-keeping ordinances and treaties to enable a *modus vivendi* that largely preserved the political and legal order inherited from the late Middle Ages [29–30]. The tendency of historians to separate the 'medieval' from the 'early modern' sometime around the year 1500 has obscured these continuities, and it is hoped that readers of this book will profit from examining the late medieval and sixteenth-century evidence side-by-side, regardless of whether their primary interests lie in the Middle Ages or the Reformation era.

Throughout this period, the monarch and princes presided over a primarily German realm and political community, and they increasingly identified it as such, even as they maintained their universal imperial pretensions. Since at least the mid-thirteenth century, literate inhabitants of the Holy Roman Empire had explicitly tied their polity to notions of 'Germanness'.[19] The relationship between 'Germany' and 'the Empire' was complex and multifaceted, and evolved over time. We have seen that the division of the Carolingian empire caused the imperial title to pass to Germanophone monarchs whose core support stemmed from German-speaking regions such as Saxony, Franconia and Swabia. Although the high medieval kings and emperors emphasised the universal and sacral quality of their Roman imperial office, their opponents deflated their pretensions by identifying them instead with a putative 'German' kingdom. After the Staufer era, this German association shed any lingering pejorative implication. Political actors and chroniclers in the Empire referred to the 'German lands' as a matter of course (*deutsche[n] Lande[n]* in the vernacular – rendered variously as *Germania, Alemannia,*

---

18 See Hardy, *Associative Political Culture*.
19 For the themes in this paragraph see Scales, *German Identity*, especially chapters 4–6.

Teutonia and even occasionally as *regnum Teutonicorum* in Latin). That these German lands formed a coherent if imprecisely delineated core of the imperial polity, in which the most politically engaged nobles and communes were all of the German tongue, was an uncontroversial and obvious reality, despite the Empire's claims over Bohemia, northern Italy, Lorraine and elsewhere. The conceptual anchoring of the imperial polity in Germany in no way lessened the potency or plausibility of residual claims to Roman and Christian leadership. On the contrary, these claims were underpinned by the flattering notion that the virtuous German people (above all its warrior aristocracy, the nobility and princes) had been chosen by divine providence to receive the mantle of imperial rule, passed on from the Romans (via the Byzantine Greeks) through the classical and Biblical tradition of *translatio imperii* [2].

To the vaguely spatial label of the 'German lands', inhabitants of the Empire increasingly added the communitarian idea of a 'German nation' (*deutsche Nation, natio Germanica*). As with many proto-national or ethnic categories, this idea originated in ecclesiastical circles, notably to describe regional groupings of students at universities and the Central European clergy at the great international councils of Constance and Basel in the first half of the fifteenth century. By the 1450s to 1470s, letters and treaties emanating from the chanceries of most princes and cities were evoking the 'German nation' to refer to the elite community of members or estates that constituted the Empire. Soon afterwards, the formula 'Holy Roman Empire of the German nation' began to appear intermittently in connection with imperial assemblies and policies.[20] By the early decades of the sixteenth century it was employed frequently, and it seems to have acquired quasi-official status in the legal jargon of the imperial diets by the 1550s [30].

If most denizens of the Empire in the mid-fourteenth to mid-sixteenth centuries took for granted that they lived in an entity that was both imperial and German, the content of German identity was inevitably less clear and agreed upon. Germanness might be defined by language, myths of origin, supposed virtuous characteristics and much else besides.[21] Even centuries-old ideas about the Germans could be rearticulated in new ways in this period. German

20 Nonn, 'Zum Nationen-Begriff'.
21 Scales, *German Identity*.

humanists in the late fifteenth and sixteenth centuries employed rediscovered texts and new methods of source analysis pioneered in Renaissance Italy to give longstanding historical narratives empirical legitimacy, and to pit their vision of Germany against the rival patriotisms advanced by their learned counterparts in other realms in a rhetorical competition for national honour.[22] A consistent theme for Germans across time and space was the diversity of dialects and regions encompassed within their 'nation'. From Saxony to Swabia and from the Rhineland to Thuringia, regional identities rooted in their own mythologies and ethnic stereotypes could be of central importance, and this is likely to have been especially true of less literate and mobile people lower down the social hierarchy.[23] Equally, regional and national identities could co-exist readily within the same political worldview. Thus, a humanist such as Jakob Wimpfeling (1450–1528) could comfortably extol the virtues of his native Alsace while writing patriotic propaganda about Germany (*Germania*) and its worthiness to bear the Roman and Christian imperial mission.[24]

The sheer complexity of medieval and early modern 'Germany' and the Holy Roman Empire, and the difficulty of apprehending these entities with our modern vocabulary of statehood and nationhood, has given rise to spirited debates among historians since the waning years of the Empire itself, which was dissolved during the Napoleonic Wars. Scholarship of the pre-modern *Reich* has been further influenced by the ideological priorities of the various regimes in nineteenth- and twentieth-century Germany, each of which produced tendentious and sometimes dramatically divergent interpretations of the Holy Roman Empire. Even if we restrict our search to the last two generations of scholarship, beginning with the resurgence of interest in the late medieval Empire in the 1970s and 1980s, we will find multiple ongoing debates and questions, of which the following are only some of the most prominent.[25] Was the Empire a uniquely

---

22 Hirschi, *Origins of Nationalism*, chapters 5, 7–8.
23 Scales, *German Identity*, chapter 11; Graf, 'Aspekte zum Regionalismus'.
24 Mertens, 'Jakob Wimpfeling'.
25 Foundational interpretations include Schubert, *König und Reich* and Moraw, *Von offener Verfassung*. For up-to-date surveys of major debates relating to this period, see the relevant volumes in the encyclopaedic Gebhardt series: Hesse, *Synthese und Aufbruch*; Boockmann and Dormeier, *Konzilien, Kirchen- und Reichsreform*; Reinhard, *Reichsreform und Reformation*.

decentralised or dualistic entity, justifying a narrative of a German 'special path' (*Sonderweg*), or were there comparable formations elsewhere in late medieval and early modern Europe? Should the Empire be considered a 'state'? Conversely, should that term be applied to its constituent 'territories', and if so, in which chronological period is it appropriate to begin using that label for them? Can we consider the institutional reforms in the Empire around 1495 a radical turning point in German history, or do these reflect longer-term processes that continued long before and after that symbolic year? Was political and legal agency mostly restricted to princes in this period, or should we include a wide array of social groups in our analysis? Was the Reformation a 'German event' enabled by the unique political configuration of the Holy Roman Empire? The aim of this book is to allow Anglophone readers to begin to formulate their own ideas in response to these questions, and to articulate new ones – admittedly in response to a deliberately broad selection of evidence across time and social and geographical space. This selection reflects the author's conviction that the Empire is best understood through a holistic approach that takes into account multiple layers of political activity in parallel and in connection to each other, and pays attention to continuities and gradual changes over time.

The nature of the evidence from the German lands c. 1350 to 1550

It is a truism that we cannot study the past *per se*, but only the fragmentary pieces of evidence which survive from it, which we must decipher and interpret, and through which we can make imaginative attempts to reconstruct the most plausible possible understanding of a given culture and time period. In the case of late medieval German political and legal history, the most pertinent textual evidence is strewn across multiple Central European archives, reflecting the fates of the monarchy and the various principalities, lordships and cities of the Holy Roman Empire over the centuries. For example, the eventual monopoly of the imperial office attained by the Habsburgs has ensured that much of the material produced by the chancery of the kings and emperors of the Romans has ended up in Vienna, even though in the fourteenth to sixteenth centuries the monarchs were most effective in intervening in imperial politics when they pursued itineraries in core Upper German regions like Franconia, Swabia and the Rhineland. It should be stressed that the surviving documentation in Vienna, such as the imperial registry books (*Reichsregisterbücher*) containing miscellaneous privileges and mandates issued by the monarchs, constitutes only a fraction of the total material produced by the imperial chancery, and that chancery's output was fairly modest in scale compared to the more centralised and bureaucratised regimes of Western European kings. Especially for the earlier part of this period, such as the reign of Charles IV, a handful of chance survivals make tantalising references to much larger bodies of documentary evidence that must now be considered *deperdita* (sources which we know existed but are now lost).[26]

The evidence for the activities of the wider elite community of princes, lords and cities that came to regard itself as constituting the Empire and the German nation is even more fragmented, dispersed and multifarious. The imperial diets, for instance, were occasions of multilateral consultation and decision-making, so a given assembly may be attested by reports and letters written by and for dozens of princely and urban governments, and now kept in any number of regional archives. The free and imperial cities kept comparatively good records for their unusually literate governing elites, so we are often confronted with the paradox that we have a predominantly urban perspective on events in which the princes played the leading role, and the cities were only marginally influential. The documentary outcomes of collective actions at the diets, such as the issuing of legal ordinances and treaties, are reflected in the survival of multiple official copies in urban and princely archives, and the importance and effectiveness of a given legislative document can be roughly gauged from the number of copies that exist and their geographical distribution. Again, though, the distorting priorities of later generations should be factored in. Late medieval principalities such as Bavaria and Saxony, which became powerful early modern territories, and still enjoy some form of institutional continuity as federal states in contemporary Germany, have relatively coherent and well-preserved archives. By contrast, posterity has often had little incentive to preserve the records of long-extinct

---

26 See, for example, Hohensee et al. (eds), *Monumenta Germaniae Historica. Constitutiones*, p. vii.

noble families or religious institutions affected by the Reformation, however important and revealing their documentation may have been as a window into the period between *c.* 1350 and 1550.

A type of document that is often well represented in the archives, and which is very pertinent to the history of law and government, is what late medieval people called an *Urkunde*: a charter or treaty with legal force, often produced to high standards and formalised by seals or bulls.[27] We can still access large numbers of charters and treaties because their legal status made them worth preserving and copying. After the advent of printing in the mid-fifteenth century, documents that enacted important legislation for the whole Holy Roman Empire might even be distributed in printed editions. This category was very broad. Charters and treaties could range from the documentary proofs of a local transaction or grant (such as the enfeoffment of a nobleman or patrician with some minor lands or assets, or the sale or financial pledging of offices or jurisdictions) to landmark pan-imperial peace-ordinances agreed by monarchs, princes and cities collectively at major political assemblies. Often *Urkunden* cemented agreements and regulated interactions between horizontally ordered elites – such as princes, prelates, nobles and urban patricians, all of whom saw themselves as immediate 'members' of the Empire – although we must always be alert to the underlying asymmetries of wealth, power and social status that shaped relations between supposed political peers. We must also keep in mind that charters were primarily normative and prescriptive, reflecting how their creators believed things ought to happen rather than how events necessarily transpired in practice. Indeed, the repeated need to issue peace-ordinances such as those found in sections II and III attests to the difficulty of enforcing more ambitious legislative and governmental agendas. Nevertheless, even legal documents that were not respected in practice can be invaluable windows into the mentalities, ideals, assumptions and conventions of German political actors in this period.

If charters and treaties took pride of place in medieval and early modern archives, and remain an indispensable resource for the themes illustrated in this sourcebook, they were nevertheless only one type of written evidence. A much more voluminous – but

---

[27] For the next three paragraphs, see Hardy, *Associative Political Culture*, chapter 1 with further references.

unfortunately less well preserved – category consisted of all kinds of written correspondence and record-keeping, known generally in German palaeography and diplomatic as *Akten*. Through letters, reports, lists of people or financial information and a range of other written artifacts produced for day-to-day purposes, we can get a little closer to the processes of negotiation (what late medieval Germans often called *Handlungen*) that lay behind charters, although we should still guard against the assumption that any source gives us direct access to events or the authentic beliefs and intentions of the people involved in them. For contemporary insights produced with a somewhat greater degree of distance, although usually equally inflected by specific agendas, we can look to chronicles and other narrative accounts. The German lands had a rich tradition of chronicle-writing throughout this period and in a range of contexts, from monasteries to city councils to princely courts. Finally, learned theorists in this period made lengthy polemical interventions through law-books and treatises, which might purport to summarise the essence and key rules of the legal and ecclesiastical order (as in the *Saxon* and *Swabian Mirror* [1]) or could advance more-or-less concrete blueprints for the reform of the Empire and the Church.

A notable feature of the sources pertaining to legal and political history is the language in which they tended to be written. The centuries encompassed by this book lie in the period that immediately followed the triumph of specific forms of the German vernacular in imperial, princely and urban chanceries and in manuscript workshops and scriptoria across the core lands of the Holy Roman Empire. In the decades around 1300, first the princes and cities and then the Romano-German monarchs shifted from mostly issuing documents in Latin to predominantly using German. In the southern half of the German lands (including what are now Alsace, Switzerland and Austria), this was a somewhat standardised type of early new High German (*Frühneuhochdeutsch*), with some influence from regional dialects, while in the lordships and cities near the North Sea and Baltic coasts it was Low German, with a transitional zone roughly between Westphalia and Brandenburg. While these chancery languages corresponded only loosely with spoken German in some regions, they were clearly a conscious and pragmatic choice for the political elite of this era, in which a steadily growing proportion of princes, nobles, patricians and their officers and personnel could read or write, but mostly only (or primarily) in the vernacular.

This is strikingly illustrated by a letter from Margrave Albrecht 'Achilles' of Brandenburg, an elector and one of the most powerful princes in Germany, from November 1474. Emperor Frederick III had recently contacted Albrecht about an alliance with France in the context of the brewing imperial war against Duke Charles of Burgundy [7]. Unusually, the emperor's missive was in Latin. Albrecht responded (in German) requesting that Frederick 'have the letter translated into German in the style of your chancery, so that I may understand it, for you know well that I am not a good Latinist'.[28] We must be cautious about taking this request at face value: Albrecht probably understood more Latin than he implies here, and in any case would have had many learned translators at his disposal, so this was most likely a strategic claim to delay having to implement Frederick III's demand to prepare for the looming conflict with Burgundy. Nonetheless, that a fifteenth-century prince could feign a relative ignorance of Latin and express a strong preference for written correspondence in German is revealing in itself. Long before the end of the traditionally defined Middle Ages, German political actors could reasonably expect that almost all their textual interactions, not to mention their governmental records and laws, would be in the vernacular.

Thus, the majority of sources in this book are translated from German. The small number of Latin exceptions come from highly specific contexts, such as correspondence with non-German speakers, humanist epistles in which a key aim of the author was to demonstrate mastery of Ciceronian rhetoric, materials produced by and for clerics regarding ecclesiastical affairs and learned treatises about the Church and the Empire. Even these last two categories might also contain texts in the vernacular. Late medieval bishops issued German texts and documents like their secular counterparts when engaging in everyday politics and customary or feudal litigation [39, 41]. The author of the much-copied reformist tract titled *The Reformation of Emperor Sigismund* [32], who was almost certainly a cleric at the Council of Basel in the 1430s who would have mastered Latin, chose to write in the vernacular to

---

28 *das ich nicht ein guter latennist bin.* Priebatsch (ed.), *Politische Correspondenz*, vol. I, no. 983.

reach a wider audience. The most famous German writer of this era, Martin Luther (1483–1546), was a cleric and skilled author of Latin theological and ecclesiological treatises of the kind that proliferated in late medieval universities. Most of his early publications fit this mould, but he deliberately chose to write his 1520 exhortation for the nobility to reform the Church in the German vernacular that his target audience was much more likely to understand [35]. There was clearly a well-developed 'public sphere' among the political elites of the German lands between the mid-fourteenth and mid-sixteenth centuries, even if its inner workings and the networks of people who sustained it are only obliquely accessible to us.[29] Even before the rise of the printing press, the vernacular was a practical choice not only for everyday legal and governmental business, but also for the circulation of more developed and idealistic political polemic. Once printing had become well established in the last decades of the fifteenth century, the potential audiences for such writings grew exponentially.

While the number of literate people capable of producing or consuming texts of any kind increased throughout this period, we should not forget that writing was only one form of communication, and not always the most important and valorised – even among the social strata involved in law and government. Visual communication through iconography and architecture could be just as significant in shaping political worldviews, and could potentially reach much wider audiences. The sense of belonging to the Holy Roman Empire, for instance, was animated by the proliferation of the imperial heraldic motif – the black eagle (increasingly double-headed from the fifteenth century) – and other unmistakable symbols of the Empire, such as schematic depictions of the seven electors in frescoes and sculptures.[30] Heraldic iconography more generally was a powerful visual medium for organising and categorising the Empire's complicated and multifarious political landscape, as attested by the many books of arms (*Wappenbücher*) that survive from these centuries. Legal and political custom in the German lands of this period favoured face-to-face interaction wherever possible, whether to arbitrate in disputes or to consult at diets over collective policies within a principality or league, or

---

29 Kintzinger and Schneidmüller (eds), *Politische Öffentlichkeit*.
30 Scales, 'The Illuminated Reich'.

indeed within the Empire as a whole. Records of such meetings are often laconic, conveying only abridged and highly edited versions of the course of events. Particularly telling is the importance of oaths in German political culture. Throughout the Middle Ages and the sixteenth century, people gave assent and authentication to legal documents and mandates by swearing prescribed oaths, promising before God and their peers to live up to the commitments being made. Many documents are therefore not merely records of events that took place, but served as props within a ritualised *mise-en-scène* which – as much anthropologically inflected scholarship has shown – aimed to reinforce social and political ties and obligations and defuse and manage tensions and conflicts. In short, much of the written evidence that survives served its purpose within what historians have described as a culture of 'pragmatic literacy': specific genres of texts interacted with oral, visual and ritual or performative media of communication to various symbolic and practical ends, which may not be entirely clear to us as modern readers who can usually only access the written components of this culture. We should therefore try to keep the multidimensional nature of German legal and political culture in mind when interpreting the archival sources.[31]

Finally, it is worth emphasising that the translated sources in this book – as with any translations – are the result of interpretive choices by the author. This is especially true of the late medieval German evidence. There is no consensus around appropriate English equivalents for specific legal and political terms, and there are few pre-existing translations from which to draw inspiration. Sometimes the choices are largely technical. For instance, I have opted to render *Kammergericht* as 'cameral' rather than 'chamber' court, although either would be a reasonable approximation of the term. Other choices are more contentious. For example, should *Landfrieden* (a word variously applied to regional alliances and pan-imperial ordinances) be translated as 'public peace', 'provincial peace', 'territorial peace' or simply 'land-peace'? None of these choices is self-evident and each has different connotations, so some of the sources that follow have different renderings of the term depending on their context. Precisely because these choices are

---

31 On oaths, ritual and pragmatic literacy, see Hardy, *Associative Political Culture*, chapter 1 with further references.

interpretations, which in effect present a set of implicit arguments about how I understand the political culture of late medieval and Reformation Germany, I want to stress that they are not the final word. Scholars and students are encouraged to consult the original sources where possible, and to formulate their own analyses of the Holy Roman Empire.

I
THE IMPERIAL MONARCHY IN THEORY AND PRACTICE

The student of late medieval German history must confront a paradox. The kings and emperors who ruled most of the German-speaking lands, and the broader Holy Roman Empire that contained them, claimed the most exalted rank among the temporal rulers of Christian Europe. Yet the resources available to them and the extent of their control in most regions were very modest indeed. In the absence of much permanent governmental infrastructure under their direct purvey, their rule was perhaps the least intensive of any European monarchy in this period, especially relative to the vast areas they notionally oversaw.[1]

To understand how these situations could co-exist, we need to move beyond the nationalist narratives that have sought the origins of modern centralised nation-states in the pre-modern past, giving late medieval German history an especially bad reputation as a time of pointless fragmentation and anarchy, but also to treat more recent, overly irenic interpretations of the Holy Roman Empire as a kind of pragmatic, implicitly secular proto-federation (foreshadowing the European Union) with caution. The ideological basis for the imperial monarchy's implausibly lofty status was not rooted in practical conditions that pertained in the fourteenth to sixteenth centuries, but in a centuries-old providential narrative about the ordering of the Latin Christian world. Alongside the pope, the emperor (or king, pending imperial coronation) was the wielder of one of two 'swords' bestowed by God. The swords represented the division of universal authority and jurisdiction into spiritual and temporal spheres.[2]

This narrative manifests itself clearly in two extremely popular vernacular law-books that survive in almost a thousand manuscripts, the so-called *Swabian Mirror* (*Schwabenspiegel*) [1] and its northern

---

1 This situation, and the long historiographical tradition of bemoaning it, is surveyed in Scales, *German Identity*, pp. 65–97.
2 See Whalen, *The Two Powers*, p. 37.

German counterpart, the *Saxon Mirror*.³ Both were composed in the thirteenth century and proliferated in the fourteenth to sixteenth, informing judicial and social realities. They open with a distillation of this 'Two Swords Theory', effectively announcing that the universal temporal authority supposedly granted to the monarch underpinned the legitimacy of the entire socio-political hierarchy and the customary and feudal laws that governed it. This point is reinforced by the *Swabian Mirror*'s rapid transition from the divine bestowal of authority in the world to an outline of the idealised order of feudal ranks (*Heerschilde*) flowing downwards from the monarch.

The kings' and emperors' unique claims to authority over the temporal realm also rested on the notion that they were the heirs of the Roman Empire and its universal civilising and (after Constantine) Christianising mission – hence the Latin title *rex* or *imperator Romanorum* ('king' or 'emperor of the Romans'), typically rendered into German as *römischer König/Kaiser*. (A ruler became 'king of the Romans' by dint of election to the throne; the title of 'emperor' required a second coronation in Italy, and not all kings were able to acquire it.) The peculiar situation whereby German-speaking noblemen occupied and supported the Roman imperial office could be readily explained by another providential narrative: that of divinely guided 'transfer of empire' (*translatio imperii*). The Frankish king Charlemagne had resurrected the title of *imperator* in 800, and, following the fragmentation of the Carolingian polity, it was revived once again in East Francia by the Saxon family we call the 'Ottonians' in the tenth century, inaugurating an 844-year period in which the Roman imperial office would be borne by German-speakers. High medieval political theorists posited that God had steered this handing-over of the imperial mantle from the Romans to the Greeks (Byzantines), then to the Franks and finally to the Germans as a people. The wide diffusion of this narrative by our period, and the collective sense of pride and responsibility that it engendered, is suggested by its inclusion in the work known in English as the *Nuremberg (World) Chronicle* [2]. Written in Latin by the humanist Hartmann Schedel and printed in both Latin and German by Anton Koberger in 1493, it proved hugely popular with urban and noble readers: the German version was reprinted in Augsburg in 1496 and 1500.⁴

---

3 Translated into English by Dobozy (ed./trans.), *The Saxon Mirror*.
4 Reske, 'Schedelsche Weltchronik'.

Importantly, it was well established by the late Middle Ages that the king's or emperor's authority was formally delegated to and shared with high-ranking nobles who claimed to embody the community of the realm. By the latter half of the thirteenth century, this principle extended to the succession to the imperial throne. A group of seven leading spiritual and temporal princes – the 'electors' (*electores*, *Kurfürsten*) – regularly exercised the right to elect each new king of the Romans, a right that was codified in the Golden Bull of 1356 [14] (discussed further in section II). Thus, the electoral process is portrayed as deeply significant even in the *Little Book about the Imperial Monarchy* (*Libellus de Cesarea monarchia*) [3], composed in 1460 by Peter of Andlau, a professor of law at the University of Basel, and described by its modern editor as 'the explication of an idealised picture of the traditions, history and structure of the Empire from the specific perspective of a late medieval canonist, wherein the rule of the emperor is foregrounded'.[5] The electors did not see their role as being limited to choosing monarchs. Many involved themselves closely in the ongoing government of the Empire, acting almost as co-regents with the king or emperor (sometimes in his absence) at its ritualised assemblies and in the organisation of the associations that enforced peace and justice within it. The visual and material iconography of the late medieval and early modern imperial polity often depicted these so-called 'pillars of the Empire' alongside the king or emperor, collectively incarnating a body politic of multiple, diverse 'members'.[6] The image on the front cover of this book, from a mid-fifteenth-century manuscript of the Golden Bull, is a prime example of this iconography.

While the electors' relationship with the occupant of the throne could be characterised by a mixture of collaboration and tension, depending on individual and factional interests, they proved capable of acting decisively as a group to shape and constrain the monarchs' freedom of manoeuvre. Several times between the thirteenth and fifteenth centuries the electors threatened to depose a sitting monarch for his alleged failure to manage the Empire's problems at a time of crisis. In the right circumstances they could even make good on this threat, as they famously did in 1400 by deposing

---

5 R. Müller (ed./trans.), *Libellus de Cesarea monarchia*, p. 324.
6 Begert, *Entstehung und Entwicklung*; Gotthard, *Säulen des Reiches*.

King Wenceslas [5] and electing one of their number, Rupert of the Palatinate, to replace him. As in all electoral machinations, the individual ambitions and interests of the electors played a key role here, but their actions were also framed by well-established 'public' norms and expectations pertaining to the leading princes of the Empire. Wenceslas's deposition, which was justified by reference to his failures to attend to the 'Town War' of the 1380s and the Papal Schism, among other complaints, provides fascinating insights into responsibilities that the monarchs and electors could claim – and were expected to fulfil – within the Empire and Christendom. These would crystallise further and become still more formalised over the course of the century and a half that followed. While still relying on the kings and emperors as founts of legitimacy, the electors took it upon themselves to spearhead assemblies and judicial and military initiatives against the backdrop of external threats (such as the Hussites of Bohemia) and internecine conflict within the Empire. After the death of Maximilian I, the intensely competitive election campaign to succeed him put the electors in an especially strong position to negotiate with their chosen candidate, Maximilian's grandson Charles V. The electoral contract [9] (called a *Wahlkapitulation* by modern historians) that Charles was obliged to enter into with the electors reflects the prerogatives and responsibilities that these leading princes claimed for themselves by the early sixteenth century. It leaves little doubt that the Empire was now a formally multilateral entity, with power officially distributed among many actors and layers of authority, even if its ultimate source was notionally located in the monarchy and its divine mandate.

If the Romano-German monarchs of this period faced material, legal and ideological constraints quite unlike those in rapidly institutionalising kingdoms such as England and France, it would nevertheless be a mistake to assume that they had no tools at their disposal for asserting themselves within the Holy Roman Empire's decentralised political landscape. The fourteenth-century kings and emperors inherited a residue of jurisdictions and revenues attached to the crown in some densely urbanised areas of southern and western Germany (regions dubbed 'close to the king' – *königsnah* – by Peter Moraw).[7] By mobilising these remaining resources and working with the grain of local

---

7 Moraw, *Von offener Verfassung*, p. 71.

dynamics – notably by encouraging local alliances and associations for keeping the peace (see section V) – an energetic monarch who frequently travelled through the German heartlands of the Empire could impose his will to a degree, and be perceived as a ruler who fulfilled his peace-keeping and justice-enforcing duties. Charles IV was especially successful in this regard. A narrative of his endorsement of a regional land-peace and its successes (and limitations) in Franconia in 1373 [4], stemming from an anonymous compilation of chronicle accounts written in late fourteenth-century Augsburg, exemplifies the modest yet meaningful results that a partnership between itinerant monarchs and local associations could yield.

Although Charles IV and Sigismund pledged many of the remaining imperial properties and offices in the *königsnah* regions in return for loans to keep their governments afloat, a determined emperor could still exploit traditional prerogatives to extract resources from the Empire a century later. Frederick III responded to military incursions in the Rhineland by Duke Charles 'the Bold' of Burgundy in the 1470s by calling on all the imperially immediate members of the Empire, including the free and imperial cities, to supply troops for a collective imperial army to repel him [6]. While by no means all members responded, and those that did offered less assistance than requested in Frederick's letters, an impressive army of some 33–40,000 troops did assemble and force Charles to retreat in 1475.[8] The victories that followed in the rest of the Burgundian Wars (1474–77) led to Charles the Bold's death and propelled the Habsburgs to European and global pre-eminence through their acquisition of the Burgundian Low Countries.[9]

The case of the Habsburgs' vertiginous ascent in the late fifteenth and early sixteenth centuries highlights the importance of familial power and patrimony (so-called *Hausmacht*) in enabling successful monarchical rule in the Empire, and the interdependent – if sometimes tension-ridden – relationship between imperial and dynastic resources and spheres of activity. Indeed, the importance of this relationship was already clear a century earlier, during the Luxemburg emperors' temporary dominance founded on a Central European complex of kingdoms and principalities. An older generation of historians bemoaned the tendency of Luxemburg and Habsburg

8 Leukel, *Das Reichsheer*.
9 Moraw, *Von offener Verfassung*, pp. 411–15.

monarchs to alienate imperial properties and cajole denizens of the Empire into supplying resources for the sake of their dynastic power bases.[10] Yet this misses both the normativity of the imperative to provide for one's familial patrimony and honour as a late medieval prince, and the extent to which these dynastic power bases supplied most of the resources for the modest imperial institutions (such as the chancery and judicial apparatus attached to the court of the king or emperor). The crescendo of negotiations between the monarchs and nascent estates at assemblies in the decades around 1500 (see section III) were stimulated in part by requests for ad hoc taxation and troop provision by Frederick III and Maximilian I. The latter's exhortation to an imperial diet in 1509 for assistance [8] demonstrates how the Habsburg emperors tried to link the dynastic concerns and 'foreign policy' of the 'house of Austria' (*Haus Österreich*) with the interests of the Empire and its political community. While we must approach this polemical and self-serving text with caution, Maximilian's speech (or rather, the printed and widely circulated written version of it) highlights the vexed issue of the vastly greater expenditures he made from his 'hereditary lands' (*Erblande*) compared with funding provided by the imperial estates – a dynamic borne out by the surviving evidence, even if his figures are exaggerated.[11]

In the final analysis, it would be misleading to portray the relationship between the monarchs and the wider Romano-German polity as either purely co-operative or purely adversarial. While context-specific crises and hostilities arose from time to time, individual elites and networks of princes, prelates, nobles and cities relied on the kings and emperors to legitimise their own claims to authority, and so the monarchs were the most essential component of the political framework in the Holy Roman Empire, whatever the practical and emerging 'constitutional' constraints that they faced. Rituals of enfeoffment and grants of charters of privileges make this especially clear, and serve to remind us that the late medieval and early modern Empire was animated as much by symbolic performances and visual and material culture as it was by rules and obligations fixed in writing.[12] Such events left a profound impression

---

10 As discussed in, for example, Monnet, *Charles IV*, pp. 191–98.
11 Brady, *German Histories*, pp. 107–29.
12 On 'symbolic communication' in the Empire, see Stollberg-Rilinger, *The Emperor's Old Clothes*.

on their audiences, as attested by Ulrich Richental's vivid description of Sigismund's enfeoffment ceremonies [6] at an assembly in his hometown of Constance in 1417. (The assembly coincided with the ecclesiastical council held there between 1414 and 1418, the subject of the chronicle Richental wrote roughly a decade later.) Following the breakdown around 1400 of the *modus vivendi* that had prevailed under Charles IV, such assemblies and their attendant rituals, at which both monarchs and the imperial 'members' and 'estates' played crucial political roles, grew dramatically in importance, as will become clear in sections II and III.

1. The 'Two Swords Theory' in the *Swabian Mirror* (thirteenth–fifteenth centuries)

Derschka (ed./trans.), *Der Schwabenspiegel*, pp. 23–25.

Since God is called a 'prince of peace', he left two swords on earth for the protection of Christendom as he ascended to heaven. God bestowed both of these on St Peter, one imbued with spiritual jurisdictional authority and the other with temporal jurisdictional authority.[13] The temporal sword of jurisdiction is lent by the pope to the emperor. The spiritual sword is appointed for the pope, that he should preside as judge with it.

[...]

Concerning the seven *Heerschilde*.[14]

Origen prophesied in times of yore that there would be six Ages of the World, and that each age would pass away after a thousand years, and that in the Seventh Age the world would perish entirely and the Day of Atonement would come. Now, it is announced to us in the Holy Scriptures that the First Age of the World began with Adam, the second with Noah, the third with Abraham, the fourth with Moses, the fifth with David, the sixth with the birth of God [i.e. Jesus]. And these six Ages of the World each passed away after a thousand years. Now we are in the Seventh Age of the World, without a certain number, for the six thousand years have elapsed, and the Seventh Age lasts as long as God wills it.

And the seven *Heerschilde* are arranged in the same way. The king has the first *Heerschild*. The bishops and the abbots and abbesses, if they are of princely rank, have the second *Heerschild*. The lay princes have the third. The barons have the fourth. The middling

---

13 This notion, based on a laconic reference to two swords in Luke 22:38, developed during the Middle Ages into the so-called Gelasian theory, rooted in a letter of Pope Gelasius I to Emperor Anastasius I in 494 which came to be interpreted as an argument for the division of the world into temporal and spiritual spheres of authority (*regnum/imperium* and *sacerdotium*), whose relationship was a constant source of debate. See Robinson, 'Church and Papacy'.
14 The 'military shield' (Latin *clipeus militaris*) that stood for a person's notional feudal rank.

freemen[15] have the fifth. The servitors[16] have the sixth. And in the same way as it is not known when the Seventh Age of the World will come to an end, it is not known whether the seventh *Heerschild* may receive fiefs or not.

---

15 *Mittelfreien* – fief-holding freemen, possibly but (in practice) not necessarily of knightly status.
16 *Dienstmannen* – this would have implied ministerials (fief-holding unfree nobles) in this ideal hierarchy at the time the *Swabian Mirror* was first written, although ministerials were becoming freemen and turning their fiefs into heritable family estates already in the thirteenth century. In the fourteenth to sixteenth centuries, a servitor more generically referred to a person, usually noble, in the employ of a prince or city.

2. The origins of the Holy Roman Empire and its transfer to the Germans in the *Nuremberg Chronicle* (1493)

Schedel, *Buch der Croniken und geschichten*, p. clxxviii.

On the origin and derivation of the imperial office and how the same was eventually transferred to the German nation.

The imperial office, which was taken by the Romans, the Gauls and the Lombards, and subsequently received by the aforementioned [Emperor] Otto [I, r. 962–73], first came to the German nation at that time, and has been retained within it until the present day. The glory, praise and adulation due to this most splendid imperial dignity bears remarking upon.

The royal Roman authority (which is known as the holy emperorship) derives its origins from mankind's natural reason (which is a guide to the best way of life, and ought to be obeyed in all matters). For when our first ancestors were driven from paradise and the garden of delights, and mankind wandered like cattle in the fields and the woods, man (whom God endowed with reason) thought to himself that the most beneficial thing for humanity would be to lead a just way of life. Thus, those men who had formerly lived in the woods like wild animals came together, either through practical experience or the will of God, master of all nature. They made societies, built houses, surrounded towns with walls, invented all kinds of crafts and led a seemly, citizenly and neighbourly existence together. But just as much of value derives to man from others, so too many bad things spring forth. And so people began to do things that were injurious to society, to break faith and trust, to harm the peace, to bear secret grudges against one another, to steal things from others and to deviate from the path of virtue into the error of vice.

As many people were now oppressed by the mighty and the powerful among them, they sought refuge with exceptionally virtuous men who protected the poor from the rich and powerful and maintained the multitude in equity, justice and fairness. As a result, many kings were chosen by their peoples, and as the principalities multiplied, the numerousness of kings and princes caused much division and upheaval. For they were oftentimes divided among themselves over landownership, and later over jurisdiction, and there was nobody who could resolve the disputes among these various parties. And as the one did not wish to be seen as lesser than the other, they resorted to the sword and pursued their causes through wars, and thus were unbound all the beneficial communal ties within human society. But the benign precaution of human nature, which is ever inclined to the best things, thought it best to bring all things under a single principality, for otherwise one would have no semblance of collective peace. Based on this principle, the Assyrian empire emerged. In the same way, the Greek principality expanded out of Europe into Asia and Libya through the power and fortune of Alexander the Great, and also the Carthaginian empire.

But since the same empires never subjugated all of the earth, and were unable to impose collective peace, so it seemed favourable to human nature – or to God, the lord and governor of the same nature – to summon up the Roman Empire. Now, Rome was originally governed by seven successive kings, and after their passing by combinations of two successively appointed men,[17] and finally by one man alone. And Julius Caesar was the first originator of such a sole government in the Empire. The populace gave all authority and power to him. And over time there were two emperors at the same time, such as Diocletian and Maximian, and at times even more, which happened more as a result of violence than of justice. Over time, someone might acquire this imperial dignity through the choice of a council, and sometimes through acclamation by the populace, occasionally through the favour of the knighthood and at other times on the order of an emperor. And this empire was governed at times by Latins, Spaniards, Africans and Dalmatians, and also by the Greeks, and for a long time it was governed with glory and great worthiness from Constantinople.

But since in the end the Greeks were neglectful towards Rome, such that they allowed the Romans to be encumbered by myriad atrocities of war, so the Roman people – which had made this imperial office through its own blood alone – appointed Charlemagne the German by birth and king of the Franks, who came to their aid, Roman emperor with the approval of the pope. From this Charlemagne until Emperor Ludwig the son of Arnulf, this empire expanded modestly over a hundred and ten years under the Gauls,

17 The consuls of the Roman Republic.

and after that it passed to the Lombards, and at last it was turned over to the Germans, to Duke Otto, son of King Henry [I 'the Fowler', r. 919–36]. And from him it has come through orderly election to the present time, to Emperor Frederick III and his son King Maximilian, to whom is entrusted from heaven the highest authority in temporal matters, that they should pursue war with good fortune, enhance the peace and maintain the common good, for which reason all peoples, all nations and kings and princes should submit to this empire with a willing disposition.

3. The procedure for electing a monarch in Peter of Andlau's *Little Book about the Imperial Monarchy* (1460)

R. Müller (ed./trans.), *Libellus de Cesarea monarchia*, pp. 176–82.

While this text by Peter of Andlau (d. 1480), doctor of canon law at Basel, found few readers during his lifetime, it attained widespread popularity in early modern Germany for its lucid distillation of the historical narratives and legal and political principles and procedures underpinning the monarchy of the Holy Roman Empire. The first half of the book summarises commonly held ideas about the origins of temporal authority, the merits of monarchy and the history of the Roman Empire and the *translatio imperii* process. The second focuses on the functioning of the Empire in Andlau's day, based on laws, customs and his own (sometimes idiosyncratic) observations. This extract comes from the crucial chapter on how the election of a king of the Romans should work, synthesising the procedures codified in the Golden Bull [14] and including some of Andlau's glosses on them.

With the most serene emperor having died and the Holy Empire being without a leader, it has been customary for the archbishop of Mainz, as president of the illustrious college of electors, to summon his remaining fellow electors to the city of Frankfurt in the diocese of Mainz (once founded by the true Franks, that is, the Trojans) through his public letters for the election of the future king of the Romans who, with the Lord's favour, will later be elevated to the emperorship. After the said electors have entered the city of Frankfurt, immediately at dawn on the following day they should have the Mass of the Holy Spirit solemnly chanted in the Church of St Bartholomew in that city in all of their presence. After the Mass has been carried out in this fashion, all the spiritual electors reverently place their hands on their hearts in the presence of the Gospel of St John the Evangelist that begins 'In the beginning was the Word' [John 1:1], which should be placed before them there. However, the temporal electors, who should attend there unarmed with all their retinues, touch the said gospel with their hands.

And then the archbishop of Mainz gives them the form of the oath which they should take in the vernacular in this way: 'I Theodoricus,[18] bishop of Mainz, arch-chancellor of the Holy Empire in Germany and elector, swear by and in the presence of these holy gospels of God that have been placed before me, through the faith that binds me to God and the Holy Empire, that I want – according to all my powers of discernment and intellect, with God's help – to elect as temporal head for the Christian people, king of the Romans and future emperor, one who should prove to be suitable for this, as far as my discernment and good sense direct me; and I will cast my vote without any bargain, payment, reward or promise, whatever they may be called.'

When all the electors have given the oath in this way they proceed to the election, and they are not permitted to distance themselves from the said city of Frankfurt until the majority elects the temporal head of the world and the Christian people. But if they take longer than thirty days to accomplish this, from the time of these discussions onwards they will have to eat only bread and drink only water until a head of the believers is elected, as mentioned before. The archbishop of Mainz has the duty of inquiring after and examining the individual votes in this order: first he will examine the vote of the archbishop of Trier, who has the first vote; second, that of the archbishop of Cologne, to whom falls – because of his rank – the task of placing the first crown of the realm on the king of the Romans; third, that of the king of Bohemia, who holds the highest position among the lay electors because of his royal status; fourth, that of the Count Palatine of the Rhine; fifth, that of the duke of Saxony; and sixth, that of the margrave of Brandenburg. With this done the said princes conversely ask the archbishop of Mainz and examine his vote, as all this is made more fully manifest in Charles IV's ordinances promulgated through the Golden Bull [14]. However, customarily the king of Bohemia is only summoned to the election if the other votes are equal in number [i.e. tied], and that is the practice today. That holds true

---

18 Andlau's Latin word 'Theodoricus' corresponds with the German name 'Dietrich' or 'Diether'. Whereas the Golden Bull ([14], chapter 2, section [2]) prescribes a generic, nameless oath, Andlau adapts it to the specific office-holders at the time he wrote his treatise: Dietrich Schenk of Erbach was archbishop of Mainz from 1434 to 1459 and Diether of Isenburg one of the claimants in a split election from 1459 to 1461.

provided that he continues steadfastly in union with Holy Mother Church.[19] Otherwise, if two elected candidates should have the same number of votes, it is necessary to have recourse to the pope, who can elect one of the two, whomever he may wish. The gloss on the *Liber Sextus*, title *de [sententia et re] judic[ata]*, chapter *[ad] apostolicae*[20] says that the king of Bohemia does not have this right of old. Certainly, though, after the majority of them elects someone, such an election must be considered and thought of in the same way as if it had been proclaimed by all of them harmoniously with nobody dissenting.

After the election has been carried out in this fashion, he who was elected as king of the Romans ought soon after he has begun to administer the laws of the Holy Empire to confirm and sanction to all the electors, ecclesiastical and temporal – who are known to be like the joints and limbs of the Empire – all their privileges, rights, liberties and old customs and whatever they had received from the Empire up to the day of the election, and he should renew all of these after he has been crowned with the imperial insignia.

[The new king should inform the pope of his election and offer him an oath of loyalty via a messenger, paving the way for the monarch's coronation as emperor by the pope in Italy in due course. Andlau discusses the canonical basis for this at length.]

However, after the elected candidate has been declared king of the Romans – to be elevated later to the emperorship – he will hurry as soon as he can to the city of Aachen in the diocese of Liège to receive the crown of the realm from the archbishop of Cologne.

---

19 At the time Andlau composed this treatise, the king of Bohemia was George of Poděbrady (r. 1458–71), a Hussite – and therefore a heretic in the eyes of most of the rest of Catholic Christendom.
20 The so-called *Liber Sextus* was a canonical collection from 1298. In modern scholarship this citation would be rendered VI 2.14.2. The relevant chapter, and the gloss mentioned by Andlau, can be found in *Liber sextus decretalium*, pp. 375–80.

4. A chronicle account of Emperor Charles IV's peace-keeping approach (late fourteenth century)

Die Chroniken der Schwäbischen Städte. Augsburg. Erster Band, pp. 33–34.

After a phase of relative calm, a series of conflicts erupted across Swabia and Franconia in the 1370s, including a major battle between a local knightly society and some imperial cities in 1372. Charles IV responded using the methods honed over the preceding decades: by sending an agent (in this case, his Bohemian retainer Borso of Riesenburg) to renew the local land-peace and use its forces to proceed against the parties deemed to be troublemakers, as recorded here in an Augsburg chronicle soon after these events took place.

In the year of our Lord 1373 Emperor Charles established a land-peace in Franconia, because the region had suffered great depredations. This [i.e. the depredations] vexed both the lords and the towns, and they took to the field between St Margaret's Day [13 July] and St Jacob's Day [25 July]. The army was composed thus: the host of Borso of Riesenburg rode out into the field in great numbers, as did that of the burgrave of Nuremberg, the bishop of Bamberg, the bishop of Würzburg, the bishop of Eichstätt and the cities of Nuremberg, Rothenburg and Weißenburg and other towns and lords who belonged to the peace – they all came out into the field, every lord and every town according to the requirements of the peace. The entire host remained at Ornbau, Heilsbronn and Spalt and thereabouts around the river for a good eight days. Thereafter the lords and towns agreed to returned home, because the Swabian knights and retainers wanted to start a fight with the lords. The lords and towns feared that they would sustain heavy damage, because Riesenburg had left them to ride to join Emperor Charles in the Mark of Brandenburg.

5. The deposition of King Wenceslas (1400)

Weizsäcker et al. (eds), *Deutsche Reichstagsakten. Ältere Reihe*, vol. III, pp. 255–58.

In the name of God, amen. We Johann [II, r. 1397–1419], by the grace of God archbishop of the Holy Church in Mainz, archchancellor of the Holy Empire throughout the German lands, declare this to all people, both present and future:

How many and various great and deplorable transgressions, errors and dissensions have arisen for many years and long periods of time in the Holy Church,[21] and are still ongoing and daily resurge more harmfully, because of which the Holy Roman Empire – from which the Holy Church and Christendom should derive comfort, protection and assistance – is, alas, so injuriously dismembered and diminished and so delinquently administered! It is not only our writing that makes this apparent; it is also clearly demonstrated by the flagrant and evil occurrences taking place daily. Because of this, our lords and fellow electors of the Holy Roman Empire and also we, at the insistent appeal of the Holy Church, which desires a protector, and of the princes, lords, cities, lands and peoples of the Holy Empire, which profoundly desire a prudent administrator, have long frequently and emphatically exhorted and called upon the serene prince Lord Wenceslas, king of the Romans and king of Bohemia, by means of ourselves, our associates and our letters, and we also privately and publicly presented our exhortations to him in person, concerning his inappropriate and shocking lifestyle and management of the Holy Empire and also such transgressions, errors and dissensions in the Holy Church and Christendom and such grave dismembering and diminishment of the Holy Empire that he has injuriously carried out and inflicted, against the dignity of his title:

[1] Namely, that he never assisted the Holy Church to remain in peace (which has been and remains a matter of great urgency for Christendom), as is his duty as an advocate and protector of the Church, and he was frequently requested, exhorted and entreated to do.

---

21 This is above all a reference to the Papal Schism: since 1378 there had been rival papacies in Rome and Avignon, and the authorities of the Empire (and Latin Christian Europe) divided their loyalties between these two popes.

[2: The electors criticise Wenceslas for giving away titles in northern Italy to Gian Galeazzo Visconti of Milan in return for an illegal payment.

3: The electors accuse Wenceslas of allowing peripheral regions to fall away from imperial jurisdiction.

4: The electors allege that Wenceslas had the imperial chancery send blank sealed charters to his friends, which they could complete with any imperial privileges they desired.]

[5] He has never paid any attention to all the discord and wars that, unfortunately, have gravely and ruinously taken place many a time in the German lands and elsewhere in the Holy Empire and are still ongoing, on account of which great pillaging, arson and murder have arisen and daily more damagingly arise; and neither priests nor lay people nor farmers nor merchants – men and women alike – have experienced peace on land or on the waterways; and churches, monasteries and other houses of God, which the Holy Empire ought to administer and protect, are also being ruinously pillaged, burned down and totally impiously annihilated and displaced. Therefore everyone has been following their own motives vis-à-vis the other, against propriety and justice, and continues to follow them now, without concern for or attention to the Holy Empire that has been managed in this negligent way, and now nobody knows before whom they can defend their rights in court, that they might be preserved and protected by virtue of the Holy Empire.

[6] He has also – which sounds shocking and inhumane – murdered, drowned and burned with torches honourable and eminent prelates, priests and clerics, and also many other honourable people, by his own hand and by means of other evildoers that he keeps around him, and has had them wretchedly and inhumanely killed against justice, which sounds and is unbecoming of a king of the Romans.

These above-written articles and many other worse ones concerning his evil deeds and transgressions are so clearly manifest and well known throughout the land that they can neither be justified nor concealed. And we have therefore frequently, many times and very zealously requested of him and exhorted and called upon him, as is written above, that he should abandon this inappropriate lifestyle and work to restore the Holy Church, which has called upon him very often as a king of the Romans, its advocate, to peace and unity, and the Holy Empire to its dignity, lands and possessions, and to ensure with all diligence that it is governed more profitably in order to be able to assist and comfort Christendom, which has also been gravely devastated and oppressed on his account. Although we have at times clearly stated and described to the above-named Lord Wenceslas as king of the Romans these and many other great transgressions affecting him himself and the Holy Empire, after his answers and our counter-responses and earnest exhortation, and after we informed the See of Rome about all this concerning him, we have still not seen him endeavour to behave in the proper manner for a king of the Romans, namely that he should strive to establish peace in the Holy Church (on account of which a profound crisis continues in the whole of Christendom) and restore the Holy Empire to its dignity, lands and possessions and govern it more profitably, as is all too evident and manifest in all the lands of the Holy Empire.

And since we cannot be silent about or tolerate these above-named and many other transgressions that are gravely, harmfully and deplorably affecting the Holy Church and the Empire, because of the above-named appeals and also because of our oaths, through which – as the highest-ranking and most proximate members of the Holy Empire – we are especially bound to the said Empire, we must, as appertains to us and is our obligation, consider and act to ensure that the Holy Empire – from whose unprofitable and neglectful handling these transgressions have arisen – may henceforth be more profitably administered for the assistance and comfort of Christendom. We therefore recently issued a renewed missive to the above-written Lord Wenceslas as king of the Romans and personally reminded, requested and demanded of him regarding our earlier entreaty that he should want to come to us at Oberlahnstein on the Rhine and be with us by the second day after the upcoming St Lawrence's Day [11 August 1400] in order to establish the Holy Empire on a more profitable footing and to cast off these great transgressions. And because we would have gladly seen this happen, we also fully and earnestly called upon him and demanded of him that if he should not come to us in this way to the above-written town and assembly, then we would have to – because of the appeal of the whole land and our oaths – consider and do what was necessary to ensure that the Holy Empire was more profitably administered, as our letters to him clearly spelled out. We therefore appeared at the above-written town and assembly, and also fully summoned our other fellow electors together with other princes, lords and cities of the Holy Empire, and waited from day to day to see whether the above-written Lord Wenceslas might appear in order to cast off these before-written transgressions and establish the Empire on a more profitable footing. And yet he has not come to us regarding all this, nor has he sent any of his people to present to us on any of these matters.

And since that time we have frequently approached him alone and secretly in amicable terms regarding these above-written deplorable and harmful transgressions and, as none of that has helped, earnestly arraigned and sentenced him before the princes, lords and cities of the Holy Empire at several assembly sessions, which has been onerous and costly for us (and when that also proved useless, we instead brought this matter to the Holy See of Rome, as is written above), and he has paid no heed to all of this. We can and may therefore do no other than to observe and esteem that he no longer has, or henceforth wants to have, any consideration or concern for the Holy Church and Christendom and especially the Holy Empire.

And since this may no longer be suffered or tolerated without ruinous harm to all of Christendom, so we have completely agreed – with a well-considered disposition, by means of much and various discussion and counsel, which we have earnestly undertaken concerning this among ourselves and with many other princes and lords of the Holy Empire, for the assistance of the Holy Church, the comfort of Christendom and the honour and profit of the Holy Empire – that we want fully and specifically to remove and depose the above-written Lord Wenceslas as a neglectful procrastinator, dismemberer and one unworthy of the Holy Empire from the same Holy Roman Empire and all the dignities pertaining to it with immediate effect.

And we Archbishop Johann, called first in God's name, seated over the judicial court, remove and depose with this, our judgement, which we make and render with this written document, the said Lord Wenceslas as an unprofitable, neglectful, inattentive dismemberer and unworthy administrator of the Holy Roman Empire from the same Roman Empire and from all the dignities, honours and lordships belonging to it, in the name and on behalf of our above-written lords and fellow electors of the Holy Roman Empire and also ourselves, because of these matters that have just been mentioned and many other great transgressions and matters that have moved us to this decision. And because of this we declare to all princes, lords, knights, retainers, towns, lands and people of the Holy Empire that henceforth the oaths and homage that they have done to the person of the above-named Lord Wenceslas with regard to the Holy Empire are fully and specifically void, and we exhort and call upon them by the power of the oaths by which they are bound to the Holy Empire that henceforth they should no longer be obedient nor devoted in any way towards the above-named Lord Wenceslas as a king of the Romans, nor should they give him or follow him as a king of the Romans with any legal assistance, service, revenues, goods or other contributions – whatever they may be called – but rather they should reserve these things for the one who, by the grace of God, will be elected as a more profitable and suitable king of the Romans.

So that this may be certified and documented, we Johann, above-mentioned archbishop of Mainz, have had this our present letter drawn up, with an open-ended format with these public notarial subscriptions that follow,[22] and had our great seal attached to it. The above-written judgement and sentence was read out and pronounced by us, Johann, above-named archbishop of Mainz, in our name and on behalf of our above-named lords, our fellow electors, in Oberlahnstein on the Rhine, in the diocese of Trier near Braubach, while sitting on a chair there that was elevated to a seat of judgement, while our above-named lords the electors and we ourselves sat in a judicial session in that place, in the year after Christ's birth 1400, in the eight indiction,[23] on Friday the twentieth day of the month of August, shortly before the ninth hour [i.e. 3 pm], in the eleventh year of the papal authority of the most Holy Father and lord in Christ, Lord [Pope] Boniface [IX, r. 1389–1404], by divine

22 On the original copies of the document, space was left for clerical notaries to sign and thereby witness that the sentence against Wenceslas had indeed been pronounced in the manner asserted in the document, and that the document itself was authentic. Indeed, the surviving original copies have multiple different notarial hands in the subscription; see Weizsäcker et al. (eds), *Deutsche Reichstagsakten. Ältere Reihe*, vol. III, p. 254.
23 'Indictions' (*indictiones*) were fifteen-year cycles used for tax assessment purposes in the late antique Roman Empire.

providence the ninth pope of this name, in the presence of [a long list of princes and noblemen follows, mostly clients of the Count Palatine who was elected to replace Wenceslas as King Rupert on 21 August 1400, although it also included the influential Burgrave Friedrich VI of Nuremberg [6]] and many other lords, knights and great and notable numbers of people both spiritual and temporal, called and solicited as witnesses to these above-written things.

6. King Sigismund's staging of royal authority in Ulrich Richental's chronicle (1417)

Buck (ed.), *Chronik*, pp. 87–90.

Written over an uncertain period starting in the 1420s, this chronicle by Ulrich Richental, proud burgher of Constance, provides (in the words of its most recent editor) 'an admittedly retrospective view that romanticised and idealised in hindsight some of what took place in Constance between 1414 and 1418' but nevertheless offers 'an astonishingly realistic and authentic perspective on the turbulent and sometimes dramatic events' surrounding the ecumenical council based in the city during those years.[24] Richental's narrative encompasses both the great acts of kings, princes and prelates and mundane but often entertaining and revealing details about the experience of everyday life during these four unusual years in the city. This extract is part of a sequence of enfeoffments described by Richental in his coverage of the spring of 1417, when Sigismund returned in triumph to Constance after a whirlwind diplomatic tour of Western Europe, enabling him to devote himself more fully to the internal affairs of the Empire – including his longstanding ally the burgrave of Nuremberg, who had been administering Sigismund's own margraviate of Brandenburg in his absence, and was now rewarded with the formal receipt of that title and its attendant electoral dignity.

On Tuesday of Holy Week [6 April 1417] our lord the king came from Radolfzell to Constance. On the same Tuesday three dukes of Bavaria also rode into Constance two hours after midday. They were Duke Wilhelm [III of Bavaria-Munich, r. 1397–1435], Duke Ernst [of Bavaria-Munich, r. 1397–1438] and Duke Heinrich [XVI of Bavaria-Landshut, r. 1393–1450]. Extravagantly adorned, they rode towards all the temporal princes.

On the Thursday of Holy Week, Margrave Friedrich [IV] the Elder of Meissen [r. 1384–1440] arrived with thirteen counts, his servitors. And our lord the king, the three dukes of Bavaria, who had just arrived, Duke Rudolf [III] of Saxony[-Wittenberg, r. 1388–1419],

---

24 Buck (ed.), *Chronik*, p. XV.

Duke Ludwig [II] of Brieg [r. 1399–1436], Duke [i.e. Count Palatine] Ludwig [III, r. 1410–36], the burgrave [Friedrich VI of Nuremberg, 1371–1440] and all temporal princes and lords rode out to meet him. Sixteen wagons laden with baggage and twenty-eight horses with appended bags proceeded before him. And more than 500 horses arrived, all with full armour and silver and gold chains. And it was the most beautiful entry that had ever been seen. They proceeded towards the monastery in Kreuzlingen. And his livery was a lion, half silver and half gold.

After that, on the Sunday on which one sings *Quasi modo geniti*, that is on the eighth day during Easter, on the eighth day of April,[25] the highly esteemed prince Burgrave Friedrich of Nuremberg received his electorate, the margraviate of Brandenburg, at the eighth hour of the day, just before the mealtime, at Constance's upper market. There, before the tall house called 'At the Harbour', a wide stepped stage had been constructed over which was a vaulted canopy with archways, and in front of the archways was a flat area on which a good thirty people could stand. The flat area was covered with a large, beautiful golden cloth. And both corners next to it were also covered in golden cloths. And against the wall there was also a golden cloth, so that a person who gazed upon it got the marvellous impression that there was a fountain of gold.

And early on the same morning, as the day began, all the trumpeters rode around the city. The burgrave's servitors rode with them, as did many other people who wished to enter his service. Each carried a stick in his hand that was one cubit long. At the end of the stick was a red banner. The bottom of the stick was pointed and the top a hand-span wide.

And then two knights on two steeds led the way, one with a banner with the arms of the margraviate of Brandenburg on a lance and the other with the shield of the burgraves of Nuremberg. They rode through the city three times. Upon their third ride, which was just before the ninth hour of the day, all the princes and lords who wished to serve him at that moment gathered before his lodgings, which were near the small butchery, in Heinrich Tettikofer's tall house. And each was given a little red banner to hold in his hand.

25 This actually took place on 18 April 1417. Ibid., p. 88, n. 588.

And they rode with him thusly attired through the little alley and Morder Lane, New Lane and St Paul's Lane to the upper market. The two banners on lances were borne before him. The people on horseback were so numerous that some of them had to stop between Ring Lane and St Paul's fountain. And all the houses with a view onto the market were packed full of people.

And as the burgrave arrived at the market with the banners and with the people bearing him along on all sides, a beautiful chair covered with a golden cloth was on the wide stage next to the house, against the walls made of golden cloth coverings.

And Duke [i.e. Count Palatine] Ludwig of Bavaria, from Heidelberg, emerged first from the house through a wooden shutter, and he was dressed in a tunic like that of a deacon who reads the gospel-book, had colourful fur around his neck, a felt hat on his head and an unsheathed sword in his hand. He positioned himself on a chair near the wall, so that many people could easily see him, and turned his face towards the market. Just before this, three cardinals and archbishops and the king's chancellor had gone up onto the stage. They had documents in their hands stating what oaths he should swear to the Holy Roman Empire.

After Duke Ludwig came Duke Rudolf of Saxony the Elder, the elector, dressed in the same garments as Duke Ludwig, and he carried a golden sceptre in his hand and positioned his back to the wall on the right-hand side and looked out over the upper market so that many people could easily see him.

After that came Duke Heinrich of Bavaria; he was not as well instructed as the two electors, but he proceeded as well as he could in his expensive attire, and carried a sceptre in his hand, which was like a large sphere and was entirely made of gold, and on top of it there was a golden cross. He positioned himself next to Duke Rudolf of Saxony and also turned his back to the wall and looked out over the upper market. Then a sudden silence descended on the crowd. Our lord the king arrived, and he was dressed in golden garments like a cleric reading the gospel-books, and also wore an amice around his neck and a tall golden crown on his head. And in either archway in front of him were placed two large burning candles. And as he emerged the bishops and cardinals stood opposite him. He then bade them to sit down, and also sat on a cushion and turned his back to the wall and his face to the market, so that many people could easily see him. And the duke of Saxony put the sceptre in one of his hands and Duke Heinrich put the sphere in his other hand. Duke Ludwig laid the sword in his lap. Then the trumpeters began to trumpet in competition with the pipers. After that total silence reigned. During the silence Burgrave Friedrich was called up. He dismounted and went up to the stage, and he was accompanied by people carrying the two banners. And as he arrived up there and knelt down before the king and took each banner in his hand, words were read out to him which explained that he should swear an oath and seal a document to the Holy Empire. Once the document had been read out, our lord the king handed back the sceptre and the sphere. Then Duke Ludwig removed the sword from his lap and held it high aloft, and rested its point in the king's crown.[26] Then the king received both banners in one hand. Then Burgrave Friedrich swore an oath before all the world. The king accepted this oath and enfeoffed him with the electorate, the margraviate and also the burgraviate of Nuremberg. And then all the trumpeters trumpeted and all the pipers piped and many people rode home.

[Here many copies of the Richental chronicle include illustrations of this enfeoffment, showing King Sigismund enthroned, the kneeling burgrave with his banners, the chancellor reading out the words of the feudal oath to the Holy Roman Empire and the three princes holding the imperial insignia.]

The same Margrave Friedrich of Brandenburg, burgrave of Nuremberg, invited our lord the king, all the electors, counts, knights and retainers and many bishops and other priests and learned people to the meal that followed – except the cardinals. They do not eat with any lay men. And on the same day he honestly compensated the king's chancellor, doorkeeper, the trumpeters, pipers and all the musicians, such that none had any complaint about him.

Our lord the king always used this order of ceremonies and these decorations whenever he enfeoffed princes. However, when he enfeoffed barons or other lords with their fiefs, he only did so in the street or in lodgings or wherever he wished.

---

26 On this curious symbolic tableau, see Paravicini, 'Das Schwert'.

7. A letter of Emperor Frederick III requesting troops from the imperial cities (1475)

Lünig (ed.), *Reichs-Archiv*, pp. 85–86.

The 1470s saw rising tensions between the ambitious Duke Charles 'the Bold' of Burgundy (r. 1467–77) and several parties within the Holy Roman Empire, culminating in all-out war on several fronts. His attempts to persuade Frederick III to grant him a royal title alienated the emperor, even as the latter pursued a marriage alliance between Charles's daughter Mary and his son Maximilian. Charles made enemies in Alsace, Outer Austria and Switzerland through the exploitation of lands he purchased in pledge on the Upper Rhine. He also intervened militarily along the Middle Rhine on behalf of his ally, Archbishop Ruprecht of Cologne (r. 1463–80), against the towns in Ruprecht's archbishopric. When Charles began to besiege the town of Neuss in July 1474, the emperor called upon the princes and cities to provide troops for an imperial army to expel the Burgundians. Frederick led a force in person to relieve Neuss, which he achieved in May 1475. In the months leading up to that victory he extracted several other towns from Burgundian control, and this letter was written during that phase before the final advance on Neuss.

We Frederick, by the grace of God Roman emperor, ever augmenter of the Empire, king of Hungary, Dalmatia, Croatia etc., duke of Austria, Styria, Carinthia and Carniola etc., announce to our and the Empire's honourable and well-beloved faithful people, the mayors, councils and communities of the cities everywhere in the Holy Empire, our grace and all good things.

Honourable and well-beloved faithful people, we have (after our great period of instability, now some time ago) betaken ourselves hither to the See of Cologne in person, together with our and the Empire's electors, princes, counts, those of the cities and other faithful people; and, for the deliverance and preservation of the Holy Empire and German nation, with the assistance of Almighty God, we intend to offer mighty resistance against the duke of Burgundy in his improper, arbitrary undertaking that he has carried out in the See of Cologne, which is an electorate and a notable member of the Holy Empire, to the truncation, severance and injury of the Holy

Empire and German nation, against the prohibition issued against him by our Holy Father the pope and by us. And to that end we have conquered – with great effort, expense and labour – certain towns and fortifications along the Rhine in which the same duke of Burgundy's people have been, and we are now in daily military preparations to meet the same duke of Burgundy in the field and to defy and defeat him with armed force, through God's help.

And given that you have sent far fewer men than you are obliged to provide in our lists of planned troop levies[27] – as you yourselves should be aware, as faithful subjects of the Holy Empire – we consider that, for the sake of the honour and salvation of the Holy Empire of the German nation and of you yourselves, you ought to have sent more men and offered more assistance to us as Roman emperor, your natural lord, for such a significant cause (in which we have personally committed ourselves, for your good and preservation and that of other subjects of the Empire). But you have not yet done so.

Therefore we call upon you once again to fulfil the obligations, vows and oaths by which you are bound to us and the Holy Empire, and also remind each of you of your illustrious traditions and present status. Furthermore, we mandate earnestly and firmly, by our Roman imperial authority and integrity of office, that you should assemble immediately in light of this, our imperial letter with all your people and those who belong to them, and that on the upcoming Laetare Sunday [5 March 1475] you should appear in the field with one-quarter of all the male people that you have among you in the cities of the Empire and otherwise in the countryside or in other locales in order to help accomplish this resistance and contest. And you should not delay in doing this, considering the notable urgency of the issue, on pain of losing all fiefs, tolls, graces, liberties, letters, privileges, jurisdictions and whatever else you hold from us and the Holy Empire and other individuals, and additionally on pain of our and the Empire's ban and double ban and all other penalties, punishments and fines which we as a Roman emperor might want to impose on you in this matter.

---

27 *Anschla^egen* – the name given to proportional lists drawn up at imperial diets of troops and funds that all members of the Empire were supposed to provide to joint initiatives (see [16]).

And inasmuch as you care about avoiding our and the Empire's grave disfavour and the penalties, punishments and fines mentioned above, in doing this you will be following our earnest intentions and doing us a special favour as well as acting justly, which we will recognise with all grace and benevolence towards you, and which will never be forgotten. However, if you do not do this, and are disobedient towards this, our imperial command, which we do not expect of you as a matter of justice in view of your obligations and the causes mentioned above, we recognise and declare you to have fallen instantly herewith into all the penalties mentioned above, to their greatest extent and in all their forms, as if you had been recognised and declared to be under the same penalties – all with judicial verdicts and adjudication – by us and the Empire's electors and princes and others who can exercise such mandates. Keep this in mind!

Given at Andernach on the Saturday after the Feast of the Conversion of St Paul [28 January], in the year of our Lord [14]75, in the thirty-third year of our emperorship.

8. King Maximilian I's exhortations to an imperial diet in Constance (1507)

Bock et al. (eds), *Deutsche Reichstagsakten. Mittlere Reihe*, vol. IX, pp. 274–90.

A short summary, hastily drawn up, of the form and content of what the most serene, very mighty prince and lord, Lord Maximilian, king of the Romans, ever augmenter of the Empire, king of Hungary, Dalmatia and Croatia, archduke of Austria, duke of Burgundy, Brabant etc. and Count Palatine etc., our most gracious lord, expressed about what he has dealt with, undertaken, devoted himself to and done in the time of his Majesty's reign up until now on behalf of the Holy Empire and German nation's common good and welfare, and also what succour and assistance his Majesty has had and received for that purpose from the Holy Empire, and how his royal Majesty informed the electors, princes and estates of the Empire at the present imperial diet about this, reminded them of it, and thereupon made exhortations for an expedition to Rome to retain the imperial crown within the German nation.

By way of introduction, it should be considered that nine imperial diets have been held in the times and reign of his Roman royal Majesty on account of the concerns and necessities of the Holy Empire and German nation, as will in part be recounted and described hereafter, and now the tenth will be held, which concerns the Holy Empire and German nation more than all the previous nine ones, in view of the great power of the king of France, by which means he has conquered Milan and Brittany. Therefore it is good and necessary for the Roman royal Majesty and the electors, princes and estates of the Empire to consider and examine properly the preceding nine imperial diets and what was negotiated and established there. For these imperial diets and negotiations were all undertaken and held and all took place through his Roman royal Majesty, whose only good and aspirational will and intention has been to preserve, strengthen, set right and bring peace and justice to the frontiers of the Holy Empire and German nation, and now to recover the imperial crown for the praise and honour of the Holy Empire and all Germans.

And for all that, his Roman royal Majesty has not received any more in money and troops than 500,000 florins from all the designated imperial diets in the sixteen years that his royal Majesty has governed,[28] plus between roughly 300,000 and 400,000 outstanding florins that are still owed to his Majesty. However, this estimate does not include the assistance granted during the reign of Emperor Frederick of praiseworthy memory for the freeing of his royal Majesty from the Flemings that took place,[29] as covered below.

Conversely, his Roman royal Majesty has expended and devoted over 10,000,000 florins – and so much more besides that it can scarcely be calculated or conceived – from his Majesty's hereditary lands of Austria and Burgundy, for the deliverance and preservation of the same, so that they remain with his Majesty's dynasty, the praiseworthy princes of Austria, and so that they may be a shield and refuge for the Holy Empire and the Germans against myriad nations such as the French, Hungarians and infidels [i.e. Ottomans], and also for the maintenance, benefit and good of the Empire and German nation. Additionally, his Majesty has foregone sleep on thousands of nights, and in all his Majesty's days he has expended more in effort and work than any human, living or bygone, has ever done before, as many know. He still does so, day and night, and will continue to do so willingly and voluntarily for as long as his Majesty's age and physical condition permit. Hence it is well to be believed and accepted that for every one florin handed over by the Empire to his royal Majesty for his Majesty's and the Empire's undertakings and necessities, his royal Majesty has correspondingly devoted 100 florins overall from his own patrimonial domains and whatever else has come to his Majesty from God and fortune, and also from his Majesty's Burgundian and Austrian lands for the benefit and good of the same and the Empire and German nation, as noted above, such that his Majesty is so denuded and impoverished that he no longer enjoys such a good condition as before (which he suffers willingly).

Alongside this, his Roman royal Majesty has always proved and conducted himself faithfully, obediently and clemently as a born

---

28 Maximilian was elected in 1486, but the first imperial diet convoked in his name was at Nuremberg in 1491.
29 In early 1488 Maximilian was imprisoned in Bruges during a Flemish uprising in the Burgundian lands. With assistance from the imperial estates, his father Frederick raised an army to free him.

archduke of Austria and obedient German prince by divine providence, who also proffers the oath to the Empire like other obedient German princes, and in relation to everything else (in terms of kingdoms, lands and peoples) that has become his Majesty's property through marriage and other natural succession in various ways, according to his royal Majesty's bloodline, which is well known and one of the mightiest among the Germans. And now he has been taking up arms for thirty-one years for the sake of the administration of the Roman Empire and German nation, and the preservation of their natural jurisdictions and welfare.

[Maximilian launches into a lengthy and tendentious account of his life and career. He begins with the Burgundian Wars of the 1470s and his acquisition of the Burgundian lands through marriage, triggering rivalry and war with France. He covers his election as king and his conflicts in Flanders and against King Matthias Corvinus of Hungary in the 1480s. His recollections of the 1490s discuss the imperial diets he convoked in that decade, mentioning only the insufficient funds granted at those occasions by the estates, and his many ongoing wars against France, the Turks, the Swiss, factions of Hungarian nobles and the powers competing in Italy from the outbreak of the Italian Wars in 1494. He complains about the short-lived attempt to usurp his authority through the establishment of an imperial council in 1500–01 [24] and mentions his victory over the Wittelsbachs in the War of Landshut Succession in 1504–05. He then emphasises the danger presented by the French conquest of Milan, which threatens to give them control over the pope and 'ultimately to bring the Roman emperorship (which the Germans chivalrously conquered many years ago through the shedding of their blood and have held ever since) under their authority'. He accepts that the estates will need to discuss all these events and their implications.]

Yet for the greater good, his Roman royal Majesty highly, earnestly and amicably requests of and appeals to the electors, princes and estates of the Empire that they should personally and sedulously take to heart and consider the events that have taken place so far, narrated above, and the concerns and necessities of the Holy Empire and German nation, as well as what ignominy, dishonour and encumbrance might result from them, not only for his Majesty but for all of us, even the lowest-ranking, if we do not do and undertake something to address them swiftly and with consideration and seriousness. And he requests that they stalwartly tackle them with counsel, assistance and succour to the Holy Empire, German nation and all of themselves, for the sake of especial honour and good; that they do not weigh down or delay any effort or expenditure; and that in the end they strive and assist to ensure that the imperial crown is attained for all of our common good, honour and praise, and also that the papacy is kept aligned with our will, and the king of France's endeavours are thereby checked and overturned. Also, that whatever is consequently decided here should be carried out and fulfilled swiftly, faithfully and without prolongment, and not refused in any way.

His Majesty is not only inclined towards all this but also entirely desirous and prepared, God willing, to render a greater service towards the Holy Empire and all Germans this year than ever before, and indeed to expend his Majesty's body and all that Almighty God has granted his Majesty in terms of allies, servitors, money and possessions, faithfully and unsparingly. Furthermore, his Majesty will sedulously show and educate his young [grand] sons and descendants [the future Charles V and Ferdinand I] (who are even now fully at the service of the Holy Empire and German nation and wish to be a good shield and refuge against the enemies of the same, just as his royal Majesty has been for thirty-one years now, but may not be capable of being for much longer on account of his age) to serve the Holy Empire, its estates and the German nation in these matters forevermore.

Carried out and printed during the praiseworthy imperial diet at Constance in the year of our Lord etc. 1500 and in the seventh [year] etc.

9. An electoral contract between the electors and King Charles V (1519)

Kluckhohn et al. (eds), *Deutsche Reichstagsakten. Jüngere Reihe*, vol. I, pp. 864–76.

We Charles V, by the grace of God king-elect of the Romans, archduke of Austria etc., king of Spain, both Sicilies and Jerusalem etc., duke of Burgundy and Brabant etc., count of Habsburg, Flanders, Tyrol etc., publicly acknowledge and proclaim to all:

In the last few days, by the providence of the Almighty, we were elevated, exalted and installed to the honour and dignity of the Roman royal name and authority through election by the highly worthy, honourable and high-born Albrecht, cardinal of the church titled St Chrysogonus, archbishop of Mainz [r. 1514–45] and Magdeburg, administrator of the See of Halberstadt, Hermann [V] of Cologne [r. 1515–47] and Richard of Trier [r. 1511–31], archbishops, arch-chancellors of the Holy Roman Empire in Germany, Italy and Gaul and in the kingdom of Arles, Ludwig [V], Count Palatine of the Rhine and duke of Bavaria [r. 1508–44], Friedrich [III 'the Wise'], duke of Saxony, landgrave of Thuringia and margrave of Meissen [r. 1486–1525] and Joachim [I], margrave of Brandenburg, duke of Stettin, Pomerania and of the Kashubians and the Wends, burgrave of Nuremberg and prince of Rügen [r. 1499–1535], arch-steward, arch-marshal and arch-chamberlain of the Holy Roman Empire, our well-beloved associates, relations and electors – an honour and dignity which we have also accepted as an onus on ourselves, for the praise of God, the honour of the Holy Empire and the sake of Christendom, the German nation and the common good.

Accordingly, we united ourselves with, entered into a treaty with and promised to our same well-beloved associates, relations and electors, out of our own gracious free will, to accept, concede and hold to these following articles in the manner of a legal contract and pact, knowingly and by the power of this document.

[1] First, that during the period of this royal dignity, office and reign we will maintain Christendom and the See of Rome, as well as his papal Holiness and the churches, in good order and protection as the advocate of the same. Additionally, we ought and desire

to propagate, build up and enact peace, justice and unity, especially in the Holy Empire, such that they have, attain and preserve their proper course for the poor and the rich alike, and that these same may be judged according to the ordinances, liberties and old praiseworthy customs.

[2] We especially ought and desire to confirm, renew and – where necessary – improve, with the counsel of our and the Empire's electors, princes and other estates, the previously issued Golden Bull [14], royal public peace [21] and other ordinances and laws of the Holy Empire, as circumstances might require at any time in the Empire's affairs.

[3] Additionally, to set up and establish – in the manner considered most intelligent – a praiseworthy, honourable governing council consisting of pious, agreeable, serious, judicious, honest people of the German nation alongside some electors and princes, as was conceived and held power once before,[30] so that the flaws, transgressions and burdens everywhere in the Holy Empire may be deflected, reformed and brought into good condition and order; yet without harming the rights and liberties of our well-beloved cousins the electors of the Palatinate and Saxony, from which they derive their vicarial offices.

[4: Charles promises to respect the status, rights and privileges of the electors and other imperial estates.]

[5] We also permit that from time to time they – the six electors just mentioned – may come together, per the requirements of the Golden Bull [14] and the circumstances in the Holy Empire, according to their necessity and what burdensome responsibilities they might have, in order to deliberate and counsel one another regarding the same. Furthermore, we ought and wish neither to prevent nor to disturb them in this, and will therefore show no disfavour or reluctance towards them collectively or individually, but will behave graciously and impeccably in this and other matters, in keeping with the Golden Bull.

[6] We also ought and desire to quash and abolish all the inappropriate and troublesome alliances, associations and bands of the subjects, the nobility and the common people, and also the

---

30 A previous *Reichsregiment* [24] had briefly operated from 1500 to 1502.

insurrections, uprisings and illegal violence that have been undertaken and henceforth might be carried out against the electors, princes and others, and so to act with the counsel and assistance of the electors, princes and other estates as to ensure that these – as is befitting and just – are forbidden and prevented in the future.

[7] Additionally, we should not and do not want to make any alliance or union with any foreign nation nor within the Empire for ourselves as king of the Romans with regards to the Empire's affairs, unless we have first notified the six electors about it at an appropriate time and at an appointed representative council, and obtained their collective or majority consent to do so.

[8: Charles promises to restore to the princes and estates possessions that were violently seized from them in the past.

9: Charles promises not to alienate any of the Empire's lands or possessions without the electors' permission, and to strive to restore those that have already been lost.

10: Charles promises to return to the Empire any illegitimately acquired feudal possessions and titles.

11: Charles promises to pursue peaceful diplomacy with the Christian powers neighbouring the Empire, not to bring foreign troops into it without consulting the estates and to assist the Empire against external attacks.]

[12] Likewise, we ought not to burden or encumber the electors and other estates of the same Empire with imperial diets, chancery fees, military service obligations, impositions or taxes unnecessarily and without honest, serious cause. Also, in acceptable, necessary cases, we ought not to assess or announce the taxes, troop levies and imperial diets without the knowledge and consent of the six electors having first been obtained, as mentioned above, and especially not to undertake or announce any imperial diet outside of the Empire of the German nation.

[13] We also ought and desire to fill and provide our royal and the Empire's offices, at court and more generally in the Empire, with people from no other nation than born Germans, who should not be of low estate or status but distinguished, upstanding people from the nobility, of princely, comital or lordly and otherwise of good, sound origin; also, to preserve the above-named offices in

their honours, dignities, cases, rights and jurisdictional powers and not to deprive them of the same or to allow them to be deprived of them, without deceit.

[14] Additionally, in the documentation and affairs of the Empire, we ought not to allow any other tongue or language to be used except the German or Latin tongue, except in places where another language is in common practice and usage, in which case we and our people may also employ that same language there.

[15: Charles promises not to summon the imperial estates to judicial or arbitrational court cases outside of the German nation, but only to do so within the Empire.

16: Charles promises to uphold the concordats and other treaties between the German nation and its princes on the one hand and the papacy and Curia on the other, and to address the grievances regarding abuses which contravene these concordats.

17: Charles promises to seek to abolish the great mercantile trading companies.

18: Charles promises not to levy new tolls or to increase old ones without the electors' permission.

19: Charles promises to repeal exemptions from the tolls of the Rhenish electors.

20: Charles promises not to interfere in princes' and other estates' litigation concerning their liberties, privileges and rights.]

[21] Also, we ourselves should not and do not want to violate the rights of the electors, princes, prelates, counts, lords and other estates of the Empire. Nor should we bring this about, or order others to do so, but where we or anybody else has a dispute with them or one of them in particular, or has any claim to bring, for the avoidance of agitation, division and other harmful dangers in the Holy Empire and the preservation of peace and unity, the same is to be referred to and allowed to play out in its entirety in the proper investigative and judicial setting, and in those or other cases in which they are willing and glad to accept orderly justice, it is in no way to be allowed that they be harmed, attacked or assailed with robbery, abduction, arson, feuding, war or other things of this nature.

[22: Charles promises not to place anybody in the imperial ban or double ban without cause and without the appropriate judicial processes being followed.

23: Charles promises to restore to the Empire those imperial taxes paid by the cities that have been alienated into the hands of various individuals.

24: Charles promises not to hand out unowned and escheated fiefs, but to use them to build up the Empire's resources and restore its status.

25: Charles promises to hand over to the Empire all lands and possessions that he conquers with the help of the imperial estates, or without their help where the conquered items appertain to the Empire.

26: Charles promises to approve all the activities of the two imperial vicars, i.e., the Palatine and Saxon electors.]

[27] And since up until now there have been and still are many complaints about and flaws in the coinage in the Empire, we desire above all to deal with it with the counsel of the electors, princes and estates of the Empire, and to employ all possible diligence to establish it in a stable order and condition.

[28] And in particular, we should not and do not want to claim, arrogate to ourselves or in any way put to the test or aspire after endeavouring to assign any succession or inheritance of the oft-named Roman Empire onto ourselves, our heirs and descendants or anybody else. Rather, if it should come to legal disputes, as necessity and circumstances might require, we – and likewise our children, heirs and descendants – should leave the said electors and their descendants and heirs in peace and fully undisturbed at all times with respect to their free electoral votes, which have been entrusted to them by age-old tradition, empowered by the Golden Bull, papal rights and other laws and liberties. However, if somebody should pursue or act against this or coerce the electors regarding their electoral rights, which ought not to happen in any way, all that should be void and baseless and regarded as such.

[28] We also ought and desire to set and announce our first courtly assembly to be held in Nuremberg, as is the old tradition in the Empire.

[29] We the above-mentioned king-elect of the Romans have vowed, promised and pledged all of this, and every specific point noted above, by our royal honour, dignity and words, in the name of truth. We also do the same herewith and by the power of this document, just as if we had sworn a corporeal oath to God and the saints: to hold the same constantly, firmly and inviolably, to comply with it faithfully and not to be or do anything against it, nor to allow anything to be carried out against it by any means or methods that might be thought up.

[30] We also desire to include in this, our promise, that we will not allow to be issued or permit to take place in any way any rescript, mandate or any infringements or as-yet unheard-of things against the Golden Bull and the ordinances and laws of the Empire that have been made until now or might be established in the future by us with the counsel of the electors and princes and other estates of the Holy Empire.

[32] If, however, anything contrary to this or the other above-mentioned articles and points should come to pass or be issued, all of that should be considered powerless, void and removed, just as we also annul, void and dismiss it herewith, now as then and then as now, and, where necessary, commit to providing documentary evidence of this to any party that requests it, which we ought indeed to be obliged to give and have rendered, without fraud and deceit.

[33] We also ought and desire as soon as possible and convenient to betake ourselves in person into the Empire of the German nation in order to receive the Roman royal crown, as well behoves us as king-elect of the Romans, and to do the other appropriate things related to that; and also to have and maintain our royal residence, presence and holding of court in the Holy Roman Empire of the German nation most of the time, as far as possible, for the honour, benefit and good of all the members, estates and subjects of the same; and subsequently, once we have received the royal crown, as stated above, to make our best effort also to attain the imperial crown as soon as possible, at an appropriate and opportune time; and, as far as possible, to show and conduct ourselves in all of this in such a manner that no shortcomings occur or be noted on our part.

To authenticate this we have made six copies of this document with identical wording and sealed them with our attached royal seal, and handed one over to each of the above-mentioned electors. Given on the third day of the month of July, 1519 years after Christ's birth, in the first year of our Roman reign and the fourth year of our Spanish reign.

II
ASSEMBLIES AND ORDINANCES TO THE MID-FIFTEENTH CENTURY

Even if one focuses only on the Romano-German kings and emperors (see section I), it soon becomes apparent that the political landscape of the late medieval German lands was exceptionally fragmented, and that power within it was dispersed among multiple actors and centres. The period between the mid-fourteenth and mid-sixteenth centuries saw many authorities in the Holy Roman Empire take on more formal roles in the co-governance of the realm. Assemblies were the most important sites for their involvement. (Other more regional and local forms and contexts of governance are illustrated in sections V–VII.) In themselves, assemblies were nothing new. It had been customary since the early Middle Ages to negotiate political and judicial questions at meetings of prominent figures in most European societies. However, an ever-larger number of surviving sources in the later Middle Ages and into the early modern period permits us to see more clearly just how many assemblies – often called 'diets' (*dietae, Tage*)[1] – were held in the German lands at multiple levels of society, and that the political assemblies at the apex of imperial politics were changing and institutionalising in significant ways.

By the end of the fifteenth century, these 'central' assemblies were known as 'imperial diets' (*Reichstage*). They functioned as the settings for legislating and policymaking on behalf of the entire Holy Roman Empire, with the formal participation and approbation of the princes, nobles and city councillors who increasingly claimed to represent and embody the realm. Nineteenth-century historians in Germany were tempted to see in these assemblies the precursors of a modern parliament for the German nation. They even projected this nationalist-constitutionalist interpretation of assemblies back into the mid-fourteenth century (the starting point of the *Deutsche Reichstagsakten* series – the monumental edition of sources pertaining to the imperial assemblies and diets, begun in 1867 and

---

1 See Hardy, '*Tage* (Courts, Councils, and Diets)'.

still ongoing).² Late twentieth- and early twenty-first century scholarship has entirely rejected this anachronistic and teleological view. It is clear that assemblies before the fifteenth century were qualitatively different from those that followed. Rather than being conceived as gatherings of a multilateral community incarnating the entire polity, they were usually sparsely attended and closely attached to the court of the king or emperor (the Latin word *curia* could refer both to this court and to an assembly held within the court's orbit). Modern historians have coined the term *Hoftag* to characterise these assemblies.³ These became more frequent and inclusive in the course of a series of crises of authority during the reigns of Wenceslas, Sigismund and Frederick III, against the background of external dangers and/or internal disorder. It would be premature to characterise these assemblies as a fully formed, systematic 'imperial diet', but they clearly derived their legitimacy from the involvement of actors other than the monarchs, notably the electors (as indicated by a new terminology of *gemeine Tage* – 'collective diets'), laying the foundations for this later institutionalisation around the year 1500.

The sources in this section provide readers with glimpses of this process unfolding. Wenceslas's summons to Strasbourg in 1383 [11] has some features reminiscent of the assemblies of his predecessors: it was the planned presence of the monarch's court that occasioned the meeting, convened for a traditional purpose – the customary right of the king to request help for a coronation expedition to Italy. However, with the vernacular now being used in royal correspondence, the meeting is called a 'diet' (*tag*) in the source, which was also the name for a variety of non-courtly assemblies.⁴ The summoned princes and cities were clearly expected to consent in some way to the topics under discussion, and not merely offer counsel, since the letter requests that the envoys be fully empowered to make decisions. By the 1420s, with King Sigismund kept out of Germany by crises in his other realms of Bohemia and Hungary and the Hussites presenting a perceived military and religious threat, the electors themselves were convoking pan-imperial diets in the monarch's absence. Their summons to an assembly

---

2 Annas, 'Die Geschichte der "Deutschen Reichstagsakten"'.
3 Annas, *Hoftag – Gemeiner Tag – Reichstag*.
4 Hardy, '*Tage* (Courts, Councils, and Diets)'.

in Nuremberg in 1422 [12] leaves no doubt about their claim to co-govern the Holy Roman Empire and manage its affairs on behalf of Christendom. The summons issued by Frederick III to a diet in Regensburg in 1454 [13] displays yet more changes. While the emperor was still convoking an ad hoc assembly on his own initiative, there was now a well-established formula encompassing all the would-be attendees as a systematic list constituting and representing the community of the realm ('spiritual and temporal electors and princes, prelates, counts, lords, cities and communes of the Holy Roman Empire'), with each member of this list receiving a summons. Frederick was cajoling them into attending because he needed their presence (or that of their envoys) to give legitimacy to proceedings. An axiom of the medieval Romano-canonical tradition held that *quod omnes tangit ab omnibus tractari et approbari debet* ('what touches all should be considered and approved by all'),[5] and the principle was well known to contemporary German princely councillors.[6] The preparations for this diet represent an important change in another sense, too. In the wake of the Ottoman conquest of Constantinople, the perceived danger of the Turks was now a central justification for internal political action within the Empire, and it would remain a catalysing factor into the period of greater consolidation illustrated in section III.

By the mid-fifteenth century, foreign contemporaries could be struck by the extreme frequency with which the German-speaking political community of the Holy Roman Empire held assemblies to negotiate the burning issues of the day, seemingly without reaching firm resolutions. The Sienese humanist Aeneas Silvius Piccolomini (b. 1405, subsequently elected as Pope Pius II, r. 1458–64) was a keen observer of events in the Empire, having been crowned poet laureate and given a post in the imperial chancery in the early 1440s. A letter of his written to Juan Carvajal, a papal envoy, complaining about the princes' penchant for endless yet seemingly futile sequences of diets [10], is perhaps the most famous observation made about late medieval German political culture. The context for his sarcasm was a series of diets held in 1443–44 to address the German princes' position in the schism between the conciliarists at the Council of Basel (1431–49) and Pope Eugenius IV.

---

5 See Watts, *Polities*, p. 76.
6 For example, Daniels, *Diplomatie*, p. 220.

Recent scholarship has underlined the need to read this letter critically: it is full of studied classical allusions, and Piccolomini's implicit frustration with the apparent inability of attendees to make decisions beyond convoking future diets obscures the symbolic role such diets played in instantiating the political community.[7] Nevertheless, this letter usefully conveys the sense of fascination and irritation that the culture of constant multilateral negotiation in the German lands elicited in observers.

While reaching consensus on contentious questions, and articulating that agreement in legislative form, often proved challenging at the Empire's main assemblies, these could nevertheless yield some substantial and durable ordinances and other legally binding outcomes. The most significant of these was the Golden Bull [14] issued by Charles IV in two stages at courtly assemblies in Nuremberg (January 1356) and Metz (December 1356). Its name – the 'Golden Bull' (*bulla aurea, goldene Bulle*) – gained currency around 1400 (Charles himself referred to the text as 'our imperial law-book').[8] It derives from the gold seal-like 'bull' which the imperial chancery used to authenticate especially important legal documents. Though very much the product of the 'pre-diet' phase of imperial political history, when assemblies were known as 'courts' and closely intertwined with the monarch's agenda and itinerary, the Golden Bull also inscribed the multilateral structure of authority in the Empire into law. It codified the procedures for electing a new king or emperor of the Romans and the extensive powers and prerogatives of the seven electors. The Golden Bull's emphasis on personal encounters and hierarchical ceremonies also highlights the importance of ritual in staging and bringing to life the idea of the Empire as a political community, a characteristic that would endure even as the emerging imperial diets became more institutionalised. A complex mix of motivations factored into the Golden Bull's content. After centuries of divisive papal intervention in imperial politics, the emperor and electors shared a desire to regulate succession to the imperial throne in a way that excluded the papacy.[9] Many of the Golden Bull's stipulations represented a

---

7 See Annas, 'Kaiser Friedrich III. und die Reichsversammlungen', pp. 29–31.
8 Fritz (ed.), *Monumenta Germaniae Historica. Constitutiones*, p. 539.
9 The most recent and detailed explanation of this background can be found in Schlotheuber and Theisen, *Die Goldene Bulle*,

compromise between acknowledging the extensive rights the electors had already enjoyed de facto for decades (while adding some new ones) and granting Charles unique privileges in his kingdom of Bohemia.

The Golden Bull would have a lasting and significant impact on the German lands. It came to be seen as a quasi-'constitutional' document: one of the Empire's foundational laws, alongside the 1442 'Royal Reformation' [17] and the public peace-ordinances [20–21], with which it was frequently bundled in fifteenth- and sixteenth-century manuscripts and printed editions. This translation is of the earliest German version of Golden Bull, translated from the Latin original in the 1360s, which served as the basis for almost all subsequent German versions of the text.[10] This German version outnumbers the Latin text in fifteenth-century manuscripts and, from the 1470s, printed editions,[11] suggesting that it was more widely used in practice – which makes its subtle differences from the Latin text all the more significant. (A complete translation of the Latin version was produced by Ernest Henderson in 1892,[12] and is now widely available in the public domain.)

For its part, the 'Royal Reformation' of 1442 [17] shows how the dynamics of high politics had changed in the century since the Golden Bull. Its content was the fruit of 'reform' debates among princes and cities in the later years of Sigismund and Albert II, a time when monarchs were absent from the realm. These factions sought to curtail destructive feuds and the much-resented Vehmic courts – self-appointed, itinerant courts staffed mostly by Westphalians and backed by violent vigilantism. (In the legal terminology of this time, new judicial regulations were often called 'reformations', so this peace-ordinance came to be known as the *königliche Reformation* – 'Royal Reformation'.) When Frederick III travelled from Austria to the western German lands for his coronation in 1442, the princes and cities presented him with this agenda to promulgate as legislation. As mentioned above, the Royal Reformation joined the Golden Bull in legal compilations. While it would be anachronistic to speak of 'constitutional law' in the Empire at this time, these

---

10 Heckmann, 'Zeitnahe Warnehmung und international Ausstrahlung', p. 940.
11 Ibid., pp. 976–1036 (catalogue of manuscripts and incunabula containing the Golden Bull).
12 Henderson (ed./trans.), *Select Historical Documents*, pp. 220–61.

ordinances created at the evolving assemblies formed the bedrock of a new kind of universally applicable, trans-regional law in an imperial polity that was otherwise highly decentralised.

The negotiation and improvisation that went on at the assemblies in this period produced other outcomes, too. Though more modest in impact, they tell us a great deal about the mentalities and customary methods favoured by the growing number of elites in attendance. In the mid-fourteenth century, peace-keeping associations were entirely regional affairs, sometimes sanctioned by the king [4, 37]. During the crisis of the 'Town War', in which coalitions of south German cities, nobles and princes waged a series of interlinked conflicts in the 1380s, participants in the emerging pan-imperial diets began to envision larger scale alliance projects as a means of restoring peace.[13] The Town War concluded with the decisive defeat of the Swabian and Rhenish city leagues. At a diet in Eger (modern-day Cheb) in 1389, the victorious princes imposed reparation payments, and Wenceslas encouraged or coerced all parties into accepting a peace treaty that was in effect a vast association, subdivided into subsidiary regional land-peace alliances [15]. This was not the only implementation of regional ways of doing things at the level of the Empire. Late medieval German alliance treaties often prescribed troop contribution quotas to be fulfilled by each member, commensurate with their wealth and population (e.g. [40]). As the Hussite crusades forced princes, lords and cities to collaborate militarily at the level of the Empire as a whole, the result was the first ever 'plan' for proportionate military contributions in 1422 [16] on the model of an alliance treaty, which by necessity required a novel form of information-gathering: a list of all imperially immediate members of the Empire. This document has gone down in German historiography as the first *Reichsmatrikel* ('imperial register'),[14] though the principle was not new, as we have just seen. These customary formats that were scaled up at the assemblies until the reign of Frederick III would feed into the institutionalisation of the Holy Roman Empire around 1500, as section III makes clear.

---

13 See Hardy, *Associative Political Culture*, chapter 9.
14 For example, Whaley, *Germany*, p. 30.

10. Aeneas Silvius Piccolomini's observations about German diets in a letter to Juan Carvajal (1444)

Wolkan (ed.), *Der Briefwechsel*, vol. II, no. 139.

Aeneas Silvius Piccolomini (elected pope as Pius II, r. 1458–64) was the most famous and widely read non-German commentator on the Holy Roman Empire. This Sienese humanist first travelled to Germany as an idealistic conciliarist and represented the Council of Basel in debates with papal envoys, including Juan Carvajal, the cleric addressed in this letter, with whom Piccolomini went on to maintain a decades-long correspondence. By 1444 he had been offered employment in the imperial chancery, whence he continued to observe an especially busy sequence of diets at which papalists and conciliarists sought to win allies among the German princes.

To the reverend father Lord Juan Carvajal, jurist and *auditor causarum* of the apostolic palace,[15] the poet Aeneas Silvius extends many greetings.

I was thrilled to hear that you have returned to Germany,[16] for I hope to see you again and would gladly speak and share a meal with you. Although we often disagree about ecclesiastical matters, still that disagreement is neither stubborn nor offensive, but that which is customary among philosophers who do not engage in disputation to show off but to arrive at truth. Nor again am I the one who would wish to present myself as the leader in this disagreement. This dispute is for the theologians, and it was enough for me to hold an opinion held by many others.

You ask me about the progress of the diet, so that I might report back to you what I expect will happen. The chancellor is doing as much as he can to satisfy your desire.[17] It is right that I neither know nor indicate more than that. If, nevertheless, you want

---

15 A judge of the Roman Rota (the appellate tribunal at the Curia).
16 *Germani[a]* – this singular form occurred frequently in medieval and Renaissance Latin, unlike the vernacular 'German lands' (*deutsche Lande*), which was almost always in the plural and only appeared as the singular *Deutschland* around the mid-sixteenth century.
17 At this time the chancellor of the imperial chancery was Kaspar Schlick, also a councillor of Frederick III, who was closely involved in organising a diet in

my prediction – for it is the prerogative of the poets to write prophecies – I will add a few words. To tell you the truth, I do not think that this diet will be any more fruitless than the others. You know what I mean by this? All diets are fecund; each one has another in its womb. In the land of the Arabs is a bird called the Phoenix, famous in the songs of the poets. Whenever it senses its death approaching (for it lives for 540 years) it prepares with incense its own funeral pyre, from the ashes of which soon rises another; and there is only ever one Phoenix. Make of this what you will. We have held diets for many years now, and the end is not near. Things are turbulent, opinions are divided. It delights certain people for neutrality to prevail, for it offers a new kind of fowling;[18] those in possession[19] are enemies of union, because none of them wish for power to be given back.

I saw and heard the snake whom you regarded with mistrust,[20] and he was not other than as I had imagined. If you feel his bite, you will die unless you have an antidote. Even Mithridates[21] would scarcely be protected against this poison.

You now have what I expect and whatever I can say without injury to my office. Farewell; and if it is in you to love someone who does not agree with you in all matters, then love me too.

From Vienna. 20 May 1444.

    Nuremberg in 1444. Piccolomini's letter was sent to Carvajal together with Schlick's own news. See Weizsäcker et al. (eds), *Deutsche Reichstagsakten. Jüngere Reihe*, vol. XVII, no. 133.
18 *novum est aucupium* – an idiom from Terence's play *Eunuchus*, line 247, said by the parasite Gnatho.
19 *possessores* – a word with a strong implication of material or financial occupation, especially in light of the Terence reference, perhaps imputing greed to the conciliarist faction of German princes.
20 It is unclear whom Aeneas is referring to with this cryptic analogy. Wolkan (*Der Briefwechsel*, vol. II, p. 318, note (a)) suggests it might be Jakob of Sierck, archbishop of Trier and leader of the conciliarist party among the princes (see [33]), although Sierck was in western Germany throughout 1444 (see the itinerary in Miller, *Jakob von Sierck*, p. 295), so Aeneas could not have literally seen and heard him.
21 Mithridates, king of Pontus (120–63 BCE), who was reputed to be quasi-immune to poison.

11. King Wenceslas summons Strasbourg's envoys to a diet in Nuremberg (1383)

Weizsäcker et al. (eds), *Deutsche Reichstagsakten. Ältere Reihe*, vol. I, pp. 366–67.

In the early years of his reign, Wenceslas (r. 1376–1400) convoked a diet roughly once per year, mostly to seek counsel and generate consensus about the papal schism and peace-keeping solutions in the increasingly troubled German heartlands. Wenceslas was also seeking assistance for a planned coronation expedition to Rome – a traditional justification for calling an assembly in the Empire – though this did not transpire in the end.

To the mayors, the council and the collective citizens of the city of Strasbourg, our and the Empire's well-beloved faithful people.

Wenceslas, by the grace of God king of the Romans, ever augmenter of the Empire, and king of Bohemia.

To my well-beloved faithful people. With God's help, we intend to travel to Rome in order to receive the imperial crown there. And so as first to bring order to the Empire in the German lands, we want to be in Nuremberg on the third Sunday of Lent, which is called *Oculi* [22 February]. We have also ordered the electors and other cities and faithful people belonging to us and the Empire to come there. Therefore we request of you that you extend assistance to us for this expedition of ours, as we trust you will do so; and, to this end, and because of the league and also other matters that we have to discuss with you,[22] that you send your associates with complete and full authority to us at the aforementioned diet in Nuremberg. The same associates of yours, dispatched for these matters, should be oriented and informed that their decision-making may not be restricted by any obligation to consult with you

---

22 This probably refers to Strasbourg's membership of a league of Rhenish cities formed in 1379 and embroiled in the conflicts that consumed Upper Germany until a truce in 1382. It may also be a reference to the peace-keeping league, or *Landfrieden*, into which Wenceslas hoped to draw the competing parties at the Nuremberg diet, but which ultimately failed to include all of them or preserve the peace. See Weizsäcker et al. (eds), *Deutsche Reichstagsakten. Ältere Reihe*, vol. I, pp. 368–74.

and your associates, as the noble Heinz Pflug, our councillor, servitor and liege, will properly instruct you on our behalf, concerning which you should fully credit him.

Given in Prague on the Sunday after Epiphany [11 January], in the twentieth year of our Bohemian reign and the seventh year of our Roman reign.

12. The electors summon Strasbourg's envoys to a diet in Nuremberg (1422)

Weizsäcker et al. (eds), *Deutsche Reichstagsakten. Ältere Reihe*, vol. VIII, pp. 125–26.

In the 1420s, two circumstances coincided that enabled the electors to play a leading role in convoking and presiding over diets of pan-imperial relevance: the Hussite Wars and the prolonged absence of King Sigismund in Bohemia and Hungary. Two crusades against the alleged Bohemian heretics, both involving substantial participation by German princes, failed in 1420 and 1421, and the electors called for a diet to discuss a third in 1422.

To the honourable, wise mayors and council of the city of Strasbourg, our well-beloved notable people.

Conrad [III] of Mainz [r. 1419–34], Otto of Trier [r. 1418–30], Dietrich of Cologne [1414–63], archbishops etc., Ludwig [III], Count Palatine of the Rhine [r. 1410–36], Albrecht [III], duke of Saxony [r. 1419–23] and Friedrich [I], margrave of Brandenburg [r. 1415–40] etc., all six electors of the Holy Roman Empire.

We extend our affectionate greetings to you, honourable, wise, well-beloved notable people. You and other subjects of the Holy Empire, and all Christian people, have surely heard about the disgraceful error that has unfortunately arisen in the land of Bohemia, and has now lasted for a long time, and still rapidly strengthens and grows from day to day, not only through those who live in the land of Bohemia, but also through some others whom they have ensnared and brought under their control. We have therefore been called upon and urged very often by prominent messengers of our Holy Father the pope and our gracious lord the Roman (etc.)[23] king to consider how such unbelief might be resisted. In particular, our gracious lord the Roman (etc.) king has advised us through the reverend lord Dietrich, archbishop of Cologne, our beloved relative and fellow elector, to inform you and others who belong to the Holy Empire via messengers to come to his Grace and to us at a diet for this purpose.

---

23 Sigismund also held the titles of king of Hungary, Croatia, Dalmatia and Bohemia.

And as we are also inclined towards the same with our full disposition, and it grieves us in no small way, as is well justified, we have also now gathered together at many diets for this purpose on quite a few occasions, considered and taken these matters in hand using all our faculties of reason and – by engaging in this work to the best of our ability – adduced the extent to which Holy Christendom has not been as effective as we would have liked to see. And since these matters now concern the whole of Christendom, and it is to be feared that, if they are not resisted in time, this would greatly weaken the holy Christian faith and might inflict a great fracture on the Holy Empire and the land of Bohemia (which is, after all, a notable member of the Empire), so we six electors have gathered together in Wesel, and reached a consensus on convoking a diet in Nuremberg on the upcoming feast that is called 'Dispersion of the Apostles' [15 July], which we all want to attend in person. We have also written about and announced the same diet to our aforenamed lord the king, and intend that he will attend the same diet in person, as we have in fact asked him to do.

Concerning this, we request, urge and call upon you with all diligence, as earnestly as we ever can and may, as you are well obliged and bound towards the Empire in this, that you should also participate in this diet in Nuremberg with decision-making authority, and that you do not allow yourselves to be diverted or prevented from doing so for any reason, in order to be united with us there and to thoroughly consider – for the praise of almighty God, the strengthening and restoration of the holy Christian faith and the profit and honour of our gracious lord the king and the Empire – how these matters should be dealt with, so that such unbelief and opposition to Holy Christendom may be removed and exterminated, and the named land of Bohemia may not be stripped and alienated from the Holy Empire, to which end we want to work most diligently with you. And may you prove yourselves and be present in this, as we have full faith in you and also expect that you will justly do. We, together with the above-named Roman (etc.) king, our gracious lord, want to regard you favourably in this.

Given at Wesel on the sixth day after the Feast of the Blessed Martyrs Vitus and Modestus [19 June], in the [14]22nd year etc.

13. Emperor Frederick III summons the imperial princes to a diet in Regensburg (1454)

Weizsäcker et al. (eds), *Deutsche Reichstagsakten. Ältere Reihe*, vol. XIX/1, pp. 108–10.

On 30 September 1453, a mere four months after the fall of Constantinople to the Ottomans, Pope Nicholas V issued a bull calling for a crusade against Sultan Mehmed II. Frederick III was under particular pressure to participate, both because every emperor was understood as the defender of the Church (*advocatus ecclesiae*) and because papal legates travelled to the German lands to drum up support for the project in the winter of 1453–54. As a result, he and the leading German princes convoked three diets in quick succession in 1454–55, ostensibly in order to prepare a crusading expedition against the Turks. This summons was to the first of the three diets, which was held in Regensburg.

Frederick, by the grace of God Roman emperor, ever augmenter of the Empire, duke of Austria etc.

High-born, well-beloved relative and prince. Our Holy Father the pope has just had the reverend Giovanni, bishop of Pavia, our well-beloved pious man, on a legation with us, in order to inform and relay to us the great tribulation now hanging over the whole of Christendom because of the notable and unconscionable evil of the infidel Turks. Before, during and after their conquest of the worthy ancient city of Constantinople, the same Turks have dreadfully perpetrated many and various acts of bloodshed and inhuman occurrences and evils against Christian people old and young, clerical and lay, female and male; and they are still carrying out such things every day with a hardened resolve. Increased and irrevocable ruin, the singular extermination of Christian people and the great affliction of the Christian faith might follow from this if worthy and serious resistance to the cruel enemies of Jesus Christ does not take place. And indeed, before this papal legation mentioned above, we confidentially and sorrowfully informed, entreated and solicited his Holiness and also other Christian kings and princes, cities and communes of Italian and other nationalities regarding the brutal actions of the Turks, for the consolation of the Christian faith. And as Roman emperor this intolerable evil justly displeases us more than anything else, and it should not only be inimical and deeply grievous to us but also to you and all people who are devoted to God and members of the holy Christian faith.

As Roman emperor we have therefore undertaken with timely counsel and good consideration to schedule a diet and to convene there your well-beloved self and other spiritual and temporal electors and princes, prelates, counts, lords, cities and communes of the Holy Roman Empire, our and the Empire's well-beloved faithful people. Thus, by the power of this letter we set and designate the same diet for the upcoming St George's Day [23 April] in Regensburg. We want to come to the same diet in person, if we have not been impeded by unavoidable legitimate causes, or to send our people with full authority. And concerning this we request of your well-beloved self with especial diligence, and also order you by our Roman imperial authority, that you – as a Christian prince and one devoted to the cross of Jesus Christ, our saviour – come to Regensburg on the aforenamed St George's Day, and that you do not procrastinate in any way in this matter. Our Holy Father the pope and also our well-beloved cousin King Ladislaus ['the Posthumous', king of Hungary, r. 1440–57, and Bohemia, r. 1453–57] will also send their envoys there, as we asked them to do for the better promotion of the cause, and the other aforementioned spiritual and temporal electors and princes, prelates, counts, cities and communes have also been called upon and should come, in order to unite there with considered counsel around plans for praiseworthy resistance and an expedition against the enemies of Christ and an honest assessment of any necessary contributions, defences and ordinances, so that – for the preservation of the Christian faith – the enemies of Christ are struck by those under the banner of righteousness, the wretched and martyred believers are avenged and the friends of God and Christian people are consoled, the Christian faith is maintained in its dignity and praiseworthy delightfulness and all those who assist in this partake of the grace of God and, beyond that, the indulgence granted by the pope for the salvation of souls and eternal life. In so doing, your well-beloved self will be doing us as well as justice a special, thankworthy favour and carrying out our earnest intention. We want to graciously recognise this with regard to your well-beloved self in the future, and not to forget it, to your benefit.

Given at Wiener Neustadt on the Friday after Epiphany [11 January], in the 1454th year after Christ's birth and the second year of our emperorship.

14. The 'Golden Bull' (1356)
Fritz (ed.), *Monumenta Germaniae Historica. Constitutiones*, pp. 563–633.

In the name of the holy and indivisible Trinity, blessedly, amen. Charles IV, by the favour of divine clemency Roman emperor, ever augmenter,[24] and king of Bohemia, for the eternal consideration of this matter.

Each kingdom divided against itself will be destroyed [Matthew 12:25; Luke 11:17], for its princes have become the companions of thieves [Isaiah 1:23]. For this reason, God set a spirit of confusion among them [Isaiah 19:14], such that they stumble in the middle of the day as if in darkness [Deuteronomy 28:29], and He has removed their lampstands from their places [Revelation 2:5], and they are blind and leaders of the blind [Luke 6:39]. And whoever walks into the darkness ends up stumbling [John 11:10], and with a blind disposition they commit many misdeeds, which occur because of division. Say, O Pride: how could you have held judgement over Lucifer, had you not been helped by division? Say, O inimical Satan: how would you have thrown Adam out of paradise, had you not divided him from obedience? Say, O Lust: how could you have destroyed Troy, had you not divided Lady Helen from her husband? Say, O Wrath: how could you have so thoroughly destroyed the Roman Republic, had you not, by means of the division of Pompey and Julius [Caesar], aroused internecine war with injurious swords?

And especially you, O Hatred: as regards the Christian emperorship, the foundation upon which the most Christian Empire is blessedly secured, which is strengthened by God with the divine virtues of faith, hope and love [1 Corinthians 13:13] in the manner of the holy, indivisible Trinity, you have wickedly vomited your ancient venom like a snake onto the imperial vine and the first and foremost members of the Empire,[25] in order to crush the pillars,[26] that you might cause the collapse of the Empire. In myriad ways, you

---

24 Already in the 1360s, vernacular translations rendered *semper augustus* as *allezit merer* – 'ever augmenter'.
25 A botanical and corporeal metaphor for the emperor and electors.
26 Another metaphor for the electors, this time architectural.

have led to division among the seven electors of the Holy Empire, through whom the Holy Empire ought to be illuminated, as though by seven blazing lampstands in the unity of the seven-banded spirit [Revelation 1:12].

Truly, since we are duty-bound to obviate future damage stemming from division and discord among the electors – on account of the office that enables us to exercise the imperial dignity, and also as one of their number, we being a king of Bohemia, and hence for two reasons, both our emperorship and the rights conferred by our electorate, which we employ in the traditional manner – we have promulgated, established and confirmed by way of an imperial pronouncement, with convictions based on ample counsel, and by the fullness of our imperial authority, the laws written below, for the protection of the law and the pursuit of unity among the electors, and to ensure a unanimous election, as well as to forestall the furtherance of the despised division mentioned above, and the myriad injuries it entails. This occurred while we were holding court publicly in Nuremberg upon our very mighty imperial throne, adorned with the emperor's mitre,[27] robes and crown, as all the electors (spiritual and temporal) were seated with us alongside numerous other princes, counts, barons, lords, nobles and urban envoys, in the year of our Lord 1356, in the ninth indiction, on the fourth Ides of January [10 January], in the tenth year of our royal reign and the first year of our emperorship.

The first chapter: how the electors should receive safe-conduct

[1] We establish with certain knowledge and by the plenitude of our imperial authority, and confirm with this imperial mandate, that whenever it should occur and as the necessity might arise hereafter that a king of the Romans and future emperor needs to be elected, and the electors have to travel to hold the election per the old, praiseworthy custom, each elector – if and when this is requested of them – is obliged to offer safe-conduct to each of his fellow electors or their envoys sent for this purpose, through his lands, districts and towns and as far beyond as they can be escorted, and to

---

27 *ymfeln* – a term usually reserved for episcopal or papal headgear, and here possibly referring to the arch or hoop on top of the imperial crown of the Holy Roman Empire (probably created in the tenth century, and now in the Imperial Treasury in Vienna).

provide safe-conduct without deceit to the city where the election is to take place, and then to travel thence once again, on pain of perjury and loss of the electoral vote that he enjoys at that time. And we establish that any person or people who should be delinquent in providing the aforenamed safe-conduct, or should iniquitously revoke it, should instantly be subject to this punishment.

[2: The Empire's other princes, nobles, cities and communes should likewise offer safe-conduct to the electors. The penalty for princely and noble violators is loss of all fiefs and property. Urban violators will lose privileges and be placed in the imperial ban, and hence become fair game for attack.

3: Towns and communes should sell and provide supplies to travelling electors, on pain of the same penalties. Princes and nobles should not hinder or attack the electors, on pain of the same penalties.

4: Any hostilities between electors should be suspended for the sake of safe-conduct to the election, on pain of the penalties in article 1.

5: Likewise, princes, nobles and cities should suspend any hostilities with electors to permit their safe-conduct to the election. Electors, princes, nobles, cities and communes should certify all of the above with legal documents and oaths, on pain of the prescribed penalties.

6: An elector who violates these mandates should be shunned by the other electors and lose his dignity, imperial fiefs and vote. Other nobles should lose their imperial fiefs and suffer the penalties set out above.

7–14: The specific princes, lords and cities who have a particular responsibility to offer safe-conduct to the electors closest to them are listed, on pain of the prescribed penalties. Electors should request safe-conduct well in advance of their travels.]

[15] Additionally, we establish and mandate that the archbishop of Mainz at that time should announce the election to each elector individually via his messengers and public letters. The same letters should indicate the dates and deadlines within which they might, by common estimation, reach all of the same princes. The same letters should assert that within three months of the date indicated in

them, the electors – individually and collectively – should be present in Frankfurt on the Main, or they should send their trustworthy envoys to the same city within the same timeframe, with full and unconditional authority and bearing their public letters sealed with their great seals, in order to choose a king of the Romans to be elevated to the emperorship.[28] [The form of these letters and arrangements for these envoys are set out later in this law-book,[29] and should be kept in this form forever.]

[16] We command and establish that if it should happen that the death of the emperor or king of the Romans should become known in the diocese of Mainz, thereupon – within one month, counting from the day on which the same death came to light – the archbishop of Mainz should announce this death and how it came to be known via public letters to each of the electors individually, in the manner written above. Now, if the same archbishop should be neglectful, or perhaps remiss, regarding this death or its announcement, in the three ensuing months the same electors should – as written just above in this law-book – assemble in the aforenamed city of Frankfurt of their own volition in order to choose a king of the Romans and future emperor, without needing to be summoned, for the sake of the virtue of their loyalty, which obliges them to care for the Holy Empire.

[17] Each elector or his envoy should not ride into the aforenamed city of Frankfurt with more than 200 people on horseback during the period of the aforesaid election. Among their number he may have 50 or fewer men-at-arms, and no more.

[18: Electors who neglect to attend or to send an envoy, or who depart early, should lose their vote in that election.

19: The citizens of Frankfurt should swear oaths to protect the electors and their entourages, on pain of the punishments set out above.

20: The citizens of Frankfurt should not allow anyone else into the city during the election, and expel anyone who does make it in.]

---

28 Elevated to the emperorship in due course through coronation in Italy, that is, not as an automatic corollary of election as king.
29 Chapters 18–19 below.

The second chapter: concerning the election of a king of the Romans

[1] After the electors have entered the city of Frankfurt, at dawn on the following morning they should be fully present in the Church of St Bartholomew. There they should have a mass sung about the Holy Spirit, that He might illuminate their hearts and pour out the light of His power onto their intentions, and that with His help they might be guided towards choosing a just, good and effective person as king of the Romans and future emperor, for the preservation of all Christian people.

When the mass has finished, the electors should all go up to the altar where the mass was sung. There, over St John's Gospel opened at *In principio erat verbum* etc. ['In the beginning was the Word', John 1:1], which should be placed there for them, the spiritual princes should dignifiedly place their hands on their chests. The temporal princes should corporeally touch the gospel-book with their hands. All of them should be present there with all of their followers, unarmed. And the archbishop of Mainz should provide the form of the oath to be taken to them. And he should take the oath in German before them (or the envoys of those who are not present), and they before him, in this manner:

[2] 'I, archbishop of Mainz, arch-chancellor of the Holy Empire throughout the German lands and an elector, swear on these holy gospels that presently lie before me that by the faith that binds me to God and the Holy Roman Empire I want to choose – according to all my faculties of reason and good sense, and with God's help – a temporal head for the Christian people, that is, a king of the Romans and future emperor, who is well-suited for this, as far as my faculty of reason and my wits indicate to me. And by the same faith I want to cast my vote and express my will, and carry out the aforenamed election, without any conditions, payments, remunerations or commitments, or any such things, whatever they might be called. So help me God and the all the saints.'

[3] Once the oath has been sworn in the aforesaid form and manner by the electors or their envoys, they should betake themselves to the election, and from that moment on they should no longer depart the city of Frankfurt or leave one another until they reach the point that the majority among them has elected a temporal head for the Christian people: a king of the Romans and future emperor. If they delay in doing so for thirty sequential days,

counting from the day of the oath-swearing, once those thirty days have elapsed they should thenceforth eat nothing except water and bread, and should not depart the city in any way, until a temporal head of Holy Christendom has first been elected by them or the majority among them.

[4] After they, or the majority among them, have cast their votes, this same election should be received and upheld as if it had taken place with unanimity among all of them. Furthermore, if it should happen that some electors or their envoys should not have been present for some of the time, or should have been delayed or hindered but nevertheless arrived before the completion of the election, we pronounce that they should be permitted to participate in the election in the state that it was in at the moment of their arrival.

Since it has hitherto inviolably been the case, as a matter of old custom and praiseworthy tradition, that we proceed in the manner written hereafter, so we establish and announce by the plenitude of our imperial power:

The one who is elected king of the Romans in the manner set out above should – as soon as the election has taken place and before he undertakes any matter or business on behalf of the Holy Empire – confirm and substantiate for the spiritual and temporal electors (who, as is well known, are the first and foremost members of the Holy Empire), collectively and individually, all of their privileges, charters, rights, liberties, fiefs, old customs and dignities and whatever they held and possessed from the Empire up until the day of the election, with his sealed legal documents, without delay or objection. And he should renew all of the aforenamed things once he has been crowned with the imperial insignia. The elected one should first issue these confirmations in his royal name for each of the electors individually, and he should subsequently renew them under his imperial dignity.[30] He should never hinder the princes as a collective and individually. Rather, he is duty-bound to graciously support them, without malice.

[5] In the event that three present electors (or envoys for absent ones) should elect a fourth from among themselves or from within

---

30 That is, after the confirmations following election as king of the Romans, a monarch who later succeeded in being crowned emperor was supposed to renew these confirmations using his new title.

their electoral association – that is, an elector, be he present or absent – as king of the Romans, we declare with this law that the vote of this elected individual (be he present or represented by an envoy if he cannot appropriately be there) should have full validity, increase the number of people with the vote accordingly and be capable of establishing the majority, as with the other electors.

The third chapter: concerning the seating order of the archbishops of Mainz, Trier and Cologne

In the name of the holy and indivisible Trinity, blessedly. Charles IV, by the favour of divine grace Roman emperor, ever augmenter, and king of Bohemia, for the eternal consideration of these matters.

The adornment and honour of the Holy Roman Empire, the dignity of the emperorship and the agreeable benefit of the common good are promoted by the unanimous will of the worthy, illustrious electors, who, as the highest pillars of prudent wisdom, support the holy edifice with diligent beneficence. With their assistance the authority of the emperor's right hand is strengthened, and the more they are bound together by the great beneficent inclination of mutual favour, the more they blessedly pour out the benefit of fruitful peace and tranquillity upon all of Christendom.

So that all conflict and suspicion that might arise between the worthy archbishops of Mainz, Cologne and Trier, electors of the Holy Empire, on account of the status and dignity of their seating order at imperial or royal courtly assemblies may be abolished hereafter and for all time henceforth – and so that their hearts and dispositions remain in a peaceful state, that they might more perfectly work together through the collective favour and zeal of potent charity to help address the necessities of the Holy Empire and Christian people – we establish, with the forethought and counsel of all the electors, spiritual and temporal, and we confirm with this law that is to last in perpetuity, by the plenitude of our imperial authority:

The archbishops may and should have a seat during all the public business of the king or emperor – whether judicial proceedings, enfeoffments, banquets, advisory councils and all other occasions at which it is necessary to assemble in order to deliberate about the Empire's benefit and honour. The bishop of Trier should sit directly opposite the countenance of the emperor. The bishop of Mainz should sit to the right of the emperor in his bishopric, in his ecclesiastical province and outside of his province and in all areas under his German chancellorship, except in the province of Cologne. The bishop of Cologne should sit at the right hand of the emperor in his bishopric, in his ecclesiastical province and outside of his province in all of Lombardy and Gaul.[31] We will that the same seating order stated above should always be maintained by the successors of the aforenamed archbishops of Cologne, Trier and Mainz, so that no doubt may arise ever again about these matters.

The fourth chapter: concerning the seating order of all the electors; and the convocation of the electors to choose a king of the Romans; and the offices of the temporal electors at the emperor's court, etc.

[1] Furthermore, we establish: whenever, from this moment onwards, an imperial courtly assembly is held, in each session – at an advisory council, banquet or whatever other settings it behoves a king or emperor of the Romans to sit with the electors – the king of Bohemia, being a crowned and anointed prince, should sit right next to the archbishop, be he of Mainz or Cologne, who at that time has the right to sit immediately on the right side of the emperor, as dictated by the location of the setting and the ecclesiastical province, in accordance with their privileges. The Count Palatine of the Rhine should sit next to the king of Bohemia on the same side, but the duke of Saxony should sit on the left side of the aforenamed archbishop to whom it falls to sit immediately to the left, and then the margrave of Brandenburg.[32]

[2] Additionally, whenever the Holy Empire is vacant, the archbishop of Mainz should have the authority – an authority which it is well known that he has long traditionally had – to convoke the other electors, his associates for the election, with letters. When all of them, or those who can or wish to be present, have assembled at

---

31 While the archbishop of Mainz was considered arch-chancellor of the German ecclesiastical provinces, the archbishop of Cologne was theoretically arch-chancellor of the 'Romance' (*welsch*) provinces of Italy. The provinces of Gaul notionally fell under the arch-chancellorship of the archbishop of Trier, but here they are also attributed to Cologne for the purposes of the seating order.
32 That is, whichever archbishop of Cologne or Mainz did not currently enjoy the privilege of sitting on the monarch's right-hand side was seated to his left, with the duke of Saxony and margrave of Brandenburg to that archbishop's left.

the location of the election, the archbishop of Mainz (and nobody else) should enquire about their votes in this order.

First, the archbishop of Mainz should enquire of the archbishop of Trier, to whom the first vote belongs as a matter of old custom; then of the archbishop of Cologne, to whom belongs the dignity and the task of placing the first royal crown upon a king of the Romans; third, of the king of Bohemia, who goes first among the lay princes on account of this royal status; fourth, of the Count Palatine of the Rhine; fifth, of the duke of Saxony; sixth, of the margrave of Brandenburg. When all this has taken place, the aforenamed princes should in turn ask the bishop of Mainz, their associate, to make known his intention and his will.

[3] Additionally, during the holding of an imperial courtly assembly, the margrave of Brandenburg should proffer water for the handwashing of the king or emperor of the Romans, the king of Bohemia should serve the drinks (though only if he wants to do so voluntarily – he is not obliged to do this given his royal crown), the Count Palatine of the Rhine should bear the first course of the meal and the duke of Saxony should carry out his office of marshal, as is customary of old.

The fifth chapter: concerning the offices of the Counts Palatine and the dukes of Saxony when the Holy Empire lacks a head, etc.

[1] Whenever it should occur hereafter that the Holy Empire lies vacant, the Count Palatine of the Rhine should be the regent of the Holy Empire on account of the Palatinate, acting as deputy for a future king of the Romans in the lands of the Rhine and Swabia and in Franconian districts, with the authority to hold judicial courts, distribute ecclesiastical benefices, collect revenues and yields, make enfeoffments and receive oaths of loyalty in the stead and name of the Holy Empire. However, all that should be renewed in time by the king of the Romans who is subsequently elected, and the oaths should be sworn to him anew. The sole exception is princely fiefs and banner-fiefs[33] – we specifically reserve the right to enfeoff and install people with and into these to the king or emperor of the

---

33 *vanlehin* (Latin: *feudum vexillare*) – a fief consisting of the office and regalia of a temporal prince, who would hold a banner during enfeoffment by the monarch (see [6]).

Romans alone. However, the same Count Palatine should know that he is expressly forbidden from changing or alienating in any way the Empire's possessions of which he is regent.

The duke of Saxony should be regent of all cities that adhere to Saxon law,[34] in the same manner and under the same conditions as those set out above.

[2: If a case arises involving the king or emperor in which the Count Palatine is to act as judge, he may only exercise this prerogative at the monarch's court and in his presence.]

The sixth chapter: concerning the status of the electors vis-à-vis the other princes collectively in the order of seating, processing and standing

[No other prince may sit, process or stand ahead of the positions of the electors at courtly assemblies. The king of Bohemia should enjoy a superior position to any other kings present.]

The seventh chapter: concerning the successors of the princes

[1] Among the innumerable worries that daily exhaust our heart on account of the wellbeing of the Holy Empire, which we possess with God's awesome blessing, our concern is focused above all on how to ensure that a longed-for and ever salutary unity blossoms among the electors of the Holy Empire, and that their hearts remain united in pure affection. The more quickly and readily this turbulent world is aided through their timely ministrations, and the less disarray insinuates itself among the electors while unadulterated charity is preserved and the hidden weeds of distress are excised, the more purely justice will shine brightly on everyone.

Now, it has long been public knowledge among many people – perhaps it is known throughout the whole world! – that, by virtue of their kingdom and principalities, the illustrious king of

---

34 German town law (*Stadtrecht*) derived from several sources, including founding privileges, the customs and institutions of an influential city (e.g. Cologne, Lübeck, Magdeburg and Ulm, whose much-copied laws generated so-called 'town law families' shared by dozens of other towns) and regional legal traditions, in this case those of Saxony as reflected in the *Saxon Mirror*. See Isenmann, *Die deutsche Stadt*, pp. 192–96.

Bohemia, Count Palatine of the Rhine, duke of Saxony and margrave of Brandenburg have a rightful vote and seat in the election of a king of the Romans and future emperor alongside the other, spiritual electors, and that when they hold session together with the others, they are true and lawful electors of the Holy Empire. In order to prevent any future cause for umbrage or discord that might arise among the electors' sons or successors with regard to a lawful vote or right to participate in an election, and lest the common good be hindered by harmful future delays, we establish and proclaim by imperial authority with this present law, which is to last in perpetuity:

After one from among the same electors has died, the right to a vote and the authority to participate in an election should fall to his first-born legitimate son who is a layman. Should he no longer be alive, the electoral right should freely fall to the same's eldest-born son who is both legitimate and lay, without any objection from anyone. If, however, this same first-born son should depart from this world without any legitimate, lay male heirs, by the power of this imperial law the right to a vote and the authority to participate in an election should fall to the oldest lay brother who is truly descended in the paternal line, and thereafter to the same brother's first-born son.

This order of succession to the aforenamed voting right and electoral authority should be maintained in perpetuity for the first-born sons and heirs of the electors. However, if a prince or his first-born son or other lay sons should die and it transpires that he has left behind legitimate, lay male heirs who have not reached the age of majority, the oldest brother of the deceased should act as regent for and look after the same's children until the oldest among them reaches the age of majority. We hold the age of majority for an elector to be eighteen years, and will and establish that it should be thusly held in perpetuity. And as soon as the oldest son reaches this age, the regent is immediately obliged to hand over the right to a vote and the authority to participate in an election, with the electoral office and everything that belongs to it.

[2: Vacant electoral principalities should rightfully escheat to the king or emperor. However, this does not affect the rights of the Bohemians to elect their own king.]

The eighth chapter: concerning the privileges of the king of Bohemia and his subjects

[Nobody residing in Bohemia may be cited before a court outside of that kingdom, per established privileges and custom. If Bohemians do receive judicial summonses, or become the target of judgements, those should be considered null and void. Bohemians may not appeal to external courts.]

The ninth chapter: concerning the gold and silver mines in the kingdom of Bohemia

[Charles's successors as kings of Bohemia and all the electors may lawfully possess gold and silver, forgeable metal and salt mines in Bohemia and its appurtenances, as well as the regalian rights to tolls and jurisdiction over the Jews, as confirmed in old customs and privileges.]

The tenth chapter speaks of minting coins and other rights of the kingdom of Bohemia etc.

[Future kings of Bohemia have the right to mint gold and silver coins in the customary fashion, and to purchase or acquire in pledge any subject's properties, provided the property's tenurial conditions and customary obligations to the Empire are maintained. These rights are extended to the other electors.]

The eleventh chapter: concerning the immunities of the electors of the Roman Empire

[Subjects of the electors should be subject to their sole jurisdiction. These subjects may not be cited before courts outside of their elector's principality and – where applicable – archbishopric, and may not appeal externally, except to the emperor's aulic courts and judges in cases of denial of justice.]

The twelfth chapter: concerning the assembly of the electors

Among the manifold concerns about the common good that are severely consuming our thoughts, we have worthily considered it necessary for the electors of the Holy Empire – who are the Empire's secure cornerstone and immovable pillars – to assemble more frequently than has traditionally been the case, in order to discuss and deliberate about the salvation of the Empire and the world. Owing to their dispersed location throughout the lands, whereby they reside far from one another, they are well placed to discuss and negotiate with one another regarding the wrongful abuses in the lands that are familiar to them, and, through their prudence and sound counsel, they can offer salvific assistance and effective reformation of such abuses.

Consequently, at our exalted courtly assembly in Nuremberg – that we have worthily held, together with the honourable spiritual and illustrious temporal electors and other princes and lords – we have ordained, with the well-considered sentiments and counsel of the same electors, for the sake of the common good and prosperity, that henceforth the same electors should personally assemble every year for four weeks after Easter Sunday in a certain city of the Empire. And at this same time in this present year, we and the same princes should pursue discussions and hold court in our imperial city of Metz with this same assembly. There it should be clarified, with the counsel of the princes, the day and location on and at which the aforesaid yearly assembly should henceforth gather in ensuing years.

This ordinance should endure solely with our and the princes' consent. As long as the ordinance lasts, we grant our imperial safe-conduct to the electors to travel to, remain at and return home from the aforenamed court.

[To avoid excessive expenditure and delays in proceedings, a prince at an assembly may not entertain the entire gathering. Moderate gatherings of individuals are permitted.]

The thirteenth chapter: concerning the revocation of privileges

[Past, present and future charters of privileges issued by the kings and emperors of the Romans should not infringe on the rights and jurisdictions of the electors. Any that do are and should be considered revoked.]

The fourteenth chapter: concerning those who maliciously declare feuds against their own lords

[Servitors and fief-holders have been renouncing what they hold from their lords then declaring feuds against those lords and seizing what they formerly held within a tenurial relationship for themselves. Such renunciations should be considered invalid unless carried out honestly and with full restoration to the lord. Whoever attacks what they formerly held within a tenurial relationship, or assists such attackers, should be placed in the imperial ban, and may never hold their former fiefs or other assets again. These punishments also apply to those who injure their lords without renouncing their fiefs.]

The fifteenth chapter: concerning the malicious conspirators who form alliances against those whose lawful subjects they are

The shameful alliances and inappropriate gatherings or associations inside and outside of towns, or alliances between two or more towns, or between individuals and towns, or between two or more individuals, on account of familial ties or under whatever other pretext, as well as rituals of promising and oath-taking, forming leagues and pacts and other customs of this kind that have been introduced (and which we justly consider disturbances), are contrary to the holy laws. With certain knowledge, we repudiate, condemn and declare null and void all such things, whereby towns or individuals have entered into or intend to enter into such alliances (whether among themselves or with others, whatever their dignity, estate or condition) without the permission of the lords whose subjects or servitors they are, or in whose districts they live, and without excluding the same lords from the targets of their alliances. Just as these alliances were doubtless forbidden and abolished by the holy laws of our predecessors the Christian augmenters [i.e., previous emperors], so we, too, forbid and abolish them.

The sole exception is the contractual agreements and alliances that the princes and cities have formed and publicly confirmed with one another for the sake of the collective peace of the lands.[35] We uphold those by our especial provision and permit them to remain until we have been able to take counsel on what we should mandate regarding them.

However, any individual who henceforth initiates such sworn associations, leagues, evil alliances and pacts in contravention of

---

35 That is, the land-peaces (*Landfrieden*), e.g. [37].

this present law and the precepts of old about this issue should instantly be subject to loss of their honour and a penalty of ten pounds of gold. If a town or commune should contravene this law, they should give a hundred pounds of gold and lose all privileges and imperial dignities. Half of the penalty in gold should fall to the imperial treasury and the other half to the lord of the region harmed by the alliance. Still, the aforenamed are at least not subject to the penalties of the old precepts against malicious conspirators.

The sixteenth chapter: concerning paleburghers[36]

[Certain burghers and subjects of princes and other lords are seeking to shirk their obligations by receiving citizenship from other towns, enjoying the privileges conferred by this citizenship while continuing to reside within their lords' jurisdictions. These paleburghers should no longer enjoy these urban privileges unless they physically relocate into the appropriate town, on pain of a penalty of 100 gold marks for the receiving town.]

The seventeenth chapter: concerning feud-declarations

We declare that anyone who henceforth professes to be entering into a feud with someone for a just cause, yet declares the feud against them in their residence at an unjust time, or in a location where they do not normally reside, may not honourably harm the party against whom the feud was declared with arson, robbery or plunder. Since nobody should benefit from deceit and malice, we confirm with this law, which is to endure in perpetuity, that feud-declarations that have occurred or will occur in this manner should be null and void: those against the feud-declarer's own lord and those against other people with whom they had close ties within an association or social group, or with whom they had some other honourable friendly relationship.

And nobody should be attacked with arson, theft or plunder under the cover of a given feud-declaration, unless that declaration was personally delivered to its target three full days beforehand in a public setting or in the place where they usually reside, and unless the announcement of this feud-declaration can be securely

---

36 *pfalburgirn* – people granted citizenship by a town while residing outside of its walls or jurisdictions.

corroborated by proper witnesses. Anyone who attacks or declares a feud against someone in any other way instantly falls into dishonour, and it should be as if no feud-declaration had been made. We further establish that the same person should have a just penalty imposed on them as a traitor by every judge.

We also forbid all unlawful wars, all unlawful arson, robbery and plunder, unlawful tolls and unlawful safe-conduct (and coerced customary dues for that safe-conduct), on pain of the penalties prescribed by the holy laws established regarding the aforesaid things and among the specifications for each of them.

The eighteenth chapter: concerning the letter to the electors about the election

[The formulaic template for a letter from the archbishop of Mainz inviting an elector – in this case, the margrave of Brandenburg by way of example – to the election of a new king of the Romans follows, setting out the stipulations for participation specified in chapter 1.]

The nineteenth chapter: concerning the form of the letter of empowerment that an elector's envoy presents at the election

[The formulaic template for a letter from an elector – again, the margrave of Brandenburg serves as the example – empowering his envoys to represent him at every stage of the election of a new king of the Romans follows.]

The twentieth chapter: concerning the unity of the electoral principalities and the rights that belong to them etc.

[Since the right to an electoral vote is bound up with possession of one of the electoral principalities and its appurtenances, these principalities should remain forever unpartitionable. Any judicial decisions that might separate something from an electoral principality are null and void.]

The twenty-first chapter: concerning the procession order of the archbishops etc.

[When processing with the king or emperor of the Romans at an assembly, the archbishop of Trier should walk directly in front of him, with the bearer of the royal or imperial insignia between them, if applicable. The location of the archbishops of Mainz and Trier is determined by their ecclesiastical provinces, as set out in chapter 3.]

The twenty-second chapter: concerning the procession order of the temporal electors, and who should walk ahead of the emperor or king carrying the imperial or royal insignia

[When processing with the king or emperor at an assembly, the duke of Saxony should stand in front of him, between him and the archbishop of Trier, while bearing the royal or imperial sword. The Count Palatine should stand to the duke's right, bearing the imperial orb, the margrave of Brandenburg to his left, bearing the sceptre. The king of Bohemia should process directly behind the king or emperor.]

The twenty-third chapter: concerning the blessings of the archbishops at mass and at table in the emperor's or king's presence etc.

[One of the three archbishops should say all blessings and thanksgivings in church services and at mealtimes on a given day, with a second doing the same on the following day and the third on the third day, in a rotating order based on whoever was consecrated as bishop first. The archbishops should nevertheless charitably invite the others to officiate before defaulting to this order.]

The twenty-fourth chapter: concerning perpetrators against the bodies and lives of the electors, and the penalties for perpetrators and their offspring and dependants

We have pronounced the laws written hereafter at the courtly assembly in Metz that we, Emperor Charles IV of the Roman Empire and Bohemian kingdom, an augmenter, held in the year 1356 as one counts from Christ's birth, while all the electors of the Holy Empire were with us, in the presence of these lords: the honourable father the bishop of Albano, cardinal of the Holy Roman Church, and Charles, first-born son of the king of France, duke of Normandy and Dauphin of Vienne [later Charles V of France, r. 1364–80].

[Would-be perpetrators who seek to kill any elector(s) should face just – that is, capital – punishment, 'since the aforenamed electors are members of our body'. Their property should go to the emperor's treasury. Their descendants and wives face degrees of disinheritance and disgrace depending on their presumed capacity for complicity. Co-conspirators face the same punishment as perpetrators. A would-be conspirator who reports the plot should be pardoned and rewarded. To ensure full punishment is administered to all culpable parties, accusations and investigations can be made after the guilty party's death, and their servants and retainers may be tortured.]

The twenty-fifth chapter: concerning the successors of the temporal electors

[The principalities and lands of the temporal electors should remain intact, and never be partitioned. An elector's first-born son should succeed to all his lordships and rights, if he is fit to rule; otherwise, they should go to a second son, brother or lay blood relative in the paternal line. Other relatives should be provided for, but not in a manner that entails partitioning the principality.]

The twenty-sixth chapter: how the electors should proceed at the emperor's courtly assemblies

[1: At the opening of a courtly assembly, the electors should meet the king or emperor at his residence at the first hour – that is, around 6 am – and they should process from there as established in chapters 21–22. Additionally, the archbishop serving as arch-chancellor in that region should hold the imperial seals on a silver rod, while lesser princes bear the crowns of Aachen and Milan – that is, of the Romans and of Italy – ahead of the archbishop of Trier.]

[2] The empress or queen of the Romans should proceed to the session dressed in her imperial or royal regalia, accompanied by her great lords and the maidens of her entourage, an appropriate distance behind the emperor or king of the Romans and the king of Bohemia, who follows immediately behind the emperor.

The twenty-seventh chapter: concerning the offices of the electors at the emperor's or king's courtly assemblies

[1: Before the enthroned king or emperor, the mounted duke of Saxony should fill a silver measuring implement from a tall pile of oats and pour the oats into a passing servant's bag. He should then insert a silver staff into the oat pile and withdraw while a subordinate marshal continues to measure it out.

2: At mealtimes, an archbishop should say grace, per the order established in chapter 23. All the archbishops should then present the imperial seals on a silver rod to the emperor, who should return it to them. The archbishop who is arch-chancellor of the region where the assembly is being held should then wear the emperor's great seal around his neck during the meal and until he returns to his lodgings, whereupon one of his followers should return it to the aulic chancellor.

3: The margrave of Brandenburg should arrive mounted with two silver basins of water and a towel to wash the king's or emperor's hands.

4: The Count Palatine should arrive mounted with four silver bowls to place on the table before the king or emperor.

5: The king of Bohemia should arrive mounted with a silver drinking vessel containing water and wine to offer to the king or emperor to drink.

6: In the stead of the margrave of Brandenburg, Count Palatine, king of Bohemia and duke of Saxony, these official roles may, by tradition, be fulfilled by the imperial vice-chamberlain of Falkenstein, the kitchen-master of Nordenberg, the vice-steward of Limpurg and the vice-marshal of Pappenheim respectively. In their absence, members of the emperor's or king's household may fulfil them.]

The twenty-eighth chapter: concerning the mealtime seating order at the emperor's or king's courtly assemblies

[1: The king's or emperor's table should be six feet higher than the others in the banquet hall. He should sit there alone. The queen's or empress's table should be three feet shorter than the king's or emperor's, and three feet taller than the electors', whose tables should all be of the same height. The electors' tables should be arranged per the seating order set out in chapter 3.

2: None of the temporal electors should be seated until all have fulfilled the ceremonial duties of office set out in chapter 27.]

The twenty-ninth chapter: where the election of a king of the Romans should take place, and where he should receive his first crown and hold his first courtly assembly[37]

[1] We have also found, on the basis of true testimony and the laws of old, that everybody has long agreed that our blessed predecessors zealously observed that a king of the Romans should have his election held in the city of Frankfurt, be crowned in Aachen and hold his first courtly assembly in Nuremberg.

We therefore will, on confident grounds, that these same conventions should be maintained into the future, unless some or all of the aforenamed points should be hindered by genuine causes.

[2: When an elector cannot attend a courtly assembly in person, his envoy should not sit at the elector's designated place.]

The thirtieth chapter: concerning the princes who receive fiefs, what they should pay etc.

[1: The electors do not owe anybody payments for the fiefs they receive, since payments are usually due to officials in such circumstances, and they themselves hold all the highest offices at a courtly assembly.

2: Other princes must pay sixty-three and a quarter marks of silver for their enfeoffments, divided among court officials and chancery personnel, in part to cover the costs of wax and parchment for their fief confirmations. This payment is waived if they hold privileges exempting them.

3: From this payment, ten marks should go to the steward of Limpurg, ten to the kitchen-master of Nordenberg, ten to the vice-marshal of Pappenheim and ten to the chamberlain of Falkenstein. If they are absent, equivalent payments go to their replacements from the king's or emperor's court.

4: If a prince is enfeoffed while on horseback, the horse should be donated to the highest-ranking marshal present – in descending order of rank, the duke of Saxony, the vice-marshal of Pappenheim or a replacement from the king's or emperor's court.

---

37 This chapter title only appears in some post-1400 manuscripts. Other versions, such as the first printed edition of 1474, integrate it into chapter 28, for a total of 30 instead of 31 chapters.

5: When all events and enfeoffments at a courtly assembly have concluded, the master of the king's or emperor's household should dismantle and keep the temporary edifice that housed the monarch's throne.[38]]

The thirty-first chapter: concerning the various languages of the electors

Since the worthy rulers of the Roman Empire must consider laws and administer in many varied lands, which differ in their customs, ways of life and languages, so all the wise judge it to be appropriate and useful for the electors – who are the pillars and members of the Empire – to learn many and various languages and tongues, so that they can understand many people and make themselves widely understood, and attentively address the needs of many people.

We therefore establish that the sons, heirs or successors of the illustrious electors – the king of Bohemia, Count Palatine of the Rhine, duke of Saxony and margrave of Brandenburg – should be taught the Latin, Lombard[39] and Slavic[40] tongues, for it can be taken for granted that knowledge of the German language will be cultivated naturally through childhood learning. Thus, they should be taught these languages before the age of fourteen, insofar as God has shown grace towards them in this area. This will not only prove useful, but will come to be seen as exceedingly necessary for the aforenamed reasons. For these tongues often have to be used for the sake of the customary benefit and necessity of the Holy Empire, and are especially important for addressing the more challenging affairs of the Empire.

We therefore establish that this method of learning should be employed: it is up to the fathers (whether they have sons or immediate relatives who will foreseeably be the heirs to their principalities)

---

38 In some manuscripts, this section erroneously appears at the end of chapter 29.
39 That is, the form of Italian spoken in most of the regions of Italy under theoretical imperial jurisdiction. Some manuscripts include 'the Romance and French languages' here (*Welischer und Franczoischer zungen*) – see Fritz (ed.), *Monumenta Germaniae Historica. Constitutiones*, p. 633, note j.
40 That is, Czech.

to send their successors to the places where they can learn these same tongues, or else to introduce educators, teachers and young playmates who are fluent in these languages into their own households, so that their successors can be instructed in these tongues through mutual interaction and teaching.

15. The imperial land-peace and alliance issued at a diet in Eger (1389)

Weizsäcker et al. (eds), *Deutsche Reichstagsakten. Ältere Reihe*, vol. II, pp. 158–67.

We Wenceslas, by the grace of God king of the Romans, ever augmenter of the Empire, and king of Bohemia, declare and make known publicly with this document to all those who see it or hear it read out: that we have agreed upon a collective land-peace, for the praise of almighty God, the honour of the Holy Empire and also the benefit, peace and comfort of the lands and peoples collectively, with the well-considered resolve and good counsel of our and the Empire's electors, princes (spiritual and temporal) and lords, and based on right knowledge; and we have enacted it to all the extent that is written hereafter.

[1] First, we – both the electors, princes, counts and lords and the cities who are in this land-peace – ought to and desire to be supportive and of assistance towards one another concerning justice and honest matters, with constant faithfulness and full diligence, as per the wording of the following articles of this land-peace, as far as all of our bodies and possessions may extend, without any malice or deceit.

[2] We have also fully agreed with the electors, princes, counts, lords and cities who are in this land-peace, concerning any pillage, murder, arson, abduction and unjust feud-declaration that may arise against us or anyone who belongs to this land-peace and league, that those who are installed in a position of authority over the land-peace, or the majority among them who recognise that such crimes have occurred, should duly oversee just legal proceedings within the land-peace. And to that end, each of the above-named electors, princes, counts and lords and each of the cities should provide four men.

Additionally, we the above-named King Wenceslas have selected and provided through our royal authority a collective superior officer, with the instruction: if we or any prince, count, lord or city, or any of those who belong to this land-peace and alliance, should be damaged by somebody against the articles of this land-peace, this should be brought to the superior officer. He should then send for some of his other associates who have authority over the land-peace and alliance within fourteen days or sooner to assemble in one of four towns, Würzburg, Neustadt on the Aisch, Bamberg or Nuremberg, if he should consider it necessary under oath. And if they or the majority among them determine under oath that the deed occurred unlawfully, they should then call upon the nearest lords, cities, officers and judicial personnel without deceit to assist against the same criminals as they know best, according to their oaths. And they should provide assistance to the superior officer faithfully under oath for as long as he is redressing the damage that was done without deceit, following the suggestions of those in authority over the land-peace.

[3] Should those in authority over the land-peace and alliance, or the majority among them under oath, consider that the damaged party might be overwhelmed without assistance from their oath-bound associates, they may and ought to inform as many of the nearby lords and cities as they consider necessary without deceit that they are in need. And the latter should then assist them without hesitation according to their oaths, as is written above, without deceit.

[4] Also, those who have authority over the land-peace should extend that obligatory assistance and service to those princes, lords and cities who are in this land-peace or who will enter into it, according to their oaths, faithfully and as their resources permit, without deceit.

[5] Also, the nine men[41] who are appointed over the land-peace and alliance should swear oaths on holy relics to be faithful judges to the rich and to the poor alike, without deceit.

[6: If the superior officer dies or leaves office, Wenceslas or his successors should nominate a replacement. If any member of the land-peace finds him unsuitable, the monarch is obliged to look for someone else.

7: Those with authority over the land-peace should assemble in one of the four appointed towns in Franconia to hear and adjudicate the claims of those members of the alliance claiming to be damaged

---

41 The council established to decide if crimes have been committed and assistance should be extended, per articles 2–3.

or attacked. These assemblies should be held four times per year at minimum, on the Sundays after the Ember days, or more often if necessary.

8–9: Only the land-peace's appointed scribe may cite people before its ad hoc court, if the council set out in articles 2–5 attests that the summons is just. The council may issue majority rulings if some are absent from the meeting.]

[10] Also, should it occur – God forbid – that a war or assault should arise between lords or cities or others who are in this land-peace and alliance or have yet to join, this should be brought before the superior officer and those with authority over the land-peace. And what they or the majority of them pronounce under oath after holding council should be respected by both sides in such matters, as is written above. And whoever opposes this and disobeys it, the lords and cities and all who are in this land-peace and alliance should be supportive of and assist one another in the above-written manner in opposing them.

[11: Members of the land-peace should work together and pool resources to construct and equip fortifications under the direction of the land-peace council.

12: During collective military expeditions by the land-peace members, only the necessary provisions should be transported. Taking them home or selling them is forbidden.]

[13] It has also been agreed, and we desire this before all other things, that when [members of] the Holy Empire or this land-peace embark on military expeditions in this way, all roads, churches, monasteries, parsonages, churchyards, mills and especially all ploughs with horses and that which belongs to them and vineyards and fields and all things agricultural should be safe and be left in peace, and that nobody should attack, injure or damage them. And should anyone contravene this, it should be treated as pillage, and the land-peace should proceed against them as is written above.

[14–17: The land-peace should regulate behaviour during collective military expeditions by forbidding poaching and foraging, taking crops and other people's household goods and arson.

18: Land-peace members should unite against roving mercenary bands.]

[19] It has also been agreed: if the land-peace desires to undertake a righteous campaign or siege, each lord or city in this land-peace and alliance should send along those who participate in the land-peace on their behalf to be present for as long as the same campaign or siege lasts and until it reaches its conclusion. And if any of the same who participate in the land-peace on their behalf are not able to be present because of honourable necessity, the same lords or cities should appoint and send another respectable man who has sworn an oath to the land-peace in the stead of the person who is not able to be present, as often as necessary. And the captain of the land-peace leading its forces in the field should have our and the Empire's banner, as often as necessary.

[20: The land-peace members should use messengers to keep each other informed when a member has been attacked.]

[21] Also, if someone should commit any damage against us and those who are in this land-peace or have yet to join it, with murder, pillage, arson, theft, abduction or unjust feud-declaration, or with other things as written above, whoever knowingly aids and abets them with lodging, food or drink, that person should be considered as guilty as the perpetrator.

[22] Also, if someone should be condemned in a court, and someone else should declare a feud on their account, they should be considered as guilty as the one condemned in the court. And should there be an injurious person with a publicly evil reputation, and this be made known to the land-peace, anybody who knows this and detains or attacks the injurious person is neither guilty nor under any obligation for those actions. However, if anyone ought to or wants to answer for their reputation before the land-peace, the land-peace should extend safe-conduct to them without deceit.

[23: The land-peace council and its constituent authorities should be consulted, and their orders followed, if large-scale violent conflict breaks out over the issues set out in article 22.]

[24] Also, if someone in this land-peace and alliance or who has yet to join it has any feud declared against them because of things that take place in this land-peace, which the feud-declarer pursues after this land-peace and alliance has ended, the same lords and cities

who are in this land-peace and alliance should be supportive and of assistance towards them under oath for as long as the feud lasts until they are free of it, without deceit.

[25: Pledging by debtors should be regulated. The captain of the land-peace should oversee pledge transactions, with specifications for different types of pledges such as movable and consumable goods, and procedures to follow if somebody should arrive to claim the pledged goods.]

[26] Certainly, too, we establish that the bodies and possessions of each and all of our and the Holy Empire's and the kingdom of Bohemia's electors', princes', counts', lords' and cities' people, spiritual and temporal – priests, laity, knights, retainers, townspeople, merchants, pilgrims, farmers and all kinds of honourable, respectable people, whether of fixed abode or itinerant, from whatever lands they originate – should be safe in this land-peace. However, should any of these people suffer harm to their bodies or goods, on the waterways or on land, the lord or city or other entity belonging to this land-peace and alliance located nearest to where the harm occurred should, as soon as they hear of it or are called upon on account of it, rush to assist them with all their resources, and they should faithfully ensure that restitution is made, without deceit. And if restitution cannot be made, thereafter – as directed by the councillors appointed over the land-peace, or the majority among them – the land-peace members should assist one another as if it were a case of pillage, as is written above.

[27] Also, neither the bodies nor the possessions of any monastic communities, parish priests and other spiritual people should be pledged to anybody in any way.

[28: Land-peace members should not make verbal legal commitments contrary to its terms.

29: Nobody should give succour to those with a public reputation for causing harm.]

[30] It has also been agreed: should it occur that the lords or other people hold courtly assemblies in the imperial cities or other towns, one should grant unconditional and secure safe-conduct to all those who demand and call for it for the duration of the assembly, without deceit.

[31] Also, if someone should want to or be obligated to defend their honour through trial by combat before the lords or cities, one may grant him and his associates unconditional secure safe-conduct to the judicial appointments at which he must appear.

[32: Land-peace members should oppose armed retainers and servitors without lords.

33: The land-peace should not concern itself with wars and disputes that predate its foundation treaty.

34: The superior officer of the land-peace has discretion over whom to admit into it for its benefit. New members must swear a prescribed oath and have documents distributed to existing members.]

[35] Also, the collective league of cities which has existed until now should be terminated, and no more such city leagues should be created.[42] Similarly, the alliance which was created between us and the princes and lords should also be terminated to the extent written hereafter. Thus: whichever city, whether one or more, settles its disputes with the princes and lords who are currently in the war with the cities, either through mediation or through a judicial ruling, as was agreed before our council at Mergentheim,[43] the same city or cities should and may be taken and accepted into our land-peace which we have now made here at Eger; and our and the princes' and lords' above-named alliance should be totally ended against those same cities or that city which are accepted into the land-peace. However, whichever cities or city does not do this and remains disobedient and does not want to settle its disputes through amicable agreement or judicial ruling, as is written above, our and the princes', counts' and lords' alliance should remain in force against the same, as the alliance treaty stipulates. If the same cities which join the land-peace or want to join it then require the administration of justice in court from the above-named princes or lords, so they should provide it to the same cities, as was agreed at Mergentheim before our council.

[36] Also, whichever princes, lords or cities join us in the land-peace now or in the future, if someone should drag them into a

---

42 The 'Great Town League' founded in February 1385, consisting of the existing alliances of Rhenish and Swabian free and imperial cities. See Hardy, *Associative Political Culture*, p. 188.
43 In January 1389, the king had hosted another assembly at Mergentheim for an earlier round of peace negotiations.

feud or enmity or cause them any kind of damage, we and the above-named electors, princes, lords and cities should be supportive and of assistance towards the same against those feud-enemies, faithfully with all our resources, without deceit.

[37] Also, each and every paleburgher,[44] whoever has them, should have their status fully abolished, and henceforth nobody should have them or receive new ones.

[38] Also, nobody should receive as an urban citizen another lord's bondsperson; or an official with custodial duties, if their existing obligations cannot be accounted for; or those embroiled in pending wars that might follow them; or those who swore disloyal oaths or issued disloyal documents before the date of this charter. But if there is no dispute over the matter, the land-peace should recognise that.

[39] Also, this land-peace should exist and extend along the Rhine, into Bavaria, into Swabia, into Franconia, into Hessen, into Thuringia and into Meissen, as is defined in the ancillary treaties issued for this purpose.

[40] Also, as we have established and divided the land-peace among individual land-peaces along the Rhine, in Swabia, in Bavaria, in Thuringia, in Meissen and in Franconia, so we desire that if one of these individual land-peaces encounters an issue, they should not have to overcome or subdue it alone. The other land-peaces – one or more of them, as called upon by the captain of the land-peace whom this concerns with his public letters, in which he states together with his oath-bound associates with authority over the land-peace, or the majority among them under oath, that the afflicted land-peace indeed needs help from the other land-peaces – should then offer assistance in order to settle the matter before a court of law, as the land-peace calling upon them considers that the others should best come to its aid, without deceit.

[41] Also, the same land-peace should not make judicial claims or legal objections against the others, without deceit.

[42] Also, whoever receives an adjudication in a land-peace, they should also be considered to have received that adjudication in the other land-peaces, with the same penalties, as stated in the land-peace treaty, without deceit.

---

44 See [14], chapter 16.

[43] Also, this land-peace – which is conceived only for the common good – should cause no harm to us and the Holy Empire and the above-named electors, princes, counts, lords, knights, retainers, priests, cities and laity, and should be harmless to our and their principalities, lordships and jurisdictions, freedoms, rights and other good customs, spiritual and temporal, excepting those things which are written above, with the caveat that we reserve all rights that we should and may have by law and by royal Roman authority as a Roman king and future emperor, whether they are spiritual or temporal.

[44] And this land-peace should last irrevocably, as defined in all its points and articles, for six whole consecutive years from the date of this document, and thereafter until we revoke it.

[45] And we Wenceslas, above-named Roman king and king of Bohemia, vow by our royal faithfulness, and we Lamprecht of Bamberg [r. 1374–99] and we Gerhart of Würzburg [r. 1372–1400], bishops, Stephan III and Friedrich, Counts Palatine of the Rhine and dukes of Bavaria [r. 1375–92], Ruprecht [II] the Younger, Count Palatine of the Rhine and duke of Bavaria [r. 1338–98], Johann of Regensburg [r. 1384–1409] and Otto of Augsburg [r. 1373–1404], bishops, Wilhelm [I] the Younger, margrave of Meissen [r. 1382–1407], Hermann [II], landgrave of Hessen [r. 1376–1413], Friedrich [V], burgrave of Nuremberg [r. 1357–98], Eberhard [II], count of Württemberg [r. 1344–92], Friedrich [III], count of Oettingen [d. 1423], Albrecht [I], landgrave of Leuchtenberg [r. 1378–1404], Friedrich [II] of Heideck [d. 1423], and we the citizens and councils of the cities of Regensburg, Nuremberg and Weißenburg vow to hold to and carry out this land-peace in all its points and articles, as it is written, defined and sealed, wholly and steadfastly, without deceit and according to the oaths we have made about this with corporeal rituals.

[46] Also, according to the oaths that we have sworn, we should pass orders and make arrangements to ensure that all our officers and administrators, local custodians and representatives and judicial personnel who are located within this land-peace swear similarly constituted oaths, in our presence or that of someone else to whom we commend this task, to uphold the land-peace and the articles defined in it, without deceit. And the same should take place and be carried out without deceit within two months after

the date of this document. All our servitors, vassals, counts, lords, knights and retainers who are located in this land-peace should also swear in this way within the next two months to uphold the land-peace; if any do not want to do so, they should not enjoy the benefits of the land-peace.

[47] Also, every lord and his officers should be bound by these oaths. They should inform the captain of the land-peace and communicate in writing which of their servitors and officers swear the oaths. And should there be anyone located in this land-peace who has not sworn to uphold the land-peace, the land-peace should not adjudicate matters on their behalf, and they should not enjoy the benefits of the land-peace.

And we, the above-named King Wenceslas, have affixed our royal seal to this document to truly witness that it is a legally binding treaty, which is given at Eger, in the 1300th year after Christ's birth and thereafter in the eighty-ninth year, on Wednesday after the feast of the Apostles St Philip and St James [5 May], in the twenty-sixth year of our Bohemian reign and the thirteenth year of our Roman reign.

16. A planned levy at a diet in Nuremberg for the war against the Hussites (1422)

Weizsäcker et al. (eds), *Deutsche Reichstagsakten. Ältere Reihe*, vol. VIII, no. 145.

After two failed anti-Hussite crusades in 1420 and 1421, the electors convened another diet to discuss further measures against the perceived heretical threat emanating from Bohemia [12]. An assembly duly took place in Nuremberg in July–September 1422, at which plans for another expedition were proposed. This intriguing document was produced there sometime before 1 September, on which date Sigismund mentioned the planned levy (*anschlag*) in a letter.[45] Eight contemporaneous copies survive, so the idea of raising proportionate troop contributions in this way must have been taken seriously, even though no actual army formed on the basis of this plan. (A third anti-Hussite crusade, which was also unsuccessful, only got off the ground in the summer of 1423, and it involved only a small proportion of the lords and cities listed here.)

Military plan for the ongoing war in Bohemia

Archbishops	First, Mainz	50
	Cologne	40
	Trier	40
Count Palatine		50 with lances[46]
Saxony		20 mounted gunners[47]
Brandenburg[48]		50 with lances

---

45 Weizsäcker et al. (eds), *Deutsche Reichstagsakten. Ältere Reihe*, vol. VIII, p. 170.
46 The word used here – *gleve* – could refer to a mounted soldier armed with a lance, or a military unit of three to four men led by such a cavalryman. It is difficult to be sure which is meant here, although 'with lances' (*mit gleven*) implies the former. Later *Anschläge* tended to specify cavalry (*zu Roß*) and infantry (*zu Fuß*) numbers in more detail.
47 *schuczen* – this could indicate archers or crossbowmen, but by the 1420s it generally referred to soldiers equipped with early gunpowder weapons.
48 The six electors listed here were the same as the senders of [12].

The bishops

The archbishop of Magdeburg	30 lances, 10 gunners
The bishop of Hildesheim	5 lances, 5 gunners
The bishop of Würzburg	20
The bishop of Bamberg	20
The bishop of Eichstätt	10
The bishop of Strasbourg	5
The bishop of Constance	8
The bishop of Basel	2
The bishop of Chur	2
The bishop of Besançon	6
The bishop of Augsburg	2
The bishop of Metz	6
The bishop of Toul	3
The bishop of Verdun	6
The bishop of Lausanne	6
The bishop of Speyer	8
The bishop of Worms	2 with lances
The bishop of Verden	3 lances, 6 gunners
The bishop of Schwerin	8 lances, 8 gunners
The bishop of Halberstadt	6 lances, 6 gunners
The bishop of Bremen	10 lances, 10 gunners
The bishop of Cammin	6 lances, 6 gunners
The bishop of Regensburg	5 lances
The bishop of Münster	10 lances

Dukes and temporal princes

The duke of Lorraine [Charles II, r. 1364–1431]	
The duke of Bar [René of Anjou, r. 1419–80]	20
The duke of Savoy [Amadeus VIII, r. 1391–1439]	50
Margrave [Bernhard I] of Baden [r. 1372–1431]	10 with lances
Landgrave [Luwdig I] of Hessen [r. 1413–58]	20 lances, 10 gunners
Duke Otto [II] 'by the Leine' [of Brunswick-Göttingen, r. 1394–1463]	10 lances, 10 gunners

ASSEMBLIES AND ORDINANCES TO THE MID-15TH CENTURY

Erich of Brunswick[-Grubenhagen, r. 1384–1427]	5 lances, 5 gunners
Duke Otto of [Brunswick-]Grubenhagen [d. 1452]	5 lances, 5 gunners
Bernhard [I, r. 1388–1434] and Wilhelm [I, r. 1416–82] of Brunswick[-Lüneburg and -Wolfenbüttel] with their towns, namely Brunswick and Lüneburg	10 lances, 10 gunners
Johann [IV, d. 1422]	10 lances, 10 gunners
Albrecht [V, r. 1412–23] of Mecklenburg	10 lances, 10 gunners
Duke Ulrich [I of Mecklenburg-Stargard, d. 1417]'s children [Albrecht II, d. 1423, and Heinrich, d. 1466] in the land around Stargard	10 lances, 10 gunners
Otto [II, r. 1413–28] Kasimir [VI, r. 1413–37] of [Pomerania-]Stettin	20 lances, 12 gunners
Wratislaw [IX] of [Pomerania-]Wolgast [d. 1457]	15 lances, 12 gunners
Erich [V] of Saxony-Lauenburg [d. 1435]	3 lances, 6 gunners
Ludwig [VII] of [Bavaria-]Ingolstadt [r. 1413–47][49]	
Ernst [of Bavaria-Munich, r. 1397–1438]	16
Wilhelm [III of Bavaria-Munich, r. 1397–1435]	10
Heinrich [IV of Bavaria-Landshut, r. 1393–1450]	20
Johann [Count Palatine of Neumarkt, r. 1410–43]	10
Stefan [Count Palatine of Simmern-Zweibrücken, r. 1410–59]	5
Otto [I, Count Palatine of Mosbach, r. 1410–61]	5 lances
Adolf [I] of Cleves[-Mark, r. 1394–1448]	20 lances

---

49 The princes listed from Ludwig to Otto are bracketed under the label 'of Bavaria' (i.e. Wittelsbachs) in the manuscript. The list includes both co-rulers of the part-duchies of Bavaria and the cadet members of the Palatine branch of the dynasty.

Duke [Adolf VII] of Berg [d. 1437]	6 spears
The bishop of Utrecht with Deventer, Kampen, Zwolle and Utrecht	40 lances

Lords and counts in the Netherlands

The duke of Jülich, the knighthood of Jülich and Guelders and the four towns of Roermond, Nijmegen, Arnheim and Zutphen	60 lances
The three towns of Brabant	100
The towns of [the bishopric of] Liège	100 lances
Banner lords, knights and retainers in Holland	60 lances
Banner lords, knights and retainers in Hainault	
The towns of Hainault	
The count of Namur	20 lances
Lords and knighthood of Flanders	
The towns of Flanders	20 lances

Counts and lords

Gerhard, count of the Mark	3
Wilhelm, count of Ravensberg	2
Count of Tecklenburg	2
The counts of Rietberg	1
The lord of Lippe	2
The lord of Diepholz	1
The count of Bentheim	1
The count of Schauenburg	1
The count of Oldenburg	1
Friedrich Wilhelm of Henneberg	4
The count of Rhinek	2
The count of Kastell	2
The count of Hohenlohe	2
The count of Weinsberg	2
The count of Heideck	1
Otto	
Erich of Hoya	6
The counts of Württemberg	20

ASSEMBLIES AND ORDINANCES TO THE MID-15TH CENTURY

The count of Chalon	15
The margrave of Röteln	3
The count of Toggenburg	5
Konrad of Freiburg	5
Hugo, master of the Order of St John	10 lances
Christoph of Wenden	6 lances, 6 gunners
Albrecht	
Georg of Anhalt	5 lances, 5 gunners
Bernhard of Anhalt	4 lances, 4 gunners
Bernhard of Reinstein	3 lances, 3 gunners
The count of Wernigerode	4 lances, 4 gunners
Emicho	3
Friedrich of Leiningen	2
Philipp of Nassau	4
Johann of Sponheim	5
Friedrich of Veldenz	3
Johann	2
Friedrich the Rhinegraves	2
Philipp	
Emicho lords of Oberstein	2
The lord of Hohenfels	1
Nicklaus, advocate of Hunolstein	1
Johann of Katzenelnbogen	8
Adolf of Nassau	2
Wilhelm of Wied	3
Philipp	
Salentin lords of Isenburg	3 lances
Johann of Wied	
Reinhard, lord of Westerburg	2
Dietrich, lord of Runkel	1
Johann	
Heinrich counts of Nassau, lords of Beilstein	2
Bernhard	
Johann counts of Solms, brothers	3
Johann of Wittgenstein	1
Ruprecht of Virneburg	2
Gottfried	
Eberhard lords of Eppenstein	4
Reinhard, lord of Hanau	3

Diether, lord of Büdingen	3
Michel of Wertheim	1
Wilhelm of Eberstein	1
The lords of Arberg	3
Wilhelm of Blankenstein	1
Johann, lord of Schleiden	1
Friedrich of Moers	4
Johann, lord of Heinbserg	4
Walraf of Moers	1
Wilhelm	
Kraft lords of Saffenburg	2
Johann, lord of Rodemach	2
Johann	
Gottfried counts of Ziegenhain	2
Heinrich of Waldeck and the other Waldecker	4
Johann	
Heinrich of Vinstingen	2
The lord of Weibelkoben	1
Schenk Eberhard	
Schenk Konrad the Elder	
Schenk Konrad the Younger of Erbach[50]	3
Konrad, lord of Bickenbach	1
The lord of Neuenar	1
Eberhard of Limberg, lord of Hartenberg	2
The count of Limpurg	1
The lord of Hoorn	2
Johann of Saarwerden	1
The brothers of Bitsch	1
The count of Salm	1

The abbots

The abbot of Fulda	6
The abbot of Wissembourg	2
The abbot of Selz	1
The abbot of Murbach	3
The abbot of Maulbronn	5

50 The counts of Erbach were called *Schenken* – 'butlers'/'stewards' – because their ancestors had held prestigious ceremonial positions at the court of the Counts Palatine of the Rhine.

The abbot of Einsiedeln	2
The abbot of Bebenhausen	3
The abbot of Salmansweiler	5
The abbot of Alb	2
The abbot of Kempten	2
The abbot of Schaffhausen	2
The abbot of Petershausen	2
The abbot of Konzlingen	2
The abbot of Weingarten	4
The abbot of Elchingen	2
The abbot of St Blasien	2
The abbot of Blaubeuren	2
The abbot of Zwiefalten	2
The abbot of Isny	1
The abbot of St Georgen	1
The abbot of St Johannes	1
The abbot of Pfäfers	1
The abbot of Königsbrunn	1
The prior of Schussenried	2

The towns

The confederates of Bern, Lucerne, Zurich, Freiburg in the Üchtland etc.	250 horses
Constance	
Lindau	
Buchhorn	
Ravensburg	
Überlingen	
Radolfszell	
Diessenhofen	50 with lances or 200 mounted men-at-arms
Schaffhausen	
Waldshut	
Laufenburg	
Säckingen	
Reinfelden	
Winterthur	
Rapperswil	
Frauenfeld	26 gunners
Kempten	
Isny	

Wangen	
Leutkirch	
Memmingen	
Augsburg	
Biberach	
Pfullendorf	
Kaufbeuren	
Ulm	
Giengen	
Nördlingen	
Aalen	
Gmünd	
Dinkelsbühl	
Esslingen	
Reutlingen	
Rottweil	
Buchau	100 with lances and 100 gunners
Hall	12 with lances and 12 gunners
Heilbronn	
Wimpfen	
Weinsberg	24 men-at-arms who are mounted
Basel	16 with lances
Strasbourg	20 lances
Mulhouse	
Colmar	
Munster	
Kaysersberg	
Turckheim	
Sélestat	
Obernai	
Rosheim	
Haguenau	
Wissembourg[51]	30 lances
Freiburg	
Neuenburg	

51 The ten towns from Mulhouse to Wissembourg were allied within the 'town league of the Alsatian bailiwick [*Landvogtei*]'.

ASSEMBLIES AND ORDINANCES TO THE MID-15TH CENTURY

Breisach	
Kenzingen	
Endingen[52]	10 lances
Metz	20 lances
Toul	5 lances
Verdun	10 lances
Sarrebourg	3 lances
Trier	4 lances
Speyer	
Worms	
Mainz	24 lances
Cologne	
Aachen	30 lances
Dortmund	6
Frankfurt	15
Friedberg	2
Gelnhausen	3
Wetzlar	2 lances
Nuremberg	30 lances, 30 gunners
Rottenburg	12 lances, 12 gunners
Windsheim	6 lances, 6 gunners
Weißenburg	5 lances, 5 gunners
Schweinfurt	5 lances, 5 gunners
Regensburg	15 lances, 15 gunners
Lübeck	30 lances, 30 gunners
Hamburg	20 lances, 20 gunners
Mühlhausen	8 lances, 6 gunners
Nordhausen	15 lances, 10 gunners
Goslar	10 lances, 6 gunners
Aschersleben	10 lances, 10 gunners
Halberstadt	10 lances, 10 gunners
Quedlinburg	10 lances, 10 gunners

Summa totalis 754 lances, 777 armed cavalry from the towns[53]

52 The five towns from Freiburg to Endingen were possessions of the Outer Austrian Habsburgs for most of this period, but briefly held the status of imperial cities from the mid-1410s to mid-1420s in the wake of Sigismund's imperial war against Duke Friedrich IV of Austria-Tyrol.

53 This does not tally with the numbers enumerated above, which amount to 548 lances and 24 cavalry (or 398 lances and 224 cavalry, based on the two choices listed for the towns around Lake Constance). The gunners are also not counted here.

17. A peace-ordinance promulgated at a diet in Frankfurt (the 'Royal Reformation') (1442)

Weizsäcker et al. (eds), *Deutsche Reichstagsakten. Ältere Reihe*, vol. XVI, pp. 401–07.

We Frederick, by the grace of God king of the Romans, ever augmenter of the Empire, duke of Austria, Styria, Carinthia and Carniola, count of Tyrol etc., impart our grace and all good wishes to all and every one of our and the Holy Roman Empire's honourable and high-born electors, princes (spiritual and temporal), counts, barons, servitors, knights, retainers, burgraves, advocates, mayors, magistrates, councillors, judges, officials and communes, and all and every one of the towns, markets and villages and all of our and the Holy Empire's other subjects and well-beloved faithful people, whatever their dignity, estate or condition.

Since the time when we, by the undeserved grace of Almighty God, were elevated to and placed into the dignity of Roman royal authority, we have been well and justly concerned to prove ourselves in our duties towards everyone in such a way that peace and tranquillity might blissfully be enjoyed in the Holy Empire. Yet now, at the outset of our rule, and also now after our royal coronation, we have heard and learned from many reliable sources that many ruinous events – violent, inappropriate and dishonourable attacks and injuries – have taken place in the Holy Roman Empire, and especially in the German lands, and are still taking place every day, with robbery, murder and arson. Because of this, the Holy Empire, of which we have been named an augmenter, is greatly and harmfully diminished, and many of the Empire's subjects and faithful people, both spiritual and temporal, daily suffer great affliction, devastation and injury. Consequently, a great complaint sadly echoes throughout the lands. The common good is greatly led astray, undermined and oppressed by all of this.

Therefore, because of the burden of our royal office (which we have taken upon ourselves for the praise of God and the honour of the Holy Empire, and for the sake of the common good), we have agreed that we want to work with all diligence and to the best of our capabilities, with timely counsel and the help of God as well as the assistance of our and the Empire's faithful people, to obliterate such ruinous and evil occurrences. And to this end, through this proclamation, and in the presence and with the counsel of our and the Empire's electors, other princes (spiritual and temporal), counts, barons, knights, retainers and cities whom we have summoned and ordered to come to us in person or through their empowered envoys for the sake of this matter in particular, we earnestly and firmly establish, will and mandate with this document, by our Roman royal might, power and authority, and also exhort you – all and every one of our and the Empire's subjects, whatever your dignity, estate or condition – by the faithfulness and dutifulness that you are obliged and duty-bound to show towards God, the Holy Empire, us as king of the Romans, your supreme lord, the common good and yourselves:

That you should uphold, carry out and extol each and every part, point and article of this, our ordinance written below, entirely, faithfully, righteously and without deceit; and also earnestly ensure that it is mandated and implemented among your people and those who belong to you or are your subordinates, so that they likewise uphold it entirely and faithfully – if, that is, you wish to avoid our and the Empire's severe disfavour and the penalties set out hereafter in this, our ordinance.

[1] Firstly, nobody should cause or inflict damage upon another, unless they have first sought impartial, fair justice from them according to the customs of the region. And should they be unable to find or benefit from such justice as quickly as they might wish for it or request it, they should nevertheless neither attack nor harm the other party unless they have first fully and unreservedly done and carried out everything that is contained and stipulated in detail in the chapter on feud-declarations in the Golden Bull [14] of Emperor Charles IV of blessed memory, our predecessor in the Empire.[54]

[2] Item, if anybody should have a known and lawful debt to another, and if the creditor has guarantors and documents proving the debt, they may demand repayment and collect their debt according to the terms and declarations of these documents of theirs and the promises made to them concerning repayment.

[2a] However, if one party cannot obtain repayment according to the terms of their documents or the promises made to them about

---

54 See [14], chapter 17.

how repayment should proceed, and they are now entitled to seize something belonging to the debtor as a pledge, they should handle this pledge in the manner written hereafter, though without affecting the salesperson involved in these transactions. They should repay one another, and each should collect their interest, revenues and fees, in the customary manner.

[2b] And before a person who wishes to seize pledges in this way does so, they should request – in writing, verbally or in person – repayment in full from the person who is in their debt within two consecutive months of the request being made, by amicable means or according to the fair, just customs of the region.

[2c] And if the debt is not repaid in full within this time in the manner written above, the creditor may then apprehend the debtor and seize their property and assets in pledge. However, they should then handle these pledges in accordance with the laws and customs of pledging. Thus, they should transport all of these same pledges without deceit to the nearest town or castle containing a court that does not belong either to the one seizing the pledges or to the one whose assets are being seized in pledge. And the apprehended debtor and property seized in pledge should be taken into custody and guarded in the same castle, town or court, and they should not be permitted to extricate themselves from there. During this time, the creditor should enjoy peace and safe-conduct with regard to the same pledges, without deceit. And if the pledges consist of consumables or livestock, they should be left there for three days and three nights. If they are other kinds of pledges, they should be left there for four consecutive weeks. And no companion should be permitted to take any of them as booty or as a portion. Rather, the same items of property should be left there together, undisturbed.

[2d] And if someone should come to redeem the apprehended debtor and pledges, they should be handed over to this redeemer as lawful collateral, with the approval of the judge or official in whose court they are located, or that of other honourable people who are there.

[2e] However, if nobody wishes to redeem the pledges within the aforenamed timeframe, the pledge-taker may then sell the same pledges for as high a price as they can, without deceit, again with the approval of the official into whose court they were transported,

or that of other honourable people there. And the resulting money should be deducted from the debt of the one whose property was seized in pledge. Whatever expenses they incurred during the same pledging should also be deducted, provided they are genuine and can be demonstrated before the lord or official of the court.

[2f] Also, if someone should have been taken into captivity as part of this pledging, these same prisoners should also all be redeemed as lawful collateral. And if they cannot agree about the guarantees and collateral decided by the presiding court, that decision should stand. Where necessary, the said court should decide in these kinds of disputes.

[2g] Also, should it happen that the pledge-taking creditor does not transport these same pledges to the next castle or town containing a court and hold them there, as written above, this should thenceforth be treated as a robbery. And should the lord or official of the same castle, or others based nearby, be called upon, they should offer faithful assistance with their allies, pursue the perpetrators who are *in flagrante delicto* and proceed to bring the same pledge-taker and the pledges into their (or someone else's) castle or court. They may then be dealt with in accordance with the Empire's laws (which the lord or official should be permitted to do).

[2h] Also, should it happen that a pledge-taker comes to a castle with the pledges and asks to enter, and they are then denied entry, and they can demonstrate that this took place, they may either leave the pledges there or transport them onwards to the next court. And any damages that they incur there as a consequence that can be demonstrated to be genuine, without deceit, should be compensated by the lord or people of the same castle that denied them entry.

[2i] Also, anyone who permits the pledges to be left in their castles and courts should not bear any ill will on this account or inflict any kind of damage on them.

[2k] Also, should someone else – apart from those written about above – undertake any hostile or aggressive actions against somebody, everyone who is called upon on account of these actions should pursue the perpetrators who are *in flagrante delicto* and help to (re-)apprehend the stolen property along with the perpetrators, according to the law.

[3] Item, both during and in the absence of declared feuds, farmers and winegrowers should enjoy peace and security when they are outside their houses with their possessions that are needed for the cultivation of fields, pastures and vineyards; and also when they are in the fields, pastures and vineyards; and when they are at home in their houses; and when they are harvesting the fruit, mowing the meadows, picking the wine grapes and bringing in these crops. And whether they are in a public state of feud-enmity or not, nobody should commit arson, burn and plunder buildings or set or spread fires, whether during the day or at night.

[4] Item, all clerics, women who have recently given birth, those who are severely ill and also pilgrims, travellers, merchants and wagon-drivers should be left in security along with their possessions and merchandise and not harmed.

[5] Item, churches, cemeteries and parsonages should also be left in security, and nothing should be taken from them. Nobody should seek to defend themselves within them. However, if somebody should seek to storm these places or endanger those within them, it is permissible to defend against them.

[6] Item, henceforth, itinerant mercenaries should no longer own their own horses, unless they are in the service of a lord, nobleman or town, acting as their hired, fed and salaried retainer. And if the retainer should do anything to violate the articles written above and below, the authority employing them should take responsibility for it and offer compensation. And should there be any itinerant mercenaries who own their own horses yet lack lords or noble employers, as written above, neither they nor other soldiers who lack lords or whose lords do not have lawful authority over them should enjoy peace, support or safe-conduct.

[7] Item, all electors, other princes (spiritual and temporal), counts, barons, knights, towns and the multitude of our and the Empire's subjects should earnestly and firmly ensure and establish that all their people and those whom they command – be they noble or non-noble, itinerant retainers, journeymen, household servitors, farmhands or others – do not belligerently assist anyone with carrying out an attack or hostile action, nor do so on anyone's orders, whether on water or on land, without their authority's knowledge, consent and favour. We also order all of the aforementioned, and all others who lack lords to whom they are specifically answerable, to uphold this firmly.

[8] Item, everyone, be they princes, lords or cities, whatever their estate or condition (as stated above), should also diligently and firmly mandate in their lands, towns and districts, among their officials and elsewhere that henceforth, adult men who are not afflicted with a notable corporeal disease yet behave like idle do-nothings, and lack an honourable, honest and adequate means of providing for themselves, are not to be harboured or tolerated in their lands, towns and districts, but should be spurned and driven out.

[9] Item, nobody should have safe-conduct to any destination, nor anybody be granted it, except according to the law, with the exception of safe-conduct to public diets, courts and pre-arranged duels.

[10] Item, concerning the secret courts:[55] many unlawful things have been going on and have been pursued in myriad ways in these same courts that do not belong in their competence, such that if this state of affairs were to continue it would cause no small damage to and impingement on the common good and peace in the Holy Empire.

To obviate this danger, we have – with the counsel, as written above, of our and the Holy Empire's electors, princes, cities and others mentioned above – established and ordained, and establish, ordain and mandate with our Roman royal authority, by the power of this document, that henceforth these secret courts should be staffed with proper, intelligent and experienced people, and not be held by people of illegitimate birth or who have been excommunicated, placed in the imperial ban, committed perjury or are of unfree status.

Thus, these same staff should not handle judicial matters any differently than at the very beginning, as established by the Holy Emperor Charlemagne,[56] our predecessor in the Empire, and ordained and established in the reformation issued at Arnsberg by the honourable Dietrich, archbishop of Cologne,[57] our well-beloved relative

---

55 *heimlichen gerichte* – another name for the Vehmic courts, a kind of vigilante justice administered by itinerant Westphalians that impinged on existing jurisdictions.
56 Part of the Vehmic courts' claim to legitimacy was rooted in the notion that they had been founded by Charlemagne himself.
57 Dietrich of Moers, archbishop of Cologne (r. 1414–63), sought to codify and regulate the Vehmic courts in a reform issued at a meeting in Arnsberg in 1437, which was also sent to Emperor Sigismund. See Fricke, 'Die Vemegerichtsbarkeit'.

and elector, in the presence of many counts, barons, knights and Vehmic overseers, judges and assessors,[58] as he was mandated to do by Emperor Sigismund of blessed memory, our predecessor.

In particular, nobody should cite or summon anyone before these courts except for cases that belong within their competence, or cases which otherwise lack a court with jurisdiction over the matter. If someone should be summoned before these courts when their lord or judge has jurisdiction over them, or other courts have jurisdiction over them according to prevailing regional customs, and the same lord or judge informs the Vehmic court personnel of this in person or in writing, (counter-)summons the cited party to their own court and sends firm written proof of their aforementioned jurisdiction over the case to the Vehmic court personnel in a letter sealed by themselves and two or three other neutral men, the Vehmic court's summons should then immediately be null and void, and the case should be referred back to the lord or judge in whose competence it belongs and before whom the party should be summoned, without any obstruction on the part of the Vehmic court personnel. Should the case not be transferred in this way, all judicial proceedings and enforcements and court sessions that may have occurred or may yet occur in connection with it should be entirely null and void and terminated. We pronounce and adjudge them null and void, now as then and then as now, by our Roman royal authority.

[10a] Also, nobody should be appointed as judge or assessor of a Vehmic court except those who are lawfully eligible, and who can sufficiently demonstrate their suitability for the role. Specifically, no illegitimately born people, or bondspeople or people who are otherwise of unfree status, should be appointed as assessors. Those who are in the imperial ban or double ban, or have been declared outlaws or spiritually excommunicated, should also never be appointed as assessors.

[10b] We will that what is written above regarding the secret courts be upheld by everyone firmly and inviolably. To that end, we earnestly and diligently command all and every one of the Vehmic court personnel with this document, whatever their condition or

---

58 *stuohlherren, freygreaven und freyschephen* – specific titles for the owners and staff of the Vehmic courts.

estate, that they should ordain that this be lawfully respected in their judicial seats and courts. Whenever or wherever something is done in violation of this, or following alternative practices, the overseer of the Vehmic court should pay ten marks of gold to our royal treasury, without possibility of remission, and the Vehmic judge should be removed from office. The person who obtains such an illegal summons or citation has also condemned themselves and forfeited their life, having acted dishonourably against another, and everyone should ensure that this person faces appropriate justice.

[11] Item, since the Holy Empire and German lands face urgent problems related to the gold and silver coinage, and it is necessary that they be minted and maintained to a correct standard, we establish – with the counsel and in the manner already mentioned – that the gold florin should remain at a common regional valuation of nineteen carats of fine gold, as has been the case for some time. It should not be minted at a higher or lower degree of fineness. Anyone who does it in a different way, whatever their dignity, estate or condition, should be severely punished for it, as appropriate.

[12] Item, concerning the silver coinage: since it cannot be brought to a common fineness across all regions, because of the circumstances of those regions, and for multifarious other reasons, we will and command that everyone who mints silver coins should ensure that they are minted and treated to a consistent and correct standard. Wherever they are minted and treated differently from such a fair standard, we will that this be strictly and firmly punished, and that the punishment be enforced, as appropriate.

[13] Item, any people who violate, act against or provide assistance in the contravention of one or more of the articles written above – or willingly, knowingly or deceitfully harbour, house, sustain or support those who act against these articles – should be treated as lawbreakers, and fall into our and the Empire's grave disfavour, and additionally have to pay a penalty, namely one hundred marks of pure gold – half to our and the Empire's treasury, and half to the plaintiff or injured party, without possibility of remission or mercy. Should they lack the money or gold to pay this penalty, they should suffer corporeal punishment for their misdeed, and they should be tried according to the Empire's laws. And everyone who has fiefs and privileges to lose should be stripped of all the ones that they

hold from us and the Empire or other spiritual or temporal authorities or individuals, as well as incurring the aforenamed penalties in their entirety, as if this were the consequence of a judicial process.

And those who commit such violations, or those who harbour them, make contributions to them or encourage them, should never enjoy any kind of safety, peace or safe-conduct in any settlements or places. Rather, everyone should and may have the right to attack them and their property without this being treated as a violent crime, in the same way and in all the same respects as if the violators had been cited before the Empire's aulic court (or other relevant courts) and declared outlaws following a just verdict and placed in the imperial ban and double ban. And nobody should justify or protect the lives and properties of the violators in any way. And whichever courts have jurisdiction over them should take them into custody without hindrance and pronounce justice over them, per the penalties and as written above.

[13a] However, we reserve for ourselves as a king of the Romans that if ever at any time hereafter it would be appropriate – according to the circumstances of the time and the matter – to alter, augment, reduce or abolish this, our ordinance, wholly or in part, or to issue an addition or retraction to it, we may do so or have it done, as is only right, with the counsel of our and the Empire's faithful people, excluding and repudiating all guile and deceit in all and every one of the points and articles written above in their entirety.

Given at Frankfurt, sealed with our appended royal majestic seal, in the 1400th and then the forty-second year after Christ's birth, on the eve of the Assumption of Our Lady [14 August], in the third year of our reign.

III

CONFLICT, COMPROMISE AND CONSTITUTIONAL CHANGE AT THE IMPERIAL DIETS, 1467–1555

The century between around 1450 and 1550 was arguably the most important in the entire history of the Holy Roman Empire. The loose entity of the fourteenth and early fifteenth century – with its under-resourced imperial monarchy and fragmented princely, noble and urban authorities – began to consolidate partially at a central level and to crystallise into a specific multilateral and power-sharing structure in this period, setting in place a more interconnected yet still polycentric configuration that would endure until the Empire's dissolution in 1806.

Imperial diets were at the heart of this process. While still not permanent or regular institutions, pan-imperial assemblies reached a peak of frequency in this period, especially in the immediate decades either side of 1500. The diets' internal processes became gradually more consistent, involving ritualised entries into the host city, enfeoffments by the monarch (if present), the presentation of the king or emperor's agenda and replies by the estates, deliberations in committees or councils (usually one for the electors, another for the princes and sometimes a third for the cities, though the latter often lacked a vote), the finding of consensus on key issues and the promulgation of a 'recess' (*Abschied*), containing – or issued alongside – legislative ordinances and treaties. Our knowledge of what went on at these assemblies also greatly increases in this era, thanks especially to the detailed reports of urban envoys. One, sent by Hans of Seckingen, councillor of Strasbourg, from a diet in Nuremberg in 1487 [18], sheds light on the insecure position of the cities at the diets, but also the struggle the various factions of the estates faced both in negotiating with the emperor and in keeping the topics under discussion secret within their committees.

The diets' presumed relevance for the entire Empire was reflected in a change of nomenclature: during the 1490s, alongside the customary terms 'royal diet' and 'collective diet' (*königlicher Tag, gemeiner Tag*), the new coinage 'imperial diet' (*Reichstag*) came into use. The diets of these years saw the creation of new, collective institutions for deciding and enforcing peace and justice, to be staffed by both the king or emperor and the imperial members (now known increasingly as 'estates' – *Stände*). This new vocabulary, reflecting a new degree of institutionalisation of imperial politics, is on display in Maximilian I's invitation to 'the electors, princes and estates of the Empire' to attend 'a useful imperial diet' in 1509 [19].

The more institutionalised political frameworks of the *Reich* helped determine the course of another vital new element in the German lands: the emerging division between adherents of the new evangelical teachings of Martin Luther, Ulrich Zwingli and other 'reformers' and adherents of the old faith from the 1520s onwards. The public peace, cameral court, imperial circles and ad hoc alliance treaties and contracts – all continued to be iterated by the monarchs and estates into the 1550s, through truces, conflict and eventual compromise between the new confessions. Thus, the unfolding developments of the Lutheran and Catholic Reformations in the German lands are inseparable from the ongoing evolution of the political framework created over the decades before Luther penned his *Ninety-five Theses* in 1517.

The impetus for change gathered substantial momentum during the reign of Frederick III. Extreme turbulence characterised the decades that followed his 1442 coronation expedition. Alongside many localised feuds, much of southern and central Germany erupted into open conflict during the 'Margravial War' (1449–50, see [46]) and the Princes' War (1458–63). Frederick himself faced rebellions, invasion and fratricidal war in his Austrian heartlands. The Empire as a whole seemed to be threatened by France from the west (notably during mercenary incursions in 1444–45) and the advancing Ottoman Empire. The fall of Constantinople in 1453 was a turning point in German political discourse: anxiety about 'the Turks' and the need for the Empire's denizens to defend Christendom against them became a rhetorical commonplace.[1] Under pressure from papal legates, this issue prompted the leading princes and cities to find a degree of unity by the 1460s. This cohesion was also helped by the increasing urgency with which more and more polemicists (including influential councillors in princely

---

1 Hardy, 'The Fall of Constantinople'.

entourages) decried internal disorder and called for better governance in response to it (see [33]). The many years' worth of projects drafted since the last peace-ordinance of 1442 [17] coalesced into public peace ((*Land-*)*frieden*) legislation promulgated and updated in stages: in Nuremberg in 1466 and ratified by Frederick in 1467; at a diet in Regensburg in 1471, when Frederick returned to the Empire for the first time in more than a quarter-century; and at another diet in Frankfurt in 1486, in return for promises of aid against King Matthias Corvinus of Hungary, who had invaded Austria [20].

The preambles to these ordinances touch upon themes that would prove very durable in imperial high politics. On the one hand, they denounce internal disorder and insist upon the need for measures to restore peace. On the other hand, they warn of imminent external dangers to the Holy Roman Empire and Christendom, presenting domestic peace as a prerequisite for adequate defence. Throughout the reigns of Frederick III, Maximilian I, Charles V and Ferdinand I, the Habsburg monarchs would repeatedly request military and financial assistance from the estates – to be deployed against Burgundy, Hungary, France, various Italian opponents and above all (at least rhetorically) the Ottomans – and concede some degree of institutional change in return. This is not to say that the kings and emperors consistently opposed political reforms, but on balance the initiative for institutional change came from factions among the estates, and reflected the dynamics of the Empire's fragmented heartlands, where collective solutions for peace and justice had long existed within regional associations.[2] The public peace-ordinances of this era applied the logics and mechanisms of regional land-peace-alliances to the entire community of the Holy Roman Empire. This began already with the peace-ordinances in [20], which called upon the imperial members to end their feuds, avoid harbouring peace-breakers and band together to pursue perpetrators and bring them to justice across jurisdictional boundaries.

The 'Perpetual Public Peace' issued at a diet in Worms in 1495 [21], long viewed as the turning point between 'medieval' and 'early modern' German history, was no innovation in this regard. It largely reiterated the terms of the 1467, 1471 and 1486 peace-ordinances [20]. Where it did depart from precedent was in its

---

2 See Hardy, *Associative Political Culture*, chapter 12.

duration. These earlier pan-imperial peace-ordinances had a duration of five to ten years and were renewed, whereas in 1495 their terms were established permanently, and would indeed remain part of imperial constitutional law until 1806. Furthermore, the perpetual public peace rested on a broader foundation of new institutions and practices founded in 1495, and soon even more would be added to the cluster of interlinked mechanisms promulgated at the imperial diets under Maximilian.

The most important of these was the new imperial cameral court (*Reichskammergericht*) [22]. Until 1495, the only courts with pan-imperial jurisdiction belonged to the kings and emperors of the Romans. The 'aulic court' (*Hofgericht*) was attached to their entourage in certain periods during the thirteenth to fifteenth centuries, and regional courts belonging to the crown (such as the *Hofgericht* in Rottweil) could try to exercise pan-imperial jurisdiction, but none were more than fitfully effective; they struggled to reach plaintiffs and to enforce their judgements and declarations of outlawry.[3] A new 'cameral court' (*Kammergericht*) run by councillors of Sigismund and Frederick III grew in popularity in the middle decades of the fifteenth century. By the 1470s it had been delegated to the archbishops of Mainz for its everyday running, and was increasingly staffed by jurists educated in civil law, who layered principles derived from this 'learned' law onto procedures rooted in customary law.[4] The 1495 ordinance founding a pan-imperial cameral court [22] was not, therefore, creating an entirely new institution, but transferring formal control of the existing cameral court to the estates as a collective, codifying its powers, processes, personnel and revenue sources and linking it to the public peace, such that it served as the judicial arm of peace-keeping in the Empire. (Meanwhile, in a bid to maintain a supreme court under his more direct control, Maximilian founded the 'aulic council' – *Reichshofrat* – which functioned in parallel with the new imperial cameral court.)[5] A third ordinance issued in 1495, known as 'the administration of peace and justice' (*Handhabung Friedens und Rechts*) [23], further clarified the functioning of both the public peace and cameral court, prescribing annual diets for

---

3 Baumbach, *Königliche Gerichtsbarkeit*, pp. 156–89.
4 Ibid., pp. 284–310.
5 Whaley, *Germany*, p. 33.

the imperial community to make collective decisions in these areas and for mutual defence. (The 'Common Penny' – a fourth, much shorter-term and less successful initiative in 1495 – sought to levy a tax on all denizens of the Empire to fund these institutions and Maximilian's planned campaigns in Italy.)[6]

The Worms ordinances of 1495 are therefore best seen as one important step in a longer process of constitutional evolution and experimentation, which continued into the sixteenth century. The multilateralisation of imperial governance reached its apogee at a diet in Augsburg in 1500, with the foundation of a governing council (*Reichsregiment*) of twenty representatives of the estates and one of the monarch, with sweeping judicial, fiscal, executive and military powers [24]. Probably the ambitious project of the faction around Berthold of Henneberg, the reform-minded archbishop of Mainz (r. 1484–1504), the *Reichsregiment* sat for two years in Nuremberg before dissolving once Maximilian was strong enough to undermine it. (The king and future emperor had always opposed the project as an attack on his sovereign prerogatives.) A new *Reichsregiment* was constituted in the 1520s, as requested in the electoral contract of Charles V [9], but it was mostly a partisan instrument of the Habsburgs.[7] One of the *Reichsregiment*'s innovations did endure: its division of the Empire into six 'circles', originally conceived as recruitment zones for the representatives with a seat on the governing council. Four further circles were added in the recess of the 1512 imperial diet of Trier/Cologne, and the members of these circles were now tasked with enforcing the public peace at a local level [25].

These new institutions were not static. Rather, they were constant works in progress, iterated in the recesses and ordinances of successive sixteenth-century diets as new problems and challenges arose. The public peace underwent major revisions in 1521 at the first diet of Charles V's reign [26], for instance. The recess of the 1555 diet of Augsburg, better known as the 'Peace of Augsburg' [30] because it formally accommodated Lutherans alongside adherents of the old faith in the Empire's legal framework, was in fact largely a revision of the public peace, cameral court and circles, as readers will be able appreciate from the later articles of the recess, which are presented here for the first time in English translation.

---

6 See Lanzinner, 'Gemeiner Pfennig'.
7 Whaley, *Germany*, pp. 34–35.

Indeed, from a political perspective, 'the Reformation' in the German lands can be understood as a sequence of events and developments in which emerging confessional divisions among the estates placed great strain on the imperial constitution forged in the later Middle Ages, but in which this constitution ultimately provided the flexible tools necessary to contain the crisis and enable compromise and co-existence within a decentralised, religiously mixed polity.[8] The religious question began to encroach upon the imperial diets after Martin Luther's condemnation at the 1521 diet in Worms, but became truly unavoidable after the turbulence and trauma of the Peasants' War (1524–26), perceived by many elites as the product of dangerous new religious teachings. In the recess of a diet held in Speyer in 1526 [27], the estates prescribed harsh measures against future 'rebels' and agreed on ambiguous wording to enable princes and cities that now adhered to evangelical doctrines to remain in good standing within the Empire's political community. When the old faith majority sought to impose the anti-Lutheran edict of 1521 more explicitly at a subsequent diet in Speyer in 1529, the evangelical minority issued a legal protestation [28]. These tensions continued at a diet in Augsburg in 1530, personally attended by Charles V, but the Habsburg emperor and his brother Ferdinand (now crowned king of the Romans) were also compelled to seek compromise by the urgent need for collective assistance from the estates against the Ottomans, who had besieged Vienna itself in 1529. The framework of the public peace provided a template for a temporary truce in 1532 [29], which has often been overlooked in the bigger picture of Reformation history, yet clearly pointed the way to a longer-term solution to the Empire's religious divisions.

This did not prevent escalating tensions between the evangelicals of the Schmalkaldic League [43] and coalitions of princes of the old faith, which culminated in Charles V's decisive victory in the Schmalkaldic War of 1546–47. However, Charles's unpopular peace terms in the 1548 'Augsburg Interim' paved the way for a second series of conflicts in 1552 that dismantled the emperor's commanding position. In August of that year, Ferdinand made peace with his brother's Protestant opponents in the Treaty of

---

8 The details of the key events of the early Reformation are well covered in existing English-language scholarship and will not be rehearsed here. For a comprehensive yet digestible overview, see Whaley, *Germany*, parts III–IV.

Passau, promising to negotiate a settlement for Lutherans within the Empire's laws at a future diet, which eventually took place at Augsburg in 1555 [30]. Though by no means a panacea, the Peace of Augsburg proved the viability of the imperial institutions built up over the preceding century, creating the conditions for seven decades of peace before the Thirty Years' War and its aftermath forced another reconfiguration of the Empire, including a permanent imperial diet in Regensburg from the 1660s.

18. An urban envoy reports on the negotiating process at an imperial diet (1487)

Bock et al. (eds), *Deutsche Reichstagsakten. Mittlere Reihe*, vol. II, pp. 1030–35.

The diet at which this letter was written was held in Nuremberg in 1487, against the background of a crisis in Austria: King Matthias 'Corvinus' of Hungary was at war with the Habsburgs, and close to capturing their seat of power in Wiener Neustadt. Frederick III and the recently elected Maximilian I therefore sought help from the imperial estates. At the same time, Archbishop Berthold of Mainz was acting as the ringleader of a reform-minded group that sought to persuade the estates to negotiate institutional changes at the diets. The diet began on 31 March, just over a month before this urban envoy sent his report to Strasbourg's city council.

To my stalwart and vigorous, judicious, honourable and wise, well-beloved lords; may my willing service ever be at the disposal of your judicious and honourable wisdom.

As Heinrich Eberhart, your messenger, set off home on St George's Day [24 April], the representatives of the cities were sent into the town hall, and the three electors were there together, [Archbishop Berthold of] Mainz [r. 1484–1504], [Archbishop Hermann IV of] Cologne [r. 1480–1508] and [Archbishop Johann II of] Trier [r. 1456–1503]. Afterwards they saddled up and rode to our lord, the Roman emperor, telling him that no negotiations were conducted in this session of the diet. And so our lord the Roman emperor came with the same three electors and rode to the stage, and they did this without yet bearing the imperial and electoral insignia. After that, the three dukes of Saxony came with 300 well-armoured cavalry and received their fiefs and regalia.

After that our lord the emperor went with the four electors into the hall, and they were there together for three hours. What they negotiated is unknown to the cities. The cities were then told they should take Thursday [26 April] off, as my lord the Count Palatine [Philipp I 'the Sincere', r. 1476–1508] was arriving then. And so my lord the Count Palatine came with 240 cavalry.

Item, and so on the Friday the holy relics were shown in the presence of all the princes. Those of Nuremberg had 800 armoured men on foot and 150 cavalry, who formed an outer ring. It was said that they additionally had many hidden people, who were also armed. It was also estimated by many good people that over 100,000 people were in the town square on that day.[9] That is without mentioning that all the houses around it were full of people, who were also remarkably numerous.

Item, on Saturday came Margrave Hans [i.e. Johann 'Cicero'] of Brandenburg [r. 1486–99], the elector, with two of his brothers. They had 750 very well-armoured cavalry without including their caterers and low-status followers; I counted them.

Item, on the last day of April our lord the Roman emperor ordered the electors, princes and princely representatives and the urban envoys to assemble in the town hall, and had Count Haug of Werdenberg give a speech in the presence of his imperial Majesty. He spoke thus:

> 'Your Graces, my lords, envoys, well-beloved urban associates and subjects of his imperial Majesty: his supreme Grace and lord, the Roman emperor, has on several occasions brought to your attention the notable afflictions being experienced by his imperial Majesty at the hands of the king of Hungary in his hereditary lands, and how this king repeatedly and unjustly persists against all fairness, and now Wiener Neustadt is so grievously oppressed, and how the king has carried out this attack for two whole years. Meanwhile, his imperial Majesty has now summoned you, and so a remarkable number of electors and princes and representatives and subjects of the Holy Empire is here; it is therefore his imperial Majesty's amicable request and wish, and he thus calls upon you who are associates of the Holy Empire, that you should wish to assist and counsel and act so that advantageous assistance should come about, for should Wiener Neustadt be lost, that would bring yet more damage than all that was experienced up to that point. Concerning what precise obligations his imperial Majesty can call upon from my gracious lords, electors, princes and other subjects of his imperial Majesty and of the Holy Empire, his imperial Majesty is well-disposed, and in his graciousness he will negotiate with you and will not fail to reach agreement.'

---

9 Attendance numbers in such reports are almost always implausibly high, but they do convey the sense that the diets at the end of the fifteenth century were increasingly well attended.

Item, the electors discussed this in one group, and the princes and princely envoys in another group, and the cities also in another group. Item, the electors counselled that, since the next day [1 May] would be a feast day, and our lord the Count Palatine had only just arrived, and indeed the margraves of Brandenburg, they wanted to reconvene on Wednesday [2 May] and discuss what to negotiate, and then they summoned the princes and princely envoys. The princes agreed with this; the cities also allowed it to happen. And so my gracious lord of Mainz gave this response. And his imperial Majesty insisted strongly that he would not suffer such procrastination, and requested of them on that same day that they should already come together on May Day [1 May] for a meal and hold a session about this and examine the facts of the matter. And so the electors held counsel and then asked his imperial Majesty to let the matter proceed as requested, and that he might wish to enfeoff the margraves of Brandenburg on May Day, as they wanted to hold a session on these matters on the Wednesday. His imperial Majesty was firmly against this, and the electors went to him three or four times to explain that they did not want to prolong the session. Then the margraves of Brandenburg went with the electors to his imperial Majesty and pleaded that he might wish to enfeoff them, and that they were not simply requesting this in order to be able to depart the diet swiftly afterwards. As soon as they had been enfeoffed, they wanted to remain there and help counsel and negotiate with the other electors and princes. And then my lord of Mainz debated this at such length with his imperial Majesty that his imperial Grace acceded to it. And so the marshal of Pappenheim called for the departure of the princes and princely and urban envoys, and nobody remained with his imperial Majesty except the electors. What was then negotiated is unknown to the cities.

Item, on May Day there was such heavy rain that the enfeoffments were not held that day. The cities' envoys were together, and it was agreed that the princes' council's advice should be heard before reaching a position.

Item, on Wednesday [2 May] the electors, princes and princely envoys and cities were called together. Item, my gracious lord of Mainz began proceedings and spoke thus:

> 'Since our most gracious lord, the Roman emperor, recently spoke with the electors, princes, princely envoys and cities about effective military

assistance, and since the matter arose of writing to Dukes Georg ['the Rich' of Bavaria-Landshut, r. 1479–1503] and Albrecht [IV 'the Wise'] of Bavaria[-Munich, r. 1465–1508] and also the count of Württemberg [Eberhard V, r. 1457–96], a reply has now come. We have not wanted to conceal it from you, and it should be read out to you. You may choose, after you have considered the matter, to make your position known; if not, you may consider it further. My fellow electors and I also wish to consider the speech given before us by his imperial Majesty, and also the written text. The princes and princely envoys may wish to do the same, and you from the cities the same again, as is the custom in the Empire. And as we have not yet made up our minds, we wish to call you back later; everyone can then make public the outcome of their discussions.'

And then we were given the reply of dukes Georg and Albrecht. It went no further than declaring their wish to give an answer through their own envoy. My lord of Württemberg's answer was the same. He additionally wrote that where he knew how to serve his imperial Majesty, he would gladly do so, and wanted to send his answer by his own envoy, hoping that those at the diet should look kindly upon this.

And so we held session until midday. The marshal of Pappenheim came and told us that our lords the electors could not decide among themselves yet, but they wanted to hasten and work to persuade his imperial Majesty to enfeoff the margraves of Brandenburg, and then on the next day everyone should come back and make public what they had considered about the matters under discussion.

Item, the margraves of Brandenburg were duly enfeoffed in the evening.

Item, on the Day of the Finding of the Holy Cross [3 May] the electors, princes and cities were convened and held session until eleven o'clock. They could not reach unanimity, as will clearly be observed. But the marshal of Pappenheim was sent to us, and he spoke thus:

> 'Well-beloved friends, our lords the electors have held session regarding the issues, and have not quite reached a decision, for a messenger has arrived to inform us that Duke Albrecht ['the Spirited'] of Saxony [r. 1485–1500] is returning. The electors and princes want to ride out to meet him after lunch and will send for you after that. Everyone should then make public what they have considered among themselves.'

Item, on the Friday after the Day of the Finding of the Holy Cross [4 May] the electors, princes and princely and urban envoys were convened, and my gracious lord of Mainz spoke thus:

> 'My fellow electors and I have held session concerning the grievous actions which are unfolding in dreadful conflicts in the Holy Empire, and also about how his imperial Majesty has often remonstrated with us and requested urgent military assistance. We have now convened together many times, and what was discussed in our council is openly gossiped about in the alleyways. We consider it to be a grave problem that these serious affairs are being discussed in public, for if we are meant to negotiate with one another confidentially, then necessity demands that whatever anyone should counsel in confidence and good faith should remain secret. For if the content of our negotiations is made public, many negative consequences will follow. Nobody should reveal their position in public. They should be careful where they say something displeasing to his imperial Majesty, lest they face retaliation for it. Given that we all belong together within the Holy Empire, it is our opinion that as members of the Holy Empire – whether princes, princely envoys or cities – we should wish for that which is negotiated or spoken here to remain secret. Thus, we wish to hold a session together and confidentially discuss the issues around how the Holy Empire might attain to peace and lasting strength. To that end, the princes and princely envoys should head out and consider this, and the cities likewise, and whoever wants to proceed in this way this should offer their assent. We want to hold session and confidentially negotiate the issues with them in this manner.'

And so the princes and princely envoys convened in one group, and the urban envoys likewise in another. And the princes and princely envoys vowed to take up this approach of secrecy, excluding Duke Georg's representative. He said that it was not appropriate to do so without the permission of his gracious lord. He wanted to write to him, and he would not conceal the answer from their princely Graces. And so he was allowed to do so, on the condition that in the meantime he could not be in the princely council, and he promised that.

Item, there was a similarly large amount of discussion among the urban envoys about the possibility that if we refused to take this vow of secrecy, it would go down very badly and be perceived as an offence on the part of the cities. And the answer was given that the urban envoys were well aware of what had been negotiated so far, and that it had been kept secret on their part and not been leaked by them. But they would gladly swear this vow, as long as they could nevertheless still make the content of negotiations known to their colleagues, for as their princely Graces could surely well understand, no envoy can negotiate without his colleagues' counsel.

And the cities' answer suggested that all in the council should not speak openly or write about what was discussed until a consensus opinion was reached. What was agreed could then be relayed to the envoys' colleagues. The princes' envoys could do likewise. In this way, if it should occur that something be productively negotiated and then leaked, it would be despite everything being done to avoid the council breaking its silence; everyone should take care to ensure this. And a question was raised about what to do if other cities were present at the diet without having been formally invited. Might an opinion be shared openly with them? The answer was given that one could indeed discuss, share and take counsel with any other city that also made the same promise to my lord of Mainz. And this was made known to the other cities present here. They also deliberated about this matter, and although they had not been formally invited by his imperial Majesty, they still wanted to remain, and were willing to take the vow.

So it was judged that it would be better to stay with the princes in all this, for had this assent not been given, they would have taken decisions in session alone, and the cities would just have to have done whatever the princes decided in those sessions. And those of Nuremberg requested that they might be able to discuss this with the eight men on their Elder Council. This was granted to them, on the condition that they made the promise first.

Stalwart and vigorous, judicious, honourable, wise, well-beloved lords, thus have I also had to make this promise with the others. Therefore neither I nor anyone else may write what was further negotiated in the council, for an agreement is to be formulated on this, as your wisdoms will have understood from what I wrote earlier.

And the council now holds session every day, and many good opinions have been expressed to us, but also many bad ones. However, I hope that the cities will not allow themselves to succumb to blame, for there is a desire to cause them harm. I want to record what is further negotiated myself, until I am able to make it known to your wisdoms. And if this should be contrary to your wisdoms' wishes then I am truly sorry, but I hope that things will go more with the cities than against them. Also, all envoys considered it best to keep in their own council, without damage or blame to anyone, and for everyone to express their true feelings.

With this, well-beloved lords, I consider that these matters will not come to an end anytime soon, although things have now begun to be discussed in earnest. To that end I have borrowed 50 Rhenish florins from the servant of Adolf Rusch and handed him this, my handwritten letter. I request of your wisdoms that you repay him this. Have no doubt that I would prefer it if I were able to do it. I have already been here for all too long a period of time. I also kept your messenger here for five days, so that I might (as I then hoped) be able to write rather more. The cost of living is high here. That is why I let him go. Should something come up, and if I am permitted to write, I will not keep it from you, but inform your wisdoms. Duke Otto should arrive in two days, and thus fourteen princes are here. And I hope that the princes are also bearing high costs, so that they might err towards seeking a rapid end to proceedings. Nothing more to say right now. May the almighty, eternal God ever grant you stalwart, judicious, honourable wisdoms provision and good health. Given on Tuesday after the day of the Finding of the Holy Cross [5 May] in May, in the year [14]87.

19. Maximilian I summons the estates to an imperial diet in Augsburg (1509)

Bock et al. (eds), *Deutsche Reichstagsakten. Mittlere Reihe*, vol. XI, pp. 154–58.

During the second decade of the Italian Wars (1494–1559), the Habsburgs' principal focus shifted from France to Venice. Maximilian fought a failed war against the city in February–March 1508. Soon afterwards, Pope Julius II (r. 1503–13) orchestrated an anti-Venetian alliance involving Maximilian, Louis XII of France and Ferdinand II of Aragon, known as the League of Cambrai. Maximilian sought renewed funding and troops from the imperial estates to launch a second campaign against Venice, first at an inconclusive diet in Worms (April–June 1509) and then at another diet in Augsburg (March–May 1510). This was his formal summons to the latter assembly.

High-born, well-beloved cousin, elector and counsellor, we personally travelled from our Low Countries to attend the recently held imperial diet in Worms, to make known there to the electors, princes and estates of the Empire – at least, to those in attendance – the praiseworthy alliance, league and treaty formed between our Holy Father the pope and us, and also our beloved brothers the kings of France and Aragon.

[Maximilian describes the background of the League of Cambrai in detail, emphasising the transgressions of Venice against papal and imperial lands in Italy, the specific obligations of the emperor and Holy Roman Empire to protect the Roman Church and the need to restore Italy as a preliminary step towards defending Christendom's borders against the Ottomans. The estates were not sufficiently numerous at the recent assembly in Worms to provide Maximilian with the support he needed to fulfil his obligations towards the League, and he subsequently requested a loan from them to fund his ongoing expedition in Italy.]

And following on from all that, we have moved to hold a useful imperial diet. We schedule and confirm it in our and the Empire's city of Augsburg for the eighth day after Epiphany, that is the upcoming 13 January, for you and all electors, princes and estates of the Empire, mandating with all seriousness and diligence that – by the duties binding you to us and the Holy Empire, for the sake of the necessity and good of the Holy Empire and the whole of Christendom – you contemplate and consider our faithful actions that we have undertaken so far and our future plans related above; that you do not allow yourselves to be prevented or disturbed by anything other than divine authority; and that you appear without fail at the imperial diet designated here to negotiate and act, in person or, if by divine authority you cannot, at least through your empowered envoy or official, who should not need to confer with you before making final decisions; for up until the time of the diet we are pursuing our affairs in these, our lands.

We especially exhort you to consider the honour, benefit and wellbeing of us and the Holy Empire and also of the whole of Christendom, pointed out above, and how you are duty-bound to promote them, and specifically how we have recently – through our faithful efforts and the heavy outlays and costs of our hereditary lands and people, together with those of our praiseworthy allies – brought and established our and the Empire's and the whole of Christendom's affairs onto such a good trajectory, which will make it easier henceforth to attain and accomplish that which we have taken on for many years now, together with the electors, princes and estates of the Empire, at the price of much emotional investment and financial expenditure, yet have never been able to bring about. You should therefore want to appear, obediently and usefully, and not to be absent in any way, nor to refuse, withhold assistance or delay. For if this imperial diet does not prove to be effective in this way that we have set out, on account of our not receiving the counsel and assistance of the estates, leading to us not accomplishing and carrying out our and our allies' plans – which we in no way anticipate – we and many others would be moved to consider and esteem that you and other electors, princes and estates of the Empire are not willing to avail, honour, support, promote and uphold the welfare of the Holy Empire as your duties oblige you to do, and according to the urgent concerns and necessities in which we and the Empire have hitherto been embroiled. If, following on from that, the Holy Empire, German nation and Christendom as a whole were to suffer shame, disadvantage and hardship, we desire herewith to testify that we have sufficiently laid down our abilities, body and possessions on behalf of these matters, and so we can honestly state before God and the world that it would not be our fault.

The reason we have named the city of Augsburg as a site for this imperial diet is that the same city is located close to the mountains leading to Italy, so that we can better administer these, our newly conquered lands, and attend to them, and they may have recourse to and reassurance from us, and so that we may most opportunely and liberally provision and accommodate there the estates who will undoubtedly attend in person. For we want to cater and provide for your arrival, and additionally to keep in mind and recognise your obligatory duty with all grace and good sentiments towards you.

Given in our city and castle of Rovereto on the eighth day of the month of November, in the year of our Lord 1509, in the twenty-fourth year of our Roman imperial reign.

20. Peace-ordinances promulgated at imperial diets in Nuremberg, Regensburg and Frankfurt (1467–86)

Müller (ed.), *Reichs-Tags-Theatrum*, vol. II, pp. 291–92; Weizsäcker et al. (eds), *Deutsche Reichstagsakten. Ältere Reihe*, vol. XX/2, pp. 870–73; Bock et al. (eds), *Deutsche Reichstagsakten. Mittlere Reihe*, vol. I, pp. 384–85.

Despite his promulgation of a 'Royal Reformation' [17] at the start of his reign, Frederick III faced repeated demands from some of the leading princes and cities for more effective and durable peace-keeping measures, generally conceived as treaties that would bind all members of the Holy Roman Empire to the same types of stipulations as regional *Landfrieden* [15][37][41]. Frederick was often unwilling to delegate peace-keeping powers that he regarded as monarchical prerogatives, but the need for assistance against encroaching enemies – the Ottoman sultan, duke of Burgundy and king of Hungary – forced a series of compromises at imperial diets in the 1460s to 1480s. These three preambles to the ordinances-cum-treaties of 1467, 1471 and 1486 show the rhetorical emphasis on both external defence and internal pacification that undergirded this new era of temporary Empire-wide peace agreements, paving the way for the perpetual peace of 1495 [21]. The stipulations of that ordinance closely resemble those of these three (with the exception of classifying peace-breakers as perpetrators of *lèse-majesté*, a Roman law concept that was inserted into the 1467 peace-ordinance – perhaps to mollify Frederick III – but did not appear subsequently).

The peace-ordinance of Nuremberg (proposed by the estates on 11 November 1466, confirmed by Emperor Frederick III on 21 August 1467)

We Frederick, by the grace of God Roman emperor [etc.], impart our grace and all good wishes to each and every one of our and the Empire's electors, princes (spiritual and temporal), prelates, counts, barons, servitors, knights, retainers, cities and otherwise to all and every other one of our and the Empire's subjects and faithful people, whatever their estate, dignity or condition.

As, by divine providence, grace and foresight, we were elevated to the majestic honour of the Roman royal and imperial dignity and placed in command of the Holy Roman Empire to preserve the same in a praiseworthy state, to propagate virtue and good works and not to tolerate unjust violence and offenses, so we are also fully inclined towards the praise of God with a fervent love, the protection of the Christian faith and our mother the Holy Roman Church and the promotion of the common good and peace.

And although we issued a reformation in the Empire at Frankfurt [17] when we were still in our royal estate,[10] with the counsel of our and the Empire's electors, princes (spiritual and temporal), prelates, counts, lords and subjects, ordered on pain of high and grave penalties in order to keep the peace; and although we have subsequently spent many constant days at our imperial court and other public locations of the Holy Empire and devoted assiduous diligence so that the oppressed and afflicted Christian people are liberated from the despicable Turks and enemies of our Christian faith, the same Christian faith is secured and Christian and praiseworthy resistance is made against these Turks; yet, our said reformation of peace and our faithful efforts on behalf of an expedition against the Turks have still not borne fruit as we had hoped and would, with fervent desire, have liked to see. On the contrary, since then myriad wars and upheavals have taken place, our and the Empire's subjects have been greatly damaged and the common good has been so strikingly injured and obstructed that it is beyond painful to lament. Consequently, the Turks have risen ever higher, grown stronger and subjugated many Christian lands and peoples, and continue to attempt to do so daily, so that it is to be feared that, if resistance is not offered against them, they will manifest and inflict insurmountable damage on Christendom and the Holy Empire.

And since we are responsible for the Empire, we also ought willingly and desire affirmatively to orient our efforts and apply our faithful labours to the best of our ability so that steadfast resistance might be offered against the despicable Turks, with the help of God, our Holy Father the pope and other Christian kings, lords and people. However, our and the Empire's electors, princes (spiritual and temporal), prelates, counts, lords and cities have deemed and

10 That is, before Frederick's imperial coronation in 1452.

counselled (last Martinmas [11 November 1466] in Nuremberg, in the presence of our Holy Father the pope's legation) that the German nation does not want to send anybody to fight the Turks unless a collective, praiseworthy peace lasting five years is ordained beforehand – to be carried out by us, confirmed by the pope and respected under pain of high and severe spiritual and temporal penalties imposed by his Holiness and us.

And to that end, so that the Christian faith may be relieved of the despicable Turks; our worthy mother the Holy Roman Church may be strengthened; peace and unity may be more fruitfully administered in the Holy Roman Empire; evildoers and disobedient people may be punished with the sharpness of penalties; the Holy Empire's roads may be secured and pacified; widows, orphans and the poor may be protected; and the common good may be promoted; so, with the timely counsel of our and the Empire's well-beloved faithful people, we have accepted the above-mentioned counsel proposed at Martinmas and consented to it, and accept and consent to it with this document. We order all of you and yours that – earnestly and firmly, and by the duties and vows which bind you to us and the Holy Empire – you should not initiate, engage in or pursue any robbery, feud, discord or war, either collectively or individually, for the entirety of the above-mentioned five years. Rather, whoever intends or gains cause to pursue a dispute with another should carry out and pursue it by judicial means before the conventional courts and judicial settings and locations to which a given matter appertains, without deceit.

However, if – against and in violation of this – somebody should attack, feud with or make war against another, the one(s) who do this should be subject to the penalty for injury against our Majesty, which is called *poenam criminis laesae Majestatis* in Latin, and also to being placed in our imperial ban and double ban, and everyone will have the power to detain and seize them together with their possessions and goods in all settings and locations in the Empire, and to treat them in the manner that violators of this peace and law deserve.

The peace-ordinance of Regensburg (24 July 1471)

We Frederick [etc. – an identical salutation to that of the 1467 peace-ordinance follows].

We contemplate and take to heart the unspeakable and manifold harsh actions and evil deeds that the Turks, enemies and despisers of the holy cross and our Christian faith, have carried out in the past – and still resolve to carry out more and more every day – against the holy sacraments, against the temples of Almighty God, against images of Mother Mary and other saints and against clerics and members of religious orders and others, with the shedding of Christian people's blood, the conquest and destruction of many Christian kingdoms and lands and in other ways, contrary to divine, natural and human laws and ordinances – about which we inform you with a sorrowful disposition. It is therefore entirely to be feared that if swift resistance against them does not occur, they may soon inflict insurmountable damage on Christendom and above all the Holy Empire through their great might, which is constantly growing, as we are unremittingly informed by their daily actions and creditable warnings. We are thus fervently moved to consider the martyrdom and death which our lord Jesus Christ suffered for the sake of our redemption, and also the duty to rescue one's fellow Christian that we and every Christian person has taken on through the holy sacrament of baptism, and additionally how we are bound by obligations as Roman emperor and supreme advocate and defender of the Christian faith and See of Rome, and therefore intend to orient all our efforts and to apply our faithful labours so that – with the help and support of God, our Holy Father the pope and other Christian kings, lords and people – the said Turks might not only be Christianly and steadfastly resisted, but that they might also be driven out of the lands which they have cut off from Christendom.

However, it has been counselled at all the diets held in the Holy Empire regarding this matter that – if fruitful assistance is to be forthcoming from the German lands, which necessity surely requires – a collective, durable peace should be established and administered beforehand.

To this end, so that the Christian faith may be maintained; our worthy mother Church may be protected; the evildoers may be punished with severe penalties; the courts and the law may be correctly and swiftly upheld and carried out; the Holy Empire's roads may be pacified; and the common good may be promoted; so – with the counsel of our and the Empire's electors, princes (spiritual and temporal), prelates, counts, barons and others among our and the Empire's subjects and well-beloved faithful people who have been present with us now in person or through their envoys, and with just knowledge, by our imperial plenitude of power – we have established and enacted a collective, durable peace everywhere in the Holy Empire, and thus we presently ordain and enact it by the power of this document. We also exhort all of you and yours that – earnestly and steadfastly, by the duties, vows and oaths which you owe and are bound and obliged by towards Almighty God as Christians and towards us and the Holy Empire as obedient members and subjects – you should not break or violate this peace and our same ordinance in any way, form or manner, either collectively or individually, but rather sustain, administer and uphold it fully, firmly, loyally, inviolably and without deceit in all and every one of its parts, articles, points and clauses, to the fullest extent that they pertain to each of you, if you and yours care to avoid our and the Empire's grave disfavour and the penalties contained in this ordinance, which reads word for word as follows.

[...]

And this peace should last four entire years immediately following the date of this, our ordinance.

The peace-ordinance of Frankfurt (17 March 1486)

We Frederick [etc. – a salutation similar to that of the 1467 peace-ordinance follows].

As we consider that there can be nothing in the whole world more praiseworthy nor more fruitful than peace and harmony, through which all good things and also honour and authorities, from the highest to the lowest and weakest, emerge – and conversely, that through division and discord all the highest estates of the world go from dignity to dishonour and from freedom to servitude – so it pains us to remind you about how in recent years Christian empires, kingdoms, principalities and lands, which in former times enjoyed the official status of the Roman Empire and were Christianly and praiseworthily governed, have now been subjugated by the blasphemous Turkish people. In addition to this manifest themselves before our very eyes the daily afflictions of domestic war and upheaval, which we are all the more motivated to avert – with the Almighty's and all of your assistance as well as our own capabilities – since in these times they increasingly risk injuring the Holy Empire and the German nation and supporting and providing opportunities for the designs of those others who have hardened their disposition against us and the Empire, against which we do not know how to undertake proper resistance without durable domestic peace.

And in order to curb upheaval, war and bickering in the Empire and raise up fulsome resistance to it, we have – with the counsel of the most serene prince Maximilian, king of the Romans, our beloved son, and also of our electors, princes and princely envoys, and upon the call of the counts, lords and others assembled here in notable numbers – undertaken and enacted a collective, Christian peace throughout the whole Empire of the German nation, to last for the next ten years, and we also establish, ordain and enact it herewith by our Roman imperial authority, in the form that follows, by the power of this document.

21. A peace-ordinance promulgated at an imperial diet in Worms (the 'Perpetual Public Peace') (1495)

Bock et al. (eds), *Deutsche Reichstagsakten. Mittlere Reihe*, vol. V, pp. 361–73.

We Maximilian, by the grace of God king of the Romans, ever augmenter of the Empire, king of Hungary, Dalmatia, Croatia etc., archduke of Austria, duke of Burgundy, Brabant, Lorraine, Styria, Carinthia, Carniola, Limburg, Luxembourg and Guelders, count of Flanders, Habsburg, Tyrol, Ferrette, Kyburg, Artois and Burgundy, Count Palatine of Hainault, Holland, Zeeland, Namur and Zutphen, margrave of the Holy Roman Empire and Burgau, landgrave of Alsace, lord of Friesland, the Windic March, Pordenone, Salins and Mechelen, impart our grace and all good wishes to each and every one of our and the Holy Empire's electors and princes (spiritual and temporal), prelates, counts, barons, knights, retainers, captains, deputies, advocates, custodians, administrators, officials, magistrates, mayors, judges, councillors, urban citizens and communes, and otherwise all other subjects and faithful people belonging to us and the Empire, whatever their dignity, estate or condition, who come to see, read or be shown this, our royal document, or a copy thereof.

Since we were elected to the majestic dignity and burden of the Holy Roman Empire, and latterly assumed the governance of the same,[11] we have witnessed a ceaseless assault against Christendom, which has now been waged for a very long time, through which many kingdoms and authorities within Christian lands have been subjugated by the infidels [i.e. Ottoman Empire], such that they have extended their power and dominion up to the borders of the German nation and Holy Empire, and significant violence has been carried out during this time against our Holy Father the pope's and the Roman churches' cities, lands and ecclesiastical properties, and they have also violently overrun other lands and authorities of the Roman Empire, from which grievous decline, devastation and loss of souls, honour and dignity will arise – not only for the Holy

---

11 Maximilian I was elected king of the Romans in 1486 during Emperor Frederick III's lifetime and only assumed all monarchical obligations after his father's death in 1493.

Empire, but for the whole of Christendom – if resistance against this is not striven after with substantial and timely counsel, and if – for the facilitation of the same – steadfast and efficacious peace and justice are not established in the Empire and sustained and administered in a strong condition. We have therefore undertaken, established, ordained and made a collective peace throughout the Holy Empire and German nation with the unanimous, timely counsel of our honourable and high-born, well-beloved cousins and relatives, the spiritual and temporal electors and princes, and also the prelates, counts, lords and estates; and we establish, ordain and make it in and by the power of this document.

[1] Thus, from the moment of this promulgation, nobody – whatever their dignity, condition or estate – should have a feud with, make war against, rob, abduct, attack or besiege another, whether they do so themselves or on behalf of another as a servitor. Nor should they scale walls to capture any castles, towns, markets, fortifications, villages, farmsteads or hamlets, or violently or maliciously occupy them without permission, or underhandedly damage them with arson or by other means. Also, nobody should provide counsel, help or any other kind of assistance or reinforcement to such perpetrators, nor knowingly or deceitfully harbour, house, sustain, suffer or supply food or drink to them. Rather, whoever intends to pursue a dispute with another should seek and carry out such a matter in the judicial settings and courts to which such cases conventionally appertain, or to which they have previously been agreed to be assigned for adjudication, or will now and in the future be assigned per the ordinance of the cameral court [22].

[2] And to that end, we have voided and invalidated all openly declared feuds and conflicts begun in the name of self-defence, and we also void and invalidate them herewith by our Roman royal plenitude of power, in and by the power of this document.

[3] And if somebody – whatever their dignity or estate – acts or undertakes to act against one or more of the things mentioned above in the previous articles, they should (alongside other applicable penalties) be forcefully placed in our and the Holy Empire's imperial ban, according to justice, and we recognise and declare them herewith to be in our and the Empire's imperial ban. This means that their body and possessions are fair game for anyone, and nobody may or should complain about or negotiate concerning this. Also,

all commitments, obligations and alliances to which they belong or to which they might have recourse should be considered null and void if invoked against those who might arrest them. Also, the fiefs that the perpetrator makes use of should revert to the feudal lord, and for as long as the peace-breaker lives this lord is not obliged to enfeoff them or other feudal heirs with the same fiefs or feudal portions, nor to hand over their share of the usufruct of their fiefs.

[4] And if electors, princes, prelates, counts, lords, knights, cities or others – whatever their estate, dignity or condition may be, spiritual or temporal – or the people belonging to them should be damaged against the terms of this peace, and the perpetrator is not publicly known, but there is somebody who is suspected of being the perpetrator, and the plaintiffs cannot prove their culpability yet there are good faith indications that they should indeed be under suspicion, the electors, princes, prelates, counts, lords, knights or cities or their fief-holders, prelates, counts, lords, knights, subjects or associates to whom the damage was done may and should write to the one(s) under suspicion and summon them to an arbitrational assembly in order receive an oath from them certifying their innocence. And if the one(s) under suspicion oppose the certification of innocence in any way or do not want to appear at the assembly, they should be held to be guilty of the damage and violation of the peace, and thereafter they may be proceeded against per the terms of this decree. However, the same electors, princes, prelates, counts, lords, knights or cities should guarantee safe-conduct for the one(s) under suspicion to and from the arbitrational assembly until they are back in their place of safety, both for them and all those they might bring with them to the assembly, without deceit. And if the preference is not to deliver the summonses to the assembly by hand, they should be posted in two or three locations where judicial courts are held, so that they reliably circulate and take legitimate effect.

Also, if somebody is robbed, damaged or attacked against the terms of this peace and our decree, all those who are called upon as the crime is being carried out *in flagrante delicto*, or who are simply present in the vicinity, should forcefully pursue the perpetrator(s) of the damage and proceed and seek after them with diligent earnestness, as if they were themselves the victims of the crime, in order to get hold of them.

[5] Also, nobody should house, harbour, sustain, reinforce or supply food or drink to such perpetrators and peace-breakers in their jurisdictions, possessions and domains. Rather, they should take them into custody and put them on trial with a seriousness befitting their office, and assist with all legal accusations against them without delay. They should not protect or shield the perpetrator or litigate on their behalf in any way, nor should the perpetrator receive any comfort, security, freedom or safe-conduct. Except with the consent of their legal accuser(s), they should not enjoy these in any way, for in the event of all such violations of the peace we want to exclude and not to involve comforts, forms of security, guarantees and safe-conducts, regardless of who grants them.

[6] And if the perpetrators and violators of this peace should have places to stay, fortifications or other buttresses and advantages of that nature, such that substantial military assistance or expeditions would be necessary to combat them; and also if somebody included in this public peace – whatever their estate, dignity or condition, spiritual or temporal – should be feuded or warred against or otherwise damaged by somebody whom this public peace does not include,[12] or if that party houses, sustains or extends assistance and support to the perpetrators and damagers; the same case should be brought by the victims of the damage and/or our cameral court's presiding judge before us or our representative and the annual assembly of the electors, princes and estates of the Empire,[13] at which help and assistance or deliverance should be extended without delay to those being warred against or damaged. However, if the matter should involve an invasion or otherwise be of such scope that, because of necessity, the annual assembly would be inadequate to address it, we hereby grant the cameral court's presiding judge the authority to convoke, on our behalf, us and the electors, princes and estates of the Empire immediately to a designated site for deliberation, which we and they should attend with authority, or to which we and they should send our and their representatives endowed with decision-making powers, in order to offer counsel and negotiate

12 This would perforce be somebody outside the Empire, as the introduction states that the peace was valid 'throughout the Holy Empire and German nation'.
13 The accompanying treaty for the 'administration of peace and justice' [22] calls for annual assemblies of the imperial diet.

regarding the case, as stated above. Nevertheless, our cameral court and its presiding judge should always proceed as the law requires against violators and peace-breakers when appealed to by those damaged or warred against, and also by virtue of their office.

[7] And since there are many mounted and foot mercenaries who mostly have no lord of any kind and are often bound to service contracts which they essentially fail to uphold – or the lordships to which they are committed are not strong enough to hold them to legal and just conduct, so instead they carry out mounted rampages across the lands, fighting for their own benefit – we ordain, establish and desire that henceforth such mounted and foot mercenaries should not be suffered or endured in the Holy Empire. Rather, wherever they are encountered they should be taken into custody, robustly interrogated and seriously punished for their misdeeds, and at the very least have their belongings and assets seized and distributed as booty and be bound with oaths and surety pledges, as necessity dictates.

[8] Item, if members of the clergy should act against this, our peace and decree (which we do not anticipate), the prelates who customarily have direct jurisdiction over them should, at the request of the damaged party, ensure as far as possible that indemnification and restoration of the damage is done, and that they administer robust punishment for the violation. And if they are negligent in this and the perpetrators are not punished, we hereby place them and the perpetrators outside of our and the Empire's grace and protection, and – as disturbers of the peace – we do not want to defend or make assurances for them in any way. However, if they are under suspicion, the process for certifying their innocence, as described for the laity above, should be permitted for them.

[9] Also, nobody should be in or enter into commitments that are antithetical to this peace, whether through treaties that entail obligations, duties owed to another or in any other way, for the duration of this land-peace. For we recognise and declare all such commitments to be void and non-binding by the power of our royal authority. Yet, there should be no harm or detriment to the content of the other sections, paragraphs and articles of the same treaties of obligation, duties or alliances. And this public peace should neither add nor remove commitments to or from anybody's honest obligations. And whoever falls into the imperial

ban because of their transgressions, as stated above and below, should not be absolved of it by us without the consent of the damaged party, in which case they may be removed from the ban via a legal settlement.

[10] And we hereby commend this to all and every one of those written above and to you by our Roman royal authority, by the oaths and duties which you have offered to us, especially for the sake of the Empire, and by the obedience you owe us as king of the Romans, on pain of the loss of all graces, privileges and rights that you hold from us and the Holy Empire or from others, earnestly and firmly commanding that you steadfastly and tightly hold to this above-written peace and our decree in all its paragraphs, articles and content, and that you implement it throughout your principalities, counties, lordships, domains and everywhere under your rule and command, and earnestly ensure – together with your officials, deputies, custodians, administrators and governors, or whatever they are called – that your subjects hold to and fulfil it, and that you do not delay in doing so nor strive or act against it in any way, secretly or openly, so as to avoid all the above-mentioned penalties, alongside other penalties of the customary law of the Empire, the Royal Reformation [17] and our grave disfavour.

[11] Also, we annul every and all graces, privileges, freedoms, customs, alliances and obligations drawn up and issued before now by us or our predecessors in the Empire, or by others, in which there reside or are effected any things in any way contrary to this, our peace, whatever the words, clauses or sentiments with which they are established or impose obligations. And we hereby annul them by our Roman royal plenitude of power. And we desire that nobody – whatever their dignity, estate or condition – should or might try to protect or defend themselves or make legal justifications against this peace and decree in any way by reference to such graces, freedoms, customs or alliances.

[12] And this peace and decree should not abrogate our and the Empire's law and other collective ordinances and decrees issued in the past but enhance them, and from the moment of this promulgation onwards everyone is obliged to comply with it.

Our well beloved, our reverends, cousins, relatives, in-laws and faithful people the electors, princes and princely messengers, prelates, counts, lords, knights and urban envoys have been present here in splendid numbers.

Attested by this document, sealed with our appended royal seal. Given at our and the Holy Empire's city of Worms on the seventh day of the month of August, 1495 years after the birth of Christ, in the tenth year of our Roman reign and the sixth year of our Hungarian reign.

22. An ordinance promulgated at an imperial diet in Worms establishing the new imperial cameral court (1495)

Bock et al. (eds), *Deutsche Reichstagsakten. Mittlere Reihe*, vol. V, pp. 383–420.

We Maximilian, by the grace of God king of the Romans etc., impart our grace and all good wishes to each and every one of our and the Holy Empire's electors, princes (spiritual and temporal), prelates, counts, barons, knights, retainers, captains, deputies, advocates, custodians, administrators, officials, magistrates, mayors, judges, councillors, urban citizens and communes, and otherwise all other subjects and faithful people belonging to us and the Empire, whatever their dignity, estate or condition.

Honour-worthy, high-born, well-born, honourable, noble, well-beloved relatives, cousins, electors, princes, reverend lords and well-beloved faithful people of the Empire. For compelling reasons, we have set up a collective public peace throughout the Holy Roman Empire and German nation [21] and ordered that it should be upheld. And since the same peace would struggle to remain in effect without righteous, honourable and useful justice, we have undertaken to set up and uphold our and the Empire's cameral court, with timely advice from you, the electors, princes and collective assembly at our and the Empire's diet here in Worms. And we have ordained it in the form and outline that follows:

[1] First, the cameral court should be furnished with a judge, who should be a spiritual or temporal prince or a count or baron, and sixteen assessors, all of whom we will select here and now from within the Empire and German nation with the counsel and consent of this assembly, and who should be honest and honourable in their condition, knowledge and practice. And half of them should have received a university education and honours in law, and the other half should at minimum be of knightly birth. And whatever the sixteen assessors or the majority among them determine in a given case – or, if they disagree and are evenly divided, whichever determination is backed by the judge – should be considered the final word in the matter, and no other duty should obstruct or divert them from attaining this legal determination.

The cameral judge and the sixteen assessors should persevere in this task alone and remain unburdened by other business, and they should not depart or be absent from the court without special permission, which the cameral judge should obtain from the assessors and the assessors from the cameral judge. At no point should more than four assessors be absent from the court, and neither the cameral judge nor the assessors should be allowed to leave the city in which the court is being held at a given time without an extraordinary and severe justification for absence. And should the cameral judge be prevented from overseeing the cameral court for a considerable period of time because of illness or another extraordinary justification for absence, he should – with the knowledge and consent of the assessors – delegate his authority to one of the assessors, and specifically to a count or baron who is an assessor of the cameral court. And in the absence of the cameral judge and the said one to four assessors, the other assessors should have the authority to pronounce judgements and to deal with legal matters as if they were all doing so. Only, if one or more cases litigated before the cameral court should directly involve an elector, prince or person of princely rank, the cameral judge should preside over the same case(s), or – if he cannot do so for the aforementioned reasons, and with the knowledge and consent of the assessors – he may appoint another prince, count or baron in his place. The same prince, count or baron should also swear the oath that follows, which should bind him for as long as he stands in for the cameral judge.

[2] Item, as the assessors – one or more – step down from office, we want to appoint other suitable people in their place, always with the counsel and consent of the electors, princes (or their representatives) and assembly which gathers in the same year. However, if the cameral judge should die before appointing another person to replace him until the next assembly with the counsel and consent of the assessors, and if we should not be in the vicinity, such that the cameral court would be unable to operate, the assessors should elect a person from among themselves, specifically a count or baron from among their number. He should administer the office until the next assembly, whereupon we or our representative will appoint another cameral judge in place of the departed one with the counsel and consent of the electors, princes and estates or their representatives.

[3] The oath of the judge and assessors.

Item, first of all, all of them should vow to our royal or imperial Majesty and swear on holy relics to oversee our royal or imperial cameral court faithfully and diligently; and to judge those of high and low estate equally, according to their best understanding, following the Empire's common laws and customs and also the legitimate, honourable and reasonable ordinances, statutes and customs of the principalities, lordships and jurisdictions of those that appear before them, and not to allow anything to divert them from this; and not to accept or permit to be accepted any gift, donation or benefit to themselves or others in a way that people might perceive as prejudicial, from the litigating parties or anyone else in connection with any case before the court or that might end up before the court; and not to persecute any specific party before the court or their affiliates nor to favour them unduly in their judgements; and not to advise or warn any party; and not to disclose what is discussed in their advisory sessions and in court to the litigating parties or to anyone, before and after the rendering of judgement; and not to hold up or delay cases maliciously; without any deceit.

[4] Item, no citation or summons should be sent out except at the behest of the litigant or their representative, and it should be recognised by the cameral judge and registered by the scribe appointed and ordained to read out to the cameral court. And the same citation or summons should not be delivered to the relevant parties by anyone except public notaries or the oath-bound messengers of the cameral court. These same messengers should all be able to read and write, and should write to inform the plaintiff of the execution of their task upon the copy of the citation or summons, alongside the time and location of its announcement, below their name. And they should hand over the citation or summons to the defendants, and the notary or messenger who does this should also record the delivery upon the document, alongside their name.

[5] The oath of the court scribe.

Item, two trustworthy court scribes should be appointed to the cameral court, and one reader who should handle the court's affairs. They should vow to our royal or imperial Majesty, or to the cameral judge in our place, and swear on holy relics to fulfil their office faithfully in writing and reading and other duties, and also in faithfully preserving the letters and documents brought before the court; and not to disclose to the litigating parties or to anyone else what is discussed about cases in advisory sessions of the judge and assessors; and not to disclose the confidential court discussions to anyone, nor to allow them to read or see them, and not to give any copy of submitted documents and writings to the litigating parties without the permission of the court; and not to advise or warn any party against another; and not to accept any donation nor to allow themselves to be employed for the profit of another in a way that people might perceive as prejudicial, but to content themselves with the salary that will be established by the cameral judge and assessors; without any deceit.

[6] The oath of the procurators.

Item, the procurators appointed to this role by the court should be intellectually capable individuals and should vow to our royal or imperial Majesty, or to the cameral judge in our place, and swear on holy relics that they intend to be totally and justly faithful towards the parties whose cases they take on; and to argue and litigate these cases diligently and to the best of their ability, to the benefit of these parties; and, in so doing, never knowingly to engage in any falsehood or illegality, nor to attempt to drag out cases by deceitfully seeking their transfer to another court or adjournment, nor to instruct the litigating party to do or seek this; also, not to enter into any kind of bargain or discussion with the parties beforehand to receive or anticipate a portion of the proceeds from the case in which they are acting legally as procurator; also, never to disclose to the detriment of their litigating parties confidential and legal information that they obtain from those parties or information about the cases that they themselves observe; to honour and uphold the court and its personnel, and to behave honourably and refrain from insulting language when in the court, on pain of penalties to be determined by the court; additionally, not to seek to burden the litigating parties with demands for higher payments or other conditions over and above the fee or payment they owe per the ordinance of the cameral court; and – if disputes or tensions arise between them and the litigating parties on account of the fee or payment – to leave such disputes with the cameral judge and any assessors he invites or orders to get involved, and to be content with whatever they decide among themselves and leave the matter there; and not to seek to abandon cases that they have taken on without an honest, legally recognised justification, but instead faithfully to litigate on behalf of their parties until legal proceedings conclude; all without deceit.

[7] The advocates should also swear in this manner to provide counsel and litigate faithfully on behalf of their parties, per all the content of the above-written oath, to the extent that it pertains to them.

[8] Item, so that the common man is not unfairly burdened by advocates and procurators, the cameral judge and assessors should gauge what fees should be paid by each individual based on the specifics of each case and party.

[9] Item, no party should take on and appoint more than one advocate and procurator attached to the cameral court so that the other party can also access advocates and procurators, and no deceit should be committed in this. Therefore, no advocate or procurator should offer advice to any party unless that party intends to take them on as their advocate or procurator in their case.

[10] Item, if princes, prelates, counts, lords, knights or cities want to prosecute or litigate their own cases through representatives, procurators or other people whom they send or bring with them, they should have the right do so, but these same should vow and swear *de calumpnia et malicia vitande prout de jure* ['concerning cunning and wickedness that should be avoided according to the law'].[14] Every party or their representatives should also carry out this oath, according to the preferences of the opponent or the judge.

[11: The requirements for citations and summonses set out in article 4 are repeated, with stipulations about where they should be delivered to defendants, how the messenger should report back to the court, stipends to cover messengers' travel costs and the role of the court as the adjudicator of disputes over those costs.

12: Messengers and notaries acting for the court should enjoy safe-conduct and free passage everywhere in the Empire.]

[13] Item, no appeal to the cameral court should be accepted that was not pursued *gradatim*, that is, stepwise up to the next, higher court with jurisdiction over the case.[15]

---

14 A formula used in canon and civil law.
15 In other words, a litigant could not appeal directly to the cameral court, but had to have their case heard in each of the courts within the hierarchy of relevant

[14] Item, for the effective adjudication of cases and also to give reassurance to the litigating parties and guard against the kinds of disagreements that have sometimes arisen, everyone should henceforth be permitted to bring forth their cases in writing, whether they concern many or few matters. And regardless of which party requests this, it should not affect the other party, except that this opponent may request a copy of these writings and a postponement of proceedings, as circumstances might require.

[15] Item, all citations and court letters should go out under our name and title. However, the cameral judge and assessors should also be named in court letters.

[16] Item, the cameral court should never issue a summons if it will serve as the court of first instance or the starting point of a lawsuit for anybody whose accusation or complaint is directed against those who are not immediately subordinate to our royal or imperial Majesty and the Empire[16] and those who otherwise have their own judge with proper jurisdiction over their case. It should only do so in cases in which the plaintiff sought justice before the competent lower courts and it was manifestly denied or deceitfully delayed. And if such an unauthorised summons or citation does go out to somebody, all litigation that follows should be considered null and void, and the one whose accusation caused the summons should be obliged to compensate the other party for any costs and damages they may have incurred in consequence.

[17] Item, letters of summons should specify the grounds on which somebody is being called upon or summoned, in such a manner that the defendant in the case should be well informed when they appear on the appointed day or that they can send a fully briefed representative, and so as to avoid the prolongation of cases and the costs generated by legal counsel and consultation with external parties.

[18] Item, the cameral court should be held in a suitable town in the Empire, and the cameral judge, assessors, advocates, procurators, scribes, messengers and all other people belonging to the cameral court – and all their servants and legitimate members of their households – should be free of all financial exactions and

---

jurisdictions until the cameral court was the final remaining option. In practice, determining this hierarchy and applicable jurisdiction was often controversial.
16 That is, the imperially immediate estates.

encumbrances and also any local jurisdiction there. However, they should not provide lodging to or engage in commerce with others deceitfully. Also, the litigating parties and their representatives and envoys attending the cameral court should enjoy security and safe-conduct. However, if it should occur that the people belonging to the cameral court, or the litigating parties and their representatives and envoys attending the cameral court, engage in violent or capital crimes, the judge in that local jurisdiction should immediately pursue the matter and always have the cameral judge and assessors answer for what has taken place without delay. A tower or prison should be provided to the same cameral court personnel, in which they may detain such criminals or have them punished according to their own adjudications. Also, the cameral judge and assessors should help to render satisfaction to the injured party, or, if the case entails corporal or capital punishment, to order the council of the said town to administer the punishment.

[19] Item, in view of the measures set out here, it is necessary to pay an honest salary to the cameral judge, assessors and other people who have obligations towards the court or are bound to serve it. Therefore, *sportule*[17] should be levied on the revenues from the cases it hears. Namely, at the start of a lawsuit every plaintiff should pay two Rhenish florins for every hundred, up to 1000 fl., after their complaint is heard; and thereafter one florin for every hundred, up to 2000 fl.; a further half florin for every hundred, up to 3000 fl.; and then, beyond 3000 fl., one-quarter of a florin for every hundred indefinitely, as appropriate until the requisite sum has been attained from each litigant by fair reckoning using the process set out above. This money, called *sportule*, is paid after the final adjudication by the losing party, who is obliged to cover the costs and damages and to disburse and hand them over to the winning party. The personnel of the court should derive and exact their payment from this same money. However, if it is insufficient to cover this payment in full, the rest should be paid from the Empire's revenues.

[20: A schedule of fees owed to the court for sending out various kinds of summonses, outcomes of cases, commissions, appeals and issuing of documents and letters is established.]

---

17 A civil law term for fees paid to a judge or lawyer.

[21] How to proceed against disobedient parties.

Item, if – once the litigating parties have been ordered to assemble and attend proceedings – the plaintiff does not appear or send someone in their stead, and the case has not been compiled with both the complaint and the defence, at the defendant's supplication the plaintiff should be declared disobedient and the court's costs should be imposed on them, and upon request the defendant should be absolved *ab instancia judicy*, that is, from the summons to the court. However, if both the complaint and the defence have indeed been compiled in the case, the court should see it through and render judgement in favour of the plaintiff or defendant as the judicial proceedings entail, but if the obedient party receives the losing verdict, they should not be obliged to cover the court's costs.

[22] If the defendant should prove disobedient at the outset of the lawsuit or appeal, before contestation of suit,[18] at the plaintiff's supplication the court should proceed against the disobedient defendant by placing them in the imperial ban and double ban and also enacting the handover *ex primo decreto*,[19] or, at the request of the plaintiff, the court should bring in, hear and complete the investigation of witnesses and evidence and render a final judgement. Whatever the complaint brought by the plaintiff, and whether or not the disobedient party obtains the winning verdict, the obedient plaintiff should nevertheless be relieved of the costs and damages associated with the case.

[23] Item, the cameral judge and assessors should have the authority, at the supplication of the litigating parties, to place people in the imperial ban, and the cameral judge should issue the imperial ban pronouncements and, where necessary, the instructions regarding enforcement and judicial mandates related to the ban, all in our royal or imperial Majesty's name.

[24] Item, since unnecessary and malicious appeals against interim judgements, called *interlocuterie*, are occurring daily so as to prolong legal processes deceitfully, incurring many costs and damages, henceforth the cameral court should not accept such interlocutory

---

18 *bevestigung des kriegs* – a vernacular translation of the civil law term *litis contestatio*, the preliminary phase before a judicial hearing and judgement.

19 A civil law term for the temporary handing over of a contumacious defendant's possessions to the plaintiff.

appeals if the complaint contained in the appeal could allow that appeal to modify the final verdict in the main case, as ordained and defined in imperial laws.

[25] Item, the cameral court should have free rein to issue unhindered orders for restitution, supplication and advocation or any other legal remedy that cannot be achieved through the regular operation of the cameral court or its findings via a special commission.

[26] Item, the cameral court should be held on three days of the week, except those which are set aside as holidays for the praise of God and the necessity of mankind. The cameral judge and assessors should reach agreement and issue ordinances regarding these holidays, and should also make this information publicly available.

[27] Item, so that nobody is denied justice on account of poverty, as and when necessary the cameral judge should entrust the cases of the poor (who should demonstrate their poverty by taking an oath upon request) to the advocates and procurators, who should provide legal advice and achieve a judicial outcome to the best of their ability. And whichever procurator or advocate is entrusted with such cases by the cameral judge is bound and obliged to take it on without protest in the manner just mentioned, on penalty of losing his office. However, if there is more than one such case, the cameral judge should distribute them evenly among the advocates and procurators, all without deceit. And for the avoidance of the malicious and disruptive tumult that the poor sometimes cause, any poor person requested to do so should vow – as a form of oath – to the cameral judge that as soon as they have gained restitution of goods from their opponent or otherwise attained the necessary level of wealth to afford to set aside and pay the salary of the advocate and procurator, they will do so.

[28] Item, as concerns the lawsuits of electors, princes and people of princely rank (spiritual and temporal) who have or might obtain a dispute with or claim against one another, things should proceed as follows. Whoever has entered into a separate, consensual arbitrational process with another should pursue that arbitration according to its agreed terms. However, where someone has not entered into such arbitration with another, the complaining elector, prince or person of princely rank should write to the other elector, prince or person of princely rank against whom they maintain

that they have a dispute or claim, in order to set out their dispute or claim in writing and request to settle the matter with their opponent by judicial means. Thereupon, within four weeks of receiving this written call, the elector, prince or person of princely rank (spiritual or temporal) written to and called upon in this way should suggest to the plaintiff the names of four currently governing electors, princes or people of princely rank, half spiritual and half temporal and not all born into the same princely house, without deceit. Within four weeks of the aforementioned nominations, the plaintiff should select one from among these to act as adjudicator and proclaim this to the court of the inculpated elector, prince or person of princely rank, clearly and in writing, without deceit. Within the ensuing fourteen days, the plaintiff should then ask the same chosen adjudicator on behalf of both parties to accept the request to serve and to schedule an arbitrational diet[20] for this purpose. The same adjudicator should be obliged to accept and carry out this request in the capacity of a royal or imperial commissioner, with the authority of the commission that we, as king of the Romans, hereby wish to have created in every such instance. And the same chosen commissioner should establish a workable date for the judicial diet in one of his towns, without deceit, and together with his neutral councillors he should submit the case to a just hearing and, per legal custom, render a decision. However, the possibility of appealing to our royal or imperial cameral court should not be removed or forbidden from any party, per the article concerning appeals that may or may not be accepted, set out above.[21]

And if the chosen commissioner should die before the case is resolved, the plaintiff should select another from among the other three suggested electors, princes or people of princely rank. He should also be obliged to accept and carry out this request in the capacity of a royal or imperial commissioner, as set out above in this article. And whatever was judicially negotiated before the deceased elector, prince or person of princely rank should be brought before him and the case should proceed from there, and whatever justice requires should be rendered. And the said commissioners should

---

20 *tagsatzung* – the appointment of a *tag* (an ad hoc assembly or diet, in this case of a judicial nature).
21 See article 24.

deal as efficiently as possible with everyone who comes before them in these cases and not practice or permit any deceitful objection. However, if the defendant does not complete this nominating of electors, princes or people of princely rank within the time period specified above, or does not pursue the procedures set out above, he should give swift legal satisfaction to the plaintiff with respect to the latter's claim before our royal or imperial cameral court.

[29] Item, everyone should ensure that their subjects remain within and respect their competent courts, jurisdictions and authorities, according to the praiseworthy customs and practices of each principality, county, lordship and authority.

[30] However, if prelates, counts, lords, knights or retainers or imperial or free cities of the Empire should want to lodge a legally justified complaint against an elector, prince or person of princely rank, spiritual or temporal; and if the matter concerns documented or undocumented debt, commitments or promises, allegations of violence or dispossession; or if someone is complaining that an elector, prince or person of princely rank, spiritual or temporal, has obstructed or hindered their legal enjoyment of their game and hunting rights, tolls, safe-conducts, jurisdictions or other conventional benefits or rights – in every one of these cases, or in similar ones, the plaintiff should approach the relevant elector, prince or person of princely rank to seek justice before their councillors, without deceit.

In the immediately following month, the inculpated elector, prince or person of princely rank should invite the plaintiff to address their councillors at their court for honest adjudication, and on the very day of the judicial assembly and on the days that follow they should appoint nine of their pre-eminent councillors at their court to oversee the judicial proceedings. They should be drawn from among the nobility and those educated in law, without deceit; however, any officer of the prince who is alleged to have infringed the rights of the plaintiff should not be appointed. And one of the nine councillors, whom the accused shall nominate before a judge, shall receive an oath from the other eight, in the presence of the plaintiff or their representative, and the eldest among those eight councillors shall receive an oath from him in turn: that he intends to pronounce justice in this case according to the evidence brought by both parties and his best understanding, and will not employ deceit or allow himself to be hindered in any way in fulfilling this task. With respect to the case or cases brought before them for adjudication, the same nine councillors should all be and remain free of all other vows and oaths that would or might hinder their pronouncement of justice, for as long as they have yet to reach a verdict in those cases. Also, the plaintiff should not be dragged before the councillors in a countersuit.

The adjudicatory process should be completed in the half-year following the day of the judicial assembly on which the complaint was brought before the court. If, because of legitimate and acknowledged delays, there is further prolongation, it should still reach its conclusion within a year and a day. And each party should be permitted to call upon and appeal to our royal or imperial cameral court if they feel unduly burdened by the pronounced verdict, per the aforementioned article concerning appeals. The plaintiff should be able to do so without any disfavour or hindrance on the part of the elector, prince or person of princely rank and all of their people. The sued elector, prince or person of princely rank should also assign a binding safe-conduct to the plaintiff and whoever they straightforwardly bring with them or send on their behalf, ensuring that they are secure when travelling to the adjudicatory sessions, remaining there and making the return journey. However, the plaintiff should not bring anyone with them or send anyone who might be a violator of our royal public peace or an openly declared feud-enemy or injurer of the same elector, prince or person of princely rank.

If the elector, prince or other person of princely rank, spiritual or temporal, should not wish to reach a legal settlement before their councillors in the manner set out above, or if it does not help to resolve the matter, as just stated, it should be permitted to the plaintiff to proceed against the elector, prince or person of princely rank at the royal or imperial cameral court, according to this ordinance issued about that cameral court.

[31] Item, nobody should have their authority, privileges or liberties truncated or taken from them on account of these ordinances and statutes, but rather they should be reserved to them. However, should someone be appointed to hold those in the imperial ban to account, these same liberties should not be employed to oppose the accomplishment of the verdicts of our royal or imperial cameral court, and those in the ban should not be protected from or evade those verdicts.

[32] Item, should it occur hereafter that the cameral court should require further administration, ordinances, statutes or pronouncements, in any given year the cameral judge and assessors should bring this requirement before us and our electors, princes and the assembly at which they or their representatives gather together in that same year, so that – with the counsel and consent of the same assembly – we might negotiate the matter, for the furthering and improvement of the cameral court and the accomplishment of justice and righteousness.

Attested by this document, sealed with our appended royal seal. Given in our and the Holy Empire's city of Worms on the seventh day of the month of August, 1495 years after the birth of Christ, in the tenth year of our Roman reign and the sixth year of our Hungarian reign.

23. A treaty for 'the administration of peace and justice' promulgated at an imperial diet in Worms (1495)

Bock et al. (eds), *Deutsche Reichstagsakten. Mittlere Reihe*, vol. V, pp. 449–65.

We Maximilian, by the grace of God king of the Romans etc., publicly proclaim and make known to all with this document:

Since, because of striking, concerning and urgent developments and for the benefit and promotion of the whole of Christendom and the Empire and all estates, we have established and issued ordinances for a collective peace in the Empire [21] and also our cameral court [22], per the same and the documents issued regarding them; and since – however – all ordinances, decrees and judgements are ineffective if they are not strengthened and carried out through capable administration; so, in order that this peace and justice and administration may be all the more reliably overseen and delighted in, with the timely counsel and willingness of our honourable and high-born well-beloved relatives the electors, princes and other estates at this assembly, we have assented, united and committed ourselves with them as king of the Romans, on behalf of the Empire and especially of the hereditary lands belonging to us and the high-born prince Philip, archduke of Austria and Burgundy, our well-beloved son. And we assent, unite and commit ourselves by the power of this document to administer and help implement and accomplish the said peace and justice first and foremost, with seriousness and diligence; and particularly, in our and our named well-beloved son's lands, lordships and districts, to order all of our and his officials and subjects with our public letters to carry out this administration as often as necessity requires, by their oaths.

[1] And should it occur that the disregarders and violators of our promulgated peace, and/or those who wickedly and disobediently oppose the known judgements and mandates of our cameral court or mutually agreed arbitrated settlements, receive protection in a castle or fortification or support and assistance during their crime; and also, should anybody included within this peace, whatever their estate or condition, spiritual or temporal, be attacked, damaged or feuded or warred against by somebody whom the peace does not bind,[22]

---

22 That is, parties outside of the political community of the Holy Roman Empire.

or should the latter guilefully house or accommodate or offer assistance or support to the perpetrators and injurers – in response, on account of this and other necessities of the Empire, in order to serve the administration of peace, justice and the common good, and to deliberate and make provision for them, we ordain, establish and desire that on the following eve of the Feast of the Purification of Our Lady [2 February] we and our electors, princes, prelates, counts, barons and imperial estates should assemble in person in Frankfurt (or if we or one or more of you cannot appear in person, on honest and true grounds for which we or you excuse our/yourselves faithfully in public letters, we or you should then send our/your empowered envoy with sufficient authority in writing) to deliberate, negotiate and reach final decisions there about ways and means by which the peace-violator might be punished and the damage restored, and by which known judgements that somebody was supposed to follow but has maliciously opposed might be carried out, and by which other things regarding Christendom, the Holy Empire, the common good and other potentially concerning matters might best be dealt with, and also to agree to a date and location for the next annual assembly.

[2] The electors, princes, prelates, counts, lords and estates and the envoys who attend the annual assembly ought to and should want to remain assembled together for at least one month, and to deliberate effectively and make final decisions, and none should depart from there without just cause and the permission of the assembly or the majority of its attendees.

[3] And as there is an article included in the said peace, 'if an attack against the same people occurs and somebody is called upon or is present as the crime is being carried out *in flagrante delicto*, they should pursue the perpetrators…',[23] just as it states, we ordain, establish and desire that, whenever and however often such events occur, everyone should be duty-bound to carry out this pursuit following a discovery of a crime carried out *in flagrante delicto* at their own expense and risk, without malice.

[4] However, if military encampments, long-distance expeditions, daily action or other substantial military deeds should be necessary to oppose the peace-violators, this should be ordered and arranged through the Common Penny and the military assistance gathered

---

23 A paraphrase of [21], article 4.

and brought in from the Empire, as organised through the annual assembly.[24]

[5] We also want to hold, establish and enact our royal cameral court[25] – as our and the Empire's electors, princes and the whole assembly of the Holy Empire have now undertaken and ordained for it to be held [22] – in a permanent location in the Holy Empire, and that it should remain and be held there, and in no way move away or undergo changes, unless because of honest necessity and with the counsel and will of our and the Empire's electors, princes and estates who, as stated above, are ordered to assemble together annually.

[6] Furthermore, we should and want to bring together all registers, books of fiefs, letters and documents pertaining to the Empire's affairs and jurisdictions that are under our control, or wherever else they may be located or discovered, and to duplicate them, along with all those that will be made in the future, and to deposit one set in our and the Empire's treasury in Frankfurt, to be preserved faithfully for the benefit of the Holy Empire, and to allow it to be used as needed, and to retain the other in our Roman chancery.

[7] Also, neither we and our well-beloved son Archduke Philip nor the electors, princes and estates of the Empire should initiate a war or feud without the knowledge and consent of the collective annual assembly, nor should we form any alliances or unions with foreign nations or authorities that might be to the detriment, disadvantage or prejudice of the Empire.

[8] And as concerns lands, people, towns, castles, districts, markets and villages conquered by means of the military assistance and Common Penny, they should be and remain reserved for the Empire as a collective. And other things that might be conquered should be dealt with by the ways and means agreed between the captains and us and the assembly.

---

24 The 1495 imperial diet of Worms also saw the establishment of an ad hoc method of taxation, the Common Penny (*gemeiner Pfennig*). Some authorities did raise funds in this way in the later 1490s, but it was not systematically enforced or reliable. See Lanzinner, 'Gemeiner Pfennig'.

25 Scholars call the cameral court established in 1495 the *Reichskammergericht* in recognition of its collectively managed character, but it is striking that Maximilian's chancery still refers to it here as his 'royal' cameral court, as it was called when it was solely under the monarch's control.

[9] And since among other things it is stated in the collective public peace [21] – which we, with the counsel of the said electors, princes and assembly, have undertaken, ordained and moved to uphold throughout the Holy Empire and German nation – that all public feuds and declarations of war throughout the whole Empire should be voided and invalidated,[26] we – the above-named King Maximilian, again with the counsel of our said electors, princes and assembly – establish and declare that it should henceforth be understood under the same article that anything which has occurred up until now in feuds and wars and has not been resolved judicially or through arbitration should not be considered a criminal offence, and whoever served in these conflicts should remain unpunished on this account.

[10] Item, since we, the aforementioned King Maximilian, with the counsel of our electors, princes and estates of the Holy Empire, have set out and ordained that judicial courts should be held,[27] to minimise any confusion and disruption that might arise we have established and ordained – following the counsel of our and the Empire's same electors, princes and estates – and establish and ordain by Roman royal plenitude of power and just knowledge, by the power of this document, that all matters that have hitherto arisen during feuds, wars or violent conflicts whose participants have settled, negotiated and reached agreement via judgement or amicable mediation should not be affected by these judicial processes.

[11] And we hereby command all and every one of the electors and princes (spiritual and temporal), as well as the prelates, counts, lords, knights and cities, and all others among our and the Empire's subjects and well-beloved faithful people, that they should hold to and – as written above – administer this peace with earnest and faithful diligence, earnestly ordering them by the duties, oaths and obedience which they have done for us and the Holy Empire and are obligated to do, and also on pain of paying an unavoidable fine, namely 2000 pure gold marks, with half to be paid to our royal treasury and the other half to the damaged party, and additionally on pain of losing all and every grace, privilege and right

---

26 See [21], article 2.
27 That is, as a means of resolving disputes formerly settled through feuds. See [21], article 1.

that each of you has from us and the Holy Empire. They should also order their officials and subjects to do so, and to comply with this association and obligation immediately and without demur, inasmuch as all and each one of you desires to avoid our and the Empire's grave disfavour and the aforementioned penalties.

[12] Also, should somebody – whatever their dignity or estate – disregard, neglect or fail to follow this, our ordinance, commitment and administrative instruction, and should this be public, known and indisputable, we hereby declare them to be subject to the penalties just mentioned on account of their disregard. We also will that no further judicial summons or any additional declaration or judgement should be necessary. Thereupon, the same people may be proceeded against, for the execution and judicial prosecution of these and any other penalties. Each may carry this out as they know best.

Attested by this document, sealed with our appended royal seal.

And we, by the grace of God [the names and full titles of the six German electors, five prince-bishops, the abbot of Fulda, the master of the Teutonic Order and nine secular princes follow] also acknowledge for ourselves and our successors and descendants that the above-written, our most gracious lord the king of the Romans's commitment and ordinance for the administration of peace and justice was undertaken, drawn up and made with our counsel and consent. We have also accepted it for the promotion of the common good, and have committed ourselves vis-à-vis his royal Grace and one another to uphold the said peace and justice wholeheartedly, and for our part faithfully and obediently to administer, protect and defend it, and to order our officials and subjects by letter to do the same promptly, by their oaths, per the promulgated peace. We also hereby vow and promise, by the power of this document and our princely faith and loyalty, to fulfil all and every one of the aforementioned points and articles, righteously and without any deceit.

And to authenticate this, we, the above-named [the same list of electors and princes is repeated] have also appended our seals alongside the said seal of our most gracious lord the king of the Romans on this document, which is given at Worms on the seventh day of the month of August, 1495 years after the birth of Christ.

24. An ordinance to create an imperial governing council promulgated at an imperial diet in Augsburg (1500)

Senckenberg and Schmauß (eds), *Reichs-Abschiede*, pp. 56–63.

We Maximilian, by the grace of God king of the Romans etc., publicly proclaim and make known to all:

Since we were elected to the majesty and dignity of the Holy Roman Empire and acceded to the government of the same, we now see before our very eyes the horrific and relentless assault that the Turks have waged against Holy Christendom for a long period of many years, through which they have removed from the Christian faith and brought under their authority the Byzantine Empire[28] and many kingdoms, authorities and regions, and extended their authority and power right up to the borders of the German nation, such that they will henceforth be able to strike, overrun and subjugate the German nation with great violence. And furthermore, other great powers have risen up and invaded the lands of the Empire with vast, mighty armies and harassed cities and regions. All this will inflict great destruction, devastation and loss of souls, dignity, honour, lives and possessions on the whole of Christendom, us and the Holy Roman Empire and all of its estates if it is not striven and acted against with timely provision and commensurate deeds.

However, external war is completely impossible and impracticable if there is not good and upstanding governance, jurisdiction, justice and administration, on whose foundations all realms and authorities rest. Thus, so that peace and justice are not obstructed by the multitude of governments and wars in the lands of the Empire, we have – with the unanimous and timely counsel, consent, agreement and acceptance of our honour-worthy, high-born, honourable, noble, well-beloved relatives, cousins, reverends and faithful people of the Empire, the electors, princes (spiritual and temporal), prelates, counts, barons, lords and other estates of the Holy Roman Empire – undertaken and resolved, at the present diet of the Holy Empire assembled here, how and where our and the Empire's court should henceforth be held, and also how its verdicts and their acceptance should be issued and fulfilled, and both peace and justice administered, all per the ordinances of the first imperial

---

28 *das Griechisch Keyserthumb* – literally, 'the Greek emperorship'.

diet in Worms [21–23] and other imperial diets that followed, and those now concluded here.[29]

[1] And although the ordinance for the administration of peace and justice [23] promulgated at the previous imperial diet held in Worms states and includes among other things that we and the electors, princes and other estates of the Holy Empire should assemble annually for the implementation and administration of delivered verdicts, consensual arbitration and our promulgated and proclaimed land-peace, as well as other urgent necessities facing Christendom and the Holy Empire, we have considered and adjudged that the estates of the Empire are only capable of travelling and assembling slowly and with difficulty, at the cost of great effort, work and expense. What is more, sometimes extraordinary matters of concern to Christendom and the Empire arise in which any delay is enormously disadvantageous and damaging, and which require a swift response, yet the aforementioned and other extraordinary matters afflicting Christendom and the Empire tend to prompt neglect and obstructiveness rather than a sense of obligation and mission.

Because of this, and to avoid such delay, neglect, great costs and outlays, to get a grip on the other necessities of Christendom and the Empire, to negotiate and offer counsel more durably and effectively regarding the matters indicated above and on account of other righteous causes which have moved us to action, we have – with the timely counsel, consent, agreement and acceptance of the aforenamed electors, princes, counts, barons, lords and estates – undertaken and ordained that twenty people from the Holy Empire of the German nation should serve on our and the Holy Empire's council in Nuremberg with ourselves or, when we cannot be there in person because of other weighty matters or business, with the one whom we send in our place, who should at minimum be a count or baron. We and the said twenty people should have the power to move the council to another location, but only in the circumstances of the greatest, most compelling emergency. Together with us, or – if we will not be present because of other weighty business – with the one we appoint in our place,

---

29 In addition to this ordinance creating the *Reichsregiment*, the 1500 diet in Augsburg saw renewals and iterations of the public peace and cameral court legislation of the 1490s.

the twenty people should constitute and be named 'our and the Holy Empire's council'.

And they should have for themselves plenitude of authority, power and mandate from us, which we hereby grant by the power of this document. Regarding all and every one of our (as king of the Romans) and the Holy Empire's matters: justice and peace and their implementation and administration, as well as resistance against the infidels and other aggressors against Christendom and the Empire, and whatever else is connected to or might be favourable and useful in these aforementioned issues pertaining to peace, justice, their administration and resistance; and cases that might arise from or in connection with the Empire's subjects and others – in these stipulated areas, they themselves should forfend, promote, negotiate, diligently treat and counsel and finally reach decisions, all to the best of their understanding, per the obligations set out below, for the sake of our and the Empire's honour, benefit and augmentation, etc.

[2: The electors should take turns to attend the imperial governing council in hierarchical order, in a recurring quarterly cycle marked by the four Ember days in the liturgical calendar.

3: The council should call upon the six German electors and a panel of twelve spiritual and temporal princes to assemble with them to discuss the way forward in times of dire crisis for Christendom and the Empire, with the potential to widen this deliberative group to include yet more estates if necessary, and to proceed even in the absence of the monarch.]

[4] And the aforementioned twenty people are to be drawn and ordained from the estates of the Empire of the German nation, as follows:

Namely, every single one of the six electors in turn, and from among the spiritual and temporal princes, written about below, two personally present princes, one spiritual and one temporal, who should switch out every quarter-year, as set out for the electors above,[30] so that two other princes from among them, one spiritual and one temporal, can take the place they formerly occupied. They should engage in this internal rotation in hierarchical order, as with the electors.

30 Article 2 above.

However, if one of the princes cannot appear at the appointed time for honest reasons, which he should prove with public letters adorned with his seal, he should call upon another prince of his estate from among the princes specified below, namely a spiritual prince another spiritual one and a temporal prince another temporal one, and send him in his stead. However, if he is not able to call upon any prince, and proves this with sealed letters as noted above, we or the one we will appoint in our stead, together with the Empire's governing council, should immediately have the power to require another of the princes specified below to sit on the council in his place in that same quarter-year. Nonetheless, if the prince who had previously been prevented from attending should subsequently be freed of that hindrance before the quarter-year has elapsed, he should sit on the council in the following quarter-year, in the same way as the others, so that the correct order and procedure is preserved. And the same spiritual and temporal princes just mentioned are specified and enumerated by name in the recess of this, our royal and imperial diet.[31]

Further, the other twelve people are now, through us and the electors, princes and other estates assembled here, called upon and ordained, as follows. Namely, one from our Austrian hereditary lands and another from those of our son Archduke Philip ['the Fair', 1478–1506]. Item, four prelates on behalf of all the prelates of the Holy Empire. Each of the same prelates should sit on the imperial council for a quarter-year, and this should proceed in the order of their internal hierarchy, and they should be held to all the same requirements as those written for the spiritual and temporal princes. Item, one count should also be on the imperial council on behalf of the counts of the Holy Empire; this individual shall now be elected here, and is named in the recess of

---

31 Article 49 of the recess (*Abschied*), 'Here the spiritual and temporal princes who should sit on the governing council are specified', states: 'Further: as mention is made in the ordinance establishing our imperial governing council of twelve spiritual and temporal princes, and also four prelates as well as a count and six people drawn from the circles and eight people from the eight cities, who are, however, not enumerated there by name, their names are specified here. First, the six spiritual princes are: Lord Ernst, archbishop of Magdeburg, and the bishops of Würzburg, Worms, Eichstätt, Augsburg and Münster. The six temporal princes are: Duke Albrecht of Saxony, Duke Georg of Bavaria, Margrave Friedrich of Brandenburg, Duke Wilhelm of Jülich, Landgrave Wilhelm of Hessen, Margrave Christoff of Baden.' Senckenberg and Schmauß (eds), *Reichs-Abschiede*, p. 84.

this imperial diet. Item, every quarter-year two honest, intelligent people drawn now from among the cities named hereafter, which are also specified by name in the aforementioned recess, should sit on the imperial council on behalf of the free and imperial cities. Namely, in the first quarter-year, one from Cologne and another from Augsburg. In the second quarter-year, one from Strasbourg and another from Lübeck. In the third quarter-year, one from Nuremberg and another from Goslar. In the fourth quarter-year, one from Frankfurt and another from Ulm. And they should proceed further according to their internal hierarchy, as mentioned in relation to the others above.

[5] The other six people, from among the knighthood and the doctors or licentiates of law, should be drawn from the circles specified hereafter, namely one from each circle; and these are the same circles and districts.

[6] The first circle comprises the princes, principalities, lands and domains described hereafter, namely the bishops of Bamberg, Würzburg and Eichstätt, the margraves of Brandenburg in their capacity as burgraves of Nuremberg and also the counts and free and imperial cities based and situated by or around them.

[7] The second circle comprises the bishoprics, principalities, lands and domains of the archbishopric of Salzburg, the bishops of Regensburg, Freising and Passau, the princes of Bavaria and the landgraves, prelates, counts, lords and free and imperial cities based and situated by or among them.

[8] The third circle comprises the bishoprics, principalities, lands and domains of the bishops of Chur, Constance and Augsburg, the dukes of Württemberg, the margraves of Baden, the Society of St George's Shield, the knighthood in the Hegau and also each and every one of the prelates, counts, lords and imperial cities in the land of Swabia.[32]

[9] The fourth circle comprises the bishoprics, principalities, lands and domains of the bishops of Worms, Speyer, Strasbourg and Basel, the abbot of Fulda, Duke Hans [Johann I] 'on the Hunsrück' [of Pfalz-Simmern, 1459–1509] and Duke Alexander

---

32 'Land' (German *Land*) should not be understood here as a coherent political or even geographical entity, but rather as a cultural zone defined by dialect and custom.

[of Pfalz-Zweibrücken, 1462–1514] of Bavaria, Lorraine, the Westrich,[33] the landgraviate of Hessen, the Wetterau and also the prelates, counts, lords and free and imperial cities based or situated in that area.

[10] The fifth circle comprises the bishoprics, principalities, lands and domains of the bishops of Paderborn, Liège, Utrecht, Münster and Osnabrück, the dukes of Jülich, Berg, Cleves and Guelders, the counts of Nassau, Vianden, Vierenberg, Nieder-Isenburg and the Low Countries up to the Meuse, and all other prelates, counts, lords and free and imperial cities based or situated in that area.

[11] The sixth circle comprises the bishoprics, principalities, lands and domains of the archbishops of Magdeburg and Bremen, the bishops of Hildesheim, Halberstadt, Merseburg, Naumburg, Meissen, Brandenburg, Havelberg and Lübeck, the dukes of Saxony, the Mark of Brandenburg, the landgraviate of Thuringia, the estates and domains of the dukes of Brunswick, Mecklenburg, Stettin and Pomerania and also the prelates, counts, lords and free and imperial cities based or situated in that area.

[12: In the event of a candidate not wanting or being able to sit on the imperial council, the council members should select another of the same status from the original candidate's circle.

13: An elector or prince may depart from the council with the consent of the other council members.

14: In the event of a prince dying or being too ill to sit on the council, within two months the council members should elect another of the same status and from the same circle to replace them.

15: The same process should be followed for the death or departure of a non-princely council member.]

[16] And since we have granted the afore- and hereafter-mentioned mandate and commission to our and the Empire's council, set out above, so that its dealings may have all the more force and power and nothing can arise that is contrary to them, we establish, ordain and will that the business and causes included in this commission – namely all and every one of our (as king of the

---

33 A vaguely defined historical region on what is now the northerly Franco-German border.

Romans) and the Holy Empire's matters: justice and peace and their implementation and administration, as well as resistance against the infidels and other aggressors against Christendom, the Empire and whatever else is connected to or might be favourable and useful in these aforementioned issues pertaining to peace, justice, their administration and resistance – should not be handled by any other authority than us (and whomever we appoint for this role in our absence) and our and the Empire's aforementioned council.

Also, when needed, documents regarding these matters should and may be issued under our royal title and seal in the same form and manner that we do as king of the Romans. They may be drawn up by our and the Empire's aforementioned council, and they should include a few additional words at the bottom, namely: *ad mandatum domini regis in consilio imperio* ['by order of the lord king in the imperial council']. And the assigned elector should always be personally present on the council, and will undersign the first letters of his name nearby in his own hand: *P. vel F. subscripsit*. And we establish, ordain and will, ordering everybody on this point, that nothing else should be discussed, undertaken or drawn up on our behalf or in our name in the matters specified above. Should someone do so regarding these matters, that should be considered void and non-binding, and not granted any compliance.

[17: Members of the imperial council may absent themselves if the majority is in agreement, provided that a minimum of fourteen people remains at all times.

18: Annual remuneration for non-princely council members is set at 1000 fl. for the count, 600 fl. for the prelates, 600 fl. to be divided among the rotating urban representatives, plus a suitable number of horses and servants – six horses for a count or lord, four for a prelate, knight, doctor, licentiate or urban representative.]

[19] And, with the exception of the electors and princes and others to whom they owe obligations, the people on the aforementioned council should (solely in the context of this council and mandate) be entirely released from all vows and oaths binding or entangling them to us or the electors, princes and others to whom they owe obligations. And the one we appoint in our place, as set out above,[34] and likewise the other people on our and the Empire's

---

34 See article 1.

aforementioned council, except the electors and princes, should swear the following oath:

[20] I, N., vow and swear to God and the saints on the holy gospel-book that I will be faithful to his royal Majesty and the Holy Roman Empire, according to my best understanding, mental capacity and intelligence; be alert against harms; promote that which is best and most useful; and treat, undertake, counsel, assist and negotiate with regard to the necessity, honour, dignity and benefit of his royal Majesty and the Empire in the matters and business touched upon above. Also, I swear to accomplish and uphold entirely the content of all and every one of the points and articles contained in this ordinance, or which may hereafter be issued, that relate to peace, justice, their administration and resistance against enemies, as set out above, and not to pursue envy, hatred, bitterness, partiality, bribery, inappropriate friendship or any other things that might impede the said honour, dignity and common good, nor to accept any kind of bribe or gift – small or large – for myself, nor to provide one for or allow one to be accepted by others who come before me, nor to accept or conduct any unethical procurement. Additionally, I swear to keep everything negotiated, deliberated and decided in the aforementioned council secret and confidential forever. Also, I swear to collect, request and keep safe any funds assigned and delivered to me and other members of the council by the estates of the Empire following the established plan, and not to employ or direct them anywhere except towards the matters for which, as stated above, they were imposed and ordained, all without deceit.

[21: The archbishop of Mainz should appoint honest and suitable secretaries and scribes to serve the council, and require them to swear a near-identical oath to the one set out in article 20.

22: All members, servants and employees of the council are exempted from tolls, taxes and other impositions.]

[23] Furthermore, we have observed with anguish and taken to heart how unbearably the enemy of Christ, the Turk, has extended his domination even further than before into the realms of the Christian faithful, and has cruelly inflicted appalling damage and ruination on lands and peoples, and daily stands ready to continue working and undertaking to do so; and additionally, that certain other powers have risen up against the Holy Empire, its estates and its allies, and endangered and harassed some of these same

members of the Holy Empire, because of which it is to be feared that, if they get the opportunity and can increase their power, they will seek to set foot even further into the Holy Empire.

Because of this – and in order to respond to and resist such grave matters and attacks on Christendom and the Empire valiantly, and also to maintain ourselves, the Holy Empire, its estates and subjects and their honour, freedoms, customs and rights unperturbed, and to administer peace and justice in the Holy Empire – we have united and contractually committed ourselves and reached decisions with our and the Empire's electors, princes and other estates who are assembled here to provide their counsel regarding the acceptance of the financial and military assistance and administrative plan set out below, and we hereby do so by the power of this document.

[24] Specifically, hired soldiers should be raised from all and every one of the parishes in the Holy Empire. In all places, these soldiers should be deployed and paid by the parishioners. Thus, every group of 400 inhabitants in a given parish – married or not, of fixed abode or not, men or women, children or old people, whatever their estate or condition, without exception – who have some kind of property, fixed or mobile, should annually deploy and maintain one foot soldier equipped for war. However, married men and women who form a household with their children who have not yet left home, or who simply have no possessions of their own, should be considered and taxed as if they were one single person. And if someone should be deemed not to have any property at all, they should nevertheless pay one shilling in gold, that is, one-twentieth of a Rhenish florin, and this money should go to the parish administrators as a tax. The unmarried young men and women in the parish should also pay tax to the parish administrators. Each should annually provide one-sixteenth of a Rhenish florin for every florin they receive in wages. Where there are unmarried young men and women who do not have any property of their own and no fixed wage, and serve with dispensations from rents on account of their need, these same should nevertheless pay one shilling in gold. As for those unmarried young men and women who serve a prince, count, lord or someone else and are not based in a parish, they too should annually provide one-sixteenth of a Rhenish florin for every florin in wages. And the same money should be put into a tin and faithfully assigned to the imperial council by the princes, counts, lords or other lordships whom these unmarried young men and women serve.

[25–26: Parishes should form the groups of 400 to be taxed in this way: they should be subdivided into groupings of that size, and any additional people should be combined with those from a neighbouring parish to form another group of 400, while parishes with fewer than 400 inhabitants should similarly join with people of neighbouring parishes.

27–29: All parish authorities should implement this scheme, with each individual taxed in their home parish on all their possessions regardless of their location. Where multiple authorities rule the same parish, they should collaborate to raise the funds successfully, and refer disagreements to the imperial council for resolution.]

[30] It is also envisioned that all spiritual people, men and women, whether or not they are exempt from local temporal jurisdiction, in consideration of their obligations towards the administration of the Empire mentioned above, should annually provide one florin for every forty florins from all their revenues, rents, tithes and benefits, prorated for lower figures, as set out above.

[31–32: The houses of the Teutonic Order and all other religious orders are subject to the same one-fortieth tax.

33: These measures should not affect the liberties of spiritual guilds and confraternities.

34–35: The tax should be collected from the clergy and religious orders by archbishops and bishops, who should deliver it to the imperial council, with exceptions for religious institutions with other customary lords, who should deliver it themselves.]

[36] Item, the Holy Empire's free and imperial cities, and all other communes, should also always provide one florin for every forty florins that accrue to them communally each year from their revenues, rents, tithes, fees and attributed incomes, by the obligations that bind them to the Holy Empire; and this should be credited to them. And every city should send these funds over to the imperial council annually, at the time specified in the recess of the imperial diet and without deceit. And the cities on whose behalf the money has been delivered should always receive a confirmation of this from the council.

[37] And since the electors and princes are the foremost and most high-ranking estates who sit on the Empire's ordained council and address other urgent matters of the Empire, and are also the most

directly and greatly affected by the same matters, because of which they commit themselves through their personal attendance, taking on issues and work that require attention on behalf of others, costing them considerable expense and outlay, it is only fair – so that they can handle and administer these matters all the more consistently and properly – that the effort, work and costs that they expend on behalf of others in the Empire's affairs, as stated above, should be acknowledged and recognised in this plan. Nevertheless, in addition to the financial assistance provided by their subjects per the plan set out above, the electors and princes (with the exception of ourselves and our son Archduke Philip) should have and maintain no fewer than 500 armed and mounted cavalrymen as part of the aforementioned plan.

[38] Item, the following are counted among the aforementioned princes in this plan: the Grand Master of the Teutonic Order, the abbots of Fulda, Hersfeld, Kempten, Reichenau, Wissembourg, St Gallen, Saalfeld, the prior of Ellwangen, the counts of Henneberg and the princes of Anhalt.

[39: Every count should deploy one mounted cavalryman for every 4000 fl. of his income.

40: The revenue calculations for the one-fortieth tax set out in articles 30–36 should only exclude incomes set aside for particular purposes such as pensions and dowers.]

[41] Also, the knights and retainers of the Holy Empire should also contribute something to this praiseworthy Christian work and undertaking according to their means, as pious Christian people and out of their noble natures, for the sake of the preservation and salvation of their own fatherland, honour, lives and possessions, and by way of resistance against the infidel and other enemies of Christendom and the Empire.

[42] Item, every Jewish person, be they young or old, should provide one florin annually, and the rich Jews should assist the poor ones in meeting this requirement.

[43] Item, all spiritual people who preach the Word of God, be they lay, priests or members of religious orders, should be guided to do their best during their preaching to call upon the population so as to move them to assist in this praiseworthy Christian undertaking.

[44] Item, a box should be put in every ecclesiastical foundation, parish church or monastery, wherein the money donated by pious and reverent Christians out of their own piety and free will should be placed and preserved and then faithfully delivered every year to the imperial council at the time specified in the recess of this, our royal and imperial diet.

[45] And if Almighty God grants us such good fortune and victory – as we hope and pray – that the appointed captain leading the Empire's soldiers should win or conquer something that can yield revenues for the Empire, all of that should be assigned to the Empire, and faithfully handed over to the ordained imperial council. And if it turns out that such conquered possessions provide a substantial financial yield, or some other circumstances should arise that would enable the imperial council to alleviate or reduce the military and financial levies envisioned by this plan, such an alleviation or reduction should be undertaken and conducted equally vis-à-vis both the spiritual and the temporal people.

[46] Item, this ordinance should be valid for six years, and half a year before its expiry his royal Majesty and the estates of the Empire should consider what would be best beyond that.

[47] Item, one year from the initiation of this plan, the ordained imperial council should account for all of its income and expenditure to the estates, and it should continue doing so annually after that, so that the estates are informed about the imperial council's dealings, and matters may be handled all the more honestly and durably. And if a member of the imperial estates should not attend this accounting session, but rather absent themselves, the other estates who do attend should nevertheless continue with the accounting, regardless of this absence.

[48] And this financial and military assistance in the Empire should not give rise to any new customs, nor bring about any loss, disadvantage or damage to anyone's liberties, rights or privileges outside of the stipulations of this ordinance, all without deceit.

[49] And since this aforementioned military and financial assistance cannot take place or come into existence without pre-established governance and order, and also justice, peace and the administration of the same, we have bound, obligated and irrevocably committed ourselves with our aforenamed well-beloved

cousins the electors, princes and other estates of the Empire assembled here, regarding this, the aforementioned imperial governing council and all and every one of our (as king of the Romans) and the Holy Empire's matters – justice, peace and the accomplishment and administration of both, and also resistance against the infidels and other aggressors against Christendom and the Empire, and whatever else pertains to the aforementioned peace, justice, their administration and resistance – and also so that this assistance may be all the more constant and actually be carried out. We also bind, obligate and promise for ourselves and our successors in the Empire as emperors and kings of the Romans, and also our heirs and hereditary lands, by our royal dignity and words, in and by the power of this document, firmly and constantly to hold to and carry out this ordinance and governing council – our and the Holy Empire's council – with the aforementioned mandate and power, and also with jurisdiction, peace-keeping and administration, and with the resolved and agreed assistance set out above; and not to be neglectful or to allow ourselves to be diverted in this, nor to undertake anything against it in any way, but to permit these things and everything negotiated, decided and proclaimed by us or, in our absence, by the one we appoint for this purpose and the majority of the aforementioned governing council, or by the court,[35] to be administered, maintained and carried out, all without guile and deceit.

And to authenticate this as both king of the Romans and archduke of Austria, we have appended our royal seal to this document and signed it with our own hand.

[50] And we [Archbishop Berthold of Mainz, Duke Friedrich III of Saxony, Margrave Joachim I of Brandenburg, Archbishop Ernst of Magdeburg, Bishop Lorenz of Würzburg, Bishop Gabriel of Eichstätt, Bishop Friedrich II of Augsburg, Duke Albrecht IV of Bavaria-Munich, Margrave Friedrich V of Brandenburg-Ansbach-Kulmbach, Duke Heinrich V of Mecklenburg, Abbot Johann of Kempten, Count Hugo XI of Werdenberg, Count Adolf III of Nassau-Wiesbaden-Idstein], and the mayors and councils of the cities of Strasbourg and Augsburg, on behalf of the Holy Empire's free and imperial cities,

---

35 *das Gericht* – this could refer to the cameral court, or to the powers granted to the imperial governing council to make judicial and peace-keeping decisions (see articles 1, 16).

named in the recess of the present imperial diet, and we the envoys and empowered representatives of the electors, princes, prelates, counts and lords also named in the said recess, hereby declare and make known to all, by the power of this document, for ourselves, our successors and heirs and those who have empowered us to act on their behalf that – for the causes related above, and also so that we and all of our people may retain our honour, dignity and liberties that are not contrary to the ordinance, and so that our principalities, lordships, lands, people and governments may remain with the Holy Empire, to which ends we ought to support one another – we approve and accept this ordinance and governing council and associated judicial and jurisdictional policies, including administration of peace, and the military and financial assistance lasting six years, as set out above, with our consent and counsel, just as they are ordained, undertaken and enacted by his royal Majesty and constituted in this present treaty, contract and obligation; and that we have bound, obligated and humbly committed ourselves towards and with his royal Grace with regard to all this. Thus, we hereby bind, obligate and commit ourselves, by the power of this document.

Also, we the electors and princes vow and promise, by our princely honour and dignity, and we the other aforementioned estates vow and promise in good, true loyalty and faith, in lieu of an oath, to obey this ordinance, council, administration and assistance, and to be obedient to his royal Majesty or, in his absence, the one his royal Majesty appoints in his place, and to the governing council conceived here in all the commandments and enjoinders that it may issue by the power of this document, and to carry them out, all faithfully and without deceit. The same promise is contained in the written approvals that we the aforesaid envoys and empowered representatives submit on behalf of our lordships and those who have empowered us.

And to authenticate this, we – the aforenamed electors, princes, prelates, counts and imperial cities – have each appended our own seal on this booklet[36] next to his royal Majesty's seal, doing so also on behalf of the others named in the recess of this imperial diet.

Given at Augsburg, where this took place, on the second day of the month of July, 1500 years after Christ's birth.

---

36 The length of this ordinance required its issuance in the form of a codex rather than a single sheet.

25. An ordinance to expand the imperial circles promulgated at an imperial diet in Trier and Cologne (1512)

Bock et al. (eds), *Deutsche Reichstagsakten. Mittlere Reihe*, vol. XI, pp. 1348–52.

As at most imperial diets during Maximilian's reign, the estates at the assembly in Trier and Cologne made iterative changes to the institutional architecture of the public peace and cameral court established in the late fifteenth century. This extract from the ordinance-cum-recess promulgated at the conclusion of the imperial diet contains the most significant innovations agreed in 1512: the extension of the number of imperial circles to a total of ten, and the prescription of new mechanisms to enable them to enforce the public peace.

We Maximilian, by the grace of God emperor-elect of the Romans, ever augmenter of the Empire, king of Germany, Hungary, Dalmatia, Croatia etc., archduke of Austria, duke of Burgundy and Brabant, Count Palatine etc., publicly proclaim and make known to all with this document:

As emperor-elect of the Romans and rightful lord, we have considered and taken to heart in our imperial disposition how for some time now the Empire has been in striking decline because of the many wars and uprisings that have taken place, and sometimes also because of the Empire's neighbours, and much has been taken from the Empire. And so that these challenges can be met in the future, and also to administer and defend peace and justice in the Holy Empire, such that henceforth nobody should be driven out of the Empire; and to guard against any foreign power that might seek to cut anyone off from the Empire; and to ensure that nobody violently attacks anybody else, but rather that the electors, princes, prelates, counts, lords, cities and all others in the Holy Empire remain in their honour, dignity, principalities, counties, lordships and toll-rights, and otherwise retain the possessions, liberties, rights and customs that belong to them, and be satisfied with decent and proper arbitration and justice vis-à-vis one another; and so that we, as emperor-elect of the Romans, can keep and remain with the Empire and the Empire with us, for our and the estates' successors; and also to protect against wars and uprisings and declarations of enmity and feud, which are contrary to the established public peace, plus to punish and not to permit brigandage; and likewise to resist anyone inside or outside of the Empire who seeks to attack or make war against it; and because we do not consider it acceptable for us or the estates to make war against one another or anyone else wantonly, but solely *ad conservandum et defendendum* ['for the conservation and defence'] of that which is written about in this ordinance – so we have summoned the electors, princes and other estates of the Holy Empire to a collective imperial diet, initially held in Trier and subsequently, for good and compelling reasons, relocated here to Cologne.

In response they have appeared before us in good numbers, some in person and also through envoys, and thus, for the praise of God and the preservation of our holy faith, the Holy Roman Church, his papal Holiness and the Holy Roman Empire of the German nation, we have united, obligated and contractually committed ourselves with the Holy Empire's estates and they with us, as a Christian *corpus* and assembly, regarding the following articles and intentions:

[...]

[9] And if, contrary to the established public peace, somebody answerable to the Holy Empire should attack, declare a feud, enmity or war against or violently seize possessions from us, the electors, princes or other estates who are also answerable to the Holy Empire and are subject to the Empire's plan for military and financial assistance, as set out above, where this perpetrator is caught in the act, all those called upon or who become aware of it should forcefully pursue them and help to save and protect the victims, all per our and the Holy Empire's public peace and its ordinance. However, if the perpetrators could not be dealt with while in the act and they and their allies, clients and supporters are placed in the imperial ban through our or our cameral court's denunciation, all per the Holy Empire's established ordinances; and if this denunciation plus spiritual excommunication (which may be employed as an adjunct to denunciation according to our and the Empire's ordinance) – if requested by the plaintiff or the one calling for aid, who should always have the final say in this – does not motivate others to offer assistance or support in the case; then the captain in the imperial circle in which the perpetrator and their allies and clients live or are located should immediately convene with his associates and deliberate and decide how to proceed so that the public peace may be maintained and the violators punished.

[10] Similarly, the captains and their associates within the imperial circle should also deliberate, decide how to proceed and assist one another regarding the enforcement of verdicts pronounced and put into effect by the cameral court, where the relevant executing authority fails to aid the party concerned, so that such verdicts are actually enforced.

However, where a conflict addressed by the mechanisms in the two previous articles is so severe and intractable that it cannot be resolved by the captain and associates of the imperial circle, the captain in the circle where the assistance is required should immediately and efficaciously inform us, or, if we are not close enough to be reachable, our relative the archbishop of Mainz in our place, in order that the other estates of the Empire can be convoked together at an appointed time and place to deliberate, negotiate and pursue courses of action to fend off this danger. We should always be informed of the convocation of such an ad hoc diet, so that we can also depute someone to attend it on our behalf. However, if this occurs in the period between the holding of imperial diets, it should not obstruct or divert the next imperial diet, which should be able to proceed as usual.

[11] And the costs that arise from all the aforementioned forms of assistance should be borne by and divided among us and all the estates collectively, and drawn from the collective financial levy set out below.

[12] And to this end we have ordained ten imperial circles together with the estates, as follows:

Namely, we should have one circle in our hereditary lands of Austria and Tyrol etc., and another in Burgundy with its lands; item, the four electors along the Rhine should have one circle, and the electors of Saxony and Brandenburg, together with Duke Georg of Saxony and the bishops of the lands and districts of these same electors, should also have one. And the six circles ordained earlier at the imperial diet of Augsburg [24] should remain, and all this should proceed without harming any member of the estates in their authorities, privileges or rights. Should any disagreements arise because of one or more of these circles, this issue should be dealt with at the next forthcoming imperial diet.

26. A peace-ordinance promulgated at an imperial diet in Worms (1521)

Kluckhohn et al. (eds), *Deutsche Reichstagsakten. Jüngere Reihe*, vol. II, pp. 317–28.

This extract from the first peace-ordinance of the reign of Charles V, which largely reiterated the terms of those issued under Maximilian I, highlights the rhetorical continuities in the preambles to such texts. It also includes two articles of particular concern to many members of the estates at this juncture: the relationship between the resuscitated imperial governing council (*Reichsregiment*) and the existing institutions of the public peace; and countermeasures against collectively owned castles of the lower nobility, which served as bases for the most prolific feud-declarers of the early sixteenth century.

We Charles V, by the grace of God emperor-elect of the Romans, ever augmenter of the Empire etc., king of Germany, Spain, both Sicilies, Jerusalem, Hungary, Dalmatia, Croatia etc., archduke of Austria and duke of Burgundy, Brabant etc., count of Habsburg, Flanders and Tyrol etc., impart our grace and all good wishes to all and every one of our and the Holy Empire's electors and princes (spiritual and temporal), prelates, counts, barons, knights, retainers, captains, magistrates, mayors, judges, councillors, citizens and communes, and otherwise all other subjects and faithful people belonging to us and the Empire, whatever their dignity, estate or condition, who come to see, read or be shown this, our imperial document, or a copy thereof.

Emperor Maximilian, our ancestor of benign and highly praiseworthy memory, united, committed and bound himself to a collective public peace with the electors, princes and estates of the Holy Empire [21], because of notable, great, valiant and compelling reasons and causes of the Holy Empire and the subjects of the same, for the sake of honour and welfare and the advancement of the common good. And now, at the outset of our reign, we perceive and discover that all kinds of uprisings and enmities between foreign powers are affecting the Empire's members and associates, which will cause grave decline and devastation – not only for the individual estates of the Empire, but for the whole of Christendom – and the loss of souls, honour and dignity if action is not taken against this with suitable, timely counsel, and then only if, for the furtherance of the same, durable and effective peace and justice are implemented, administered and preserved in a strong condition.

Because of this, we have been induced to follow in the footsteps of our ancestor on this issue, and we have – with the unanimous, timely counsel of our high and honour-worthy, high-born, well-beloved friends, relatives and cousins, the electors and princes (spiritual and temporal), and also the prelates, counts, lords and estates of the Holy Empire who have appeared before us here at this imperial diet – established, ordained and enacted a collective peace throughout the Holy Empire and German nation, in the same manner and with the same terms as it was first established by our ancestor at Worms and subsequently further elaborated at other imperial diets, but with a few careful and necessary additions and further elaborations. And we establish, ordain and enact it in and by the power of this document.

[...]

[11] Concerning the governing council's[37] authority against peace-breakers.

Item, as we have granted authority to the cameral judge in this, our said public peace that, where a peace-breaker's case involves armed invasion or something else of a similar magnitude, and urgent circumstances have made it impossible to convoke the annual assembly ordained to deal with such matters, he may call upon us and the electors, princes and estates to congregate efficiently at an appointed site for deliberation;[38] but as the annual assembly has been rendered obsolete by the ordained governing council established here; so we establish, ordain and desire that such appeals should henceforth be brought before and reach our regent and governing council, in the same way as this was previously supposed to take place at the assemblies. They will then surely know how to act in response, as circumstances require and according to the specifics of the case, per the instructions in the ordinance established here.[39]

---

37 That is, the resurrected *Reichsregiment* [24].
38 See [21], article 7.
39 That is, the ordinance establishing the reactivated *Regiment*: Kluckhohn et al. (eds), *Deutsche Reichstagsakten. Jüngere Reihe*, vol. II, no. 21.

Nevertheless, our cameral judge and cameral court should always proceed according to justice against violators and peace-breakers when appealed to by parties injured or warred against, or when their office requires it.

[...]

[13] Against the castles of co-heirs.[40]

Item, as we have previously heard and are still hearing great complaints about how manifold things contrary to our public peace – damage, abduction, robbery, kidnap and arson – have occurred and been committed out of and within the collective castles of co-heirs; and as it was previously declared, established and enacted at the imperial diet of Freiburg,[41] during the deliberations of the estates assembled there, to address this for the complete administration and enforcement of the public peace; so now here, with the counsel and consent of the estates of this assembly, we have renewed this, and we hereby do this presently: if declared outlaws or peace-breakers should have any share of or common living or rights within the same collective castles, they should lose these and no longer be permitted at or in those castles unless and until they have reached a settlement with us, the Empire and the opposing party regarding their actions.

This, our declaration and statute in the form set out above, should be publicly written and made known to all collective castles of co-heirs. And if, in spite of this proclamation, the collective co-heirs permit the outlaws or peace-breakers of their party to enjoy or make use of their collective living or rights, and show themselves to be disobedient in this, we declare, ordain, establish and desire that they should be subject to the penalties contained in this, our public peace, administrative ordinance and declaration, and thereupon denounced and declared to be in the imperial ban.

---

40 *der ganerben schloss* – castles and their appurtenances that were jointly owned and inhabited by various lordly and knightly families, and often served as bases for nobles engaged in feuds.
41 A diet held in 1498 in Freiburg in the Breisgau.

27. The recess of an imperial diet in Speyer (1526)

Kluckhohn et al. (eds), *Deutsche Reichstagsakten. Jüngere Reihe*, vol. V/VI, pp. 879–84, 891.

As was typical at imperial diets by this time, the estates assembled at Speyer in 1526 issued a recess that reconfirmed the cumulative institutional architecture of the public peace in the Holy Roman Empire. In the shadow of the recent and traumatic Peasants' War, the recess also specifically sought to address the discontent of the lower orders with a combination of better justice and repression, while putting off any firm decision regarding religion that might exacerbate the emerging confessional divisions among the estates. These passages are included in this extract, as well as article 30, which sought to regulate the printing of the recesses of the diets.

We Ferdinand, by the grace of God prince and *Infante* of Spain, archduke of Austria, duke of Burgundy etc., count of Habsburg, Flanders and Tyrol, etc., and, by the same grace, we Philipp, margrave of Baden, Bernhard, bishop of Trent, Casimir, margrave of Brandenburg, duke of Stettin, Pomerania and of the Kashubians and the Wends, burgrave of Nuremberg and prince of Rügen and Erich, duke of Brunswick and Lüneburg etc., appointed and empowered deputies of the most serene, very mighty, high-born prince and lord, Lord Charles V, emperor-elect of the Romans, our gracious and most gracious lord, and appointed commissioners to the imperial diet relocated hither to Speyer, proclaim and make known publicly with this document:

The aforementioned Roman imperial Majesty publicised and convoked a collective imperial diet and assembly in Augsburg on St Martin's Day (29 September) in the [15]25th year just past, and that diet was then rescheduled and pushed forward until the first day of May and relocated to Speyer by us, with the counsel and consent of the electors, princes and estates of the Holy Roman Empire and their envoys who were then present at Augsburg, for circumstantial, notable, honourable reasons. Thus, we have appeared in person, as appointed imperial deputies and commissioners, and likewise the electors, princes and estates of the Holy Roman Empire and their envoys have appeared in significant numbers, so that we, standing in for and on behalf of the aforementioned Roman imperial Majesty, can deliberate with timely, weighty counsel, together with the electors, princes, prelates, counts and estates of the Holy Roman Empire and their envoys, regarding the points and articles included in his imperial Majesty's summons and, more specifically, the sent briefing made available to us, the commissioners. And thereupon we have united and reached agreement together on a recess of all our counsels and negotiations that have taken place, which follows hereafter in writing, article by article.

[1] And firstly, as his imperial Majesty's briefing chiefly expresses and contains the requirement that no innovation or determination should be made or undertaken at this imperial diet in matters pertaining to the holy Christian faith and religion, as well as the ceremonies and traditional practices of the Holy Christian Church; and considering and reflecting on the fact that the religious dispute is by no means the least cause of the recent uprising of the common man as well as all the discord now gripping the German nation,[42] so that, if the issue is not addressed, even greater contestation and rebellion between higher and lower estates is to be feared; so, in order that a unanimous, equitable understanding may be established within the Christian faith and peace and unity between all estates in the German nation may be cultivated and preserved, we and also the electors, princes and estates have considered and adjudged that this religious matter could not be worked out by any better, more fruitful, agreeable and apt method than through a free general council of the Church, or at least a national assembly, which should be undertaken in the German lands within a year or at most a year and a half.

So that this may be achieved in the most efficacious way, we, the electors, princes and estates have collectively despatched a group of envoys to send to his imperial Majesty, namely Marquard of Stein, dean of Bamberg and Augsburg cathedrals, Count Albrecht of Mansfeld and Jakob Sturm of Strasbourg, with an urgent briefing, including humbly seeking and requesting of his imperial Majesty that he should graciously take to heart and consider the grave affliction of the German nation on account of this religious dispute and division, betake himself hither into the German nation in person as soon as possible and wish to attend to and ensure that the said general council of the Church, or at least a national assembly, be

---

42 A reference to the Peasants' War of 1524–26. See Whaley, *Germany*, chapter 18.

undertaken within the specified time without any lengthy delay, all per the more detailed content of the same briefing.

[2: The estates should make proportional financial contributions to the city of Speyer to fund the journey of these envoys.

3: The envoys should report to Ferdinand and the archbishop of Mainz upon their return.]

[4] Accordingly, we, the electors, princes and estates of the Empire and the same group of envoys have now united and reached unanimous agreement among ourselves here at this imperial diet that until such time as this council or national assembly is held, in matters relating to the edict promulgated by his imperial Majesty at the imperial diet held in Worms,[43] each of us will nevertheless live, govern and conduct ourselves with our subjects in the manner that each hopes and trusts is appropriate in answering to God and his imperial Majesty.

[5] Secondly, in the past year, horrifying, unprecedented and un-Christian uprisings of subjects against their superiors in rank and honour took place and arose in almost all places in the Upper German nation, leading to great shedding of Christian blood and the depredation and devastation of lands and peoples, wherefore his Majesty has specifically and explicitly willed and ordered in his briefing drawn up for this imperial diet that we should earnestly pay heed to ensure that in future a similar uprising and rebellion of subjects may be averted and pre-empted. Meanwhile, we acknowledge that we are bound to humble obedience towards his Majesty in this, and that we ourselves are well disposed towards this goal. Thus, for the sake of pleasing and showing humble obedience towards his imperial Majesty and also for the good of the German nation, its subjects and the common good, we have committed and promised to one another that each of us intends to treat the other with honour and good faith, and also that we want to maintain firmly and administer the public peace of the emperor and Holy Empire established previously at Worms [26], such that nobody – by themselves or via someone else – wars against, robs, abducts,

---

43 The legal proclamation that followed Martin Luther's appearances at the 1521 diet of Worms, placing him in the imperial ban and outlawing his works. For an English translation of the edict, see Jensen (ed./trans.), *Confrontation at Worms*.

invades or besieges another, nor captures or scales with ladders another's town, castle or place, nor damages them with arson or by any other means, nor violently plunders, ousts or drives out another's people. Additionally, nobody should deceitfully harbour or support another's feud-enemy or injurer, nor extend help, counsel or any kind of assistance. Rather, whoever intends to pursue a dispute with another should do so via the appropriate judicial channels, all per the more detailed content of – and on pain of the penalties and punishment contained in – the aforementioned public peace.

[6] And although the common man and the subjects rather gravely forgot themselves during this past uprising, and behaved boorishly against their authorities, nevertheless, in order that they may perceive that the grace and compassion of their superiors is greater and more clement than their own irrational deeds and behaviours, every authority should have the power and capability, according to the circumstances and what pleases them best, to re-establish their subjects who have surrendered and been punished to their former honourable estate; to qualify and prepare them to sit in councils and courts, share judicially relevant information and hold offices; and, additionally, always to hear them and others graciously regarding their grievances and complaints, and to make gracious and efficacious legal pronouncements based on the facts of the case; and not to unfairly burden them, through the authorities themselves or their officers, magistrates or other servitors, but to allow whoever wishes to avail themselves of justice to do so.

[7] Also, if the subjects of any authority have injured or damaged someone, and this latter party does not wish to renounce their dispute and claim, the subjects should then provide compensation to and make whole the plaintiff for their share of the damage, according to the judgement of the appropriate authority that governs them or that of the imperial cameral court, per the ordinances of the Empire. And what is judged by the said authority should be the last word, and thus the plaintiff should thenceforth leave the injuring parties alone, not perturbing them with deeds, legal claims or in any other way. If one party feels aggrieved by the judgement or finding pronounced by the judge with competence over the case, the same should be free to pursue their appeal via the correct hierarchy of courts, including up to the cameral court. Nothing should hereby be removed or voided from the treaties

and ordinances entered into by the Swabian League during the peasant uprising.[44]

[8] Also, every authority should proceed against those who have absconded on account of their actions during the peasant uprising on a case-by-case basis, in such a manner that all those subjects willing to submit themselves to justice may experience and discover grace and beneficence rather than severity and mercilessness. However, those who were initiators, rabble-rousers and ringleaders or particular promoters of the said uprising without any special, justifiable reason or cause, which is for each authority to determine, should not receive mercy, nor be accommodated, harboured or supported by anybody. Instead, wherever they go they should be severely treated and punished according to their crimes, as is just. And henceforth the subjects should conduct and present themselves in an obedient, faithful and peaceful manner towards their authorities of the spiritual and temporal estate, as they are duty-bound to do, and also as their obligations and oaths spell out, and not give rise to their own perdition and ruin.

[9] Hereupon, we – together with the electors, princes, prelates, counts and estates, for the sake of humble obedience to his imperial Majesty – have united and reached agreement that in the event that the subjects of any authority, spiritual or temporal, should band together once more and foment another uprising and rebellion, despite the aforementioned grace and compassion that we have shown, the neighbouring electors, princes, counts and other authorities should then, when called upon by the same authority in which the uprising has taken place, be ready to charge in with cavalry and infantry and provide succour and assistance as immediately as this arises and with the greatest haste. And if the same assistance sought in this way should prove too weak for the uprising that has taken place, the other electors, princes and estates based in the vicinity – upon request, as set out above – should then likewise charge in with the strongest possible force in order to put down the disobedient rebels, to bring them back to obedience and to punish them justly. And all of us in this should show and

---

44 The Swabian League [41] played a major role in suppressing the peasant warbands in 1525 and petitioned the estates to permit League members to make their own arrangements for compensation for damages incurred during the war: Kluckhohn et al. (eds), *Deutsche Reichstagsakten. Jüngere Reihe*, vol. V/VI, no. 202.

conduct ourselves with one another just as if such an uprising and rebellion had taken place and occurred in each of our own principalities, lordships and districts, and in the manner that each of us would want to be treated by and receive from one another.

[...]

[30] Item, as it became apparent during imperial diets held in the past that the recesses have sometimes been printed and sold with wording that is not identical to the correct original document, we desire that this recess of this imperial diet should not be printed by anybody except where Andreas Rucker, secretary of Mainz and the Empire's affairs, has shown the sealed original to the printer. And no printed edition of the recess should be trusted unless Andreas Rucker has personally proofed, verified and confirmed it.

28. The full protestation of the evangelical estates at an imperial diet in Speyer (1529)

Kluckhohn et al. (eds), *Deutsche Reichstagsakten. Jüngere Reihe*, vol. VII, pp. 1273–88.

Most serene king and most highly worthy, very worthy, high-born, honourable, well-born and noble, well-beloved, gracious lords, cousins, relatives, in-laws, associates and especially well-beloved people.

After we – upon the summons of his Roman imperial Majesty [Charles V], our most gracious lord, and additionally the amicable correspondence of your royal Serenity [Ferdinand][45] – betook ourselves here to this imperial diet, for the sake of humble obedience to his Majesty and amicable and dutiful favour towards your royal Serenity, and also the good of the whole of Christendom and the Holy Empire, we have now heard, alongside you and these well-beloved people, the reading of the instructions – including the letter of empowerment – issued in his imperial Majesty's name (but drawn up by your royal Serenity and his imperial Majesty's other ordained commissioners), and also assiduously seen and discovered in his imperial Majesty's written convocation of this imperial diet, that matters have been decided through inappropriate procedures, the decision in question being that the article in the recess of the previous imperial diet held here [27], concerning our holy Christian faith and the religion or ceremonies of the same, is to be nullified, and other highly offensive articles are to be promulgated in its place.

And yet, for good Christian reasons and for the preservation of peace and unity in the Holy Empire, your royal Serenity and you other appointees as empowered deputies and commissioners of his imperial Majesty, as well as all the electors, princes and estates of the Empire and the envoys of the same, unanimously united and reached agreement at the previous imperial diet held here in Speyer on the content of the said article, as follows hereafter:

---

45 Archduke Ferdinand, Charles's brother, now bore royal titles following his assumption of the crowns of Bohemia and Hungary in 1526–27, and continued to preside over the imperial diets as the emperor's representative on the imperial governing council.

'That until such time as a general council or national assembly is held, in matters relating to the edict promulgated by his imperial Majesty at the imperial diet in Worms, each elector, prince and member of the estates of the Empire may live, govern and conduct themselves with their subjects in the manner that each hopes and trusts is appropriate in answering to God and his imperial Majesty.'[46]

And your royal Serenity, who was at that time and now still is his imperial Majesty's deputy, together with your other named and previously appointed fellow commissioners, pronounced and promised through the adoption of the aforesaid recess, by the power of the authority then granted to you by his Roman imperial Majesty (through documents sealed and signed by his imperial Majesty's hand), to hold to and carry out firmly, inviolably and sincerely each and every thing that is written in the said recess and that might pertain to his imperial Majesty, to fulfil and observe it unhesitatingly and steadfastly, and not to do or undertake anything or act against it, nor to permit anything to be issued against it or endorse anyone else to do so on your behalf, without any deceit.

[The authors of the protestation expound further on the various ways that the 1526 recess was validated and made binding: all the estates present at that imperial diet promised to uphold it; it was sealed by and on behalf of all present parties.]

Thus, in view of this previously drawn up, mutually obligated, documented and sealed recess, and also for the well-founded reasons that follow (some of which were also shown in writing to your royal Serenity, you well-beloved people and the others at the imperial diet on the twelfth day of this month of April), we cannot and may not consent to the nullification of the aforesaid article (which was unanimously agreed and made mandatorily binding), nor to the supposed moderation of it (which is actually no such thing) that has been formulated in its place.

Namely, first of all, for the well-founded reason that we undoubtingly hold that his imperial Majesty, as a praiseworthy, just and Christian emperor, our most gracious lord, and also that your royal Serenity and you other fellow commissioners, and likewise that the majority of you other well-beloved people, are surely – no less than us – of an imperial, royal, electoral, princely and honourable, sincere

---

46 See [27], article 4.

and steadfast disposition and will towards that which all of you once – together with us – unanimously endorsed, obligated yourselves to, documentarily drew up and sealed, thereby committing to holding and fulfilling it continuously and firmly, by the letter and inviolably, and to avoiding undermining it in any way or opposing it with anything. On this point we consider and seek not only our own, but first and foremost his imperial Majesty's, your royal Serenity's and all of our honour, praise, good reputation and justness.

Second, as is elaborated above and hereafter, we could in no way do this while answering in good conscience to God the Almighty, as the only lord, ruler and redeemer of our holy Christian salvific faith, or to his imperial Majesty, as a Christian emperor.

For whereas we know that our ancestors, brethren and we ourselves, in all those things in which we have been bound to show obedience towards the deceased and currently reigning Roman imperial Majesties or sometimes had occasion to promote your imperial Majesty's and the Empire's honour, benefit and maximum wellbeing, have always acted with completely faithful, willing and ready obedience, without self-glorification and without diminishment of others, such that nobody could surpass us in this; so we are also henceforth desirous of and inclined towards amicably, graciously and harmoniously showing obedience and willingness towards his Roman imperial Majesty, as our most gracious lord, and your royal Serenity and our other well-beloved and gracious lords, cousins, relatives, in-laws, associates and other estates of the Holy Empire in all obligatory and all possible things, not sparing our bodies and possessions, unto the ends of our lives and to the grave, with the help of divine grace.

However, as your royal Serenity and you others know, these are the kinds of matters that concern and touch upon God's honour and the beatitude and salvation of each of our souls. By divine mandate and for the sake of our consciences, we are bound and obliged to respect our same Lord and God in this as the highest king and Lord of all lords through baptism and otherwise, above all, through His holy divine word, in the undoubting confidence that your royal Serenity, you well-beloved people and the others will (as we amicably requested above) excuse us amicably, graciously and with goodwill for not being in agreement with your royal Serenity, you well-beloved people and the others regarding the aforementioned article, and for not wanting to comply with the majority in this, as it has sometimes been argued at this imperial diet that we should do. We are not obliged to do this, in view and consideration of the validity of the previous imperial recess of Speyer, which demonstrates clearly – especially in the highlighted article – that the said article was resolved upon through unanimous agreement (and not merely that of the majority), and so, according to honour, equity and justice, such a unanimous agreement should, can and may not be altered other than through another unanimous agreement; as well as the fact that – even if we disregard the previous point – in matters concerning God's honour and the beatitude and salvation of our souls, each individual must stand and give account for themselves before God, and nobody in that place can excuse themselves on account of the lesser or greater deeds or decisions of another; and also for other righteously founded, good reasons.

And so that your royal Serenity, you well-beloved people, the others and everyone who might hear of this affair can once again understand our grievance for themselves, as well as the reason and cause for which, on this occasion, we cannot reach agreement in this matter with your royal Serenity, you well-beloved people and you others, let us state that it is evident and undeniable that for some time now there has been a dispute over many points and articles of doctrine in our Christian religion. The cause and course of this dispute is known first and foremost to God, to whose judgement we submit all things. And this has become well known to you, partly because of the exhortation and briefing given and delivered by the papal legate back at the imperial diet in Nuremberg,[47] and also because of many electors, princes and other estates of the Empire there, who were nevertheless partly on your side. For at the said imperial diet in Nuremberg our collective grievances were compiled in eighty articles by the temporal imperial estates and handed over to the papal legate just noted, and they later came out publicly in print.[48] For the same grievances and abuses have not yet been abolished, and many more of them are now apparent.

---

47 At a 1523 imperial diet in Nuremberg, the papal legate Francesco Chieregati delivered an oration and written briefing condemning the alleged heresies of Martin Luther. They are edited in Kluckhohn et al. (eds), *Deutsche Reichstagsakten. Jüngere Reihe*, vol. III, nos 73–74.
48 This list of grievances (*gravamina* or *beswerungen*) against perceived abuses in the Church and spiritual estate is edited in ibid., vol. III, no. 110.

And yet at that same time and ever since – as is also the case everywhere here and now – at all the imperial diets it has always been considered that no more effective method and means could be found for all sides in these matters than to convoke and carry out a free, collective Christian council, or at least a national assembly, as soon as possible. And we have nothing but a faithful, Christian, amicable, helpful and good opinion on this, and namely that your royal Serenity, you well-beloved people and you others should take away and understand this for yourselves: when one party has a different stance or conviction regarding doctrine (which pertains to God's honour and the beatitude and salvation of souls), which that party holds as Christian and promotes and spreads in their lands and districts, it is appropriate and just that it should be discussed before a free, Christian general council, so that the parties divided over doctrine and other matters about which they themselves are not certain might get a hearing and negotiate. For the issue of the said council has not been, and is still not being, discussed and negotiated often and emphatically enough by his imperial Majesty's appointed deputies, commissioners and orators, nor by the electors, princes and other estates of the Empire.

That such matters now affect us, for our part, according to the content and intent of certain points and articles proposed regarding this dispute over faith and peace that some wish to impose on us, not only secretly but also openly, can readily be appreciated and understood from the evidence that follows.

For thus have some in the committee posited,[49] in their first draft[50] – and again in the draft from the tenth day of this month of April, which was revised and modified with respect to certain other points – that the electors, princes and other estates (among whom we and likewise you well-beloved people and the others would be included and defined) would then have resolved upon with one another here: that those who until now have not

---

49 *ausschus* – 'committee' or 'council'. By the late fifteenth century, it was customary for participants in an imperial diet to negotiate matters within two or three sub-committees: one for the electors, another for the princes and sometimes a third for other estates such as the cities (who might also be invited to the other councils or general sessions; see [18]). When all the members of these committees came together for a plenary session, it was sometimes called a 'large committee' (*großer ausschus*).

50 That is, the first formulation of the recess for the ongoing imperial diet.

enforced the afore-specified imperial edict should and must also henceforth respect it, and make their subjects hold unto it, until a future council. It would be extremely grievous to us, as people who cannot in good conscience hold unto nor enforce this edict in all its stipulations (a view expressed not only by us, but by yet others among the imperial estates at previous imperial diets), if, through our collaboration, somebody of a high or low estate should be cut off from the doctrine which we, through the sound testimony of God's eternal word, undoubtingly regard as divine and Christian, and if, against our own conscience (as stated above), they should be forcibly subjected to the said edict; and we would in no way be able to answer to God if we did this.

But we have absolutely no intention of contesting how your royal Serenity and each of you well-beloved people and you others should wish to conduct yourselves and your own subjects regarding the edict or anything else in the absence of our participation in the said agreement and resolution. We merely pray to God, daily and heartily, that His divine grace may be present with all of us, that He may illuminate our own spiritual understanding justly and truly, and that He may give His Holy Spirit to lead us into all truth, that we may attain unanimity regarding a just, true, loving, salvific, Christian faith, through Christ our sole source of atonement, mediator, advocate and saviour. Amen.

[The authors of the protestation provide a further, lengthy elaboration on the reasons for which they cannot assent to the planned recess of the imperial diet, asserting the scriptural basis of their doctrinal views and 'evangelical mass', and reiterating the superior validity and binding nature of the unanimous 1526 Speyer recess over the planned 1529 recess of the majority of the estates, while highlighting aspects of the latter they find unacceptable.]

Following on from all this, we wish to place our hope in your royal Serenity, you well-beloved people and you others as our well-beloved and gracious lords, cousins, relatives, in-laws, associates and especially well-beloved people – and we also amicably request and benignly entreat – that you would and should wish to take into account the circumstances of the matter once again, and consider our grievances and the causes and reasons for them seriously, and not allow yourselves to be moved in any way against, nor act in opposition to, the unanimously resolved, mutually obligated, documented and sealed recess, which nobody has the authority, power or right to do, for the reasons we have suggested and for other well-founded reasons, which we will refrain from mentioning on this occasion out of goodwill.

And if this third airing of our important grievances before your royal Serenity, you well-beloved people and you others should not be heeded, or if you do not want to heed it, then we hereby protest and witness publicly before God, our sole creator, comforter, redeemer and saviour (who alone fathoms and knows all of our hearts, as aforesaid, and would thus judge them justly), and also before all of mankind and all creatures: that for ourselves and our subjects and on behalf of everybody, in all our dealings and in the intended recess (which, as set out above, is – in this and other matters – contrary to God, His holy word, our good conscience and the salvation of all of our souls, and also contrary to the aforementioned imperial recess of Speyer that was previously undertaken, resolved and enacted), we cannot agree nor consent to this, but hold it to be void and non-binding, for the righteous, well-founded reasons set out above, and for other reasons. And we openly publicise our urgent opposition to this, and offer his Roman imperial Majesty, our very gracious lord, further detailed and truthful information regarding this issue, which we did yesterday, as soon as the proposed recess was handed out, in our hurriedly composed protestation,[51] and which we have reiterated and publicly made known and committed here: that until the aforementioned collective and free Christian council or national assembly, we will nevertheless continue to conduct ourselves, live and govern in areas under our authority and among and with our subjects and associates in a manner that allows us to answer in faith and hope to Almighty God and his Roman imperial Majesty, our very gracious lord, as a Christian emperor, by means of God's assistance and per the content of the oft-mentioned previous imperial recess of Speyer.

As for that which relates to spiritual rents, tithes, incomes and revenues and the public peace, as compiled and expressed in the previous imperial recess of Speyer, we also hold and prove ourselves irreproachable with regard to those measures. And likewise, as regards the points that follow in the proposed recess regarding

---

51 An initial, much shorter version of the protestation was submitted on 19 April.

anabaptism and printing,[52] we wish to conduct ourselves as we had always intended to at this imperial diet: to be united with your royal Serenity, you well-beloved people and you others, and to hold to the content of the same points appropriately and in every conceivable respect. We also reserve the right for ourselves to further extend our oft-mentioned grievances and protestation, and whatever else necessity might require of all of us in this matter.

And in relation to all of this, we undoubtingly seek provision and solace in his Roman imperial Majesty, that he will conduct and show himself graciously towards us, in the manner of a Christian emperor and our very gracious lord, who loves God over all things, as he regards our Christian, honourable, righteous and unshakable disposition and obligation-fulfilling obedience. And in all this we would otherwise like to carry out and demonstrate amicable and well-meaning service to your royal Serenity, you well-beloved people and you others, as our well-beloved and gracious lords, cousins, relatives, in-laws, associates and especially well-beloved people, and congenially and graciously to do your will. This is what we are benevolently inclined to do out of friendship and well-meaning obedience and gracious and Christian love and commitment.

Done at Speyer, on the twentieth day of April, in the [15]29th year etc.

Johann ['the Constant'], elector [and duke of Saxony, r. 1525–32]

Georg, margrave of Brandenburg[-Ansbach] etc. [r. 1515–43]

Philipp [I], landgrave of Hessen etc. [r. 1518–67]

Wolfgang, prince of Anhalt[-Köthen, r. 1508–62]

Johann Förster, chancellor [of Duke Ernst I of Brunswick-Lüneburg, r. 1521–46][53]

---

52 The 1529 recess contained a proscription against anabaptists and against printing works that might foment rebellious sentiment among commoners or deepen religious confusion. See Kluckhohn et al. (eds), *Deutsche Reichstagsakten. Jüngere Reihe*, vol. VII, no. 148.
53 These signatures were personally written by each of these signatories to the original document. Envoys from fourteen free and imperial cities soon co-signed the protestation, some on 20 April itself.

29. A peace agreement and recess between Emperor Charles V and the evangelical estates (1532)

Kluckhohn et al. (eds), *Deutsche Reichstagsakten. Jüngere Reihe*, vol. X, pp. 1512–17.

We [Archbishop Albrecht of Mainz and Count Palatine Ludwig][54] proclaim and make known publicly with this present recess:[55]

Certain controversies and disputes regarding the faith have been carried out for some time between the most serene, most mighty prince and lord, Lord Charles, Roman emperor, ever augmenter of the Empire, etc., our most gracious lord, on the one hand, and the high-born princes, our well-beloved relatives and cousins, Lord Johann, duke of Saxony, Elector and Duke Johann Friedrich, his well-beloved son, Lord Georg, margrave of Brandenburg, Lords Philipp, Ernst and Franz, brothers and cousins, lords of Brunswick and Lüneburg, Prince Wolfgang of Anhalt, Gebhard and Albrecht, counts of Mansfeld and the towns of Strasbourg, Nuremberg, Constance, Ulm, Biberach, Isny, Reutlingen, Esslingen, Memmingen, Lindau, Heilbronn, Hall in Swabia, Kempten, Weißenburg, Windsheim, Lübeck, Brunswick, Magdeburg, Bremen, Goslar, Einbeck, Göttingen, Nordhausen and Hamburg on the other hand. On their account, manifold negotiations have been undertaken and pursued at previously held imperial diets over how these disputes and controversies might be brought to a fair and benign settlement, which has not, however, been realised so far. And thus, for the preservation of unity and peace in the Holy Empire, and especially so that the collective enemy of Christendom, the Turk, may be all the more steadfastly faced and his cruel, tyrannical schemes against the blood of Christians and especially the German nation may be averted, we have reached a very humble, faithful, good verdict in these matters, and – with the gracious permission of the imperial Majesty, as well as the authority, instruction and mandate given by his imperial Majesty for this purpose and the approval of our aforementioned cousins and relatives and their own relations – we

---

54 The full titles of these two electors are included in [9].
55 *abschidt* – the word used to describe the agreed and legally binding outcome of any diet. Here it was an ad hoc arbitrational diet, not an imperial assembly (*Reichstag*), which had led to a compromise and peace agreement between Emperor Charles and the 'protesting' estates.

have facilitated many varied and amicable negotiations, originally in Schweinfurt and subsequently here in Nuremberg.

Since the matters of the faith could not be brought to a settlement at the many negotiations held so far, we have considered that the tyrannical, cruel schemes of the Turk may most steadfastly be resisted through the establishment of an enduring, collective peace in the Holy Empire. To that end, we have most humbly entreated and requested of his Majesty that (following this, our negotiation that we have carried out and our humble entreaty and request, to which the Roman imperial Majesty, our most gracious lord, has recently graciously consented as the supreme head of the Holy Empire, and out of the especial devotion and wish that his Majesty bears for collective peace) a collective, enduring peace should therefore be established between his Majesty and all the estates of the Holy Roman Empire of the German nation, spiritual and temporal, to last until a collective, free, Christian council, as determined at the imperial diet of Nuremberg,[56] or, if this does not come to pass, until the collective estates of the Empire are again convoked and summoned to an assembly, as will be specified in a special article hereafter.

The peace should stipulate that between now and the same council, or until the estates assemble and something else is deliberated, as just mentioned, nobody should have a feud with, make war against, rob, abduct, attack or besiege another, on account of the faith or for any other cause. Additionally, nobody should assault any castles, towns, markets, fortifications, villages, farmsteads or hamlets or violently or maliciously occupy them without permission, or underhandedly damage them with arson or by other means, whether they themselves do it or have someone else do it on their behalf, nor provide counsel, help or any other kind of assistance or reinforcement to such perpetrators, nor knowingly or deceitfully harbour, house, sustain, suffer or supply food or drink to them. Rather, everyone should intend only just amity and Christian charity towards the other.

---

56 During the parallel negotiations of the imperial diet and arbitrational diet at Nuremberg, the electors of Mainz and the Palatinate drafted a peace-ordinance that reproduced and updated the 1524 peace-ordinance issued in Nuremberg (Kluckhohn et al. (eds), *Deutsche Reichstagsakten. Jüngere Reihe*, vol. X, no. 516), which was itself an updated version of the 1521 Worms *Landfrieden* [26], with the added stipulation that the peace should endure until a future council could be held to resolve religious disagreements.

The imperial Majesty should proclaim and promulgate this aforementioned collective peace to all the estates in the Holy Empire and order them to observe it on pain of a specified, severe, considerable penalty,[57] and also graciously employ all diligence to ensure that the aforementioned council is convened and publicised within half a year and then held within one year thereafter, and that in the event that this cannot be achieved, the collective estates of the Empire are consequently called and summoned together again at an assembly to deliberate further about what should be undertaken and done regarding the said council and other necessary matters.

The Roman imperial Majesty has also graciously consented and agreed, for the greater and more steadfast preservation of this aforementioned collective peace, that his Majesty should reschedule all judicial cases in matters concerning the faith that may have been or may yet be initiated through his Majesty's *fiscal*[58] and other judicial personnel against the elector of Saxony and his associates until the forthcoming council, or, if the council is not held, whatever other approaches for these cases might be considered by the estates, just as the imperial Majesty guaranteed in the gracious authorisation letter drawn up on this topic, and should graciously wish to hand over to us.

In turn, and for their part, our aforementioned relatives and cousins, Saxony, Lüneburg and their well-beloved associates, should and want to uphold this collective peace firmly and steadfastly; not to do anything or act against it in any way; and also to demonstrate humble and obligatory obedience to the imperial Majesty; and humbly to put into effect and send their appropriate military assistance for resisting the Turks, as endorsed and decided by the estates collectively,[59] all according to what they have vouchsafed and recounted in the reply that they handed over to us in writing.

And since in their same answer our said cousins and relatives complained about certain words and articles in the latest mandate

---

57 These were standard stipulations for a *Landfrieden* since 1495 [21] and even earlier. Charles V duly promulgated this section of the Nuremberg recess as a peace-ordinance on 3 August 1532 (ibid., vol. X, no. 559).
58 A prosecutor, here presumably at the emperor's aulic council (*Hofrat*).
59 In the recess of the parallel imperial diet in Regensburg, formally issued on 27 July (ibid., vol. X, no. 303).

of the imperial Majesty,[60] and therefore amicably and humbly requested of us that we should bring their complaint to the imperial Majesty through an envoy and seek to do the utmost to attain a gracious amendment therein, so we have agreed with our said relatives and cousins and their own relations, as an amicable and gracious favour, that we are willing to prepare an envoy to go to the imperial Majesty as quickly as possible and lay their complaint before the imperial Majesty, and to employ every effort to attain an amendment from his Majesty, and likewise to persevere and solicit that the specified guarantee, of which we are sending a copy to his Majesty,[61] should be finalised as soon as possible and personally delivered to us. And whatever answer reaches us from the imperial Majesty regarding this, we should and want to share that and make it known to our relative and cousin the elector of Saxony as quickly as possible, and whatever else his Majesty might approve and permit should come into and remain in effect as if every word were contained in this recess. However, in the event that the imperial Majesty does not want to permit or amend anything more, this agreement should nevertheless come into and remain in force and its content be carried out and followed, without hesitation, judicial challenge or deceit.

[The mediators grant the request of the envoys of the landgrave of Hessen for additional time to obtain their prince's approval for the terms of the agreement.][62]

To authenticate this, we, both of the electors mentioned above, have appended our seals to this document. And we [the parties listed in the opening paragraph, in person or via their envoys] attest that the aforementioned recess was drawn up and negotiated with

---

60 The emperor's proposed terms for the peace, drafted on 18 July (ibid., vol. X, no. 534), contained the stipulation reproduced in the paragraph immediately preceding this one about judicial cases against the evangelicals pausing until 'other approaches' could be 'be considered by the estates'. The 'protesting' party objected to this, as they feared that the religious question would simply be re-opened at the next imperial diet, and that the majority among the estates would then override the protections won in this peace agreement. See ibid., vol. X, pp. 1514–15, notes 7–10.
61 A version of the guarantee regarding anti-evangelical judicial cases that matched the 'protesting' party's preferences had just been sent to Charles V (ibid., vol. X, no. 550).
62 Landgrave Philipp duly gave his assent in writing on 13 August (ibid., vol. X, no. 561).

our sound knowledge and consent, and that we have knowingly accepted it for ourselves and our lordships and officials. We therefore vow and promise for ourselves and our lordships and officials to follow and comply with it, and not to act against it in any way. [Duke Johann Friedrich of Saxony appends his seal on behalf of the princes and counts, and the envoy from Nuremberg appends his city's seal on behalf of the free and imperial cities. The document is dated 24 July 1532.]

30. The imperial recess from an imperial diet in Augsburg (the 'Peace of Augsburg') (1555)

Kluckhohn et al. (eds), *Deutsche Reichstagsakten. Jüngere Reihe*, vol. XX, pp. 3103–58.

We Ferdinand, by the grace of God king of the Romans, ever augmenter etc., publicly proclaim and make known to all:

His Roman imperial Majesty [Charles V], our well-beloved brother and lord, issued a summons for, scheduled and planned a collective imperial diet as part of the negotiations and treaty previously worked out at Passau through our dear imperial Majesty's and our gracious intercession, and in view and consideration of his dear imperial Majesty's responsibility-giving and binding office. It was to be held on 16 August of the past year 1553 at the latest in his dear imperial Majesty's, our and the Holy Empire's city of Ulm, and he was of the firm intention to attend this scheduled imperial diet personally and deliberately, and to see it proceed, with God's help. He did this for extremely urgent, compelling reasons, above all because of his Majesty's determination that the Holy Empire's statutes, ordinances and recesses, alongside the labours, efforts and work expended collectively, graciously, faithfully and earnestly by his dear imperial Majesty, by us and by the Empire's estates and members, have not hitherto attained the desired fruitfulness and effectiveness that the current urgent necessities truly require, and also because much conflict and disorder has arisen in the Holy Empire, and – as far as justice is concerned – ordinances, statutes, old customs and traditions have encountered and been intruded upon by hindrances and all kinds of errors, abuses, deficiencies and transgressions.

[1] But because of the occurrence and eruption of hindrances and military conflicts that then arose dangerously in the Holy Empire of the German nation, it was not only burdensome but impossible for the aforenamed dear imperial Majesty, in view of the situation and circumstances, to adhere to the scheduled time and to attend the convoked imperial diet in accordance with the same. And yet, his Majesty not only deemed it a completely unavoidable necessity to have this scheduled imperial diet proceed by all means, but also fundamentally determined and recognised and deemed, in the final analysis, that it will not be possible to counteract the grievances

that concern us collectively or to promote and uphold the collective peace, tranquillity and wellbeing of the Holy Empire without such a collective assembly.

[2: Charles extended the date of the imperial diet, initially to 1 October 1553 in Augsburg, in view of ongoing warfare in the Low Countries and other obstacles.

3: Despite Charles's determination to attend and relieve the Empire of its problems, the scale of the challenges he confronted and the distance from Augsburg prevented his attendance.

4: To ensure the vital assembly went ahead for the sake of the Empire, Charles asked his brother Ferdinand to attend in his stead, and gave him absolute power to negotiate there with the estates.

5: Ferdinand loyally accepted this charge, 'so as to avert as far as possible the worrying disintegration before us'.

6: The imperial diet was extended again, to 11 November 1554. Preoccupied by affairs in his hereditary lands, Ferdinand arrived in Augsburg on 29 December 1554.]

[7] And as the appointed councillors of the electors and some princes and estates of the Holy Empire – some in person and some through envoys with full authority – faithfully appeared alongside us, and we got to know with them which points were of the greatest importance, and the shape of the discussions to be undertaken first and foremost, it immediately became clear that, as at some of the imperial diets held previously, the question of the religious division – which has for some time now produced all kinds of damage, misfortune and acrimony in the Empire of the German nation – once again stood out, unresolved, as the most urgent, prominent and important among the other burdensome afflictions of the Holy Empire, being of the highest import to all the estates and subjects.

[8] Thus, in response to our opening speech and agenda that was graciously proposed to them, the electors' councillors, the princes and estates who had appeared and the others' envoys and representatives considered it a good thing to take in hand and negotiate this very important question first and foremost.

[9: However, it soon became apparent that the deep divisions over religious questions could not be resolved quickly, and that a better-functioning public peace needed to be established first.

10: The estates therefore agreed to delay the discussion about religion until a later time.

11: The discussion then turned to the successful regulation and implementation of the public peace.]

[12] Although the public peace has been addressed, considered and improved then collectively set up at previous imperial diets, in the hope that a peaceful condition might thereby be preserved in the Holy Empire, experience has shown that the same established public peace and the ordinances for its administration have been insufficient to prevent disorder and conflict. And problems and hindrances have especially arisen on account of the assistance clause, whereby adjacent and neighbouring authorities are supposed to help attacked parties. We therefore entreated and exhorted them – the estates and envoys – to properly consider certain deficiencies of the public peace, given the issues that have been encountered and are still evident, and to think of ways of attaining a more certain and steadfast administration and preservation of the collective peace, and whether this improvement of the legislation promulgated about this so far can be delivered by addressing the said deficiencies or in other effective ways, so that disorderly people might be repelled from disturbing the collective peace, and so that obedient people might find solace in the knowledge that if someone tries to attack them violently, guaranteed assistance and rescue will be extended to them.

[13] During the aforementioned deliberations about the peace, the electors' councillors, the princes and estates who had appeared and the others' envoys and representatives immediately conveyed the following, based on their experience and what had already happened:

While myriad negotiations and deliberations have taken place for thirty or more years' worth of imperial diets (and many more regional or sectional assemblies) regarding the establishment of a collective, lasting peace addressing the religious divisions between the Holy Empire's estates, and a few truces have been established, none of this has ever been sufficient to preserve the peace. Rather, in spite of this, the estates of the Empire have increasingly remained in a state of hatred and distrust of one another, causing significant damage. Thus, if – in the face of lasting religious division – an all-encompassing debate and negotiation of peace in both religious and profane and temporal matters is not undertaken within the public peace framework and not fully worked out and agreed in these articles on the matter, such that both religions are henceforth informed about what to finally expect in their mutual interactions, the estates and subjects will not be able to find comfort in lasting, certain security, but all of them will increasingly be stuck in the uncertainty of unbearable danger.

To eliminate this deep uncertainty, restore the estates' and subjects' spirits to a state of calm and trust vis-à-vis one another once again and protect the German nation, our beloved fatherland, from final breakup and collapse, we have agreed and resolved the following with the electors' councillors and appointees, the princes and estates who appeared and the absentees' envoys and representatives, and they with us:

[14] We accordingly establish, ordain, will and mandate that [the standard order to desist from feuding and abetting peace-breakers and to use the correct courts follows, per article 1 of [21]]. Rather, in all things we – his imperial Majesty and we ourselves and all the estates, and, reciprocally, the estates, his imperial Majesty and we ourselves – should be covered by all the content of this ensuing ordinance that establishes the public peace in religious and collective matters.

[15] And so that this peace may also be all the more durably set up, established and preserved among his Roman imperial Majesty, we ourselves and the electors, princes and estates of the Holy Empire of the German nation with regard to the religious division (which constitutes the greatest necessity facing the Holy Empire of the German nation, for the reasons mentioned and cited above), his imperial Majesty, we ourselves and the electors, princes and estates of the Holy Empire should not: actively and violently invade, damage or assault any estate of the Empire on account of the Augsburg Confession[63] and the doctrine, religion and faith of the same; nor oppress them in other ways against their conscience, principles and will on account of religion, faith and ecclesiastical customs, ordinances and ceremonies relating to this Augsburg Confession that they have established, or may subsequently wish

---

63 The confession of Lutheran faith submitted at the imperial diet of Augsburg in 1530, used synonymously with 'Lutherans' and 'Lutheranism' thereafter.

to establish, in their principalities, lands and lordships; nor burden them or hold them in contempt through mandates or in any other way.

Rather, they should allow them to remain in their religion, faith and ecclesiastical customs, ordinances and ceremonies, as well as their property and assets (fixed and movable), lands, peoples, lordships, authorities, seigneurial rights and jurisdictions in tranquillity and peace. And the religious controversies should only be brought to unanimous, Christian concord and agreement by Christian, amicable, peaceful ways and means, all per his imperial and our royal dignity, princely honour and true words, and on pain of the penalties of the public peace.

[16: The 'estates adhering to the Augsburg Confession' should likewise refrain from harming 'the estates adhering to the old religion' and leave them in peace to follow their own beliefs and traditions.]

[17] However, all others who do not adhere to the two aforementioned religions are not intended to be included in this peace, but are entirely excluded.

[18] And while this peace was being agreed, disputes arose over the issue of how, where one or more clerics has left the old religion, to proceed with the archbishoprics, bishoprics, prelacies and benefices that they had occupied and possessed until then – an issue which the estates of both religions have not been able to settle.

We have therefore declared and established the following, by the plenipotentiary power and discretion that his highly esteemed Roman imperial Majesty has granted us – and we hereby do it knowingly: where an archbishop, bishop, prelate or other member of the spiritual estate leaves the old religion, the same should immediately relinquish his archbishopric, bishopric, prelacy or other benefices, alongside all the incomes and revenues he received from them, without any refusal or delay, but also without prejudice to his honour. It should also be permitted to the chapters, and those to whom this pertains under the *ius commune* or the church's and foundation's customs, to elect and appoint a person who adheres to the old religion. To them, together with the clerical chapters and other churches, should be permitted unhindered and peaceful access to foundations, elections, presentations, confirmations, old traditions, jurisdictions and properties (fixed and movable) belonging to the churches and ecclesiastical institutions. However, this should not affect any future Christian, amicable and final accommodation between the religions.

[19: Some ecclesiastical properties having already been confiscated, only those held by Lutherans before the 1552 Passau Treaty and by 'those who are immediately subject to the Empire and members of the imperial estates' are covered by this peace.

20: Spiritual jurisdiction over adherents of the Augsburg Confession should not be exercised until a final resolution of religious questions, without prejudice to prelates' other rights, incomes and jurisdictions.

21: Adherents of the old religion should still receive their rents, tithes and other revenues, and these should still fund any ministries for which they were founded, but (where applicable) these properties should remain under the same temporal authorities that controlled them when the religious divisions began.

22: Disputes over the apportionment of tithes to ministries should be resolved by arbitration.]

[23] Also, no estate should coerce any other or their subjects into adopting the coercer's religion or abandoning their former one, nor take them under their lordship and protection against their previous authorities, nor defend them in any way. Those who accepted people under their lordship and protection a long time ago should not be affected by – and are not the focus of – this.

[24] However, if our and the electors', princes' and estates' subjects who adhere to the old religion or the Augsburg Confession should seek to move out of our and the Holy Empire's electors', princes' and estates' lands, principalities, towns or districts with their wives and children to other places and settle there, such departure and arrival, sale of property and goods, redemption from serfdom for an appropriate, just fee and taxation owed to a lord when leaving (per a given place's age-old and conventional traditions and requirements) should be permitted and granted to all without hindrance, fully without prejudice to their honour and obligations. However, this should not damage or take away from the authorities' jurisdictions and traditions with regard to the right to declare a serf free or not to do so.

[25] And since an accommodation concerning the religions and the matters of the faith should be sought through appropriate and just means, and yet a Christian, amicable accommodation in religious matters will surely not be attainable without lasting peace, so – out of a love of peace and for the sake of this peace agreement, the elimination of highly damaging distrust in the Empire and the protection of this praiseworthy nation against final, imminent collapse, and so that we may more quickly reach a Christian, amicable and final accommodation in the religious division – we and the electors' councillors (in place of the electors), the princes and estates who appeared and the absentees' envoys and representatives (spiritual and temporal) have consented to upholding and faithfully carrying out this peace continuously, firmly and inviolably, in all its articles written above, until a Christian, amicable and final accommodation of the religions and matters of the faith.

If such an accommodation does not come about by means of a general council, national assembly, colloquia or imperial diets, this peace agreement should then nevertheless persist and remain valid and in force in all of the points and articles set out above until a final accommodation of the religions and matters of the faith. And with this, in the form set out above and in every other respect, a lasting, durable, unconditional peace, lasting onwards into eternity, should be established and resolved and persist.

[26: The peace agreement should include the free knights subject to the Empire.

27: Where free and imperial cities contain communities belonging to both religions, they should continue to co-exist peacefully.

28: No other imperial recesses or ordinances should contradict this peace agreement, and those sections that do are null and void.

29–30: Charles, Ferdinand and the estates commit to upholding the peace and doing nothing against it, for themselves and their successors.

31: All signatories repeat the promises not to attack one another from article 14, and will provide assistance to attacked parties.]

[32] We also hereby order and mandate by the power of this, our imperial recess, that the imperial cameral judge and assessors should legally uphold and implement this peace agreement.

Also, they should impart lawful and necessary judicial assistance to appellants in light of this peace agreement, regardless of which of the aforementioned religions they adhere to, and they should not adjudicate any case or issue any judicial mandate in a way that violates any aspect of it, nor do anything or act against it in any other way.

[33–44: The better to preserve the peace, all estates should proceed together militarily and judicially against disorderly soldiers, mercenaries and other gatherings of troublemakers in their lands.

45–48: In view of rising discontent among their subjects, the estates should strive to quell disorder by providing swift and effective justice. If subjects band together and commit acts of violence, they should be named, located and punished, and not permitted to seek refuge in other jurisdictions.

49–55: Only battalions of soldiers with a legitimate lord and mission should be tolerated in the Empire's lands. The others should be forcibly disbanded, with the help of the imperial circles and other estates if necessary. The estates should avoid employing them, and may recoup damages from them.

56–103: Commanders, deputies and members of the imperial circles should act with restraint and limit themselves to lawful missions on behalf of the Empire. Other imperial circles and estates and members should assist one another against peace-breakers, in expanding degrees of proximity to the danger. The personnel of the circles should follow prescribed processes for a range of scenarios (including selection and replacement of personnel, provision of troops, supplies and funds, joint military action, negotiation with enemies, execution of imperial and cameral court judgements and exemptions from obligations towards the circles under the public peace legislation).

104–14: The estates need to take up the improvements to the cameral court recommended in the Passau treaty. They suggest further emendations, to be enforced if necessary through visitations by an established rotation of estates. Court personnel should be appointed from both religions. Different oath rituals are to be permitted for the swearing in of old religion and Augsburg Confession personnel. Emendations to the court's procedures, such as the execution of penalties against peace-breakers, should be printed in full. A final decision on how to fund the cameral court has proved impossible to reach, and should be discussed at the next imperial diet.

115–34: Several estates have requested a hearing about reducing their customary obligations to provide troops and funds to collective imperial initiatives. They are not satisfied with how these discussions played out at recent diets. In the first instance, such reduction requests should happen through appointees within the assemblies of the imperial circles. A group of moderators will then hear these requests at a designated assembly in Worms. Their decisions may be appealed to the cameral court.

135–36: The estates amend the 1548 ordinance for social discipline[64] to include clauses regulating the sale of woollen textiles.

137–38: Previous ordinances regulating coinage quality, issued at imperial diets and special assemblies convened to address coinage, are not being respected. The estates have issued an interim mandate on the matter and call for further discussion of coinage at future diets.]

[139] The initiation, deliberation and mandating of appropriate and lawful ways of seeking and, by God's grace, attaining and accomplishing the necessary and salvific accommodation and unity over the religious divisions and matters of the faith were supposed to take place at this imperial diet. However, for many reasons, some of which are mentioned above, this proved impossible at present.

[140] The electors' councillors, the princes and estates who appeared and the absentees' envoys and representatives have therefore agreed and resolved with us, and we with them, to defer the resolution of this article to future imperial assemblies, with the specific condition that, for the sake of setting aside the damaging schism and division in our holy Christian religion and matters of the faith, his Roman imperial Majesty, our well-beloved brother and lord, or – if his dear imperial Majesty should be prevented from doing so – we ourselves, in person, on behalf of his dear imperial

---

64 *polliceiordnung* – a genre of legislation which sought to regulate social disorder through prohibitions on a range of behaviours, such as blasphemy and excessive luxury. Such regulations had long been included in more general imperial and princely legislation (see [54][56]) before the genre of the *Polizeiordnung* crystallised in the sixteenth century.

Majesty, should attend and remain at this imperial diet. Likewise, the electors and princes should also appear in person, and – with exceptions for evident physical frailty and incapacity and other lawful causes – should not absent themselves. Additionally, and in the meantime, everyone should ready and prepare themselves with their educated theologians, so that it will not only be possible to deliberate about the ways and means of seeking the accommodation, but also to then negotiate and reach decisions about the key points of contention efficaciously and fruitfully, though only as is permitted by the content of the Passau treaty.

[141: This subsequent imperial diet is scheduled for 1 March 1556 in Regensburg.]

[142] The rights and order whereby the estates enjoyed a seat and a voice at the imperial diets, and the order in which their names are listed at the end of this recess, should not be prejudicial to, cause any damage to or have any effect on each of their traditional customs and jurisdictions.

[143] We vow and promise to inviolably and sincerely uphold and carry out all and every one of the points written above that touches upon his imperial Majesty, our well-beloved brother and lord, and us ourselves, and to follow and live up to them rapidly and unerringly, without any deceit.

To document this, we have appended our royal seal to this recess.

[144] And we, the appointed electors' councillors, princes, prelates, counts and lords who appeared in person and also the absent princes', prelates', counts', lords' and Holy Empire's free and imperial cities' envoys, representatives and empowered deputies, named hereafter, also proclaim publicly with this recess that all and every one of the points and articles written above has, as stated before, been undertaken and resolved with our good consent, knowledge and counsel. We also hereby endorse all of the same, collectively and individually, by the power of this document, and vow and promise in good, true faith to truly, continuously, firmly, inviolably and sincerely uphold them and carry them out, insofar as they do or may touch upon each of the lordships or associates on whose behalf we have been sent or empowered, and to follow and live up to them to the maximum extent of our capacities, without deceit.

And we, the electors' councillors, the princes, prelates, counts and lords and the absent estates', as well as the Holy Empire's free and imperial cities', envoys and empowered deputies, are listed hereafter:

[A complete list of attendees, grouped by estate – electors, house of Austria, spiritual princes, temporal princes, prelates, abbesses, counts and lords, free and imperial cities – follows.]

To document this, we, Marquard of Stein, dean of the cathedrals of Mainz, Bamberg and Augsburg, Eberhard of Grawenratt, official of Oppenheim, appointees and councillors of the electors of Mainz and the Palatinate at this imperial diet, on behalf of our gracious lords and the other electors, Michael, archbishop of Salzburg, legate of the See of Rome [r. 1554–60] and Albrecht [V], Count Palatine of the Rhine and duke of Upper and Lower Bavaria [r. 1550–79], on behalf of ourselves and the spiritual and temporal princes, Christoph of Hausen, doctor, on behalf of the prelates, Peter Endriß Guett on behalf of the counts and lords and we, the mayor and council of Augsburg on behalf of the free and imperial cities, have appended our seals to this recess.

Given in our – King Ferdinand's – and the Holy Empire's city of Augsburg, on the twenty-fifth day of the month of September, in the 1555th year after the birth of Christ, our beloved lord, and in the twenty-fifth year of our Roman reign and the twenty-ninth year of our other reigns.

IV

IMAGINING POLITICAL AND RELIGIOUS REFORM

As in other regions of late medieval Europe, political actors and educated commentators in the German lands of the Holy Roman Empire wrote the kinds of sophisticated works focused on 'public' and social affairs that have been identified as a hallmark of this era.[1] Indeed, so numerous were the treatises, letters and exhortations addressing the problems facing the Romano-German polity that historians have coined the term 'imperial reform' (*Reichsreform*) to characterise projects for restoring or improving the Empire and 'reformist writings' (*Reformschriften*) for the genre of texts on this theme.[2] In the Empire, political reform was necessarily interlinked with ecclesiastical reform. Many leading princes were simultaneously high-ranking prelates (including three of the seven electors). The residual sense that the Holy Roman Empire had a universal mission to defend Christendom oriented its monarchs' and princes' gaze towards Rome and the papacy – which, for its part, maintained a close interest in the Empire, even if popes no longer interfered as frequently and directly as in the age of the Salians and Staufer. Most significantly of all, the German lands played host to two deeply consequential general councils in the fifteenth century, Constance (1414–18) and Basel (1431–49). Prominent members of these councils embraced radical ecclesiological theories and calls for root-and-branch ecclesiastical reforms, and they overlapped with political assemblies within the Empire. Indeed, the German princes were drawn into the schism between the conciliarists of Basel and Pope Eugenius IV in the years around 1440.[3] It is not surprising, therefore, that much fifteenth-century material adjacent to the councils calls for a simultaneous reformation (Latin: *reformatio*; German: *Reformation*) of spiritual and temporal affairs.

---

1 Watts, *Polities*, p. 392.
2 The most recent and comprehensive overview that endorses the concept of 'imperial reform' remains Angermeier, *Die Reichsreform*.
3 Stieber, *Pope Eugenius*.

Some historians have found it tempting to extrapolate from these late medieval developments into early modernity, with the rise of the movements we now call 'Protestantism' and their social and political implications, and to characterise the fifteenth and sixteenth centuries collectively as an 'Age of Reformations'.[4] Others see such verdicts as excessively sweeping: they run the risk of simplifying and conflating very diverse authors and contexts for the sake of a facile narrative of omnipresent 'reform', a freighted concept that historians have not always defined very clearly.[5] In particular, *Reichsreform* – the notion, in its nineteenth- and twentieth-century formulation, of a coherent set of theories and institutional changes to make the Empire more centralised and state-like – has come under fire for its anachronism and teleology.[6] By no means all advocates of supposed 'imperial reform' used the noun *reformatio/Reformation* and the verb *reformare/reformieren* (indeed, these terms were rare, and reserved for discussions of the simultaneous reform of the Church, or else more specific changes to coinage and/or judicial courts, e.g. [17]). Perhaps the only convincing commonality that links the disparate sources labelled *Reformschriften* is a shared language of 'peace' and 'justice'. While these were commonplaces in political discourse throughout medieval and early modern Christian Europe, they had, as Gabriele Annas has aptly put it, 'a highly distinct and explosive political-judicial resonance' in the context of debates about governance in the Holy Roman Empire.[7] This is clear from the prologues to the ordinances issued at imperial diets (see sections II and III) and to regional alliance and association treaties (see section V), which frequently bemoan the absence of order in the German lands and the need for a restoration of peace and justice. Apparently similar themes appear in more theoretical and aspirational texts, whether they were penned by central political protagonists or marginal observers and critics of events. This section contains a selection of such texts, enabling readers to interpret for themselves the extent to which they may have shared a common agenda, or at least a common set of rhetorical tropes and discursive motifs.

4 Brady, *German Histories*.
5 See the historiographical survey in Hardy, 'Reform and Reformation'.
6 Hardy, 'The Fall of Constantinople', surveys this historiographical critique with further references.
7 Annas, 'Zum Begriff der "Gerechtigkeit"', p. 247.

For a range of authors writing against the backdrop of the late medieval schisms and councils and their aftermath, questions of governance in the Holy Roman Empire seemed to be bound up with the problems besetting the Roman Church. In itself, this relationship was far from new. In the exceptionally fraught relations between the popes and councils of the thirteenth century and the kings, emperors and princes of the Empire, a simultaneous reform or restructuring of both had been a frequent point of discussion.[8] But the early fifteenth century saw a substantial increase in the volume and vehemence of writing on this topic. And whereas earlier visions of simultaneous reform had been formulated with a view to the Empire's complicated claims in Italy and Provence, fifteenth-century writings were much more focused on the re-ordering of an explicitly German political community within the Empire in tandem with a reformation of the Church. The chancery of Sigismund, who played a major role in convoking the councils of Constance and Basel, was one of the main propagators of this putative dual mission. Already in 1417, in his summons to an assembly to be held in parallel with the Council of Constance [31], Sigismund could claim that the urgent need for a two-pronged reformation of Church and Empire was widely known.

This dual mission was taken up in the most popular 'reform' tract of the fifteenth century, the *Reformation of Emperor Sigismund* (*Reformacion keyser Sigmunds*, sometimes known by the Latin name *Reformatio Sigismundi*) [32]. It was composed by an unknown author in 1439. He was clearly closely acquainted with developments at the Council of Basel, then at the height of its dispute with the papal supremacists around Pope Eugenius IV. Both his decision to write in the German vernacular and his frequent references to the imperial cities suggest that he was aiming to reach a broad audience. He was successful in this: the treatise survives in nineteen manuscripts with multiple variants. (This translation is based on the oldest version, 'N'.) Its already wide circulation expanded rapidly through the repeated publication of printed editions from the 1470s.[9] The tract bears some of the features of prophetic literature, since it ends with Sigismund having a vision of a figure called 'Friedrich' bringing the spiritual and temporal

---

8 Scales, *German Identity*, pp. 165–69.
9 Koller (ed.), *Reformation*, pp. 1–49.

reformations to fruition (a trope in 'Last Emperor' prophecies).[10] At the same time, the *Reformation* contains numerous concrete proposals, some more radical than others. Those pertaining to temporal governance in the Empire are translated here, but they should be understood as inextricably linked to the extensive spiritual reforms contained in the same text, including the dispossession of ecclesiastical institutions' temporalities, an argument for clerical marriage and vituperative polemic against the religious orders. Strikingly, some manuscripts and print editions place the *Reformation* alongside the Golden Bull [14] and 'Royal Reformation' [17], apparently treating it as a real ordinance that ought to have legal force and taking the author's claim that it was penned by Sigismund literally.

If the *Reformation* struck a chord with contemporaries, it is perhaps because leading protagonists were addressing similar issues in their own political agendas in the mid-fifteenth century, as expressed in more pragmatic documents. This is clear from a 'strategic paper'[11] drawn up in 1452[12] on behalf of Jakob of Sierck, archbishop of Trier (r. 1439–56) [33], in a meeting between his councillors and those of the two other spiritual electors. Its emphasis on the need for institutional change to restore order in the Empire presages the issues negotiated at the diets of the latter half of the fifteenth century. Equally, the focus on the need for further ecclesiastical reform at future councils both harks back to the Constance/Basel era and prefigures the mounting grievances of the German estates against the Curia in the decades around 1500.

By the end of the fifteenth century, the institutional changes promulgated at successive diets had changed the circumstances in which reformists found themselves and allayed some concerns about the practicalities of enforcing peace and justice, but these themes retained their potency as a focus of critique. One well-informed commentator from Alsace, who seems to have attended some diets in the 1490s, wrote a trenchant and increasingly jaded and apocalyptic call for the renewal of the Church and Empire in a work written and amended over a twenty-year period (*c.* 1490–1510) and called *The Little Book of One Hundred Chapters with Forty Statues* [34]. The work is indeed organised into over one hundred

---

10 Kneupper, *Empire at the End of Time*, p. 164.
11 The apt descriptor used by Daniels, *Diplomatie*, p. 225.
12 Ibid., p. 222, note 1238.

sections, and the final 'statute', which summarises most of its key themes, is translated here. The author, dubbed the 'Upper Rhine Revolutionary' by later scholars, deliberately maintains his anonymity in the text, and his identity has been a matter of lively debate.[13] Like the *Reformation of Emperor Sigismund*, the *Little Book* mixes prophetic visions and admonitions with specific 'policy' proposals for immediate implementation, all grounded in idiosyncratic scriptural interpretations, chauvinistic histories and citations from canon, civil and customary law, suggesting that these were not necessarily understood as separate genres or phenomena for contemporaries. (For ease of legibility, the in-text references that punctuate the original source have been left out of the translation.) Unlike the *Reformation*, however, this text seems not to have found an audience – it survives in only one manuscript. It is best understood as an example of what an eccentric yet university-educated and politically engaged commentator could envision at the turn of the sixteenth century.

The nature of the relationship between fifteenth-century currents of political and religious reform in the Holy Roman Empire and 'the Reformation' spearheaded by Martin Luther and others remains one of the most intriguing historical questions about this era.[14] The view that probably commands the most scholarly support, at least implicitly, is that ongoing concerns about the need for reformation in the Church and the Empire provided fertile ground for evangelical theologians to spread their message that current ecclesiastical practices had departed dramatically from the teachings of the Bible. In particular, Luther's decision to appeal – in German – to the temporal elites in the 1520 tract *To the Christian Nobility of the German Nation* [35] is seen as an attempt to harness late medieval reformist grievances to his mission after he lost faith in the ability of fellow clerics (and especially the papacy and its agents) to reform themselves.[15] If so, the fifteenth-century themes only partially resonated with Luther's preoccupations. Longstanding concerns about the Empire's weakened monarchy and political institutions receive little attention in his tract. (The sections most related to these are translated here; most of *To the Christian Nobility* focuses on

---

13 Lauterbach (ed.), *Das buchli der hundert capiteln mit xxxx statuten*, pp. 13–19.
14 See Scott, 'The Early Reformation'.
15 Whaley, *Germany*, pp. 169–70.

the trickery and corruption of the papacy, and how it might be overcome by temporal rulers or a general council.) Furthermore, Luther evinces a deep ambivalence about pan-imperial laws and the Roman identity of the imperial polity, putting him at odds with the prophetic traditions that foresaw a universal, apocalyptic role for the Holy Roman Empire. This ambivalence may help to explain why the long tradition of compiling 'grievances [*gravamina/Beschwerden*] of the German nation' – rooted in the conciliar era, continued at regional synods thereafter and expanded at the imperial diets around 1500 – saw its final efflorescence in the 1520s. The most influential grievance list was presented at Worms in 1521 and subsequently printed.[16] Five years later, growing religious dissensions among the princes and cities and the trauma of the Peasants' War made for more divergent and tension-ridden grievances deliberated and submitted by different groups of estates at an imperial diet in Speyer [36]. After the decisive split within the estates in 1529 [28], a shared agenda for the grievances (which largely addressed spiritual matters) became impossible, even if common ground remained in temporal affairs.

---

16 Translated in Strauss (ed./trans.), *Manifestations of Discontent*, pp. 52–63.

31. King Sigismund calls for the reformation of the Church and Empire in a summons to an assembly (1417)

Weizsäcker et al. (eds), *Deutsche Reichstagsakten. Ältere Reihe*, vol. VII, pp. 321–22.

We Sigismund, by the grace of God king of the Romans, ever augmenter of the Empire, and king of Hungary, Dalmatia, Croatia etc., impart our grace and all good wishes to the honourable mayor and council of the city of Frankfurt, our and the Empire's well-beloved faithful people.[17]

Honourable, well-beloved faithful people. How greatly the Holy Church and the whole of Christendom have suffered from the deplorable schism, which has now lasted into its fortieth year;[18] how much disarray and distress has arisen and come about among the spiritual and temporal estates of the Holy Roman Empire and other kingdoms, principalities, lands and peoples; how we have also, after considerable expense and effort, brought the holy council to Constance,[19] through which, with God's help, we hope that a complete and pure unification in the Holy Church and, otherwise, a good, righteous and necessary reformation of the spiritual head and its members should be carried out;[20] and also what troublesome events, strife and injustice are taking place in the Holy Roman Empire, and how necessary it is to improve them and bring them into good order – all this is so evident and ubiquitously and generally known that it would be superfluous to write about it.

By God's grace, the aforenamed council has now been secured and brought into effect, so that we fully hope that the aforenamed unification and reformation will thereby soon gain momentum, with God's help, and a unanimous head of Christendom should be

---

17 While this is Frankfurt's version of this summons, the same letter was sent to many recipients in the Empire, as the final sentence of the third paragraph indicates.
18 The schism between the Roman and Avignonese lines of popes began in 1378 with the rival elections of Urban VI (r. 1378–89) and Clement VII (r. 1378–94).
19 Sigismund played a major role in orchestrating the Council of Constance (1414–18), which affirmed the superior authority of councils over popes, tried and executed Jan Hus and would end the schism by electing a unanimous candidate, Martin V, in November 1417.
20 *widerbrengung des geistlichen houptz und siner gelider* – a vernacular translation of the longstanding ecclesiastical slogan *reformatio in capite et in membris*.

elected. And we have taken on responsibility for the Holy Roman Empire, so that we would all the more gladly see its reformation, benefit and honour, and want to seek and encourage these with all our strength, with God's help. And so we are also completely willing to strive faithfully and earnestly, with your counsel and assistance and that of our and the Empire's other faithful people, to quell the aforenamed troublesome events, strife and injustice, of which there is sadly much in the Empire at the moment, and to bring about peace and justice. And – to that end – we intend to hold a collective council with all of the Empire's electors, princes, nobles, faithful people, cities and subjects, and to handle the Empire's matters and necessities with their assistance, just as the aforenamed Council of Constance is now being held to address spiritual matters. And we have written to all of you regarding this.

And since you belong to the Holy Empire and ought justly to counsel and assist in the matters written about above, and furthermore are eminently appointed for the pursuit of the love and honour of Christendom, the Empire, the common good and the German lands, for which purpose the aforenamed council exists – so we diligently request of you, and earnestly and firmly order you by our Roman royal authority with this letter, not to neglect this, but to send your envoys with full authority to us at our royal court in Constance at the upcoming Easter festival [11 April 1417], in order to counsel and assist in the matters set out above alongside other aforenamed faithful people of the Empire, and to contribute to such praiseworthy and necessary affairs and decision-making, as is your duty, as we have complete faith that you will do. You will thereby be doing an agreeable service and favour for the Church and the honour of Christendom, and especially for us and the Empire.

And if any of you or your people, individually or collectively, have any kinds of problems in spiritual or temporal matters, these should be sent in writing with your aforenamed envoys to the aforenamed *concilium* and council in Constance, so that they may address them as best they can.

32. The Reformation of Emperor Sigismund (1439)

Koller (ed.), *Reformation Kaiser Siegmunds*, pp. 50–58, 88–90, 240–42, 276–78, 294–300, 308–12, 330.

The earliest versions of this much-circulated text are divided into three main sections, all interspersed with eschatological revelations and repurposed popular stories and political and religious metaphors. The prologue consists of an ostensibly divine appeal to the lowly people of Christendom to take up reform, in view of the failures of its heads (the popes and emperors), the inability of the Council of Basel to implement its reform proposals and the general descent of Christian society into selfishness and vice. The second and by far the longest section lists proposals for the reform of the clergy and spiritual sphere, addressing such issues as the reining in of the greed and political ambitions of the papacy and Curia, the transformation of religious and monastic orders, the just allocation of benefices, the proper fulfilment of episcopal duties and the abolition of clerical celibacy. The third and final section contains miscellaneous proposals with a vague connection to temporal government, including prescriptions for the education of an emperor, legal and judicial reforms and what we would now call economic policies, such as price controls and regulations for guilds and industries. This translation includes most of the prologue and excerpts from key passages containing the anonymous author's prescriptions for reforming the temporal sphere within the Empire.

The reformation of Emperor Sigismund etc.

Almighty God, creator of heaven and earth, give strength and bestow grace, give wisdom that we might understand and bring to fruition the most blessed conditions and have an ordering of the spiritual and temporal estates, in which your holy name and divinity may be proclaimed. For your wrath is manifest, your displeasure overcomes us. We behave like sheep without shepherds. We stray in the pasture without permission.

Obedience is dead,

justice is afflicted,

nothing is in good order.

Therefore God removes His grace from us, and justly so, for we have disregarded His commandments. We make little effort to follow what He has commanded, lacking all righteousness.

But we should know this: things will not go well any longer if there is not a just ordering of the spiritual and temporal estates, for they stand naked with their heads and limbs in disharmony.[21] All princes and lords, all knights and you worthy imperial cities are therefore collectively exhorted: the great heads [of Christendom, i.e. the pope and emperor] would alleviate the body if they had a just order, yet they are currently presiding with their authority over extreme injustice. And nobody should be exhorted more highly than the imperial cities.

We can clearly perceive this: an emperor or a king of the Empire cannot establish or maintain his position when so much has been taken from him by the electors and others that things have become very miserable indeed. Therefore you honourable imperial cities are exhorted – by God our Father, by Jesus Christ and by His rose-coloured blood that He shed for us, and be also exhorted by all Christian faith – that, together with all Christians, you contemplate our liberation: how we are made free in faith, and thus how we should conduct ourselves. Behold! All justice is in disequilibrium, and is daily subjected to transgressions and troubles.

Consider that from the beginning the imperial cities were established to support the Holy Church, protect the Empire, maintain justice for all and assist everybody collectively. All imperial cities are still bound by oaths and honour to fulfil these tasks today, where they perceive that somebody wants to oppose those things which are just, as is sadly occurring nowadays. Consider how things are now going: in the holy council [of Basel, 1431–49] we reformed that which ought to be reformed, spiritual and temporal, from the head to the lowest members. And yet when the heads see what we are trying to teach them about their injustices – namely that they should let go of that which is unjust – they turn their arses to us (if you will permit the expression) and do not seek a

---

21 *dye stend ploß on alle lidmaße* – this striking corporeal imagery draws on the common late medieval metaphor of estates, polities, the Church and the entire Christian community as 'bodies' – the 'body politic', *corpus Christianum* etc. – in need of 'reform in head and members'.

reformation,[22] and all the spiritual heads use their authority to derive income from simony, and avarice has totally free rein among the temporal and among the spiritual.

Therefore our lord the emperor, Sigismund, sought ways and means of forestalling these matters that are severely besetting Christendom, and assembled the Council of Constance, where a unification of the popes was effected. There he requested that a reformation be carried out. But the spiritual heads rejected this, and the emperor was disavowed at the Council of Pavia. Nothing came of it, and it was adjourned to Siena.[23] The empowered papal representatives, the cardinals, the universities and higher schools and those who should constitute a council were present there, and it was indeed ordained and decided per strict vows to accomplish the reformation in Basel, and there to implement and issue ordinances on these three points, which are the grave concerns of Holy Christendom:

The first point is to fend off heretical beliefs, such as are arising in those places that are failing to forestall them.

The second point: to bring about and establish peace.

The third: a just reformation of the spiritual and temporal estates.

And so matters at the council proceeded, and its decrees were issued. Behold! Who is obstructing this? Whence come the heads? Where are the electors? Where are the cardinals and archbishops? They flee![24] It seems to me that this concerns them, but they renounce it only too gladly. We cannot implement the reformation unless we ordain, under pain of violence and punishment, that it should endure. It has struck me that when Jesus was martyred, few stood by him in his great, just commands, and yet he triumphed. Thus, every just cause has only few supporters, but it still triumphs

---

22 While the author seems to be making a general point here, applicable to lay rulers as well as clergy, he is almost certainly referencing the immediate context of the breakdown of relations and mutual excommunications between the Council of Basel and Pope Eugenius IV in 1437–39.
23 In accordance with the 1417 conciliar decree *Frequens*, Pope Martin V convened a short-lived council in Pavia in 1423, which soon moved to Siena to escape a plague outbreak.
24 After the death of Sigismund in 1437 and during the dispute with Eugenius IV in 1437–39, a large number of prelates left the Council of Basel and many – though by no means all – princes and kings withdrew their support for it.

in the end. Perhaps the treasury of all righteousness is reserved for the lowly.

[...]

It should be known that everything written here in this book has been translated from Latin into German to make known what our lord the emperor, Sigismund, intended: a very brief outline of how to reform all things in the most effective way. And should a sufficiently wise person wish to improve a part of this according to their specific region's customs, this should gladly be permitted: this should be brought before a king or regent, and it should be for them to accept and uphold it. And considering that the great prelates do not want to allow themselves to be reformed, this ordinance must be enforced through the use of the sword. The weeds must be sought and rooted out of the garden.

[...]

The ordering of a temporal estate

Just as we have now set out very briefly how the spiritual estates should be reformed, likewise we should briefly set out how the temporal estates should be reformed and dealt with.

Our lord the emperor (or king, should he not be an emperor) should be established as the first in the order. And what should his role be in this order? Many spiritual and temporal lords know how our lord the emperor, Sigismund, complained about the electors: that they wrested castles and tolls from the Holy Empire, that the Empire has become weak. This has also been brought about because the kings have pawned things off and granted pernicious liberties, so that they no longer have any possessions in the Empire that would enable them to establish this order. At the emperor's exhortation, all temporal possessions that belong or formerly belonged to the Empire should be fairly compiled, wherever they are found, whether in the hands of the electors or elsewhere, so that they can be demanded and returned to the Empire, which we are legally bound to do.

What can a king now accomplish? He cannot end wars. People are not obedient, as they ought to be. All the imperial cities see that they do not have lords – that is how they perceive their situation. Thus, the Empire becomes ever sicker. Things have almost reached the point where people demand not to have any king. Without a head of the Empire, people take liberties that nobody should take. While the cat sleeps, the mice govern.

O, noble Empire! All imperial cities derive their dignity from your nobility. You worthy imperial cities, you proclaim your great honour and dignity, you think yourselves obedient. Likewise the princes and nobles, for the Empire rests on the nobility and the imperial cities, and not on either of them alone. Both are equally obligated to show obedience: the nobility through service, the imperial cities through taxes and revenues. But we can clearly see how things are actually going now; I will leave it at that.

[...]

Concerning penal authority and jurisdiction

Now, we should take note of all the law concerning penal authority and jurisdiction, as ordained by the emperors.[25] It should be known that the high-ranking princes who own much land still partially hold unto the emperors' law; but many counts, barons, knights and retainers, who are of noble status and who also possess penal authority and jurisdiction, are turning many people into property and treating them as bondspeople, extracting payments from them and, over and above those, levying extraordinary taxes on them, such that they have to pay very burdensome dues to use the woods and pastures.

It is an unheard-of outrage – a great, ongoing injustice which ought to be publicised to all of Christendom – that some are so spiritually impoverished before God that they speak thus to their fellow human, whom God has powerfully redeemed and freed: 'You are my property!' This is a heathen way of behaving. God has redeemed us from all bonds, and henceforth nobody should haughtily exalt themselves into any position of ownership over another. Our God

---

25 This primarily refers to the customary and feudal law in the *Swabian Mirror* [1], which was a major source of inspiration for the author. Koller (ed.), *Reformation*, p. 276, note 1.

Himself proves this to us: some of His disciples were of high birth, others were born into poverty, and some of them then exalted themselves in their hearts [Luke 22:24–26]; Christ perceived this clearly in their hearts, and spoke thus: 'Whoever among you exalts themselves should be the servant of all of you!' [Matthew 23:11–12] God wants to treat us all equally. Whoever is baptised and believes, they will be saved. In heaven, nobody has more freedom than anybody else. Therefore, everyone, whoever they are, should know that if they dare to say, 'You are my property!' to another, they are not a Christian. If someone does not refrain from doing this and instead give honour to God, they should be shunned as a heathen, for they are against Christ, and the commandments of God are lost on them.

[...]

Concerning judges

We should also know about courts and the pronouncement of judicial verdicts regarding property, inheritance and blood.[26] First, it should be known that a judge ordained unto and granted his office – whether he is a prince, a nobleman or a non-noble – should wield and hold in fief the rod of the emperor's authority. Nothing should be brought to or before the emperor's rod of authority except matters of justice, pure and simple. The judge should be a man of good reputation, a righteous Christian person in his works, and he should not be a usurer, nor an adulterer or speculator, nor somebody in a state of penance; if someone has had a penance imposed upon him, he should and may not justly wield or hold the judicial rod. Furthermore, if someone should have had a verdict handed down to them by such a judge, that verdict should be considered void, and the case should be sent back to another court. Likewise, the judicial findings of all co-judges[27] guilty of these things should be considered void, whether they concern property, inheritance or blood. They should not pronounce any verdicts.

---

26 That is, courts with jurisdiction over corporal and capital cases (*Blutgerichtsbarkeit*).
27 *urteylsprecher* – literally, 'pronouncers of judgements'. This was a common role in German customary and feudal law courts, involving advising a chief judge and sometimes passing verdicts by majority opinion (similar to assessors in Roman law and in the hybrid jurisprudence of the cameral court [22]).

If this does occur, and their verdicts are handed down, the plaintiff should be able to discard it and transfer their case to another court endowed with just personnel; for when this reaches the king's or emperor's court, the court with the guilty personnel should lose its judicial privileges. This is why it is necessary to know how a court and an arbitrational council should be set up. They ought to be earnestly warned to guard against any injustice entering into or occurring in their affairs, on pain of the highest fines to the king's or emperor's treasury.

At Basel, in the presence of our lord the emperor,[28] it so happened that someone appealed the verdict of a court to the emperor. He had been deprived of his father's inheritance before that court by people who were not qualified to rule in the matter, and were in ill repute on account of being guilty of adultery. Before the emperor it was determined that his inheritance should be restored to him, and the court was forbidden from issuing further verdicts according to the emperors' law, as has formerly been commanded in the emperors' laws. We can see that it is for this reason that arbitrational councils and courts should be supervised. A very severe lord indeed is coming soon to carry out judgement.[29]

Item, care should be taken in all the highest courts[30] to strive to adjudicate according to the emperors' laws, as was formerly commanded. They should derive their judgements from a book.[31] We command this on pain of the removal of a court's judicial privileges.

Item, all courts should be newly endowed in the manner set out above.

Item, care should be taken not to adjudicate spiritual matters in temporal courts, for temporal and spiritual jurisdiction should be clearly separated. All temporal courts should adjudicate that which pertains to the emperors' law, leaving papal and episcopal justice undisturbed, and vice versa.

---

28 If this actually took place, it must have been during Sigismund's stay in the city of Basel between October 1433 and May 1434.
29 A reference to the apocalyptic vision of a last emperor in the final section of the *Reformation*.
30 *heuptgerichten* – this presumably refers to courts that claimed (more in theory than practice in this period) to have the final say in cases under their jurisdiction, such as princely *Landgerichte* and urban *Stadtgerichte*.
31 The author's ideas about 'the emperors' laws' rely heavily on his reading of the *Swabian Mirror* [1], which is presumably the book referenced here.

Item, if a cleric has a dispute with a layperson over property or an inheritance, the cleric should have the case decided before an arbitrational council, which should render a judicial verdict or negotiate an amicable compromise. Likewise, if a layperson has something to litigate with a cleric, it should be decided before a spiritual judge, also via a judicial verdict or an amicable compromise. If, however, one party should consider that the matter was decided in a manner prejudicial to them, both sides may refer it for arbitration to a legally educated cleric and a wise layperson nominated for this purpose.

Item, no cleric or layperson should be excommunicated over a monetary debt – that pertains to the emperors' law – nor should any indebted churches be destroyed. Why should church services to God be struck down on account of the actions of two or three debtors? Where there are thieves or arsonists who prey on churches and committers of sacrilege, as they are legally known, they should be excommunicated and banned from all Christian fellowship. The enforcers of temporal law should help with this, and if anyone opposes this, they should indeed be excommunicated and banned, forcibly removed from churches and deprived of divine services.

[...]

Concerning peace and justice

It should also be considered that the most beneficial thing would be for an ordinance for the collective upholding of peace and justice to be promulgated among the lords and cities and throughout the land.[32] We can fully perceive that very great strife arises from wantonness and minor disputes, so that the lands and peoples are defiled and brutalised. It should be ordained that we should have four vicars, who should be considered vicars of an emperor and the rightful deputies between the seas. Each should bear the symbol of the Empire, to be used while carrying out necessary duties, such as ending conflicts and defending the faith. They should be installed in four zones, such that one is in Austria, another in

---

32 Here the author is clearly drawing on the concept and language of (*Land-*) *Frieden* ordinances and treaties, e.g. [15][17].

Milan, the third in Burgundy and the fourth in Savoy. Wherever conflicts and dissensions arise, those disputes should be brought before the vicar based in the closest proximity to see if they can be resolved. For nobody should declare a violent feud against another. It is therefore considered rightful that one should obtain justice by judicial means.

However, anyone who rejects justice and seeks to take matters into their own hands by launching an aggressive feud should lose all the rights that they possess – however many rights they might wish they had. Additionally, they should fall into the emperor's or king's disgrace, and everyone should be permitted to attack their person and possessions, and all those who might want to assist them. If a city likewise violates the peace and launches an attack – which, on account of their homage to the Empire, should be just as unlawful for them to do as for the lords – the nearest vicar should call for aid against that city, administer punishment to it and rescind its liberties.

You lords, you princes – whatever your titles are called – and you imperial cities! I call on you, for the sake of your homage to the Empire and as a holy Christian exhortation, to take care of all complaints and to avert wars and uphold the peace. Whoever ignores this exhortation violates the law of the Empire and should no longer be called a Christian, nor should their dynasty enjoy imperial privileges any longer. Among fellow Christians they should be considered a perjurious, bad Christian.

[...]

I believe that these things should now be set in motion,[33] and will proceed thus, for God never measures the righteous – he is the lord and master of righteousness. Therefore, you well-beloved faithful people, you princes and lords who enjoy fiefs from the Empire yet have not exerted yourselves in the name of the Empire for a long time, be now exhorted, according to the exhortations of your oaths and of God; and you knights, according to your knightly honour and oaths; and likewise you worthy imperial cities. When you hear of these things arising, sally forth and assist in the destruction of all

---

33 This final exhortation comes in the context of the author's apocalyptic prophecies, allegedly revealed to the late Emperor Sigismund, about a figure named Friedrich who would establish a new order in the Church and Empire.

the injustices that have caused the whole world to suffer such tribulations. And the more someone sacrifices in service of this cause, the more highly he and his family should be exalted. You nobles, act in this and live up to your nobility! Righteousness should be the hallmark of a nobleman. If you are taking to heart this worthily proclaimed sign from God, which will be heralded by the symbol of the Empire, ride now, for God and righteousness!

33. The proposals of an archbishop of Trier for reforming the Holy Roman Empire (1452)

Weinrich (ed.), *Quellen zur Reichsreform*, pp. 301–09.

Counsel or suggestion of the spiritual electors about how to raise up the Roman Empire[34]

The unity between our lords the pope and the emperor could be particularly beneficial,[35] for much good may come from it, as long as the common good is sought and all matters are undertaken in good faith. We have all seen and understood that when there has been strife between them in the past, many terrible things have afflicted the Empire and especially the princes and prelates of the Empire. At other times, many subjects could be oppressed by exactions and levies because of their concord, which occurred as a result of their lack of understanding, for they are frequently poorly counselled about the needs of the German nation. And so this matter should be considered with timely forethought, and necessary provision and means to this end should be sought.

Thus, clear and sincere unity is necessary among us electors. If such unity existed, the pope and emperor would listen all the more diligently to our counsel and about our and our peoples' necessity, and there would hardly be a prince in the Empire who would deviate from our counsel and arguments. Now we are many, and it is urgent to employ cleverness and wisdom and to find ways through which we may be brought together and into a friendly opinion and a better condition and full unity; and to that end, one must begin with a small number among us, and then with better justification approach the other princes. And it is also urgent to consider in what ways good, enduring, complete and pure harmony and understanding can be achieved among us, such that, if the pope or the emperor should wish to utilise their union for the common good, we may

---

[34] This title is probably a later addition to the text. On the contemporary manuscript it appears in an eighteenth-century hand. See Daniels, *Diplomatie*, p. 223.
[35] This is a reference to the recent Concordat of Vienna (1448) in which Frederick III had recognised papal authority in the dispute against the conciliarists at the Council of Basel (1431–49) in return for increased control over and revenues from German ecclesiastical institutions.

help all the more with that endeavour. However, if they should wish to utilise their union in some way to issue unjust orders and to encumber the Empire – and also their and our subjects – we should then, as loyal electors of the Empire who should elevate the common good above all things, seek through our good counsel to instruct their other councillors who do not take the common good quite so firmly to heart in a timely and appropriate way, and to stand for the common good ourselves.

In all the things that we have to or will have to accomplish, it is an appropriate necessity that we electors – before all others – should have a particular care for those matters which affect the Holy Christian Church and also our gracious lord the emperor and the common good of the Empire.

Thus, I anticipate two concerning things. First, no specified goal or deadline has been set for any future ecclesiastical council. Given that the law *Frequens*, that was issued at the Council of Constance[36] and obviates all concerns regarding future division in the Holy Church, is now wholly and entirely held in contempt, to the extent that, should it come to pass, God forbid, that the pope (who is quite old)[37] should die, and in the election of a new pope through the cardinals there should be a split, so that two individuals might claim to be popes, then there would be no means of settling such a split. However, if we had an agreed date for a future council, we would immediately have the available means to do so, as the law *Frequens* clearly instructs. To that end, I consider it to be to the benefit of our Christian faith, for the unity of the Holy Church, and to the honour and good of our Holy Empire, our spiritual estate and our nation, that a defined deadline should be set and a future council should take place. For it is especially appropriate for us to consider this rather than anything else, since this above-named law *Frequens* was issued in our nation in the presence of a Roman emperor [Sigismund], and also since the divisions of the Holy Church conspire to interfere with our nation to a much greater extent than others, for our nation is commonly divided among

---

36 This was one of the conciliarist decrees passed by the Council of Constance (1414–18) in 1417, mandating the regular convocation of a general council of the Church every ten years.
37 Pope Nicholas V (r. 1447–55) was in his late fifties around the time this document was written.

many lords and obediences, and does not readily allow itself to be kept under one obedience as in other nations which have their sole kings, whom everyone must obey in such matters.

And if such a split should come about, God forbid, and our nation be thusly divided, everyone would excommunicate each other as heretics, and the spiritual estate in the German lands would doubtless be suppressed in short order. We would not only lose principalities, lordships and other temporal assets. There would also be grave dangers, fears and concerns for our own bodies and souls. It is plausible that if these matters are brought before the pope and emperor and sufficiently well explained to them, they should then understand it and take it to heart more completely, and their unity and understanding should then be of a great help in all good means.

And it therefore seems to me to be urgent and good that we – as the highest members and as people who are held in no small regard, especially inasmuch as we promote the common good – should harmoniously consider how we might apply ourselves in feasible and useful ways to our highest superiors [i.e. the pope and emperor] to ensure that potential future divisions and disputes in the Holy Church, which might be a concern at some future time when we have all passed away, may be headed off in advance. It is also to be hoped that both the pope and the emperor may magnanimously and graciously understand this and assist in this, and may take on board our holy arguments as magnanimous princes.

Furthermore, we perceive that there is neither peace nor justice nor prosecution of the law anywhere in the Empire's affairs. There are many wanton conflicts, disobediences of subjects towards their lords, robberies, arsons, murders, thefts on the roads, feuds and enmities, without any justice or integrity. Neither freedom nor peace is anywhere to be found. Any given prince must defend himself with his own might. When he pursues peace or war in one place, new disputes instantly begin elsewhere. It is constantly necessary for princes, counts, lords, nobles and other good people to prepare for battle, or to pay money to avoid being attacked. It follows from this that the principalities are decayed and ruined through pledging, destruction, base and sinful usury and other day-to-day futile, pernicious, great and severe costs. In the same way, counties, lordships, monasteries and collegiate churches are also reduced to extreme poverty and ruin, and the more prestige and temporal goods they have, the greater the damage they suffer.

From this it also follows that the Roman Empire, the emperor, the princes and all the German nation is now considered the least by all other nations. As the Germans seek to use the lands and assets of other nations, our nation is now laid low, insulted and assailed by the others, and oppressed in every way. As a consequence, it may transpire within very few years that the emperor and we, his electors, will be held in no more respect than those other titled men who are greatly honoured in word but not at all in deeds. And worse still, our nation, more than any other, will be encumbered and struck with severe frequent burdens by all other nations.

It therefore seems to me to be necessary to consider a means to raise up the Empire and to put in order the matters of the Empire. First, there is no more suitable path forward in our nation than to awaken the Empire, on account of which this nation is fairly placed above all other nations. We would then be held in the greatest respect above all other princes. I will gladly offer counsel and assistance for whatever is urgent and worth considering in the service of this end. It also seems to me to be an urgent necessity, so long as so much evil occurs and increases, and other nations clearly know very well about and daily experience our discord, weakness and affliction. And if this is not shortly dealt with, we could easily lose the Empire through our divisions and discord, and we will doubtless sink in our own mire.

It is urgent that we electors weigh up, consider and accomplish these things with these ends in mind – collectively, individually and extensively. However, as I stated earlier, one must begin with few people, yet work with such diligence that we should be completely united, and to the benefit of these necessary things remain indissolubly together in this endeavour. When two of us have discussions with our closest colleagues, we will convey a single set of arguments. Let us bring the others over to our point of view without neglect, until we are one in all things, for truthfully it is most urgent for us spiritual princes that it soon be dealt with, above all other matters. For we can see clearly how deleteriously the spiritual princes are daily assailed and crushed. I am also full of hope: if this thing is taken up in order to bring collective benefit, justice and peace through good ordinances to our nation, everyone will fall in line with us, for there is no estate in the German lands which has not severely suffered and does not suffer daily. So I desire to add myself and assist with my life and goods in these matters, insofar as my wits and capacity allow.

To go further in these matters, it seems to me to be even better that each among us three spiritual electors ordain two of our closest councillors, whom we trust the most, that they should discuss among themselves ways and means to consider how to initiate these matters, namely that there be a defined date for a future council, and that the Empire be established in peace and obedience.

These practices will serve many purposes. When the pope seriously envisions holding a future council, he will behave more justly and customarily in all matters. For when this occurs, he will have to fear a future council, and will turn away from many causes and innovations that take place daily at the Roman Curia, and he will be more attentive to the highest individuals of this nation, and will grant them unbidden those things which he currently refuses when they request them. Item, if the emperor comes to know and perceives the desire that we electors gladly hold – that we should awaken and elevate him, and seek the benefit, good obedience and respect of the Empire – he will be all the more willing to fall in line with us in all things, and will much more gladly follow our counsel.

The way by which the Empire might be raised up

First, that the emperor should come to an imperial city roughly in the centre of the realm, with a view and desire to remain there in person for some time. Item, that at the same time we electors should also come to him personally and remain in the same way, just as the cardinals remain with the pope and their secret consistories, in order to achieve as much as possible.

Item, that a court should be ordained, with a defined number of people from all the estates, who should constantly sort matters out by judicial means, in the same manner as the *parlement* of Paris (as has been done there since ages past, and can indeed still be seen in that form today).

Item, for the accomplishment of justice, three secular princes should be ordained as captains in three parts of the Empire, and they should be the three temporal electors,[38] each of whom should be a captain for the execution of justice in the part of the German lands that is assigned to him. Item, for this purpose, all subjects of the Empire should accede to this execution of justice when called upon by the prince who is a captain over the part of the Empire in which they are located.

Item, it is also to be believed that when such a good order of justice is brought about, the emperor's declarations of imperial ban will be carried out justly and sincerely, and all those placed in the imperial ban and double ban should then be fully shunned and treated as people of their status ought to be treated. And if they do not respect their ban, justice should nonetheless be executed against them as prescribed. Item, provision should be made for dealing with such cases, and for the question of how cases should be relayed from the lower courts to this court.[39]

Item, the chancery and treasury of the Empire should be restored in a proper condition, and they should be maintained in the same way as at the Curia in Rome.

Item, each and every thing required for this establishment of justice and organisation of the emperor's court should be properly ordained by us, the electors, and the councillors whom we appoint for this purpose, in the presence of the emperor. For many unforeseen issues might come up. When embarking on a project, one issue after another arises as part of the process.

Money is required for all these purposes, but the Empire has such small revenues that the emperor cannot bear the burden of maintaining this political order, unless other steps are taken. And it is necessary to consider ways of raising money, and how this can be achieved with the least difficulty.

If the emperor and we electors come together in this way and remain with each other, we will surely find ways to obtain money. For there is no doubt that when the subjects of the Empire (spiritual and temporal) perceive good order in the Empire, along with courts, peace and a reduction of wanton wars, and when they see

---

38 Presumably, the three German temporal electors (with the king of Bohemia excluded from the scheme).
39 That is, the new pan-imperial court proposed two articles above.

principalities, lordships and roadways pacified as a result, and the serious intentions of the emperor and we electors, it will not be difficult for them to recognise that they should gladly suffer[40] for this purpose. And should there be some malicious people who do not desire to have peace, and who would be sorry to see it, the majority will nevertheless gladly fall in line for the sake of their own benefit.

Item, when this occurs, no princes in the world ought to be so greatly respected as we electors. For through us the emperor will be respected, and we through the emperor, and that should bring about great benefit for our nation, such that our emperor should be held in great esteem. For in terms of people, towns, fortifications and all other things which bring glory and greatness, our nation is the master over all other nations, as long as it is in just order and under good government.

When Italy perceives that the Empire is in such good order, the cities which are ruled by tyrants – which is the majority of them – will also fall in line, and no longer tolerate the great and severe burdens with which they have been afflicted and encumbered for many years until today, which they otherwise never dare to challenge, as long as they know the Empire in the German lands to be in a state of disorder. Item, when this happens, the pope will prioritise us electors, for in this good order we and the emperor should be able to protect the pope and the Holy Church so much better than any other captains or men-at-arms can.

Item when other kings of Christendom see such good order in the Empire, they will be so happy that they will do what the emperor and we electors desire, and will seek refuge with us in times of trial.

Finally, to draw together many issues in a few concluding words, it is hard to articulate just how much honour and benefit would accrue to the German lands from this plan. For all the potential obligations this might impose on the Germans because of these dangers, they should consider them bearable in order to obtain such honour and benefit. If things go this way, it would be a simple matter to oppose the infidels, for an emperor, as a lord ordained by God, would always have an easy task. If, however, things do not go this way, clear signs indicate that the emperor, we and other Germans would be held in the lowest esteem. And other nations

---

40 That is, tolerate financial exactions.

will fully and wholly demolish and cast down our nation with shame and great confusion, as we ourselves observe happening all around us.

How one should advise regarding the future council

First, it is urgent that the emperor be advised to hold a future council, for he is the initiator of the declaration that took place with Eugenius and also with this pope,[41] and a future council was promised to him in a bull,[42] and it is therefore urgent that he be persuaded of this argument before all other things.

Item, this should be the way to bring the emperor around to this position. He should be told that Emperor Sigismund, his predecessor of blessed memory, worked to achieve two great things at the Council of Constance:

First, that the schism was brought to an end.[43]

Second, that the law *Frequens* was issued, which contains the stipulation that every ten years a *generale concilium* should be celebrated, and that at the conclusion of a given council another should be appointed to be celebrated ten years later, so that at all times there should either be a council or at least a defined date for a future council. It is also stated in the law *Frequens* that if a schism occurs within the time before a future council, one should without hesitation have recourse to the council, and through it procedures are also laid down to bring the schism to a complete end. And that was the second great thing that Emperor Sigismund did, through which the path was closed off to future divisions in the Holy Church.

At present there is no council. Nor is there a defined date for a future council, and so at this time the holy law *Frequens* is fundamentally ignored, wherefore God is enraged, and the imperial Majesty and our nation, in whose womb this healing law was

---

41 This is another reference to the 1448 Concordat of Vienna. The pontificate of Eugenius IV, the predecessor of Nicholas V, lasted from 1431 to 1447.
42 Eugenius IV made this commitment in 1447.
43 The election of Pope Martin V in 1417 ended the two- and then three-way papal schism between Rome, Avignon and Pisa that had lasted since 1378.

conceived, is held in great disrepute and suffers scorn and shame. I do not even mention the inconceivable damage to our nation which could follow from this. It is therefore urgent that we request of his imperial Majesty, for the honour of the Almighty and of the holy faith and all good Christian people and the Holy See of Rome, and for the sake of his Majesty of the Holy Empire and our nation's honour and benefit, that his Grace should appreciate that a date for a future council should be set.

Item, it is also to be hoped that when we electors show the way in rendering appropriate respect to the emperor, and also when the emperor sees our earnest desire for the elevation of his Majesty and of the Holy Empire in the German lands and thereafter in other nations, he will come around all the more gladly and seek to convoke a council. And the nation will then have embarked on the process, and the council will be convoked by the pope through the emperor and we electors, for the pope will not dare to do otherwise.

The council is a holy matter, on which the emperor and we electors should work with all our means and without ceasing. Then things will proceed successfully, as I trust in God, and unspeakable honour and good things will accrue to us from this, and all our urgent difficulties will easily be overcome, and in a short time.

34. The Little Book of One Hundred Chapters with Forty Statutes (c. 1490–1510)

Lauterbach (ed.), *Das buchli der hundert capiteln mit xxxx statuten*, pp. 591–97.

The author divided his long text into a prologue (which claims that the book contains revelations from the Archangel Michael for amending Christian society's many sins, and that it was entirely written in 1490), a table of contents summarising the one hundred chapters on a variety of themes and the forty 'statutes' that would purportedly restore unity with God, if respected, and the chapters (of which the author only wrote ninety in full) and statutes themselves. This extract is a translation of the final statute, which ties together many of the text's recurrent concerns and demands.

Concerning the status of the highest ruler – the fortieth statute (XL)

The fortieth statute is about the emperor and his subjects, such as the pope,[44] and knights and retainers.

An emperor is lord of the entire world. An emperor is lord over all kings. All authority is placed under his sceptre. And I state this with the support of the laws.[45]

The Empire receives its name from God alone. Therefore, a double-edged sword is bestowed on the emperor from the throne of eternity. This is so that he should govern both estates, spiritual and temporal.[46] And the greatest honour for an emperor is to administer the common good and preserve it in an honourable condition, to defend widows and orphans, to maintain good coinage, as stated above in

---

44 Earlier in the work – notably chapters 55 and 59 – the author contends that an emperor has authority over the pope and, as protector of Christendom, is charged with reforming the Church.
45 Here, as throughout his work, the author inserts parenthetical citations, quotations or paraphrases at the end of most sentences to back up his claims, mostly from civil and canon law (especially the *Digesta* of what we now call the *Corpus Iuris Civilis* and Gratian's *Decretum*, and the myriad glosses on these corpora). Full details, with references, can be found in the cited pages of Lauterbach's edition. They are not included here for ease of reading.
46 Contrast with the 'Two Swords Theory' in [1].

the fifty-seventh chapter, and to be in his palace just as God is in heaven, and to ordain a good, pious vicar for our holy mother the Christian Church – that is, to appoint a pope – and to examine him to ensure that he has sufficient faith to take custody of the Church.

An emperor should always be in armour, ready to suppress evil crimes and anything that is contrary to the common good. He should not permit the profligate use of resources for dishonourable purposes, and reclaim ecclesiastical endowments for himself when they are misused. This is why I said above that an emperor should not have any property of his own, but should live according to the established laws and draw his expenses from the commonwealth. Therefore, no ill-conceived last will and testament should be permitted for an emperor.

But the greatest thing there is that should adorn the imperial Majesty is that he should conduct himself according to the written [Roman] law, for *de auctoritate iuris nostra pendet auctoritas*.[47] The Empire should also live according to the instituted law, no more or less than the emperor.

Everyone can understand from this that an emperor should not burden the common good, whether with tolls, fees, taxes etc., and that he should uphold good, high-quality coinage, and not allow any evil authority to go unpunished. His imperial Majesty should not craft any statutes that are against the common good. Likewise with privileges which contradict the written laws – his imperial Majesty is obligated to abolish and rescind them.

An emperor is of the very highest knighthood.

I read that an emperor is the most exalted knight,[48] that is, a judge placed over the entire world. This knightly jurisdiction is conferred upon his imperial Majesty by God. It behoves him to fight for the sake of the common good, and he may fatally strike down his enemies. This is like what was written above about the Cimbri; they

---

47 'our [the emperor's] authority depends on the authority of the law' – a precept laid down in Justinian's *Codex*.
48 A view advanced in one of the glosses on customary law in the *Swabian Mirror* [1] – see Lauterbach (ed.), *Das buchli der hundert capiteln mit xxxx statuten*, p. 593, note 1092.

said 'it is better to protect widows and orphans than to be overcome with riches'.[49] And where an emperor does not do this, God's peace eludes him.

The legal glosses say regarding this that where an advocate hands out a sentence but does not administer the punishment, he is obligated to pay all the damages himself. And Cato says about this that an emperor should not tolerate any unfit, unjust judge. He is also obligated to exile any knight who flees from the battlefield. Also, he should not take any adulterer with him into battle, for there is an old saying: 'What good can someone who does not even wish their own soul well do for another?' As the legal texts say, illegitimate children – namely the children of cursed seed, who are justly called the children of Antichrist – are not steadfast in battle.

Regarding this, the *lex Cornelia*[50] says that an emperor should abolish and rescind everything that causes damage to anyone's neighbour. And Jeremiah, chapter 8:[51] an emperor should learn from the past punishments that God visited upon us because of our sins. To this end, Emperor Justinian confirmed the statute *C[odicem] de su[mma] tri[nitate] et fi[de] ca[tholica]*,[52] on which an emperor or pope should base their decisions.

It follows from this that all laws should be inscribed in an emperor's heart, and that he has the authority to govern on earth as God governs in heaven. And his highest duty is to defend widows and orphans.

Thus, tithes and offerings are established for the protection of the land and the common good, per the highly learned St Augustine in a homily: *omnes decimas* are established for the protection of the Christian faith. As mentioned above, parishes should be graciously permitted to collect this tithe. And whoever collects it should give a fifth of all tithes directly to the emperor, without going through any

---

49 The Cimbri were a tribe that fought the Roman Republic in the late second century BCE. The Roman historian Valerius Maximus presented them as spartan and virtuous. Ibid., p. 593, note 1096.
50 A law attributed to one of the many Roman officials called Cornelius, transmitted via the *Corpus Iuris Civilis* (references in ibid., p. 594, note 1103).
51 An allusion to Jeremiah 7–10, in which the punishment of the kingdom of Judah by God for its people's impiety is prophesied.
52 The first section of the first book of Justinian's *Codex*, on correct Christian doctrines, originally an edict from 380.

middlemen, as mentioned above in the thirty-third statute and in the fifty-fifth chapter (on who should make offerings, and what the offerings should be). And the *pastores* – that is, those who can anoint us – should keep the other four-fifths safe as pious shepherds, as stated above, for the benefit of the common good. For Jesus said to Peter, 'Do you love me?', to which he replied, 'Yes, Lord, you know that well'. And then Jesus ordered him to tend to His little sheep and to share the food of the pasture with them [John 21:15–17]. And where they do not do this, they are called *sacrilegi*, that is, thieves whose crimes entail the emperor's punishment. Thus, the *pastor* (that is, the priest) is owed an appropriate amount for subsistence, and the rest should be spent on the common good, the sick and pilgrims.

It is therefore forbidden for priests to take possession of funds for any other purpose. Instead, they should be obedient in serving the poor and proving themselves virtuous, and only concern themselves with God and spiritual affairs. A priest should be a good example to his flock. He should not charge money for reading the mass, nor for performing baptisms or hearing confessions.

It is forbidden for women to serve at the altar.

A cleric should not beg. It is therefore a great abuse that healthy monks, who could readily earn their bread, are permitted to beg. This also applies to the mendicants, who tell lies so they will be given money. A pope may rightly be forced to return the money he has obtained through letters of indulgence. As Pompeius states in his statute: each is obligated to return any gain which he has obtained unjustly.[53] For the popes and their legates have always claimed that one should and wants to use the money received in the jubilee year to oppose the Turks. They should not be permitted to make dukes of their children.[54]

I read that an emperor is obligated to love righteousness, just as God does, per Deuteronomy 33: 'I have the almighty authority to issue my commands to the whole world.'[55] This is why I said in chapter 41 that the entire world and all infidels should be made

---

53 Another reference to the *Digesta*. See ibid., p. 596, note 1120.
54 Presumably a reference to nepotism at the Curia, and perhaps more specifically to the careers of the illegitimate sons of Pope Alexander VI.
55 A loose summary of God's characteristics in the Song and Final Blessing of Moses (Deuteronomy 32–33).

obedient, and thereafter in chapter 44 that the princes and lords should demonstrate this with their deeds. Knights and retainers should always be prepared to protect widows and orphans.

Another example is needed to make the point about why adultery should be eliminated. We see how David was punished with death because of Bathsheba; how their son Solomon strayed from the faith because of impure behaviour; how this likewise happened to Solomon's son Rehoboam, as mentioned in chapter 37, whereby he drove away the ten tribes;[56] and how Sergius, a monk, ended imperial rule over Antioch and led it out of the faith along with thirty-two kingdoms.[57]

Restoring all this into our hands will not happen easily unless we first reform ourselves, and live according to the words of Christ, and take up the cross to contemplate the suffering of Jesus Christ. So will His word be fulfilled; as He was preparing to depart from us, He said to His disciples: 'I am ascending to my and your Father, and will send you the Holy Spirit, which will teach you righteousness. That is, the one who believes and is baptised, and the one who holds unto the commandments of God, will be blessed.' [John 16:5–14; Acts 1:8] And we should condemn anyone who does not want to accept baptism [Mark 16:16].

I therefore exhort all the mighty, serene princes and lords not to receive this, my written work, as something produced out of malice, but rather in my humble way, made to provide the young with something that will take them a long time to read. If it should occur that someone were to be displeased by it, it is always my intention to make improvements.

Thus, you highly learned scholars and specifically those of you who have fat benefices, or you lay people who have received usurious income or other goods from the churches or the parishes, which damages the common good, you should live your lives according to this little book and turn away from excess, as set out above,

---

56 2 Samuel 11 (David commits adultery with Bathsheba); 1 Kings 2 (David's death); 1 Kings 11 (Solomon's idolatry, God's promise to remove ten tribes of Israel from his son Rehoboam as punishment); 1 Kings 14 (Rehoboam's idolatry).
57 According to one medieval tradition, a Nestorian monk called Sergius helped the Prophet Muhammad to write the Qur'an and secured the peaceful surrender of Antioch to the Caliphate. See ibid., p. 566, note 934.

before the wrath of God appears. And for those who may have acted against the commandments of God, I advise all Christian people who have been born in Christ Jesus to have the radiant cross of Christ before them as a meditation and to contemplate the suffering that God endured for us sinners upon the wooden beams of the holy cross on Good Friday, after which He died, was buried and led the community of souls out of hell. Just as He told the thief on the cross that he would be led into paradise on that same day [Luke 23:39–43], so we should also be prepared for this, as long as we carry out His commandments.

May God the Father and God the Son impart this to us, and send His Holy Ghost, so to live in this time as to merit eternal joy. AMEN.

35. Martin Luther, *To the Christian Nobility of the German Nation Concerning the Improvement of the Christian Estate* (1520)

D. *Martin Luthers Werke*, pp. 427, 457–60, 462–65.

The year 1520 saw the propulsion of Martin Luther, Augustinian friar and doctor of theology at the University of Wittenberg, to international notoriety. Following the publication of his *Ninety-five Theses* in 1517 and acrimonious debates with cardinals and fellow scholars in 1518 to 1519, 1520 saw Luther develop his anti-papal ideas to new levels of radicalism in three widely read treatises: *To the Christian Nobility of the German Nation*, *On the Babylonian Captivity of the Church* and *On the Freedom of a Christian*.[58] While the last two dealt with theological and ecclesiological questions, the first sought to influence temporal politics, primarily through prescriptions about how rulers should interact with the papacy and clergy. This extract offers a new translation of key passages near the end of the text, in which Luther offers his most fully articulated ideas about the improvement of law and politics in the Holy Roman Empire as part of his broader call for reining in papal and spiritual authority in the name of reform.

[Luther begins his text by bemoaning the terrible situation in 'Christendom, and above all the German lands', blaming this on the devilish schemes of the popes and their supporters, the so-called 'Romanists'. Three 'walls' have obstructed any improvements: the separation of clergy and laity into spiritual and temporal estates, with the former claiming superiority over and immunity from the latter, whereas the Bible teaches that all are of equal spiritual status before God; the papal claim to be the exclusive interpreter of Scripture; and the papal reservation unto itself of the right to convoke a council. The temporal authorities ought to ensure the convocation of a general council to address Romanist avarice and tyranny. In the final, longest section, Luther presents his proposals to redress Christendom.]

Now, while I am too lowly to put forth articles, in the interest of improving this outrageous situation I will nevertheless play the fool

---

[58] See Roper, *Martin Luther*, pp. 159–68.

by singing and stating out loud, as far as my standing enables, what really might and ought to take place, by the agency of temporal authority or a general council.

[...]

[25] The universities also really need a good, vigorous reformation. [...] I leave it to the medics to reform their faculties; I take the jurists and theologians in hand, and firstly say that it would be a good thing if spiritual [i.e. canon] law were totally annihilated, from the first letter to the last, especially the decretals.[59] What is written in the Bible is sufficient to inform us about how we should behave in all matters. Such canonistic studies only hinder Holy Scripture. Most spiritual law is characterised by vanity, avarice and pride, and even if there were many good things in it, it should nevertheless be exterminated, for the pope has taken all spiritual laws captive in the letterbox of his breast,[60] such that henceforth it is worthless and of no benefit to study them, and they contain only deception. 'Spiritual law' nowadays does not mean what is written in the books, but whatever resides in the immoral desires of the pope and his sycophants. If you have a case that can be supported by spiritual law to ensure the very best outcome, the pope can nevertheless hold his *scrinium pectoris*[61] over it, and all law and the whole world has to be directed by that. Oftentimes the same *scrinium* is governed by a scoundrel and the devil himself, and yet it is extolled that it is governed by the Holy Spirit. This is how the pope treats the poor people of Christ. He lays down much law on them and does not obey any of it himself, yet coerces others to obey it or release themselves from it with money.

Seeing as the pope and his adherents have retained the entire spiritual law for themselves, yet do not observe it and pursue only their own immoral desires while lording it over the whole world,

---

59 The cumulative body of law formed by the letters of the popes (*litterae decretales*) and their glosses, most famously compiled alongside laws from other sources in Gratian's *Decretum* and subsequent corpora of canon law (e.g. Gregory IX's *Liber extravagantium decretalium*) that expanded it.
60 A vernacular rendering of *scrinium pectoris*, which appears two sentences below.
61 Literally, the 'letterbox/document-holding chest of his breast' (a *scrinium* being a storage box used in medieval chanceries). Pope Boniface VIII (1294–1303) employed the metaphor of his *scrinium pectoris* to justify a papal right to modify canon law at will. See Buck, 'Papal Antichrist', p. 356.

we should follow their example and also discard the law-books. Why should we futilely study them? Anyway, we could never fully learn the pope's wanton will, which is what spiritual law has now become. Oh! May this, which has arisen in the devil's name, be cast down once and for all in God's name, and may there no longer be a single *doctor Decretum*[62] on the face of the earth, but only *doctores scrinii papalis* ['doctors of the papal letterbox'], who are the pope's sycophants. It is said that there is no finer temporal government anywhere than under the Turk [i.e. the Ottoman sultan], even though he has neither spiritual nor temporal law, but only his Qur'an.[63] We therefore have to acknowledge that there is no more nefarious government than ours because of spiritual and temporal law, as a result of which no estate is in conformity with natural reason, let alone Holy Scripture.

As for temporal law – God help us, what a wilderness it has become! Although it is much better, cleverer and more honest than spiritual law (about which nothing is good beyond its name), there is still far too much of it. Truly, reasonable rulers would, alongside the Holy Scriptures, constitute sufficient law; as St Paul says in 1 Corint[hians] 6[:5–6]: 'Is there nobody among you who can judge his neighbour's case, that you have to take your quarrels before heathen courts?' I likewise think that customary law and regional consuetudes should be preferred over the emperor's laws and the common law,[64] and the emperor's laws only employed when necessary. May God will that just as every region has its characteristic mores and gifts, it would also be governed according to its own, brief laws, as the regions were once governed before such laws were invented, and indeed as many regions are still governed without those laws! Laws that apply over large areas and allow litigation to be pursued far away are only a burden to the people, and more of a hindrance than a source of support in judicial cases. Still, I hope that these issues are already being considered and examined by others in more depth than I can expound them.

62 A holder of a doctoral degree in canon law.
63 *Alkoran* – a Germanised form of the Latinisation *alcoranus*.
64 Here Luther could be referring both to ordinances and statutes of the emperors and diets (e.g. [21]) and to the *ius commune*, the body of primarily civil law (especially as compiled in the *Corpus Iuris Civilis*) which could be marshalled in legal arguments alongside local customs and German customary law as found in law-books like the *Swabian Mirror* [1], and which was playing an increasingly prominent role in imperial jurisprudence, as at the cameral court [22].

[26] I am well aware that the Roman Curia will set forth and presumptuously boast about how the pope allegedly extracted the Holy Roman Empire from the Greek emperor and conferred it on the Germans,[65] for which honour and blessing he has supposedly earned and obtained just servitude, gratitude and all good things from the Germans. It is perhaps because of this that they will try to cast any kind of initiative to reform them to the winds and not permit any consideration of anything other than this conferral of the Roman Empire. They have therefore so wantonly and arrogantly harassed and oppressed many a magnificent emperor up to the present that it is lamentable to talk about it, and they have used the same cunning to make themselves overlords of all temporal jurisdictions and authorities, contrary to the holy gospel, about which I must therefore also speak.

It is indubitable that the true Roman Empire, announced in the writings of the prophets in Numbers 24[:17–24] and Daniel [2:36–45], was destroyed and came to an end long ago, as Balaam clearly announced in Numbers 24 when he said: 'The Romans will come and scatter the Jews, and thereafter they, too, will be destroyed.'[66] And this occurred through the Goths, but more especially with the commencement of the empire of the Turks[67] some thousand years ago. Thus, with the passage of time Asia and Africa fell away, then Francia and Spain, and most recently Venice rose up, and nothing remains unto Rome of its former sphere of authority.

And since the pope was then unable to coerce the emperor of Constantinople, who was the Roman emperor by right of inheritance, according to his arbitrary will, he came up with a ruse to rob the emperor of the same empire and name and to confer it on the Germans, who were great warriors and enjoyed a good reputation at that time, so that they[68] might subdue the Roman Empire's sphere of authority under themselves, and that it might be held in fief from their hands. And so it therefore occurred: the Roman Empire was taken from the emperor of Constantinople,

---

65 The venerable theory of *translatio imperii*, as set out in [2].
66 A historically creative interpretation of Numbers 24:24.
67 The original Islamic Caliphate.
68 This passage is ambiguous, as the group last mentioned before this clause was the Germans, while the pope was in the singular, but in the context of this paragraph 'they' presumably refers to the popes.

and the name and title of the same ascribed to us Germans, and in this way we became servants of the pope. And now there is a second Roman Empire, which the pope has constructed on the backs of the Germans, for the first one was destroyed long ago, as I said.

Thus, now the See of Rome has fulfilled its perverse desire and occupied Rome, driven the German emperor therefrom and bound him with oaths not to live within Rome. He is supposedly the Roman emperor and yet does not occupy Rome, and additionally must depend on and displace himself at the arbitrary pleasure of the pope and his adherents, such that we have the Roman name and they the Roman territory and city. For they have always exploited our naivety to benefit their arrogance and tyranny, and they call us foolish Germans who allow themselves to be duped and mocked at will.

[Luther cautions the Germans to remain humble about having been chosen by God to bear the Roman imperial mantle, in contrast with unjust papal arrogance and thirst for power.]

So may God, who has thrust this empire upon us through cunning tyrants (as I said) and ordered us to govern it, help us to perform the duties associated with this name, title and coat of arms, and to speak eloquently of our liberties, so that one day the Romans see what we have received through them from God. If they want to pride themselves on having conferred imperial authority on us, well then, so be it; let it be so, and may the pope accordingly hand over Rome and everything that he holds from the imperial authority, and may he leave our lands free of his unbearable financial levies and afflictions, restore our freedoms, jurisdictions, possessions, honour, bodies and souls and leave the imperial authority in the condition that befits an imperial authority, so that he may live up to his words and assertions.

If he does not want to do this, what kind of a charlatan is he, with his false, concocted words and skulduggery? Have we not had enough of him grossly and ceaselessly leading this noble nation around by the nose for so many hundreds of years? It does not follow that the pope is superior to the emperor just because he crowns or elevates him. For the prophet Samuel anointed and crowned King Saul and David by divine mandate, yet he was subject to them. And the prophet Nathan anointed King Solomon, yet was not appointed his superior as a consequence. Item, St Elisha had his servant anoint King Jehu of Israel, yet they remained obedient under him. And it has never happened anywhere in the world that the one who anoints or crowns the king should be superior to him, except in the single case of the pope.

36. The 'grievances of the German nation' at an imperial diet in Speyer (1526)

Kluckhohn et al. (eds), *Deutsche Reichstagsakten. Jüngere Reihe*, vol. V/VI, pp. 617, 641–42, 678, 723–24, 732, 737.

Opinion of the council of electors concerning the abuses and grievances of the German nation (20 July 1526)

What our gracious lords the electors' councillors have considered and advised regarding the recently issued mandate about abuses, per the goodwill and desire for amelioration of their gracious lords the electors, etc.

By way of introduction, since the temporal princes submitted certain grievances against his papal Holiness and other clerics to his imperial Majesty at the recently held imperial diet of Worms,[69] and have subsequently pointed out and informed him about the same grievances lengthily and sufficiently, our highly esteemed gracious lords the councillors of the electors have reckoned and considered it beneficial and necessary that the aforementioned grievances shown at the same imperial diet be taken in hand and examined article by article, and that deliberations be held about the ways in which the same grievances might be remedied and restored to good order, for the preservation of the unity and peace of the spiritual and temporal estates. And given that it is well known that the grievances confronting the Holy Empire because of his papal Holiness are by no means minor, and were undoubtedly part of the cause of the recent peasant uprisings,[70] having hitherto moved the common people against their local clergy to no small degree, the same grievances should not be ignored. Rather, it is necessary to consider their content as a matter of primary importance. And the councillors' well-considered reflections and deliberations follow hereafter, that their reckonings may serve to remedy the same grievances etc.

---

69 The list of 102 grievances against the clergy introduced at the 1521 diet, which formed the reference point for the debates about the reform of abuses in the German lands throughout the 1520s. Kluckhohn et al. (eds), *Deutsche Reichshtagsakten. Jüngere Reihe*, vol. II, no. 96. Translated in Strauss (ed./trans.), *Manifestations of Discontent*, pp. 52–63.
70 The so-called 'Peasants' War' of 1524–26.

[96 of the 102 grievances presented at Worms are re-copied here, with additional commentary. They begin with grievances against the papacy, including the Curia's inappropriate jurisdictional claims and judicial activities and its financial exactions and handling of benefices, and then cover similar topics at the levels of dioceses, parishes and other ecclesiastical institutions and communities, while also touching on behavioural and moral failings of the clergy.]

Opinion of the council of princes concerning the abuses and grievances of the German nation (23 July 1526)

Upon receipt of their mandate from our gracious lords the princes, the envoys of the same and the counts and prelates, their empowered representatives have considered that three prominent aspects should be discussed (but this is absolutely not final, and subject to additions, removals and changes upon their Graces' approval).

Namely, first of all, what the good, truly traditional Christian practices and ordinances might be that should be preserved in the Empire, per the request of his imperial Majesty and his commissioners.

Second, and to the contrary, that evil and noxious traditions, which are abuses, should be abolished or amended and re-established.

Third, how whichever grievances in the German nation that the temporal estate has against the spiritual and vice versa should be amended, and also how the grievances of the common man about unfair practices should be considered and alleviated.

And it is first and foremost considered that this intervention should begin with a protestation, which should also be inserted into the recess, namely that it is not the will and intention of the imperial commissioners[71] and all the estates to make any determination in the question of the Christian faith, nor in the matters related to it, nor to modify the good, truly traditional statutes and ordinances of

---

71 The commissioners were Bishop Bernardo Clesio of Trent, Margrave Kasimir of Brandenburg-Kulmbach, Margrave Bernhard III of Baden-Baden, Duke Wilhelm IV of Bavaria and Duke Erich I of Brunswick-Lüneburg-Calenberg-Göttingen (ibid., vol. V/VI, p. 300). They were simultaneously princely members of the imperial estates, hence this formula.

legally assembled and universally recognised Christian councils – indeed, the collective estates were not assembled or convoked here with this opinion or purpose in mind.[72] But (as is obvious to everyone) all kinds of schisms, divisions, discords, confusions and imbalances have erupted in the Holy Empire of the collective German nation, among the high and low estates, the learned, the uneducated and the common man – so much so that if this is not examined and as much equitability pursued and ordained in this as possible, it is to be feared that not only will insurrections and uprisings spring up (as has already occurred), but many more afflictions of Christian consciences, souls, bodies and goods may arise, and ultimately result in the renunciation of certain critical aspects of the Christian faith. For what we have learned up to this point is that one error begets another.

For these reasons, and per the imperial briefing and mandate we received, the imperial commissioners, together with estates collectively, have pursued the following measures, remedies and ordinances, which do not have the status of a new statute or determination, but would only be held until amended by a free general council, and upheld so that the members of the Empire might preserve equity, peace and unity.

[The princes take up 72 of the grievances listed by the council of electors, but also include a section addressing religious practices such as preaching and the sacraments, sometimes implicitly taking up evangelical ideas and sometimes tacitly or openly forbidding them.]

Advisement of the temporal estates.

In this context, it is the humble opinion of the representatives of the temporal estates – considered for his imperial Majesty and for the benefit and wellbeing of the Holy Empire – that it is no small burden on the Roman Empire and German nation that the archbishops, bishops and exempt prelates[73] have such extensive

---

72 The proposals of Archduke Ferdinand and his commissioners for the diet, submitted on behalf of Charles V on 25 June, had asserted, in view of the spread of the alleged Lutheran heresy, 'that in matters touching upon our holy Christian faith and religion, no innovation or pronouncement should be undertaken by the same imperial estates and German nation'. Ibid., vol. V/VI, p. 301.
73 Prelates who were not under (arch-)diocesan oversight, and answered only to the Holy See.

duties for his papal Holiness and the See of Rome, and yet hold all their temporal properties and jurisdictions from his imperial Majesty and the Holy Empire, or they are at least located within the Empire and the prelates are princes and members of the Roman Empire. Sometimes their extensive duties that are owed to the Holy See hinder them from being able to counsel and assist for the benefit and wellbeing of his imperial Majesty and the collective Empire of the German nation, which they would otherwise undoubtedly be inclined to do. We should note that for the sake of the recovery, preservation and wellbeing of the German nation it is worth considering whether the clergy's obligations towards the See of Rome should always be subject to his imperial Majesty and the Roman Empire, and any cleric who might oppose this should not be enfeoffed with his regalia by his imperial Majesty. If his papal Holiness should seek to oppose this, the archbishop, bishop or prelate should nevertheless be protected and supported in his enjoyment of his lands, peoples, regalia, possessions and properties.

Nota. All kinds of articles have been submitted herein which were previously considered in connection with the holy sacraments and abuses involving them, some having been consolidated and some having been postponed until a deliberation about the grievances of the subjects.

Opinion of the large committee[74] concerning ecclesiastical abuses and the grievances of the subjects (18 August 1526)

Regarding the second article of the imperial briefing,[75] concerning the insurrection of the subjects, two principal points are considered by the committee:

First, how uprisings of the subjects should be pre-empted.

---

74 *des grossen usschus* – the third of the three sub-councils that conventionally met during the imperial diets of the sixteenth century, representing all the estates collectively (including the free and imperial cities and imperially immediate nobility who were not represented in the electoral or princely councils). Its right to a voice was often contested by the princes.
75 The briefing called on the estates to discuss measures for opposing the further spread of peasant uprisings. Ibid., vol. V/VI, p. 304.

Second, if insurrections and uprisings occur among the subjects, how the same should be fended off, quieted and faced down.

We firstly reckon that it would be of no small assistance to pre-empting the insurrections of the subjects if the common man's grievances about unfair practices by spiritual or temporal authorities were appropriately and fairly remediated. Hence the following articles: the articles previously submitted by the temporal estates at the imperial diets of Worms and Nuremberg in the first section, and those considered just now by the committee in light of the experience of the recent insurrections in the second section, with the good will of our most gracious lords the electors and princes and our gracious lords the estates, as follows hereafter.

[The committee takes up 100 of the grievances of the German nation submitted by the electors and princes.]

It is further considered that each authority ought to guard against unfairly burdening their subjects; and they should ensure that their advocates, custodians or officials do the same; and always graciously and benignly listen to their subjects about their concerns; and, according to the nature of the matter, fairly and effectively keep them informed at all times; and not leave any subject who requests an audience unheard, nor proceed against or punish them at the mere denunciation of an official, forest overseer or some other person in the service of a lord. And whoever must go through a judicial process should be treated justly throughout, and not burdened outside of the bounds of the law.

[The committee drafts a total of twenty-five proposals to lessen the burdens on subjects in the German lands, touching upon vineyard harvesting, tithes and rents, free movement, game hunting, common lands and waters, corvées, inheritances, interest on loans, investigation of crimes, the costs of courts and the fairness of their penalties.]

Since usages and customs in the Roman Empire have by now become innumerable, and one place has different traditions from another according to the circumstances of the mores and practices of the region, such that it is surely impossible to pursue one single collective statute and ordinance that could encompass every location's subjects (it would be an unfair burden on them), it is generally thought that each authority, when addressing their subjects' pressing complaints, should conduct themselves and behave according to the form, situation and tradition of the mores and practices of their region, as their own conscience, divine and natural law and fairness dictate, and as they feel able to answer to Almighty God regarding this. And in particular, no authority should burden their subjects with innovations.

V
ALLIANCES AND ASSOCIATIONS

The Holy Roman Empire's vast size and decentralised political landscape presented its political elites with a structural problem: managing basic tasks of regional governance and defence when they were invariably too weak and atomised to do so as individual princes, nobles, cities or communes. Associations offered a solution to this problem. In this context, the word 'association' can be understood to encompass a range of specific types of treaty-bound and oath-sealed agreements between two or more parties of a similar juridical standing (if not social rank or military and financial strength) as members of the Empire or subsidiary entities within it.[1] Common vernacular terms for such quasi-horizontal organisations included *Einung*, *Bund*, *Bündnis* and *Gesellschaft*, which might variously be translated as 'alliance', 'league', 'union' and 'society'.

The study of these formations was long confined to regional and local historiographies, but recent scholarship has shown that they were actually integral to the functioning and conceptualisation of the medieval and early modern Empire at every level.[2] The prevalence of feuding (see section VI) made alliances an important tool for mutual defence, and this was their primary purpose, as the extensive military stipulations in the sources in this section show. Equally, the fragmented configurations of lordship that underpinned political actors' authority (see section VII) and the lack of effective and widely accepted judicial resorts for much of this period made associations attractive as a multilaterally agreed framework for resolving disputes. Whether they prescribed detailed mechanisms for arbitrating between association members or simply stipulated that specific judicial pathways should be followed in existing courts, the treaties that founded and renewed leagues and alliances almost always sought to regulate and channel 'internal' conflict. Some alliances enabled other joint initiatives, such as collective actions against insurrections

---

1 Hardy, *Associative Political Culture*, esp. chapter 5.
2 Ibid.; Close, *Shared Sovereignty*.

within member cities or regular assemblies to discuss shared challenges. These organisations not only sought to manage mundane local interactions, but were also vested with significant ideological content by their members. The preambles to association treaties tend to reference the need for divinely ordained peace and justice within a given locality and group of communities. The similarity between these legitimising discourses and those in Empire-wide ordinances (see sections II and III) is not coincidental, and points to the conceptual prominence of multilateral structures for many German-speakers in the fourteenth to sixteenth centuries.

Alliances' ideological resonance and perception of relevance to the essence of the Holy Roman Empire as a polity is clear from the phenomena labelled *Landfrieden*. In the period encompassed by this book, discourses that evoked this term could apply to the monarchical duty to enforce peace, pan-imperial peace-ordinances (e.g. [20–21]) and alliances that claimed to exist to maintain peace in a given region. The practical means by which these different pathways to peace-keeping operated overlapped substantially. In the fourteenth century, Charles IV's approach to governance relied heavily on collaboration with local 'land-peace' alliances, which he fostered and sanctioned from afar or in person during his itineraries. The 1356 renewal of the Swabian land-peace, consisting of twenty-nine free and imperial cities [37], is a case in point, and its wording reveals how much deference was accorded to the emperor in arranging these regional formations when he was at the height of his influence. We know from narrative sources (e.g. [4]) that these land-peaces really did operate in practice, albeit with mixed results. Yet these were only one type of regional alliance, and many had little to do with the monarchs, even while they tapped into the same legitimising discourses about *Landfrieden*. The prohibition against alliances that were not officially recognised as vehicles for upholding 'the peace of the land' in the fifteenth chapter of the Golden Bull [14] proved futile. While coalitions could foster conflict, as in the 'Town War' of the 1380s, they were essential for managing and resolving it, and there was no ready alternative in the absence of a more centralised government capable of running vertically integrative institutions that could take on the functions of alliances and associations.

The highest-ranking figures in the Empire made use of this same format to put into practice their professed goals on behalf of the Romano-German political community. The six German electors frequently formed alliances, as in the treaty of 1424 that ostensibly aimed to support their shared mission to oppose the Hussites (sometimes called the 'Electoral Union of Bingen') [39]. This was only one of several such treaties – other generations of electors entered into similar agreements in 1399 (before Wenceslas' deposition [5]), 1446, 1461 and 1503. Alongside their high-minded claims to uphold the Empire and its mission, the electors also used such alliances to defend their corporate interests, including against monarchs, as signalled by the implicit criticism of the failures of Sigismund to maintain the Empire and defeat heresy in the 1424 treaty.

The electors were not alone in embracing alliances at the highest level of imperial politics. The king and leading princes and cities employed the customary template of the alliance as a practical method for organising and implementing peace throughout the German-speaking lands of the Empire. The 1389 land-peace of Eger [15] was an early experiment in this direction. It ordered all imperially immediate members of the central and southern German regions to organise themselves into a series of regional associations, which were in turn supposed to assist one another trans-regionally in keeping the peace. The lack of central institutions and the quasi-absence of the monarchy prevented this system from working in practice, but the concept was revived in the public peace-ordinances of the later fifteenth century [20–21], which functioned by having all imperial members behave as if they were part of a pan-imperial alliance, assisting one another against enemies and peace-breakers and using prescribed judicial resorts to resolve their disputes. The imperial circles [25] further elaborated this system. It did not replace other associations, but worked in concert with them, relying on existing networks to carry out the aspirational peace-keeping methods prescribed in the peace-ordinances. It is in this context that the Swabian League, founded in 1487–88 [41], should be understood. The League was not created *ex nihilo*. The emperor sanctioned the consolidation of a nexus of existing noble, urban and princely alliances in southern Germany. The idea was to bring together competing parties in an exceptionally fragmented area of the Empire in a way that chimed with the Habsburg monarchs' interests (notably in opposing the Bavarian Wittelsbachs), and for the resulting League to act as an enforcing arm of the developing public peace legislation. This was largely successful, in that the Swabian League expanded rapidly, assisted Maximilian I in his major wars and opposed knightly and peasant uprisings in the 1520s, disintegrating only in the face of confessional strife in the 1530s.[3]

If associations proved readily adaptable at the apex of the Empire's affairs, it is because they were deeply embedded as traditional ways of regulating interactions in every locality of the German lands, from what is now Switzerland to the Baltic coast. Indeed, in these more peripheral regions, longlasting nexuses of alliances could develop into important local power structures, existing in symbiosis and occasionally in rivalry with the Holy Roman Empire's evolving institutions. The cluster of cities and rural communes that came to be known as the 'Swiss Confederation' (*Eidgenossenschaft*) in the fifteenth century grew out of strong alliances forged between the Upper Rhine and the Alpine passes over the preceding 200 years. The league between Zurich and Lucerne and its rural allies Uri, Schwyz and Unterwalden in 1356 [38] was typical of fourteenth-century association treaties in most respects, except that it was supposed to last in perpetuity. It was only by the sixteenth century that the Confederation was starting to detach itself from the rest of the Empire, and this outcome was by no means predetermined in the late Middle Ages.[4] At the opposite end of the Empire, the Hanseatic League – composed mostly of Low German-speaking cities with trade interests along the North Sea and Baltic coasts – proved almost as durable as the Confederation, though it was much looser and more ad hoc and sprawling, lasting in various configurations from the thirteenth to seventeenth centuries. The renewal of the alliance among a subset of Hanseatic cities in 1443 translated here [40] shows that their treaties were similar to those of associations elsewhere in the Empire, but with additional emphasis on the commercial concerns of the merchant-dominated city councils.

The changes of the sixteenth century – including the political consolidation of the Empire and its constituent authorities and the religious fractures among the estates – did not reduce the attractiveness of the alliance format. It was repurposed as a vehicle for confessional solidarity in the form of old faith and evangelical

---

3 Close, *Shared Sovereignty*, chapter 1.
4 Hardy, *Associative Political Culture*, pp. 118–19.

associations, including, most famously, the Schmalkaldic League founded in 1531 [43] and expanded over the ensuing years to include most Protestant princes and cities. But perhaps the most enduring legacy of associations was their role in shaping the internal configuration of emerging principalities. These were by no means bounded unitary states under the direct control of a prince, but fragmented agglomerations and bundles of properties and jurisdictions gaining gradual coherence, under the intermediary management of local elites who demanded their own say in governance.[5] Even the strongest principalities in the more consolidated northern half of the Empire had their own incipient 'estates'. These were not an impersonal constitutional force in the *Ständestaat*, as older German scholarship tended to portray them, but networks of political actors who could identify themselves corporately when defending shared interests.[6] This is clear from the 'alliance' (*voreynynge*) of the prelates, knights and towns of Mecklenburg in 1523 [42] – a multilateral format (an association embodying a principality) that would have a long afterlife, ensuring that 'associative' structures endured well into the early modern period in the German lands.

---

5 Ibid., chapter 4.
6 Ibid., chapter 8.

37. An alliance and land-peace in Swabia (1356)

Fritz (ed.), *Monumenta Germaniae Historica. Constitutiones*, pp. 459–61.

We the imperial cities of Augsburg, Ulm, Memmingen, Kempten, Kaufbeuren, Donauwörth, Nördlingen, Dinkelspühl, Bopfingen, Biberach, Ravensburg, Lindau, Buchhorn, Überlingen, Pfullendorf, Constance, St Gallen, Schaffhausen, Leutkirch, Wangen, Esslingen, Reutlingen, Schwäbisch Gmünd, Schwäbisch Hall, Heilbronn, Rottweil, Weil der Stadt, Wimpfen and Weinsberg proclaim publicly and unanimously and make known to all with this document:

Since the land-peace ordered and established by our gracious lord Emperor Charles of Rome is now ending and will have expired on the upcoming Martinmas [11 November], and since our same gracious lord Emperor Charles has now shown and performed for us the especial grace, for the sake of the peace and comfort of the cities and region, that we should and may ally with and commit ourselves to one another to be mutually helpful and supportive in all just and honest matters, and that it is his imperial order and will that we reach agreement and bind ourselves to one another for the causes of peace and justice, until the emperor should call this off or repeal it – so, to this end, we have all collectively reached agreement with one another that we want to truly and firmly have and uphold for ourselves the peace recently established by our gracious lord Emperor Charles, in all its points, commitments and articles, without deceit, just as the same peace was previously established, until the upcoming St George's Day [23 April 1357] and then for an entire year after that.

And we have committed ourselves and allied together to uphold the same peace. We have now therefore ordered and divided ourselves into three groupings, but all of us should and want to uphold the one single alliance and land-peace together. First, these cities have been ordered together: Augsburg, Ulm, Memmingen, Kempten, Kaufbeuren, Donauwörth, Nördlingen, Dinkelsbühl and Bopfingen. And then we have ordered these cities together: Biberach, Ravensburg, Lindau, Buchhorn, Überlingen, Pfullendorf, Constance, St Gallen, Schaffhausen, Leutkirch and Wangen. And after that we have ordered these cities together: Esslingen,

Reutlingen, Schwäbisch Gmünd, Schwäbisch Hall, Heilbronn, Rottweil, Weil der Stadt, Wimpfen and Weinsberg.

And we have all collectively promised and committed to uphold the land-peace together. Therefore, if anyone – whoever they are – located within the boundaries of this land-peace should be the victim of illegal robbery, abduction, murder, arson or damage, or if someone unjustly declares a feud against them, the city located closest to where this took place – if the perpetrator is discovered in the act or as soon as the misdeed is heard about, and if the same city's council recognises under oath that it is the kind of case that requires an immediate reaction to the misdeed – should make every effort and mobilise all its resources to ensure that restitution is made in the matter. However, if the same city assesses under oath that it might not be able to handle such a case alone, it may call upon as many nearby cities from its grouping as might be needed to get the situation under control. But if a situation is so severe and large-scale that the same city located close to it assesses under oath that it needs to call for aid, the same city, or the one(s) being damaged, should call the cities in its grouping to an appointed diet at the most convenient time for deliberation within their city. And every city in the same grouping should send honourable envoys from its council there. And if all or a majority of those sent there by the cities recognise under oath that the misdeed on account of which they were summoned should be acted on, the same cities in that grouping should accomplish and carry that out unhesitatingly and without any objection. If the same envoys sent by the cities because of such a situation assess under oath that the case is so severe and large-scale that the same grouping among which the situation arose might not be able to carry this out alone, they may and should call on as many men from the nearby cities of the other grouping as they assess under oath that they might need to accomplish this and get the situation under control, and the other cities should assist them in this unhesitatingly and without any objection.

[If a city itself is attacked in these ways, it may likewise call on its nearby allies in the order stipulated above. The allies should help provide one another with goods, equipment and finance as these joint campaigns against perpetrators and enemies might require. The provisions set out above apply whenever a member city and its allies have a conflict with a lord and his allies.]

And if one or more cities among us, the aforenamed cities, should prove delinquent, disobedient or obstructive vis-à-vis the points and articles written above and below, and all or most members of the grouping to which the same city or cities belong consider and determine under oath that the same city (whether one or more) has indeed broken and violated the articles, the same city should be expelled from this peace and never re-enter it for as long as this peace lasts. And nobody should be bound to assist the same city in any way. And the same city should be considered to have acted unjustly and dishonourably.

Also, if some issue should arise within this peace during its period of validity, and then after its expiration someone should have a dispute or pursue justice over this issue with the lords and cities who were sworn members of this peace, we should then stand by and assist one another collectively after the peace's period of validity as fully and firmly as if this peace were still in effect, as described above, until the same city or other members of this alliance (whether one or more) facing judicial pursuit is entirely rid of the matter.

Also, if violations, arguments or conflicts emerge or arise between one city and another, or between citizens within cities that are in this alliance, both disputants (or, if one is unwilling, one party) should call the cities in their grouping to an appointed diet, in the way set out above. And the same cities should set and provide a date for both parties on which to hear and take into account the arguments and causes of both sides and adjudicate and issue a decision about their conflict and case, through informal negotiation or the rendering of an amicable judgement, and both sides should follow and obey the cities in this without any objections. And if either party does not want to follow the cities' decision, the cities in the same grouping and all the other cities – as many as necessary – should stand by and assist the obedient party to ensure it receives restitution from the disobedient party.

Also, if lords, knights or retainers should wish to join us in this landpeace, regardless of whichever of our groupings this is requested, if the same grouping or the majority of its members considers that the same lord, knight or retainer would be beneficial and good for the peace, they may indeed accept them into this land-peace with us. And the same, whether he is a lord, knight or retainer, should swear an oath on holy relics and promise to uphold and carry out this land-peace truly and firmly, as written above.

We have also collectively agreed under oath that we should all assemble together in Ulm twice per year without needing to be summoned, once on St Walpurga's Day [1 May] and once on St Gallen's Day [16 October], in order to deliberate with one another there about necessitous matters facing us collectively or as individual cities.

Also, if it should come to it that all the cities collectively were called to arms and required each other's assistance, the cities should be summoned to the interior of the city of Ulm, and all the cities summoned there should come to Ulm according to their oaths, as we have sworn collectively to do.

And we have all collectively and unanimously sworn oaths according to a prescribed formula, on holy relics and with raised fingers, as has each of us cities with all of its citizens, to have and uphold this land-peace and all matters on which commitments have been made truly and firmly until the upcoming St George's Day and then for an entire year after that, without deceit, unless our gracious lord Emperor Charles of Rome should call off or repeal this peace and related matters beforehand, in which case this peace and related matters should duly be ended.

And to authenticate this truly, we the cities of Esslingen, Reutlingen, Schwäbisch Gmünd, Schwäbisch Hall, Heilbronn, Rottweil, Weil der Stadt, Wimpfen and Weinsberg have appended each of our cities' communal seals to this document.

Which was given on the Monday before St Martin's Day [7 November], there in the year of God's birth 1300 and in the fifty-sixth year.

38. The eternal alliance of Zurich, Lucerne, Uri, Schwyz and Unterwalden (1351)

Segesser (ed.), *Abschiede*, pp. 260–63.

In God's name, amen. We the mayor, councillors and collective citizens of the city of Zurich; the mayor, council and collective citizens of the city of Lucerne; and the mayor and community of landpeople of the lands of Uri, Schwyz and Unterwalden make known to all who see this document or hear it read out:[7]

That we have agreed to an eternal alliance and friendship, with good counsel and judicious consideration, for the good peace and protection of our bodies and possessions, our cities, our lands and peoples, and for the sake of the collective benefit and favour of the region. We have vowed and sworn corporeal, public oaths together on holy relics following a prescribed formula, for ourselves and our successors, who should be eternally bound to and included within this, that they should uphold and have an eternal alliance with one another, which should eternally remain – now and hereafter – unalterable, unbroken and uninjured in all things, continually and firmly, in good faith. And since all perishable things are forgotten, and the events of this world pass away, and in the course of the years many things are altered, so we the aforenamed cities and lands endow this, our mutual faithful society and eternal alliance with a tangible witness – with documentation and with writing, as follows.

We should faithfully offer assistance and counsel to one another to the maximum extent that our physical capabilities or material resources allow, without any deceit, against all those who might violently or illegally commit injustice against us, impair, attack or injure us or inflict any harm or damage on us, whether it affects our bodies or possessions, our honour or our privileges, or we ourselves or anyone else in this alliance, now or hereafter, within the boundaries and areas written below.

---

[7] The offices translated here as 'mayor' had many variations (*burgermeister* in Zurich, *schultheisz* in Lucerne, *amman* in the Uri, Schwyz and Unterwalden). In each case, by the fourteenth century the figure was elected (or selected from a leading oligarchy) by the commune. Uri, Schwyz and Unterwalden were rural communes, sometimes translated anachronistically as 'cantons', but known as *lender* at the time, and embodied by the leading *landlute* ('people of the land'), the community of men with a say in local governance.

[The spatial remit of the alliance, principally bounded by the Aare, Rhine, Thur and Rabiosa rivers to the west, north and east and the Gotthard Pass to the south, is defined in detail. As in [37], the alliance treaty stipulates that any attack on any member justifies calling for aid if the majority of the council of the injured city or land recognises this under oath, and the other alliance members must provide assistance at their own cost when called upon and congregate at Einsiedeln to deliberate about how to proceed in large-scale conflicts.]

If it should happen that we the aforenamed of Zurich should enter into a conflict or dispute with our aforenamed confederates of Lucerne, Uri, Schwyz or Unterwalden or with one of them individually (may God long forfend this), we should hold a diet about this at the aforenamed Einsiedeln Abbey, and the city of Lucerne or the lands collectively or one specific one (whichever has entered the conflict with us of Zurich) should depute two honourable men, and we should also depute two. The same four men should then swear on holy relics to adjudicate the case and conflict without delay, through amicable negotiation or the rendering of a judicial verdict, and whatever the four (or the majority among them) adjudicate should be fully accepted by both sides, without any deceit.

However, if the four nominated for this purpose are evenly divided and disagree, they should – per the oaths they will have sworn – choose and take on a neutral individual residing within our confederacy whom they consider to be a suitable, neutral arbitrator in the matter. And whomever they choose, those in the city or land in which he resides should request of and indicate to him that he should accept the case with the four and bind himself to acting as adjudicator with an oath, without any deceit.

Also, no lay person in this alliance should summon someone to an ecclesiastical court over a financial debt, for everyone should seek justice from others in the settings and courts that are located near and have jurisdiction over those claims and to which such cases belong. And such cases should be adjudicated there promptly under oath, without any deceit. However, if a plaintiff has provably been denied justice in these settings and courts, after that they may seek justice as and wherever necessary, without any deceit. Also, nobody in this alliance should capture or restrain another, apart from legitimate creditors or guarantors, who may do this to debtors who made a promise that included this possibility, without any deceit. We also unanimously agreed that no confederate within this alliance should be held in pledge by another for any cause, without any deceit.

Also, if someone in this alliance should be exiled, once they have been publicly banished by their local court and this is made known to other courts with a sealed document from their city or land, those same courts should also consider them to be banished in the same way as in their local court, without any deceit. And whoever knowingly houses or harbours them or supplies food or drink to them, they should be considered equally guilty, though not liable to bodily punishment, without any deceit.

We have also collectively agreed that the following is necessary and convincing: if at any time we collectively or one of our cities or lands individually should wish henceforth to make plans or form an alliance with lords or cities, we may indeed do so, with the proviso that we should in all things always uphold this alliance with one another eternally, continually and firmly, as agreed and prescribed in this document, above all other alliances into which we might enter, without any deceit.

It is also verily agreed that if someone should impair or damage Lord Rudolf Brun, a knight, who is currently mayor of Zurich, or whoever may be mayor in the future, or the councillors, guilds and citizens collectively of the same city, affecting their jurisdictions, guilds or laws that they have issued and which are included in this alliance – when we the aforenamed of Lucerne, Uri, Schwyz and Unterwalden are called upon regarding this by a mayor alone or by a Zurich council, with a mayor's or council's sealed letter, we are oath-bound to offer assistance and counsel unhesitatingly, so that the mayor, the councillors and the guilds remain in their authority, their jurisdictions and their laws, as they existed when they joined this alliance, without any deceit.

[The alliance members exclude the following parties from the terms of the treaty: the king of the Romans and Holy Roman Empire; the dukes of Austria and their jurisdictions; and existing allies in other alliances. All communes within the area encompassed by the alliance should have their privileges and traditions respected.]

It is especially agreed, so that this alliance may ever henceforth be all the better known to the young, the old and all those who belong to it, that these promises and this alliance should be proclaimed and renewed verbally, in writing and with oaths and everything necessary to them every ten years at the beginning of May (or shortly beforehand or afterwards, without deceit, as one of us, the four aforementioned cities and lands, may require of the others under oath). On these occasions, all men and youths over the age of sixteen should also swear to uphold this alliance firmly in perpetuity, with all the articles written in this document, without any deceit. If, however, the renewal were not to take place at these same appointed times, and someone were to neglect or renounce it for any reason, this should not harm this alliance in any way, for it should endure eternally, continually and firmly with all the articles written above, without any deceit.

We have also, after careful consideration, issued the stipulation and reservation that if we should ever hold counsel together about any matter in which we reach unanimity for the sake of our common good and necessity, now or hereafter, and which differs from what is prescribed and agreed in this alliance – whether this would add to or subtract from its content – we may indeed proceed with this together and should have the authority to do so, as long as all of us in this alliance reach unanimous agreement while holding counsel that we consider this beneficial and appropriate, without any deceit.

And to document publicly that what is written above should remain true and firm in perpetuity, for us and for all our successors, we the aforementioned cities and lands of Zurich, Lucerne, Uri, Schwyz and Unterwalden have publicly appended our seals to this document, which is given in Zurich on St Walpurga's Day at the beginning of May (1 May), as one counts from God's birth 1350 years and thereafter in the first year.

39. An alliance of the six German electors (1424)

Weizsäcker et al. (eds), *Deutsche Reichstagsakten. Ältere Reihe*, vol. VIII, pp. 347–51.

By the grace of God, we Konrad of Mainz, Otto of Trier and Dietrich of Cologne, archbishops of the Holy Roman Empire in the German and Romance lands, arch-chancellors in the kingdom of Arles and in Italy, Ludwig, Count Palatine of the Rhine, arch-steward of the Holy Roman Empire and duke of Bavaria, Friedrich, duke of Saxony, arch-marshal of the Holy Roman Empire and margrave of Meissen and Friedrich, margrave of Brandenburg, arch-chamberlain of the Holy Roman Empire and burgrave of Nuremberg, all electors of the same Holy Roman Empire, proclaim and make known publicly with this document to all who see it or hear it read out:[8]

Since great and severe heresy and unbelief has sadly arisen in the crown and kingdom of Bohemia, and increased as time has worn on, and rises up, expands and grows further everywhere day by day; and although we have previously deliberated about this with other princes, counts, lords and cities of the Holy Empire, and resolved to oppose it with all our capabilities, and also expended great financial and material cost on this account; yet, these endeavours, expenditures and efforts of ours have still not achieved the beneficial and favourable outcomes necessary for Holy Christendom and the holy Christian faith. For Almighty God has now deemed us worthy and appointed us to this task: that in view of such disgraces in the Holy Church and Christendom and especially all that is happening contrary to the holy Christian faith, we should – with the counsel, help and assistance of our most gracious lord the Roman (etc.) king – justly assist, inspire, exhort and make requests of the Holy Roman Empire's other princes, counts, lords, knights, retainers, cities and all other Christian believers regarding this, as it rightly falls to Christian princes and the Holy Roman Empire's first and foremost members to do.

---

8 Five of these electors were also authors of [12], and their full details are given there. With the extinction of the Ascanian dynasty in 1423, the new duke and elector of Saxony was from the house of Wettin: Friedrich I 'the Belligerent' (r. 1423–28).

And after timely counsel that we have held about this at some length – with one another individually, and also in the presence of our faithful councillors, both spiritual and temporal – we have come to no better conclusion or understanding than that the best starting point for resisting the aforementioned heresies, unbeliefs and errors is surely that we the aforementioned electors should enter a collective alliance with one another and embody an amicable and Christian union together, and – with the help of our aforementioned most gracious lord the Roman (etc.) king – call and draw the Holy Empire's other princes (both spiritual and temporal) to ourselves.

And to this end we have collectively entered into an alliance and league with one another, as Christian princes, to resist and oppose such matters and disgraces, which ought rightly to pain us, and for the praise of Almighty God, the strengthening of the Holy Church and the whole of Christendom and the honour, benefit and favour of our most gracious lord the Roman (etc.) king, the Holy Roman Empire and all the Christian believers who belong in and to it. We therefore ally and league ourselves collectively with one another by the power of this document, as is written hereafter:

[1] First, we the aforementioned lords should and want to be together and uphold one another, collectively and individually, with good, just and total faith and intentions, for as long as we live. And we should never – on account of any matter or event that might arise or develop – enter into any kind of war or enmity with one another in any way, without any deceit.

[2: Disputes within the alliance should be settled at a diet for mediation attended by associates of the disputants, with a chief arbitrator appointed by the other electors having the final say.

3: The electors should assist anyone who is fighting against heretics.

4: The electors should extend counsel and military assistance to one another if any of them should be attacked or have their rights and jurisdictions impaired. They may call on the king in such scenarios. Judicial encroachments should be dealt with at arbitrational diets to be held in Frankfurt or Aschaffenburg.]

[5] Also, should a schism break out in the Holy Church (may God forfend), we should and want to assemble to deal with that, alongside our educated clergy and associates, at a diet in Frankfurt or Aschaffenburg (the current bishop of Mainz at that time should

select one of these cities for this purpose), and come together to negotiate the matter as Christian princes, without deceit.

[6: The electors should work together in all matters that affect the Holy Roman Empire's powers and jurisdictions. If they are unable to agree on an issue, a diet should be held in Frankfurt or Aschaffenburg, and they should deliberate there until they reach a common position.]

[7] If someone – whatever their status – should seek to diminish, dismantle, dismember or alienate the Holy Roman Empire or any of its constituent parts, we should collectively oppose this, and should not apply or give our endorsement, favour or permission for this in any way. Rather, we should call on our most gracious lord the Roman (etc.) king to administer and preserve matters. If anything of this kind occurred before the date of this document, henceforth we should not apply or give any confirmation or endorsement of it, without any deceit.

[8: The electors should call on the king for support if anyone seeks to oppose them in some way because of their alliance, and unite and commit all their resources against such opponents.

9: The electors should rotate in and out of the role of chief arbitrator in a set order. The arbitrator's competence is established in articles 2, 4 and 6.

10: A new elector may join the alliance upon the death of their predecessor.]

[11] We the aforenamed electors have promised, on our princely faith and honour and by clasping each other's hands, to respect each and every one of the sections, points and articles written above. After that we swore to one another, on holy relics and with corporeal rituals, to uphold, carry out and do this truly, firmly, continuously and inviolably, and not to seek or do anything that is opposed to it, in the spiritual or temporal spheres, secretly or openly, in any way, entirely eliminating any guile or deceit.

And to document and fully secure this, we, Conrad, archbishop of Mainz, have appended our secret seal or *secretum* to this document, and we, all the other aforenamed, have appended each of our seals.

Given at Bingen in the year (as one writes) after Christ's birth 1424, on the Feast of St Anthony the Holy Confessor [17 January].

40. An alliance of Hanseatic cities (1443)
Urkundenbuch der Stadt Lübeck, pp. 201–05.

We the mayors and councillors of the cities of Lübeck, Hamburg and Magdeburg, as leaders of the three groupings of the cities of the German Hanse written hereafter,[9] via our suitable envoys assembled at a diet in Lübeck on behalf of the above-written cities and on our behalf, proclaim publicly to all with this document:

After good consideration, well-thought-out reflection and good counsel, and with free will, for the praise of Almighty God and the honour of the Holy Roman Empire, for the sake of the manifest necessity, succour, benefit and favour of the lands and cities and to resist violence, and also for the succour, assistance and protection that we may accomplish for one another against unjust violence whenever necessary and required, we and the other cities have unanimously entered into and formed an amicable arrangement,[10] alliance, mutual commitment and league against everyone, excluding the Holy Roman Empire and that which each of us cities honourably and justly owes our rightful lords, per the points and articles written below.

First, we cities of the aforementioned arrangement and alliance have divided and split ourselves into three groupings. In the first are these cities: Lübeck, Wismar, Rostock, Stralsund, Greifswald, Anklam, Stettin [modern-day Szczecin], Kolberg [modern-day Kołobrzeg], New-Stargard, Frankfurt on the Oder, Berlin and Kölln, the New and Old Town of Brandenburg on the Havel and Kiel. In the second grouping are these cities: Hamburg, Bremen, Stade, Buxtehude, Lüneburg, Uelzen, Stendal, Salzwedel, Seehausen, Osterburg and Tangermünde. In the third grouping: Magdeburg, Halle, Aschersleben, Quedlinburg, Halberstadt, Helmstedt, Brunswick, Goslar, Göttingen, Northeim, Einbeck, Hildesheim, Hameln and Hanover.

And each and every one of us, the aforenamed cities, should and wants – wherever we can and are able to – to faithfully secure, protect,

---

9 This tripartite division of the alliance is elaborated two paragraphs below.
10 *tohopesate* – a Middle Low German word especially linked to the Hanse, literally meaning 'assemblage' and indicating any kind of treaty-based relationship.

defend and support the Holy Roman Empire's roads that lead to and from our cities, and those who travel on these roads: merchants and their goods, pilgrims and common people on their journeys. And if someone should have their goods taken away or stolen from them or be abducted or harmed on the roads, the city of the grouping that has this under its protection should work with the other cities to help so that the goods are returned to the merchant or they are financially compensated, and so that the abducted people are released.

And we should all collaborate in this and, if necessary and required, hold a diet about it and other matters, as long as we can safely come together for this purpose, so as to deliberate about how to help the merchant get his property back and how the abducted people might be released. Should we be unable to help the damaged parties get their stolen goods back from the attackers and the abducted people released from their captivity in a suitable timeframe, we should then neither wish to nor or be obliged to suffer or tolerate these attackers and those who house, protect and harbour them in our cities, or to permit them to sell any of their goods or wares in our cities, or to extract them from our cities, until they have returned the stolen goods to the merchant or paid him compensation of equal value and released the abducted people from captivity.

Should it happen (may Almighty God forfend) that any lord, prince or retainer or the inhabitants of a region should seek to harm any of us aforenamed cities with violence, vigilantist feuds and sieges, since we, the other cities written above, want to militarily assist and powerfully support the city facing attack, within four weeks of it informing us that it is under attack we, the other cities written above, should send succour and help in the form of a number of mounted men-at-arms, with each man-at-arms given three horses,[11] in the manner written below:

Specifically, those of Lübeck: 20 men-at-arms. Those of Hamburg: 15. Those of Wismar: 8. Those of Rostock: 5. Stralsund: 10. Greifswald: 5. Anklam: 3. Stettin: 8. Kiel: 3. Buxtehude: 2. Stade: 4. Bremen: 12. Magdeburg: 12. Halle: 12. Aschersleben: 6. Quedlinburg: 6. Halberstadt: 6. Goslar: 4. Lüneburg: 12. Brunswick:

---

11 As in the pan-imperial plans for proportional contributions to an army [16], it is probably implicit that each cavalryman would be supported by a larger number of infantry.

12. Northeim: 2. Göttingen: 8. Einbeck: 6. Hanover: 5. Hildesheim: 8. Helmstedt: 3. Uelzen: 2. Hameln: 3. New-Stargadt: 6. Kolberg: 4. Stendal: 6. Salzwedel: 4. Berlin: 6. Frankfurt: 7. The Old Town of Brandenburg: 3. And the New Town of the same: 5.

[Each city should supply its share of the troops at its own cost. The city defending itself in a feud should provide sustenance to men and horses when the collective army resides within it. Spoils of war should be shared proportionately among the cities, with some reserved for the one facing attack. Indebted or impoverished cities unable to afford to send troops may pay 6 Lübeck marks to the city facing attack in lieu of each specified man-at-arms. The cities located nearby are especially exhorted to offer help. As in [37–38], in the case of an unexpectedly large threat the cities should assemble and deliberate about how to proceed. The cities should also co-operate against the threat of lordless retainers who commit crimes against merchants and farmers.]

Furthermore, since certain malevolent people are plotting, intending to inflict strife, insurrection and the ousting of the governing councils in the cities, should any of us learn of this, in secret or openly, they should wish to and be obliged to inform the nearest neighbouring city, and the city should immediately work with whichever of us cities they want to call on first for this to ensure that the strife is settled or contained, and that no further damage stems from it. If (may God forfend) these people should have initiated something like this, we should nevertheless wish to and be obliged to ride there to guard against further damage and to judge the perpetrators if we can. Also, if circumstances should dictate and necessitate it, we should all wish to and be obliged to help in this, so to forcibly constrain the seditionists as to ensure that things follow a better course and righteous order is restored.

If an uprising should occur that were led either by members of the guilds or by certain individual guild members in a city, whoever they may be, collectively or individually, the professional associations or guilds should distance themselves from this, so that through their actions these people would ensure that they would no longer possess or have any guilds in our cities. However, the professional associations themselves should not be abolished on account of the criminal activity. Also, if someone should be suspected and accused of participating in this criminal activity, he should prove his innocence as the judicial process requires. However, should he become a fugitive and refuse to prove his innocence, we should not wish to or be obliged to house or protect him in our cities or to support him, as long as any city he has entered is informed by the city in which he committed the crime.

[Individual cities' pre-existing alliances should be allowed to continue unbroken, provided these are cleared with fellow members of the Hanseatic alliance. They should not undertake future alliances that might harm this alliance, for the duration of its validity. No cities should assist any lord, prince etc. involved in attacking an alliance member. Any city entering arbitration on account of the alliance should ensure the other member cities are included in the proceedings. The allied cities should faithfully assist one another against those who might make legal claims against the alliance and use them to justify feuds.]

And if any of us cities included in this amicable alliance should be found to have committed an injurious offence, the leaders of these three groupings should have full authority to adjudicate the matter as appropriate.

This alliance and arrangement should continue until the upcoming Michaelmas [29 September 1443] and then last continuously for another three years after that. And a half-year before the expiration of these three years, we the aforenamed cities should wish to and be obliged to assemble and deliberate about whether to accept and uphold this agreement and alliance for a more extended period of time.

For greater witness to and knowledge of the truth, three identically worded copies of this document have been drawn up, all cut from one another[12] – the first for those of us from Lübeck, the second for those of us from Hamburg and the third for those of us from Magdeburg, to keep safe on behalf of the other aforenamed cities.

Given in Lübeck in the year 1443 after Our Lord Jesus Christ's birth, on the Friday after the Feast of the Beheading of St John the Baptist [30 August].

---

12 As the document survives in a near-contemporaneous copy, it is not clear if the three original treaties were written on paper or parchment. Either way, the practice in northern Germany was to authenticate documents by cutting them from the same sheet (like a late medieval English 'indenture').

41. The first treaty of the Swabian League (1487)

Bock et al. (eds), *Deutsche Reichstagsakten. Mittlere Reihe*, vol. II, pp. 768–73.

We, N. and N.,[13] proclaim and make known publicly with this letter:

Since the most gracious, very mighty prince and lord, Lord Frederick, Roman emperor etc., our most gracious lord, allowed a collective public peace to be promulgated and ordered it to be upheld [20]; and since we are imperially immediate subjects of his imperial Majesty, and he subsequently demanded via his imperial Majestic order that we should ally with one another and assist in establishing order, that we might persist in and with the said public peace, his imperial Majesty, the Holy Empire and our privileges, and be of service to his imperial Majesty; so, in order that we might be obedient subjects of his imperial Majesty and the Holy Empire, and with the help and counsel of his imperial Majesty's envoy – the high-born lord, Lord Haug, count of Werdenberg-Heiligenberg etc. – sent to us for this purpose, we have undertaken the ordinance written hereafter out of a sense of obligation and duty and allied and leagued with one another, and thus we do this knowingly and by the power of this document:

[1] First, that for the period specified hereafter, no party among us should undertake anything against or act towards another with hostility. Instead, every party should allow the others to remain in the same public peace and their rights, and we should justly arbitrate the disputes and cases that might arise between us during this time, and we should not trouble or aggress one another further or in any other way, in the form and manner that follows:

So, if we prelates, counts, barons, knights and retainers, collectively or individually, or our people or those who answer to us, should enter into a dispute with the cities, collectively or individually, this matter should be adjudicated before a chief arbitrator, whom we should recommend, select and choose from among the collective cities, with assistants of equal status. [The cities should

---

13 The league's treaty was drafted before anyone had formally committed to joining it, so the *intitulatio* contains these placeholders. It was to lightly modified versions of this treaty text that the Upper German princes, knights and cities who joined the Swabian League in the late 1480s and early 1490s agreed.

likewise select an arbitrator from among the prelates and nobility to settle disputes with them.] And as soon as the selection and choice of those who will serve as chief arbitrators has taken place, they should be declared free of their obligations and oaths by the side to whom they belong.

[2] However, if we members of the Society of St George's Shield, individually or collectively, or our people or those who answer to us, should enter into a dispute with communes in towns or villages which are subordinate to the cities or answer to them, this should be arbitrated before a chief arbitrator (with assistants of equal status) selected and chosen from the councils of two cities near to the same city to whom the commune is subordinate. [Likewise, the cities should settle disputes with the Society via arbitrators drawn from two of its members who are based near to the disputant. A chief arbitrator should be freed of existing commitments, unless he made those commitments under oath before the alliance began, in which case another should be chosen.] Upon taking on the case, the same chief arbitrator should also appoint an arbitrational diet within one month, and not delay the matter in any way, as justice requires.

[3] However, if any party among us, or among our people or those who answer to us, should enter into a dispute, collectively or individually, with the citizens, peasants, inhabitants or subjects of another, this should be adjudicated in the settings and courts with competence over the area where the defendant is based. Nevertheless, the plaintiff should receive effective and legally sound assistance against them.

[4] If one of our cities' people or those who answer to them should enter into a dispute with the Society of St George's Shield as a whole, every aspect of the adjudication of the matter should proceed as if we, the cities themselves (collectively or individually) had entered this dispute.

[5] However, if such a dispute only pertains to individuals within the Society, the matter should be adjudicated before the Society's captains and councillors.

[6] And if such disputes should pertain to wanton criminality, inheritances or fiefs, they should be adjudicated and decided in the judicial settings with competence over the areas where they occur, are located or to which they belong.

For another thing, we on both sides during the said duration of the aforementioned public peace should and want to commit to tranquil and undisturbed enjoyment of our and their freedoms, graces, legal documents, privileges, old customs and held possessions, and to administer and retain just rights, for ourselves, our people and those who answer to us, per the content of this alliance, entirely faithfully, without deceit.

[7–8: All parties should defend one another against peace-breakers and feud-declarers against any individual League member, through mutual consultation between the cities and nobles and per the stipulations of the peace-ordinances of this period [**20–21**].]

[9] And if during such wars we or our people should win castles, towns, markets or villages, or take someone prisoner, the same castles, towns, markets or villages and prisoners should be held collectively by all of us in the League.

[10] However, should it occur that we enter a war with lords or others who hold fiefs from some within this alliance, and the fiefs are rescinded from the same, we should not accept any final settlement in the matter until they have had their fiefs returned to them and been re-enfeoffed with them as before.

[11] Item, if somebody outside of this alliance, whoever he or they may be, should seek to trouble or aggress us, collectively or individually, or our people or those who answer to us with alien jurisdictions, spiritual or temporal, to which we are not legally subject, we should support, protect and defend one another in and against this, so that we or our people may justly avert being summoned by the same or having to reject their summons, and so that we and our people may be unburdened by such external and alien jurisdictions and persist in our appropriate and just rights. However, if we or our people should be affected and drawn into spiritual courts by someone outside this, our alliance on account of spiritual matters, that should not be impeded by this, without deceit.

[12] However, if someone should pursue a dispute with us (collectively or individually), our people or our people's people, in Westphalian courts,[14] using procedures other than those outlined in the ordinance and law pertaining to the same courts and the

---

14 Also known as the Vehmic courts – see [**17**].

reformation [17], we should also support one another as written above against that.

[13: The captains and councillors of the League should facilitate the just settlement of disputes in the appropriate settings between members and external parties.

14: If a member voluntarily initiates a war beyond the confines of the Leage, the other members are not obligated to assist that member.

15: Where the League should get into a feud, its members should not abandon or separate from one another until that feud's resolution.

16: If a ruler who is a member should die, his properties and people should remain affiliated with the League.

17: Members should not give away properties in a way that might jeopardise their commitments to the League.

18: Members should not allow one another's subjects to become citizens of their town(s).

19: Members should not bind themselves in treaties of protection, alliance or service to anyone except by arrangement of the League.

20: League captains and councillors may accept other parties into the League upon receipt of a sealed document committing to upholding all the articles of this treaty.]

[21] If princes, lords of princely rank or powerful communes should request to join this, our alliance, or we should solicit them to join, they should be accepted following a unanimous or majority endorsement.

[22: No League member should assist an outside party against a fellow member at judicial diets and arbitrational meetings.

23: If outside parties should pursue disputes over matters stemming from the League's activities after the League's duration has elapsed, the former members should assist one another in that case as if the League were still in effect. The League has no obligation to defend individual members' servitors or citizens in their private property disputes, except for those of the Society of St George's Shield. No member should purchase claims to be pressed against a fellow member from an outside party. Enemies of the League should not be granted letters of safe-conduct by its members.

24: Disputes that led to feuds or a final judicial settlement before the League's foundation should not be taken on by its members.]

[25] Whatever is discussed in councils following a call for aid should, per the oaths we have sworn about this, be kept secret and not transmitted to anyone else.

[26] And this, our alliance should begin today, on the date of this document, and thence last twenty-five entire years.[15]

And hereupon we have all – each and every one – sworn special oaths to God, on holy relics, with corporeal rituals, prescribed words and raised fingers, to faithfully uphold this document in all its content and not to do anything nor arrange anything to be done against it in any way, without any guile or deceit.

---

15 This version of the treaty was drafted on 28 July 1487. A subsequent draft from the following month specified a thirty-year duration. Bock et al. (eds), *Deutsche Reichstagsakten. Mittlere Reihe*, vol. II, p. 778.

42. An association of the prelates, knighthood and towns of the duchy of Mecklenburg (1523)

Sachsse (ed.), *Mecklenburgische Urkunden*, pp. 214–16.

We the prelates, fief-holding knights and towns of the principalities and lands of Mecklenburg, Wenden, Rostock and Stargard publicly proclaim with and by the power of this document, for ourselves and our heirs and successors:

As and since many conflicts and troubles are currently happening in the Holy Empire, and it is daily to be feared that more will arise in the future, so we have bestirred ourselves with prudence and mature counsel to prevent such things as far as possible. Thus, we have allied and contractually committed ourselves on account of this, for the praise of Almighty God and the honour, benefit and wellbeing of the serene, high-born princes and lords, Lord Heinrich and Lord Albrecht, brothers, dukes of Mecklenburg, princes of Wenden, counts of Schwerin, lords of the lands of Rostock and Stargard etc., our gracious lords, and their princely Graces' lands and peoples, in the manner that follows.

First, most importantly and above all, that we should wish to and ought to show willing, humble obedience to our gracious lords of high renown in all areas in which we are duty-bound and obliged to do so towards their princely Graces and their successors on account of God, honour and rightfulness, and foster regular justice for every individual, so that we may be all the more graciously protected, supported and maintained in our rights and in our privileges, liberties and praiseworthy customs by their princely Graces.

However, if it should happen hereafter that we – collectively or individually – should have our said privileges, liberties, rights, praiseworthy customs and old traditions impinged upon, harmed or violated by someone, contrary to justice and fairness, whether with violence or by any other means, we should not wish to and ought not to abandon them to the same harms against their rights, but offer help, counsel, succour and support, as justice requires, to the maximum extent that we have the power to do so under the law.

Also, should it happen that, as mentioned above, somebody should be forced or pressured into any kind of harm, against justice and with violence or judicial claims, we likewise should wish to and ought to offer assistance, firmly persisting and bearing with it, per the counsel of the prelates, fief-holding knights and towns, until the matter reaches a negotiated settlement.

We also want to assist and provide oversight with faithful diligence and to the maximum extent of our capacities, so that peace and unity may henceforth be promoted, upheld and administered here among us. And furthermore, the wanton perpetrators of damage who will not content themselves with the existing legal order should not be housed or protected by us or any of our people in a way that might harm another. (For all towns, castles and houses should be open as legal and necessary refuges to everyone whom we recognise as entitled to use them under the law.)

Also, we wish to and ought to issue a response to the request of any plaintiff who has suffered damage, in the place or town relevant to the case (at the plaintiff's own cost and expense) and per whatever is determined in our arbitrational council. And it is our unanimous recommendation that these people written hereafter should serve on the council. From the prelates, our gracious lord the bishop of Schwerin or his Grace's regent at the time, the abbot of Doberan and the dean of the cathedral of Schwerin. From the fief-holding knighthood in the land of Mecklenburg, Lord Nikolaus Lützow, knight, Detlef of Bülow, Matthias of Oertzen and Hennecke Plesse; in the land of Wenden, Wedinge Moltzan, Achim Hahne, Dietrich Flotow and Lütke Bassewitz; in the land of Stargard, Melchior Barvoth, commander of Mirow,[16] Heinrich Hahne of Pletze, Poppe Blankenberg and Engelke Helpthe. And in addition to these, two people from each of these towns written hereafter, who should be appointed by their governing councils: Rostock, Wismar, Neubrandenburg and Güstrow. And these aforenamed people should be empowered, at the request of a plaintiff who has suffered damage, to hold a judicial council about how justice should be rendered for them and anyone else, and to offer just assistance, as set out above.

However, if they reckon and acknowledge that the matter is of sufficient magnitude, they should summon the prelates, fief-holding

---

16 *kumpther* – that is, overseer of the *Komturei* of the Knights Hospitaller in Mirow.

knighthood and towns to a suitable time and place, to hold further deliberations there and make decisions commensurate with the necessity of the matter. Also, if one or more of these aforenamed people should go to be with God in death, the others from the same land as the deceased should summon some of the families of the regional nobility to themselves and elect and choose another from among them who, in their opinion, would be beneficial and useful for this task.

We do not wish by and with this, our alliance, to have detracted in any way from the authority of our gracious lords, their princely Graces of high renown and their heirs and successors, nor indeed from the oaths and obligations that we have undertaken up to this point. May we hereby be found and regarded as nothing less than ever faithful, humble and obedient. We also wish to have stipulated and reserved here that we may always extend, shorten and modify this, our mutual commitment and treaty, as often as might be necessary and required.

So that everything written above should be firmly, eternally and irrevocably upheld, without any subterfuge or human deceit, we have collectively and individually committed ourselves to one another and endorsed this through the making of promises on our honour and faith with mutual hand-clasping in lieu of oaths.

And to document this and enhance its security, we [a list of five clerics representing the prelates, twenty-two knights representing the fief-holding knighthood and an undisclosed number of mayors and councillors representing the cities] knowingly append our seals to this document for ourselves, for our dynasties and heirs, for our successors as prelates and in the towns and for all other collective estates and their heirs and successors. We, all of the collective estates, hereby avail ourselves of their seals for ourselves and our heirs and successors.

Given and written in Rostock on the Feast of St Peter in Chains, on the first day of the month of August, in the 1523rd year after Christ's birth.

43. The founding treaty of the Schmalkaldic League (1531)

Fabian (ed.), *Die Entstehung des schmalkaldischen Bundes*, pp. 347–53.

By the grace of God, we Johann, elector and arch-marshal of the Holy Roman Empire, and Johann Friedrich, father and son, dukes of Saxony, landgraves of Thuringia and margraves of Meissen, Philipp, Otto, Ernst and Franz, brothers and cousins, all dukes of Brunswick and Lüneburg, Philipp, landgrave of Hessen, count of Katzenelnbogen, Diez, Ziegenhain and Nidda, Wolfgang, prince of Anhalt, count of Askanien, lord of Bernburg, Gebhard and Albrecht, brothers, counts and lords of Mansfeld and the mayors, councilmen, guild masters, councillors and communes of the Upper German, Saxon and coastal cities named hereafter – Strasbourg, Ulm, Constance, Reutlingen, Memmingen, Lindau, Biberach, Isny, Lübeck, Magdeburg and Bremen – hereby proclaim and make known to all:[17]

The course of events in these times is proving and appearing at once frighteningly and rapidly volatile, and playing out such that some may be seeking through violence and forceful deeds to coerce those who, through the grace and bestowal of the Almighty, allow the preaching and proclamation of the bright, clear, pure and unblemished Word of God in their principalities, cities, lands and districts (whereby all kinds of abuses may be remedied and amended) into abandoning these Christian enterprises of theirs. And yet every Christian authority is nevertheless officially obliged not only to have the holy Word of God proclaimed to its subjects, but also to endeavour with all diligence, seriousness and capabilities to prevent them from being coerced against or falling away from the Word of God. Our highest necessity and official obligation as authorities therefore requires that if now or henceforth it should occur or happen that somebody should undertake to coerce us or our subjects away from the Word of God and divinely acknowledged truth through violence or forceful deeds (which beneficent and merciful God may graciously forfend, and

---

17 Most of the founding members of the Schmalkaldic League also signed the 'Protestation of Speyer', and their details can be found in [28]. The most notable addition here is Johann Friedrich, son of Duke Johann of Saxony and his successor as elector from 1532 to 1547.

which we hope will not transpire for anyone) and to require us to return once more to the abolished and emended abuses, we should make every effort to guard against this, so that such violence might be averted and the ruination of our and our subjects' bodies and souls might be prevented.

Thus, we have agreed, resolved, established and accepted a Christian and amicable alliance treaty with one another, for the praise of Almighty God, the increase, flourishing and growth of free Godly teachings, the revival and promotion of a Christian, unanimous condition and peace in the Holy Roman Empire of the German nation and all that is honourable, and additionally for the good, wellbeing, honour, benefit and favour of our collective principalities, cities and communities, solely for the purpose of self-defence and self-preservation, which is allowed and granted not only by natural law but also by written laws. And we do this presently in and by the power of this document, in the manner, form and extent set out hereafter:

Namely, that all parties among us ought and want to be heartily disposed towards one another, to conduct ourselves faithfully and to warn each other of dangers. Also, nobody should openly or secretly lead through, support or take in another's enemy or opponent. And so that this contractual alliance should only serve for self-defence and self-preservation, and none of us should at all be perceived as wanting to start any war, if it should occur that any party among us, whoever they might be, should face oppression or attack or actually be feuded against and attacked on account of the Word of God, evangelical teachings and our holy faith – or on account of things which follow and depend on the Word of God, evangelical teachings and the holy faith, or if another matter should be raised against one of us as a pretext, but we and the others who are not facing attack at that time should determine that the matter is in fact primarily about this issue of the Word of God – and the same attacked party seeks rapid, decisive justice from us others, then all of us – the other members contained in this Christian alliance – and each of us in our individual capacity should, as soon as we are informed, notified and made aware by the attacked party, or otherwise receive credible reports, allow the matter to affect us just as if each of us ourselves were being attacked, feuded against and invaded, and as if it were our very own cause. Thereupon, each should assist, succour and defend the party being feuded against or oppressed with their greatest capabilities, without any deceitful delay and without waiting for the others, creating room for the rest of us to consider most aptly and fruitfully what, given the circumstances of the matter at that time, might be a good and serviceable course of action, and what is indicated to each of us by Christian love and faith and our own conscience and wellbeing. And thus should we help one another faithfully to carry out the matter. And no party should permit or enter into any arbitration, treaty or truce without the knowledge and consent of the others.

Also, this Christian alliance of ours should not be directed against his imperial Majesty, our most gracious lord, or any estate of the Holy Roman Empire, or anyone else. Rather, it should only be undertaken for the preservation of Christian truth and peace in the Holy Empire and German nation and protection against unjust violence against us and our subjects and associates, as a matter of self-defence and self-preservation, as set out above – for each of us is still subject to the giving and receiving of justice.

If someone further wishes to enter into this Christian alliance of ours who was not previously included in it and who has accepted the holy gospel, they should be admitted and accepted with all of our knowledge and consent.

And this Christian alliance should begin on today's date and last for six consecutive years, and be carried out and upheld by all of us, collectively and individually, faithfully, honestly, righteously and without any deceit.

And if it should happen that we should enter into a war with someone on account of the Word of God, or causes stemming from it, and this war should not have fully ended before the aforementioned six years have elapsed, all parties should nevertheless faithfully persevere in that war and see it through to the end, regardless of the fact that the six years will have passed and this Christian alliance will have come to an end, and no party should withdraw or exclude themselves from it.

And this Christian alliance may then readily be extended, if this pleases all parties.

We, the aforenamed elector, princes, counts and urban councillors promise and vow on our honour, dignity, truthful words and good faith, in lieu of an oath, for ourselves and our heirs or successors etc., in and by the power of this present document, to uphold, entirely fulfil and live up to all and every one of these stipulations, firmly and inviolably, and not to do anything against it nor have anything done against it in any way, all with honour and faithfulness and without deceit.

And for the better documentation, security and enactment of this in every respect, we, the aforementioned elector, princes, counts and cities, have knowingly had our seals appended to this document – we, Duke Johann, elector, for ourselves and our son, Duke Johann Friedrich of Saxony; and Duke Ernst for ourselves and our two brothers, Dukes Otto and Franz of Lüneburg. And it is given on the Monday after *Invocavit* Sunday [27 February], in the 1531st year after the birth of Christ, our beloved lord.

VI
FEUDING, WARFARE AND ARBITRATION

Even by the standards of its time, late medieval Germany was a violent place. Complaints about public disorder and injustice suffuse reformist writings (section IV) and the preambles to ordinances and associations (sections II, III and V). Although they could undoubtedly be exaggerated rhetorical exercises in the service of other agendas, these complaints would not have had much purchase, and would not have been so widespread, if openly violent attacks had not been a genuine threat to the lives and livelihoods of many contemporaries. The comments of foreign observers, like the Franco-Burgundian diplomat Philippe de Commynes (1447–1511), also suggest that outsiders perceived the German lands as unusually violent.[1] The way in which this violence publicly manifested itself was through a spectrum of conflicts – 'feuds' (*Fehden*) and wars (*Kriege*) – seen by their initiators as legitimate and customary means of defending their honour and interests.

The structural causes of feuding are much debated, with most historians having abandoned long ago the economic explanation that poverty drove 'robber knights' (*Raubritter*) to banditry in favour of political, social and cultural interpretations. These include the decentralisation of authority requiring 'self-help' solutions (*Selbsthilfe*); the frequent frictions entailed by fragmented configurations of lordship that provoked daily disputes over property, jurisdiction and revenue; and – perhaps most importantly – the sense that feuding had become a deeply embedded, quasi-legal custom throughout the German lands by the late Middle Ages.[2] The controversial yet influential historian Otto Brunner even thought that the customs surrounding the feud revealed something essential about the spirit and mentality of pre-modern German communities.[3] Historians have since uncovered a coherent set of procedures that underpinned feuding, often by drawing on

---

1 Zmora, *The Feud*, pp. 1–4.
2 Ibid., Introduction; Hardy, *Associative Political Culture*, chapter 3.
3 Brunner, *Land and Lordship*.

sociological and anthropological theory to illuminate its functions and meanings. One or more noblemen (for it was usually noblemen, even if princes, cities and even farmers[4] also had recourse to feuds), perceiving themselves to have suffered some unfair disadvantage in a dispute, would escalate their demands vis-à-vis their opponents and, if unsatisfied, send a feud-declaration (*diffidatio, Absagebrief*) to the party that had allegedly slighted them. This act created a state of 'enmity' (*inimicitia, Feindschaft*), wherein violent attacks against the opponents' property and subjects were legitimate and generally carried out with the goal of forcing them to the negotiating table and extracting acceptable concessions. The 1395 feud-declaration of Wolf of Wunnenstein against the city of Strasbourg [44] is a classic example – it laconically sets out the letter-sender's grievances against the recipient (in this case, over lost revenue from damaged property), argues that fair resolution was sought but not received through peaceful negotiation and declares that a feud must follow both to defend the sender's honour and to enable him to seek compensation.

Clearly, then, recent research has revealed that feuding was not a sign of chaos or anarchy, as older, pejorative views of the Empire implied, but a comprehensible framework for socio-political interaction, with its own – potentially rational – logic. Particularly significant in this regard is the close connection between feuds and the multilateral, highly negotiated forms of conflict resolution that invariably followed them: arbitration and mediation at diets (*Tage*).[5] While this term came to be used for political assemblies (sections II and III), it was far more commonly deployed to describe more-or-less formal, para-judicial resolution of disputes within regional networks. Arbitration did not have to follow violent conflict, but where feuds and wars did erupt, they were invariably followed (if not always fully resolved) by parleys at diets.

All this being said, it is worth considering the limits of this functionalist model of feuding. It may broadly characterise how most feuds played out, but risks underplaying the potential of any conflict to spiral out of control (not least because violence is linked with emotions – including anger and hatred – that do not always entail rational calculation and are not amenable to optimally negotiated

---

4 Reinle, *Bauernfehden*.
5 Hardy, '*Tage* (Courts, Councils, and Diets)'.

outcomes). It also obscures the capacity of actors involved in a feud to improvise within and beyond agreed 'rules of the game' and the fact that some parties increasingly questioned the legitimacy of feuding (which helps to explain gradual moves towards its prohibition) – not to mention the suffering inflicted by a form of 'negotiation' that often involved raiding and extorting one's enemies' most vulnerable subjects.

Indeed, the large, trans-regional wars that could develop from local feuds show that feuding always contained destabilising possibilities within it, even if most conflicts played out in predictable and contained ways. One of the most damaging and consequential wars of the fifteenth century has come to be known as the 'Margravial' or 'Second Town War'. It erupted in 1449–50 from growing tensions between a coalition of princes and nobles centred on Margrave Albrecht 'Achilles' of Brandenburg-Ansbach on the one hand and the city of Nuremberg and its urban, noble and princely allies in Franconia and Swabia on the other.[6] Several feuds born of other local disputes, such as that of Count Ulrich V of Württemberg-Stuttgart (r. 1433–80) against Esslingen and its allies in the league of Swabian cities [45], became interlinked via the sprawling networks of allies and clients on all sides of the voluminous feud-declarations sent in 1449 (which number in the thousands).[7] Such a multifaceted conflict was not easy to resolve, and negotiations extended across multiple diets between 1450 and 1453, arbitrated by some of the highest-ranking figures in the Empire, independently and on behalf of the monarch. The earliest successfully arbitrated settlement between the parties was negotiated at Bamberg in June 1450 [46]. While such written negotiated agreements (called *Abschiede*, like the recesses of imperial diets) often say frustratingly little about the detail of the negotiations that led to their creation, they still reveal the key themes and practices in the Empire's internal wars, including not only the conquest of strategic places and the taking of hostages, but also the gathering of revenues from occupied properties and the coercion of enemies' clients into oaths of loyalty or homage.

While the majority of parties involved in initiating feuds were male, women in the right circumstances could also be protagonists

---

6 Zeilinger, *Lebensformen*.
7 Ibid., p. 32.

in late medieval German political culture. Widowed noblewomen acting as regents and – to an even greater extent – abbesses enjoyed considerable room for manoeuvre in this world.[8] The most striking example from this period is Hedwig of Saxony, the skilled and ambitious abbess of Quedlinburg between 1458 and 1511. Hedwig was involved in long-running conflicts with town of Quedlinburg over her rights over the commune, then with Bishop Gebhardt of Halberstadt (r. 1458–79) regarding advocatial jurisdiction over her abbey (the right to exercise justice and collect revenues from the religious house and its appurtenances, including the town of Quedlinburg). Hedwig was supported by her brothers, the dukes of Saxony, throughout these disputes. An arbitrational judgement attempted to end the conflict in 1477 [47], but it would ultimately be decided by decisive force the following year, when Saxon troops occupied Quedlinburg and the town submitted to Hedwig.[9]

The late fifteenth century saw the theoretical prohibition of feuding within the Empire, and a growing institutional apparatus to enforce this prohibition, born of a convergence of interests among the 'reformist' factions of princes and the crescendo of criticism generated by the frequent violence in the German localities (sections II–IV). Feuding was riskier in this landscape, but it did not disappear immediately. The semi-autonomous lower nobility, in particular, perceived feuding as a deep-seated right and a method to avoid the extinction of its way of life.[10] (It is also worth noting that the line between 'illicit' feuding and the activities of these men as military commanders serving princes was quite blurry.) Götz of Berlichingen (1480–1562), the one-handed knight and prolific feud-declarer immortalised by Goethe, is the emblematic example. His feuds saw him placed in the imperial ban in 1512 [48], a sign that flagrant violations of the public peace now prompted official responses, even if their effectiveness varied. However, the ongoing effectiveness of informal negotiations is attested by the fact that Berlichingen was able to redeem himself from the ban in 1514 through the mediation of the Swabian League. Indeed, the institutionalisation of the imperial framework did not prevent the continuation of customary negotiation and arbitration as a form

---

8 Rückert, Thaller and Oschema (eds), *Starke Frauen?*.
9 Lyon, *Corruption, Protection and Justice*, pp. 318–19.
10 Zmora, *The Feud*, chapter 5.

of conflict resolution well into the early modern period, in tandem with the new judicial and political apparatus – as exemplified by the successful appeal of the allies of Margrave Albrecht 'Alcibiades' of Brandenburg-Kulmbach (r. 1541–54), who had been outlawed after waging a vicious war in Franconia in the early 1550s, to have his case heard by arbitrators at the imperial diet of Augsburg in 1555 [49].

44. The feud-declaration of Wolf of Wunnenstein against Strasbourg (1395)

Fritz (ed.), *Urkundenbuch der Stadt Strassburg*, no. 946.

As was typical for late medieval cities, Strasbourg was constantly involved in feuds and negotiations with nearby nobles whom its councillors perceived as threats to their interests. In the early 1390s the city seems to have been involved in military action against the Society of the Lion, one of several knightly alliances operating along the Upper Rhine at the time. Whether as a member of that Society or simply another implicated party, the minor nobleman Wolf of Wunnenstein claimed to have suffered property damage during that action. In a letter written on 14 April 1395 he demanded compensation from Strasbourg or a chance to discuss his grievances at a diet. This subsequent feud-declaration is his only other surviving piece of correspondence with the city.

Wolf of Wunnenstein, known as the 'glistening wolf', to Strasbourg:

I am letting you know, as I wrote to you previously regarding losses that I have suffered on your account at the time of the matter of the Society of the Lion, that I would gladly have ridden to meet you at appointed arbitrational diets regarding this, and would certainly have been satisfied with a just verdict offering equivalent compensation from you; yet I cannot obtain this from you. And I therefore want to become your enemy and that of your people, and I want to make this commitment before you: that I want to take this compensation and want to have defended myself against you and yours on account of this with this public letter.

Given on the Monday before the Feast of Corpus Christi [7 June], in the [13]95th year.

45. The feud-declaration of Count Ulrich V of Württemberg against Esslingen (1449)

Schneider (ed.), *Ausgewählte Urkunden*, no. 16.

Ulrich, count of Württemberg[-Stuttgart, r. 1441–80]:

Mayor, council and commune of Esslingen! Know that since you established a new toll in your city, and thereby harshly and severely burdened our land and roads and all commerce, the toll has inflicted such damage on us and our land that we can no longer tolerate it, because of our great necessity. And we have therefore sought amicably to get you to abolish the toll before your fellow league members, namely Ulm and other allied city councils,[11] and after that at other arbitrational diets before the high-born prince and lord, Lord Heinrich [XVI], Count Palatine of the Rhine and duke of Lower and Upper Bavaria[-Landshut, r. 1393–1450], our well-beloved lord and in-law, but none of this has yielded a successful outcome so far.

Additionally, one of our poor retainers was murdered by certain people before your city's defensive fortifications, which were closed off to him, and there he had his life taken from him over a blameless matter. After this deed, the same people immediately went back inside your city. Furthermore, one of your citizens kept watch over the same perpetrators from beneath your city walls, that they might all the more easily carry out their deed. Some of your people have been reminded of this occurrence by some of our people. Yet you have never demonstrated any regret over the matter, which it was your duty not to neglect in the event that we and our people did not look into it, as happened more than a year and a half ago now. And we have recently heard news from your city that once again one of our poor men was slain therein by mercenaries in your city's employ, and had his life taken from him over a blameless matter. Justice demands that you ought to have acted on your own people to ensure that this injustice was redressed. This has also remained incomprehensible to us. Thus, may everyone – if God wills it – readily understand that we find this behaviour of yours intolerable.

---

[11] Esslingen belonged to a longstanding league of Swabian cities (which would later form part of the Swabian League [41]).

On account of all this, we want to be your enemy and that of your people, and thereby to have preserved our honour vis-à-vis you and yours with this, our public letter.

Documented through sealing with our imprinted seal on the back.

Given at Stuttgart on the Tuesday after the Feast of St Peter in Chains [5 August], in the year 1449.

46. The arbitrated settlement of the 'Margravial War' (1450)

Bader (ed.), *Erhard Schürstab's Beschreibung*, pp. 127–31.

The 1440s saw rising tensions between Nuremberg and the margrave of Brandenburg-Ansbach, Albrecht 'Achilles', especially over disputed rights and jurisdictions in Franconia. They went to war in June 1449, when Nuremberg stepped in to defend Konrad of Heideck, a local nobleman with whom the city council had an alliance and service contract, from a feud-declaration by Albrecht. The situation escalated rapidly and drew in dozens of princely and urban allies and thousands of retainers on both sides. Skirmishes and sieges ensued for nine months, while by early 1450 powerful third parties were seeking to broker peace agreements at diets in Heidelberg and Munich. However, this arbitrational meeting held in June 1450 was the first successful settlement, which paved the way for three further years of negotiations until the outstanding disagreements between Nuremberg and the margrave were durably resolved.

By the grace of God, we Gottfried of Würzburg and Silvester of Chiemsee, bishops, and we Friedrich [I 'the Victorious], Count Palatine of the Rhine, duke of Bavaria, guardian etc. [r. 1451–76]; and we, those written hereafter: Hans of Neitperg, Master Ulrich Riederer, on behalf of the most serene prince and lord, Lord Frederick, king of the Romans, ever augmenter of the Empire and duke of Austria, our most gracious lord,[12] Count Georg of Henneberg, Georg Fuchs of Schweinshaupten, master of the household of the aforenamed bishop of Würzburg, Jobst of Venningen, Master of the Teutonic Order in German and Romance lands, Count Hesso of Leiningen, Peter of Talheim and Ulrich of Rosenberg, master of the household and marshal of the aforenamed Duke [i.e. Count Palatine] Friedrich, Johannes Duster, dean of the cathedral of Breslau, the very worthy father in God and lord, Lord Friedrich, archbishop of Salzburg, Otto Penzenauer of Kemnath and Jakob Pütreich of Reichartshausen, councillors of the high-born prince

---

12 Neitberg was a Swabian knight and Riederer a clerical jurist. Both were in the service of Frederick III. All the people listed here are included in the comprehensive prosopography of Heinig, *Kaiser Friedrich III*.

Lord Albrecht [III], Count Palatine of the Rhine and duke of Bavaria[-Munich, r. 1438–60] etc.; proclaim and make known to all:

That at this present diet, on behalf of our aforenamed most gracious lord the king of the Romans, we have negotiated and arbitrated matters on account of the divisions, wars, feuds and enmities that have hitherto arisen, come about and taken their course between the high-born prince Lord Albrecht, margrave of Brandenburg and burgrave of Nuremberg on the one hand and the noble Konrad, lord of Heideck on the other, and also between the aforenamed Margrave Albrecht on the one hand and the honourable, wise mayor, council and citizens of the city of Nuremberg on the other, along with their allies, allies' allies, their people and all those who are implicated in or associated with these matters on both sides, in the form and manner defined hereafter:

Namely, as regards everything in contention between the aforenamed Margrave Albrecht and Konrad of Heideck, they should give and receive and receive and give their informal justice[13] before our aforenamed most gracious lord the king of the Romans, as is just. [The same formula is applied to the disputes between Margrave Albrecht and Nuremberg.][14]

Item, the towns and castles written hereafter should remain in the hands of Margrave Albrecht without deceit until the final negotiation of his rights that will take places in the manner just set out before our aforenamed most gracious lord the king of the Romans: Heideck (the castle and the town), Lichtenau, Bruckberg, Uehlfeld and Lonnerstadt with their appurtenances.

Item, whatever things remain apart from the aforenamed fortifications and their appurtenances – be they castles, houses, immobile properties, freeholds or fiefs with their appurtenances, and wherever and however they are located and named – that were

---

13 *unverdingt recht* – a legal term referring to matters dealt with outside of a formal court of law or criminal case, such as so-called amicable arbitration.
14 In effect, the arbitrators were admitting that these disputes remained unresolved and moving them to a future diet for further negotiation – a very common tactic. The matter would indeed be arbitrated by jurists at Frederick III's court for several years, before Duke Ludwig IX of Bavaria-Landshut negotiated a final settlement at Lauf in 1453. See Zeilinger, *Lebensformen*, pp. 35–36.

captured or subjugated by one side in this war from the other side, or by their allies and allies' allies, these occupied things should be released back into the possession of that same other side in their current condition, without opposition, delay or deceit. And the people on both sides who have had their fiefs revoked because of each of their participation in these feuds, be they citizens, allies or servitors, should be re-enfeoffed, and the same people should be given access to their fiefs without delay or deceit.

Item, whatever may be in contention between Margrave Albrecht and the citizens and inhabitants of Nuremberg who hold fiefs from the same Margrave Albrecht which he has not revoked, their final negotiation of the matter should occur through giving and receiving and receiving and giving justice before our most gracious lord the king of the Romans, as is just.

Item, if somebody among the aforementioned parties or their allies or allies' allies should have been coerced or constrained into doing homage or other commitments, he or they should all be considered and made free and unbound by these, apart from those who belong to the aforenamed towns and castles which should stay and remain in Margrave Albrecht's hands. They should remain in the obedience of the aforenamed Margrave Albrecht until his rights have been fully negotiated, as set out above, without deceit.

Item, any taxes, usages and revenues levied on or from properties, fiefs or pledges before the date of this document, on whichever party or their allies they were levied, should be ceased on both sides. However, any taxes or revenues that have lapsed or not been levied should be paid and obediently entrusted to the lords to whom they belong, as they were before these wars.

Item, the negotiated instructions and agreements regarding usufructs, perpetual revenues, pledges or other contractual or known debts on either side should be upheld by everyone without prejudice, alongside their just rights, without deceit.

Item, whatever possessions, goods, documents or other things (how and whatever they may be) were secured or placed in good faith by any one party or its people for safekeeping by someone else in the castles, towns or markets of another party during these wars, all of those things should without exception be returned and released directly back to each relevant individual or their heirs.

Item, whatever acts of killing, arson, abduction and devastation occurred during these wars should never be subject to judicial proceedings. However, if someone in either party or their ally should wish to treat a matter as a violation of the peace,[15] or if something should have occurred before these present feuds, that should be recognised as subject to justice, and the appropriate judicial procedure should ensue, with the proviso that it should not be claimed or adjudicated as anything more than a matter of minor damage. For Margrave Albrecht should relinquish his claims regarding the abductions, arson and killings carried out by those of Nuremberg at Emskirchen, Roßtal, Veitsbronn and Schwand. And in return, those of Nuremberg should relinquish any claims to compensation from Margrave Albrecht for the loss of their revenues derived from the aforementioned pledges and villages in their possession, if indeed they should have any claims to assert regarding such losses, per the stipulation about this.

Item, while all killings, abductions, arson and devastation should be considered settled and remain ineligible for judicial pursuit, in the manner touched upon above, each party may nevertheless make reference to this point in support of any other judgement they may be seeking.

Item, as soon as they request it from the date of this document, all prisoners taken by either party or their allies during this war should be proclaimed and allowed to go free without delay, upon the swearing of an old, customary oath of release,[16] provided that each prisoner pays for the food they received.

Item, all unpaid taxes and ransoms should be considered void and relinquished by both sides, and any guarantors freed of their commitments regarding these.

Item, it has also been agreed and negotiated that the aforementioned parties have reached an arbitrated settlement and judgement on all this, and that these aforementioned wars and feuds should be entirely terminated and dispensed with, and this agreement and reconciliation should take effect in the manner set out above at

---

15 *fridbruch* – while there was not yet a pan-imperial ban on feuds (the first came in 1467 [20]), jurists would still have recognised transgressions against the provisions of the Golden Bull [14] and 1442 Reformation [17] as a violation of the *Landfrieden*.
16 *urfehde* – see [51] for an example.

sunrise on the upcoming Friday after the Feast of the Visitation of the Blessed Virgin Mary [5 July 1450].

To authenticate this, each of us – the aforenamed arbitrators and mediators – has appended his seal to this document. And now that this agreement and arbitrated settlement set out above has taken place and been carried out with the consent and knowledge of the aforementioned Margrave Albrecht, the lord of Heideck and those of Nuremberg, and as we also endorse it by the power of this document, so we Margrave Albrecht, on our princely honour and dignity, and we the aforenamed lord of Heideck and we the mayor, council and collective citizens of the city of Nuremberg, on our true faith, proclaim and promise in lieu of oaths to uphold this agreement and arbitrated settlement, and all the paragraphs, points and articles contained within it, faithfully and firmly, excluding any deceit, for ourselves and for each of our sides' allies and allies' allies, and for all those who are involved or associated with our and all sides. And we have appended our seals to this document alongside the aforementioned arbitrators' seals.

Carried out and given at Bamberg on the Monday before St John's Day on the solstice [22 June], in the 1450th year after Christ's birth.

47. The arbitrated settlement of the war between Abbess Hedwig of Quedlinburg and Bishop Gebhard of Halberstadt (1477)

Janicke (ed.), *Urkundenbuch der Stadt Quedlinburg*, no. 560.

We Wilhelm [I] the Elder, by the grace of God duke of Brunswick and the Brunswickian lands on the River Leine and in Lüneburg, count of Everstein, Wunstorf, Hallermund and Wölpe etc. and lord of Homberg [1392–1482], proclaim and make known with this, our document to all who see it or hear it read out:

Discord, disagreement and conflict have arisen on account of the advocatial jurisdiction, authority and other usufructs and rights in the foundation and town of Quedlinburg and in the village of Groß-Ditfurt between the highly worthy and high-born princess, Lady Hedwig, born a duchess of Saxony etc., abbess of the secular foundation of Quedlinburg,[17] our well-beloved cousin, alongside the high-born princes, Lord Ernst [1441–86], arch-marshal of the Holy Roman Empire, elector, and Lord Albrecht [1443–1500], brothers, dukes of Saxony, landgraves of Thuringia and margraves of Meissen, our well-beloved cousins, on the one hand, and the honour-worthy father in God, Lord Gebhard, bishop of Halberstadt, our well-beloved lord and ally, on the other, involving attacks and damage committed by, from and through the agency of the subjects of the bishopric of Halberstadt against the well-beloved lady and lords of Saxony and their subjects and associates. The shedding of blood and the ruination and devastation of the land could have resulted from this. To avert and anticipate such eventualities, we have undertaken to amicably arbitrate between our named cousins and the named bishop, and to see all their disputes amicably adjudicated, settled and resolved, with respect to every party.

So: the honour-worthy bishop of Halberstadt, for himself and his episcopal successors, together with his chapter, should withdraw from and relinquish everything that he and his predecessors have held for some time from and within the advocacy, jurisdictions and other authorities and appurtenances of the foundation of

---

17 So called because it was a community of secular canonesses, that is, noblewomen who led pious lives but had not made monastic vows.

Quedlinburg, its towns and the village of Groß-Ditfurt and that our aforementioned cousin of Quedlinburg and her abbatial predecessors have demanded and claimed as their foundation's property. And he should allow it to be assigned to her well-beloved self and her foundation unhindered, and henceforth no longer go after or in any way grasp or take for himself the said foundation of Quedlinburg's authorities, fiefs and jurisdictions and everything else that pertains to the same foundation.

And if anyone should cause any form of damage, loss or injury to the aforementioned foundation of Quedlinburg, whenever the bishop or his successor is informed or told about this, he should help to guard and protect against this faithfully, with no less effort than if it affected him and his bishopric's own property.

Also, the named Lord Gebhard, bishop of Halberstadt, and his episcopal successors should not permit our aforenamed well-beloved cousins of Saxony etc., their people or the people linked to them by fiefs or otherwise associated with them to be harmed by or from his bishopric and its men. And if it should occur that our aforementioned well-beloved cousins or their people, as just mentioned, should incur some damage by or from his bishopric or its subjects, and this is made known to the bishop or he otherwise finds out about it, he and his successors should immediately and without hesitation handle the matter and ensure through faithful diligence and with all his capabilities, alongside our aforementioned cousins and their heirs and with the help of his other lords and allies, that the perpetrators make restitution and provide sufficient compensation. He and his episcopal successors should also not employ his spiritual courts via his *officialis*[18] and spiritual judges in the diocese of Halberstadt against the diocese of Magdeburg, the counts and lords of the Harz and other subjects of our afore-specified cousins of Saxony etc. in any way except the way clearly prescribed and articulated in the earlier treaty between the high-born prince of praiseworthy memory, Lord Friedrich, former duke of Saxony, relative of our aforenamed well-beloved cousins, and the predecessor of the named bishop.[19]

18 The leading judicial vicar of the bishop in his diocesan courts.
19 In July 1442, the bishop and chapter of Halberstadt accepted a treaty with several princes and counts, including Duke Friedrich II of Saxony (r. 1428–64), whereby any disputes over the bishopric's spiritual jurisdiction would be settled via arbitration. Janicke (ed.), *Urkundenbuch der Stadt Quedlinburg*, no. 373.

Also, the aforementioned Lord Gebhard, bishop of Halberstadt, should give and pay 15,000 Rhenish fl. of the old regional currency valuation to our oft-mentioned cousins of Saxony etc. as compensation for certain damages and abductions and significant costs that they incurred. Alternatively, he should pay them an annual sum of 850 of the same Rhenish fl. of security money[20] every year, to be raised from all of his bishopric's usufructs and revenues on two days each year, namely 375 fl. on or as soon as possible after *Invocavit* Sunday [the first Sunday of Lent], and the second half on the Feast of St Laurence [10 August]. The payment is to be made at the castle of Quedlinburg or somewhere else within six miles of it, to be indicated by our well-beloved cousins, until he or his successors have paid off the sum of 15,000 Rhenish fl. to the well-beloved lady and lords.

[As a token of their commitment, the bishop and chapter of Halberstadt should nominate five or six prominent knights or burghers to assist Abbess Hedwig and the Saxon dukes in the event that the articles above should be violated in any way, until restitution has been made.]

To document this, we have knowingly appended our seals to this document, which is given on the field before Quedlinburg on the Tuesday after the Martyrdom of St Laurence [12 August] in the 1477th year after Christ's birth.

---

20 *wehrzins* – a financial arrangement whereby one party paid a fixed sum to another at regular intervals, with the stipulation that the sum would increase if the payments were not made on time.

48. The imperial condemnation of Götz of Berlichingen and his allies for violating the public peace (1512)

Berlichingen-Rossach (ed.), *Geschichte*, pp. 129–32.

We Maximilian, by the grace of God Roman emperor-elect [etc. – the same formula of greeting as in [21] follows.]

Honourable, high-born, well-beloved relatives, cousins, electors and princes and well-born, noble, honourable, reverend and well-beloved faithful people. Although it is ordained and set out in the public peace that we undertook, concluded and promulgated to all with the counsel of our and the Holy Empire's electors, princes and imperial estates, for the good of the Holy Empire and Christendom as a whole, in these specific and explicit words, among other things: [the content of articles 1 and 3 of [21] is copied verbatim]; yet, in spite of this, as we have been credibly and truly informed, Götz of Berlichingen, Hans of Selbitz and Leonhard Birckner have – together with some of their allies and associates – attacked without justification a large number of citizens and merchants of Augsburg, Nuremberg, Ulm and other cities of the Holy Empire and other nations as they were harmlessly riding from the Leipzig trade fair on the Feast of St Eric after *vocem iocunditatis* Sunday just past [18 May 1512]. They also rapaciously seized their property and goods, physically assaulted them in a tyrannical manner without necessity and in the face of no resistance, wounded some of them to the point of death, took them prisoner and led them away, robbed them and still hold some of them in captivity. They did this with disdain for the Holy Empire on the Empire's roads and our property, as well as within the fiefs, districts and safe-conduct of the honourable Georg, bishop of Bamberg, our prince, councillor and reverend, who holds his revered status in fief from us and the Empire as princely regalia; and they did it while our same prince of Bamberg was attending our imperial diet in Trier.

Thus, as per the aforementioned public peace and our and the Empire's other ordinances, statutes, mandates and prohibitions, because of the aforementioned crimes they and all their allies, adherents, accommodators, supporters and all others who lent or sent them retainers or horses to assist them in this evil conduct have thereby fallen into our and the Empire's ban, double ban and other penalties, fines and punishments, defined in the aforementioned public peace and our and the Empire's other statutes and ordinances, namely those called in Latin *criminis lese majestatis* ['of treasonous crime against his Majesty'] and *rebellionis* ['of rebellion'], as well as notorious breach of the public peace and the ban for robbery, oppression of a region and violation of safe-conduct. And they have thereby forfeited all their movable and immovable property, which escheat to us as Roman emperor on account of the demonstrated guilt, forfeiting and criminal deeds, and which should be delivered to our and the Empire's treasury.

[The denunciation of the alleged peace-breakers and their accomplices is reaffirmed, and all estates and subjects of the Empire are enjoined to enforce the provisions of the public peace against them.]

49. A letter of safe-conduct to arbitrational proceedings at an imperial diet in Augsburg (1555)

Kluckhohn et al. (eds), *Deutsche Reichstagsakten. Jüngere Reihe*, vol. XX, pp. 2754–57.

The early 1550s saw the devastation of Franconia by Margrave Albrecht II 'Alcibiades' of Brandenburg-Kulmbach (r. 1541–54), a cadet member of the Hohenzollern dynasty who acted as a soldier of fortune. He served Charles V in the ill-fated Second Schmalkaldic or Princes' War. After the 1552 Peace of Passau, Albrecht plundered and extorted the allied cities and bishoprics of Franconia. His aggression earned him the enmity of several cross-confessional leagues. After inflicting a series of defeats on him in 1553–54, Albrecht's enemies succeeded in having him placed in the imperial ban and stripped of his princely authority. Albrecht appealed to his cousins and clients, who sought with mixed success to have the matter resolved in his favour through arbitration at the same 1555 imperial diet that saw the promulgation of the Peace of Augsburg [30].

We Ferdinand etc., publicly proclaim and make known to all with this letter:

On account of their unresolved disputes, an amicable arbitration with and amid the imperial commissioners, the attending estates of the Holy Empire and the absentees' envoys – all of whom are unaffiliated with the disputing parties and their quarrels – has been undertaken at the present imperial diet between the high-born Joachim [II, r. 1535–71], arch-chamberlain of the Holy Roman Empire, and Johann [of Brandenburg-Küstrin, r. 1535–71] and Georg Friedrich [of Brandenburg-Ansbach-Kulmbach, r. 1545–1603], margraves of Brandenburg, our well-beloved cousins, elector and princes, on the one hand, and the honour-worthy Weigand of Bamberg [r. 1522–56] and Melchior of Würzburg [r. 1544–58], bishops, our princes and well-beloved reverends, and the mayor and council of our and the Holy Empire's city of Nuremberg, being fellow members of the Franconian alliance, on the other.

However, it has transpired in these negotiations that the disputes and causes just mentioned may best be settled if the discord between Margrave Albrecht of Brandenburg[-Kulmbach], declared a banned outlaw by his Roman imperial Majesty and the Holy Empire, and the estates of the Franconian alliance were addressed through amicable arbitration and conciliation. And it has additionally happened that Wilhelm of Grumbach, servitor of the outlaw just mentioned, has written to the collective estates together with Christoph Straß *licentiatus*, Hans of Waldenfels, Wolf Christoph of Redwitz, Friedrich of Lentersheim and Gottfried Lochinger and requested collective or individual safe-conduct to this imperial diet.

And we and the aforementioned unaffiliated imperial estates (and the absentees' envoys) have negotiated with the members of the Franconian alliance about this and were able to get their approval for permitting the aforenamed servitors of the said Margrave Albrecht to have safe-conduct to come here for amicable arbitration. However, this should happen in such a way that they keep to the terms of the safe-conduct, and do not secretly or openly practise anything prejudicial to the members of the Franconian alliance during the safe-conduct's period of validity, nor undertake any other kinds of dealings that are against the said members of the Franconian alliance and that might be detrimental to the peace, whether they involve travelling back and forth or commerce. Rather, they should solely await the planned amicable arbitration, and otherwise abstain fully from all other objectionable matters and activities.

And thus we have granted his imperial Majesty's, our and the Empire's free, immediate security and safe-conduct to the aforementioned Wilhelm of Grumbach, Christoph Straß *licentiatus*, Hans of Waldenfels, Wolf Christoph of Redwitz, Friedrich of Lentersheim and Gottfried Lochinger, collectively and individually, in the name of his Roman imperial Majesty, our well-beloved brother and lord, and for ourselves as king of the Romans, following considerable deliberation of the esteemed commissioners of his imperial Majesty and the aforementioned estates of the Holy Empire and the absentees' envoys, so that the pursuit of amicable arbitration and the Franconian alliance members' litigation against the named Margrave Albrecht – through attainment of a verdict of outlawry, and also in the related suits before the imperial cameral court and their other judicial and jurisdictional disputes and claims – may proceed without prejudice and damage.

[The letter ends with a formulaic reaffirmation of the safe-conduct's legal validity and the penalties for violating it.] Given at Augsburg on the first of August, in the year etc. [15]55.

VII

LAW, GENDERED RULES AND SOCIAL DISCIPLINE

While the Holy Roman Empire underwent important changes between the fourteenth and sixteenth centuries, reflecting and shaping the political, social and cultural configurations that evolved within it, most inhabitants of the German-speaking lands were more directly affected by smaller and more localised legal and governmental frameworks. Indeed, some interpretations of the late medieval and early modern Empire have emphasised so-called 'territories' (*Territorien*) – understood as centralising, increasing well-demarcated subsidiary state-like units within the Empire, usually ruled by princes – as the central locus of governmental activity and political change.[1] Narratives of putative 'territorialisation' (*Territorialisierung*), and the more intensive princely-territorial rule (*Landesherrschaft*) to which it gave rise, have emphasised the top-down creation of 'territorial' institutions at princes' courts and a hierarchy of subordinate officials, enabling the consolidation of judicial and fiscal power over defined areas, and the rise of coherent estates embodying the 'territorial' community and identity in interaction with the ruling dynasty. Early modernists have also traced the rise of coercive social discipline (the regulation of public morals by consolidating authorities) and – after the Reformation – confessional conformity (a process dubbed 'confessionalisation').[2] However, other researchers have pointed to the limitations of the 'territorial' framework.[3] For one thing, there was no unambiguous language of 'territoriality' before the seventeenth century. For another, the search for discrete spatial-political units misses the more relevant interpersonal and dynastic logics of governance. The so-called 'territories' were very diverse in their internal configurations and the power bases of princes relied on fragile networks of local actors with competing loyalties. Furthermore, the (gradual

---

1 For example, Bahlcke, *Landesherrschaft*.
2 Whaley, *Germany*, chapter 43.
3 For what follows see Schubert, *Fürstliche Herrschaft*; Hardy, 'Were There "Territories"?'.

and uneven) concentration of power under certain princely regimes was layered on top of local forms of lordship that remained fragmented and overlapping to a dizzying degree. At these more local levels, we can also gain insights into the normative expectations for the lives of non-elite and marginalised groups, such as various strata of peasants, non-aristocratic women and Jews. The sources in this section illustrate the nature and limitations of legal and political frameworks at regional and local levels of German society, and the constraints and possibilities facing subaltern groups subjected to institutionalising forms of governance.

The smallest socio-political units were rural communes such as villages, of which there were some 100,000 in the late medieval Holy Roman Empire, and in which the majority of the population lived.[4] An overwhelmingly diverse array of legal and tenurial arrangements characterised these settlements, not only across but within German-speaking regions.[5] Still, most had some form of customary legal tradition, supposedly handed down by word of mouth among the leading men of the village and produced through accrued pronouncements based on a pristine law that humans did not invent, but merely drew on to 'discover' verdicts (*Rechtsfindung*). These pronouncements began to be written down in the late Middle Ages and, with increasing frequency, in the sixteenth century, effectively forming corpora of village customary law. They had a variety of regional names – *Ehaft, Willkür, Öffnung, Taiding* and *Ruge*, among others. The best-known and most self-conscious textual tradition is that of the *Weistümer* in the densely populated western Empire. Once thought to be an authentic expression of age-old 'Germanic' folk traditions, these texts are now understood as contingent, innovative and dynamic products of contests over advantageous rules between communes and their various lords.[6] In claiming that the customs they were articulating were the 'good, old law' handed down by word of mouth, leading peasants enjoyed some room for manoeuvre vis-à-vis seigneurial officials seeking to codify village law, especially where a village had multiple lords who could be played off against one another, as seems to have been the case in a 1435 *Weistum*

---

4 Kümin, *Communal Age*, p. 26.
5 Scott, *Society and Economy*, chapters 4, 6.
6 Teuscher, *Lords' Rights*.

preserved from Wagenschwend [53] (on the northern edge of modern-day Baden-Württemberg).

Such *Weistümer* point to the widespread dispersal and overlap of properties and seigneurial rights and revenues (so-called *Grundherrschaft*) among many parties at even the most localised level. These configurations were enabled by the mobility and commodification of all the fundamental building blocks of political power – such as lands, offices and titles, jurisdictions, taxes, tithes and fees – which could be held and exchanged among a surprising range of actors. Prevailing forms of tenure were amenable to such a sprawling distribution of seigneurial assets, even if they encased transactions in a specific interpersonal and liturgical framework (such as oath-swearing or liege-homage). Most items, including even offices in a princely administration and noble titles, could be sold or pledged – that is, held and enjoyed as a form of pledge-collateral (*Pfandschaft*) in exchange for a loan. An item held as a fief (*Lehen*) was supposed to be subject to the accumulated conventions of feudal law (*Lehnrecht*), but even in theory those conventions were flexible, and permitted a spectrum of protagonists to hold assets that conferred political power in a variety of creative formats. Thus, the feudal section of the popular *Swabian Mirror* law-book [50] (see also section I and [1]) admits that certain ranks of women and clerics could hold fiefs, and permits a surprising degree of fluidity even within the theoretical constraints it imposes on the holding and transferring of fiefs. Moreover, in practice a still wider range of people than those acknowledged by the *Swabian Mirror* held fiefs, used feudal courts and were involved in the nexus of 'feudal' relationships – including burghers who were not necessarily of noble status.[7] Consequently, the patterns of local governance that we can glimpse in sources such as *Urbare* (lists of a lordship or institution's properties and incomes) are extremely complex. The records of the priory of Reichenbach in 1427 [52], for instance, reveal settlements, revenues and jurisdictions shared among multiple lords, whose fragmented possessions forced ad hoc joint rule over the same spaces – a far cry from discrete 'territorial' units.

All the same, centripetal forces were undeniably at work in the leading principalities of the Empire. Some of the questions that

---

[7] Patzold, *Lehnswesen*, pp. 94–119.

remain open are how exactly this gradually centralising authority operated; how this new layer of princely authority interacted with existing structures and dynamics of lordship; and which parties came to see it as advantageous to foster and participate in emerging princely/'territorial' identities and institutions. A long-studied genre of legal source that seems to encapsulate new and explicit princely claims to judicial and fiscal supremacy – that of the 'land-ordinance' for all or part of a prince's domain(s) (*Landesordnung*)[8] – sheds light on some of these issues. One of the earliest was issued by Duke Wilhelm III of Saxony for his landgraviate of Thuringia in 1446 [54], at the outset of a war with his brother Elector Friedrich II over the division of the Saxon patrimony. It certainly exhibits his aspirations to assert his jurisdictional supremacy and channel judicial activity to his personnel, and to establish new methods of taxation. The land-ordinance also includes a variety of regulations for public morality. Equally, the provisions of the ordinance attest to the many agencies involved in 'territorial' consolidation, and the ways in which such legislation did not solely enhance princely power. Issued at an assembly in the presence of leading Thuringian nobles and towns, the ordinance was predicated on a future treaty among these elites to co-ordinate the implementation of its planned judicial and fiscal provisions. (Indeed, land-ordinances were implicitly addressed to such elite constituents and their officials, not an abstract 'territorial' population.)[9] In short, the Thuringian 'territory' was conceived and operated somewhat like an association (see section V, especially [42]). At a more granular level, other sources show that even aspects of what we would think of as 'criminal' law – exerting control and punishment over purveyors of violence – was not only a matter of vertical authority under princes, but also of negotiation within networks of allies and feud-enemies. This is exemplified by the genre of the *Urfehde*: a prisoner's or hostage's commitment, usually made under oath, to end hostilities with their captor in exchange for their release. In an example from the lordship of Henneberg in 1401 [51], elements of both 'verticality' and 'horizontality' are at play: three brothers from

---

8   The prefix *Land-* is sometimes translated as 'territorial', but this English term risks over-emphasising an anachronistically spatial dimension to a term that was more about defined groups of people: communities of custom or disparate groups united by loyalty to a princely house. See Hardy, 'Were There Territories?'.
9   Bahlcke, *Landesherrschaft*, pp. 26–27.

the 'Truchsess' family (meaning 'steward' – and implying a subordinate if high-ranking position) submit to the lords of Henneberg, but also have their right to continue a feud against the town of Schmalkalden confirmed.

The free and imperial cities also clarified and consolidated their jurisdictional and fiscal powers in this period, and nowhere more so than within their city walls. The most highly developed consequence of this process was so-called 'reformations' (*Reformationen*) of urban law, undertaken in the late fifteenth and sixteenth centuries. In 1484, Nuremberg became the first city to promulgate one [56]. Among the many areas covered by the reformation – from questions of urban jurisdiction to rules about marriage and inheritance – were legally binding oaths, including a special formula for Jews. Jewish communities existed in many German cities. The rich and diverse textual and material sources created by these communities attest to their cultural and economic vibrancy.[10] They faced deep prejudice and frequent violence – sometimes escalating into mass murders and expulsions – on the part of their Christian authorities and neighbours. Nuremberg itself expelled its Jewish population in 1499, so the oath did not appear in subsequent editions of the 'reformation'. Until that point, Nuremberg was one of many German cities that required Jews to accept what Miri Rubin has described as 'awkward – and sometimes embarrassing – forms of oath-taking'.[11] The inclusion of the 'Jewish oath' in the reformation points to the ambitions of urban governments to expand the forms of social control under their legal remit.

This same ambition impacted women, too, especially the most vulnerable. The trend is well illustrated by the increasing regulation of brothels by civic authorities, which culminated in their wholesale abolition in some sixteenth-century towns (especially those that embraced evangelical teachings). Between 1400 or so, when sex workers were mostly accepted as 'deviant insiders' within the urban population, and the disappearance of brothels was a phase in which authorities attempted to impose social discipline on sex workers in the name of good morals and public order.[12] They often did so through ordinances such as the one issued in Strasbourg in 1471

---

10 For an introduction see Toch, *Die Juden*.
11 Rubin, *Cities of Strangers*, p. 57.
12 Page, *Prostitution and Subjectivity*, p. 10.

[55]. The implications of the fines threatened by the council appear all the starker given that many sex workers were forced to work to pay off debts owed to their brothel-keepers.[13] The corollary of this tendency was an impulse by all authorities, civic and princely, to protect 'honourable' women, notably through the regulation of certain forms of sexual violence, as in the provision included in Margrave Christoph I of Baden's land-ordinance of 1495 [57]. This was not only an ethical matter, but also pertained to the perceived reputation and 'value' of a woman (especially an unmarried woman) in late medieval patriarchal culture. As was common elsewhere in Europe, fifteenth-century German ordinances sought to compel rapists to compensate or marry their victims. (Disturbingly, from our perspective, this was a legal codification of an outcome sometimes demanded by the victims' own families.)[14]

It would be a mistake to view this growing inclination towards regulation and discipline as a purely local or 'territorial' phenomenon. The estates of the consolidating Holy Roman Empire itself introduced provisions pertaining to public morals into the ordinances and recesses promulgated at the imperial diets from the late fifteenth century onwards. Notably, the long tradition of sumptuary laws forbidding luxurious dress, prevalent across later medieval Europe, found expression in the recess (legislative outcome) of the Augsburg diet of 1500 [58]. A much more ambitious project came to fruition in the early 1530s: the *Constitutio Criminalis Carolina*. This was the widely used Latin name for the first Empire-wide criminal code, which is presented in its preamble [59] as a rationalisation of judicial practice across all courts. It developed from longstanding discussions within the imperial diets and governing council of the 1520s, reaching its final form in 1532 following the return of Charles V to Germany, and was first printed in 1533 by Ivo Schöffer of Mainz. It has long been recognised by legal historians as a landmark piece of legislation, both because it effectively attempted to standardise penal law across the Empire's myriad jurisdictions (notwithstanding the exemption for existing legal customs), and because it advocated judicial norms and practices borrowed from Roman law traditions to a greater extent than any previous imperial ordinance. The ordinance was

13 Ibid., pp. 95–96.
14 Lansing, 'Conflicts over Gender'.

primarily concerned with regularising and regulating judicial processes, notably witness depositions and inquisitorial procedures including the use of torture, but also prescribed punishments for a wide range of crimes, from blasphemy and forgery to infanticide and witchcraft.[15] The scope of the *Constitutio Criminalis Carolina* is a reminder that the Empire in its entirety remained the focus of legal and governmental innovation and intensification into the mid-sixteenth century, and even the most coherent principalities – such as Bavaria, unified under one branch of the Wittelsbach dynasty from 1506 – had to take it into account. Thus, the 1553 *Bavarian Land-Ordinance* reissued the most recent imperial public peace-ordinance wholesale [60] as the best tool available for pursuing peace-breakers across the Empire's fragmented jurisdictions, illustrating the nexus of intersecting agencies in German politics and society well into the early modern period.

---

15 See Kroeschell, Cordes and Nehlsen-von Stryk, *Deutsche Rechtsgeschichte*, pp. 293–96.

50. The *Swabian Mirror* on feudal law and the fluidity and entanglement of lordship for men, women and clerics (thirteenth–fifteenth centuries)

Derschka (ed./trans.), *Der Schwabenspiegel*, pp. 236–38, 242–44, 295–96, 302.

One-quarter of the *Swabian Mirror* is devoted to feudal law (*Lehnrecht*). Amid its many prescriptions regarding fief-holding are several, translated in this extract, that highlight the recognition that groups beyond lay noblemen were involved in feudal tenure, as well as the social, political and economic complexities and entanglements created by the common scenarios in which multiple parties held fiefs jointly or exchanged them relatively fluidly between tenants.

[1] Concerning the *Heerschild* and eligibility to hold a fief.

Whoever wants to master feudal law should obey this book and its teachings. We should first note that the kings established seven *Heerschilde*. [The allegorical description of the *Heerschildordnung* is repeated in similar terms to those found in [1].] Priests and farmers and all who are not freedmen in perpetuity and not born into the knightly estate should not avail themselves of feudal law, as we set out hereafter.

[...]

[4] Fiefs for priests and women.

If a priest or a woman should receive imperial property, they may indeed hold it in fief, if both – priest and woman – belong to the knightly estate. And if it should go to another feudal lord, they may receive this property in fief from them, too. Any priest of knightly estate may hold fiefs for life or at will. However, he may only sub-enfeoff another with his fiefs, or involve the fiefs in other legal transactions, with the consent of the feudal lord.

And if a priest has a brother (or several brothers) and receives a fief with that brother through a joint enfeoffment, and shares the usufruct and possession thereof, and the brother dies without eligible feudal heirs, the right to the fief remains with the priest according to the law just written above.

And if a woman holds a fief from a lord, she has the same rights as a priest. And if a man – whoever he may be – receives it jointly with her, and they have equal rights of possession, the same law applies as for priests.

[5] How homage is sworn to a lord.

The liegeman should render homage to his lord with his oath stating that he is affectionate and faithful towards him, as the law demands that he should state when asked to do so: namely, that he will support his profit and protect him against harm, as far as he can.

[6] How the liegeman relinquishes fiefs.

And if a liegeman wishes to relinquish his fief to his lord and no longer to have it from him, the latter cannot legally deny this to the former. He must take it from him. And if the lord does not want to do so, the liegeman should speak thus: 'My lord, I proffer the fief to you, as I have it from you, and present it once, twice and thrice.' And he should do this with folded hands. And if the lord does not take it, the liegeman is nevertheless free of the feudal relationship. He should leave the asset that he had from him in fief freely available. The lord may not harm the liegeman on account of this, unless the latter has forfeited his fief, as stated later in this book.

[...]

[14] Enfeoffment of a liegeman with a monetary fief.[16]

If a lord enfeoffs a liegeman with one or more monetary fiefs drawn from an asset, and that asset yields a higher amount of revenue than the fief's value, the lord should assign money to the liegeman from that asset. If he does not do so, the liegeman should seize the entire asset and derive his money from it, and faithfully retain the rest of the revenue for the lord and give it to him without curtailment if he demands it.

[...]

---

16 *Pfundlehen* or *mangeld* – a fief consisting of a sum of money (usually paid at regular intervals) drawn from a specific asset.

[16] When two people have a joint fief.

In litigation that concerns a fief, two liegemen cannot bear mutual witness if they hold the fief jointly and undivided. If they divide the fief with one another, each may be the other's witness for the fief.

If two liegemen are enfeoffed with an asset by a single lord and both enjoy its revenues, one may not relinquish it to the lord without the other, nor may he modify the fief in such a way that this would be injurious to the other, unless they divide the fief and the revenues derived from it.

A given lord may order his liegemen who hold an asset from him in fief to divide the fief, so that he can be confident about whose service he can call upon. He should order them to divide it within six weeks and a day. If they do not do this, the asset that they hold from the lord may be denied to them, provided the lord does this in conformity with feudal law, as written above.

[...]

[21] The sale of fiefs.

When a liegeman gives a fief to another as a purchase, he should promise to effect the transfer of feudal tenure by his lord without any curtailment. The liegeman should ask his lord to take the asset from him and enfeoff the purchaser with it. The lord should then take it off him. The seller should be very grateful to the lord for doing this, as the lord may legally deny this request. And if the seller cannot sway the lord into accepting the sale, he should give the purchaser another asset of equal worth to the original. And if he does not obtain permission from his lord, he should swear on holy relics about the high value of the asset to him, and give the purchaser an asset of equal value.

[...]

[23] Enfeoffment with an asset derived from mints, mills or tolls.

Whoever holds something in fief from mints, mills, tolls or other such things should have their specific asset indicated to them by the fief-granting lord, as spoken about above.

And if a lord controls the asset of a liegeman whom he has enfeoffed with that asset, or whom he ought by rights to enfeoff with it, the lord should pay him all the revenues derived from it during that time (factoring in any damage it incurs), provided he swears an oath about the true value of the asset. However, if the lord enfeoffs people with more fiefs derived from the asset than he himself possesses of it, the liegeman may call upon him to provide a substitute for the goods that he can no longer obtain from this asset. The lord must do this by law, as soon as the goods to be provided as a substitute are freed up.

[...]

[134] Concerning courts held in fief.

Two liegemen cannot enjoy joint control of a single court in fief, for only one individual can act as judge. However, one liegeman may confer entitlement to a court he holds in fief on another.

Anyone placed in the imperial ban by the king or another judge may not legally act as a judge. The book of customary law clearly sets out who may legally be judge.

Nobody should seek justice before anyone deprived of his court because he has rendered unjust verdicts, or because of some other charge. That person may not summon anyone to his court, either. No child may legally act as judge before the age of eighteen. If a child holds a court in fief, they should have a regent to act as judge in their stead, who should also be a liegeman of the lord from whom the court is held in fief. This applies even if the child is fourteen.[17]

---

17 The age of majority for males for most other judicial purposes, as set out in the customary law section (e.g. Derschka (ed./trans.), *Der Schwabenspiegel*, p. 54).

51. Three prisoners' commitments to the lords of Henneberg in exchange for their release (1401)

Brückner (ed.), *Hennebergisches Urkundenbuch*, no. CXVI.

I Apel Truchsess and my brothers Berthold and Adolf proclaim with this public document:

That we have faithfully promised with hand gestures and then sworn an oath on holy relics with raised fingers never again to do anything of any kind against the noble, high-born lord, Lord Heinrich, count and lord of Henneberg, Lord Wilhelm, his son, and all of his heirs, nor against their lordships, lands and people (spiritual or temporal), either secretly or openly, without any deceit – with the exception of the inhabitants of Schmalkalden, against whom we may still proceed appropriately regarding damages against us. If our aforenamed gracious lord or Wilhelm, his son, or their heirs call upon us to terminate our feud against Schmalkalden, we should do so immediately and without hesitation. Those of Schmalkalden should then be considered part of the same alliances and oaths of release as our aforenamed lords' other lands and peoples, without objection and without any deceit.

It is also stipulated that if we offer our service to our aforenamed lords or their heirs and we incur damages during this service, whether to our horses or in some other way, and this is evidenced and deliberate, our aforenamed lords or their heirs should provide compensation for the damage as fairly as possible, without deceit.

So that we uphold this continuously, entirely and inviolably, each of us, the aforenamed brothers Apel, Berthold and Adolf, has appended his own seal to this public document, which is given in the 1400th year and thereafter in the first year after God's birth, on the Feast of Saints Peter and Paul the Holy Apostles [29 June].

52. Fragmented and entangled properties and jurisdictions in the Black Forest (1427)

Keyler (ed.), *Das älteste Urbar*, pp. 16–17, 140.

This register of the priory's possessions was probably compiled at the request of one its advocates, the margrave of Baden (who shared advocatial jurisdiction over Reichenbach with the counts of Württemberg). It consists of enumerated rights, properties and revenues grouped by location, with over sixty places listed in total. This extract focuses on two of those places, the small town of Horb on the Neckar and the village of Hochdorf, to illustrate the minutiae of property and seigneurial rights in such settings.

Nota anno domini 1427, item this book was then updated from the old books with the sound knowledge of old, honourable people on St John's Day [24 June]. And this was done by Lord Wolf Mayser of the Berg, then prior of Reichenbach [r. 1423–28, subsequently abbot of Hirsau 1428–60]. And included herein are the monastery's revenues and jurisdictions, which they hold in the countryside and in towns, villages, farms and other assets that they have and have held for a long time etc.

Horb

Item, in the town of Horb: one residence with a house, courtyard, barn and garden, together with its appurtenances, located in the valley and called 'the residence of those of Reichenbach'. It was traditionally and is a freehold and should remain so.

Item, in Horb: one field, called the 'Uchtet', and other acreages and properties adjoining it. They have been leased out by the parcel and furrow, as written below. And the field and acreages are divided into three tillable areas. Those who hold them and what they have is written hereafter etc.

[A long list of tenants holding portions of this arable land follows.]

Item, the following has been purchased: a wine tithe from Auberlin Welzlin, located on Wine Lane, being a quarter of a third that the late Heinrich Struchler possessed, and a sixth of a third of an entire tithe that the late Lutz possessed; and equally whatever is yielded by this tithe, be it from gardens, acreages or elsewhere, and in money, fruit, crops or other things; and equally also any revenues from the small toll, from the Bildechingen Gate on the left-hand side upwards to the Neckar Gate in the town.

[...]

Hochdorf

Item, the village of Hochdorf, written about above, belongs to the lords of Reichenbach and to one lord of Mündern Entz.[18]

Item, two annual court sessions occur at the village written about above, one on the day after May Day [2 May] and one on the day after Martinmas [12 November]. The same court sessions are to be held regularly and require no summonses, and whoever does not attend the two sessions – each held at midday – should incur a penalty for each session they miss, namely 18 Tübingen coins.[19]

Item, these two aforenamed court sessions are run jointly. In other words, one prior of Reichenbach and one lord of Mündern Entz hold the judicial rod in common, and thus form a single judge, except that a prior of Reichenbach (or whomever he confides this to) should hold the rod in his hand at the court sessions. And if the judges get into a dispute, such that they cannot resolve or adjudicate a case, the court should entrust the judicial rod to Reichenbach.

Item, if it should happen that one of the lords written above lacks the time to act as judge in the course of the year, he may and should bring his judicial rod with him to Hochdorf and ordain the judges, and whoever then fails to appear at the court sessions when summoned – whether by one lord individually or both jointly – should incur a penalty, namely 18 Tübingen coins, as written above etc.

---

18 Most likely a local minor nobleman. The name literally means 'mouths [of the] Enz'. The Enz was a nearby tributary of the River Neckar.
19 *Tüwinger* – the mint at Tübingen produced pounds, shillings and pennies. The lords and villagers would have known which applied (most likely pennies), but the text is not explicit.

53. 'Unwritten' customary law and peasant agency in the village of Wagenschwend (1435)

Kollnig (ed.), *Die Weistümer*, pp. 440–41.

Let it be known hereafter: this legal emendation was publicised and read out in the four hamlets together with their communes and special jurisdictions, in the presence of the advocates and the subjects, alongside the appended schedule of fees for transfers of loaned properties and the objection to the legal changes found at the start of the property and income register, which were individually read and publicised in each place. These age-old and hitherto concealed legal pronouncements of Wagenschwend have only just come to light again, having been found by me, the record-keeper Michel Sultzer,[20] in an old rent-book made of parchment in Heidelberg. This is how they read, word for word:

No[ta] on the Monday after *Invocavit* Sunday [17 March] *anno domini millesimo quadringentesimo tricesimo quinto* [1435] those of Wagenschwend were mandated and asked under oath to make known the lordly rights and customs of the same village. They therefore disclosed and communicated them, which have come and been brought unto them from times of yore up until now, and which their predecessors in earlier times had likewise communicated under oath in this way.

[1] Item, it falls to whomever is lord and advocate of Lohrbach[21] to order and to forbid, to interrogate and to hold court. And if other lords should have officials[22] there, they should not interrogate anyone, unless Lohrbach's official hands them the judicial rod.

[2] Item, regarding any fines that are issued, if the official of Lohrbach lets them go unpaid, nothing is owed to the other lords either. However, whatever fines are collected by the official of Lohrbach, a third as much should go to the other lords.

---

20 Michel Sultzer was active in the mid-sixteenth century as an administrator for the Palatinate of the Rhine, so this opening paragraph can be dated to some 120 years after the pronouncements themselves were written in the 'old rent-book'.
21 A settlement roughly 10 km south of Wagenschwend.
22 *schultheissen* – one of several names for an official deputised to exercise seigneurial powers in a given area.

[3] Item, if the other lords should be encamped there and the lord of Lohrbach should then arrive, and the lords should not want to remain together there peacefully and quietly, the other lords should vacate the premises for the lord of Lohrbach, despite being located on their own property.

[4] Item, all dues from all assets should go to Lohrbach, although the hens due at Shrovetide go elsewhere.

[5] Item, they also communicated that if somebody should have a judicial complaint to make, they should make it before the official of Lohrbach or his leading representative. And if the official does not help them, they may then take their complaint to whomever they wish. The lords conceded this to them and ordained it in the olden days.

[6] Item, one misdeed[23] entails a punishment of 9 ounces.[24]

[7] Item, a small fine entails 5 shillings in *Heller*.[25]

---

23 *frevel* – a term for 'misdeed' or 'crime' (or its applicable punishment) that could have a large range of specific legal and judicial meanings.
24 Payments were sometimes expressed in weight, functioning in effect as a currency denomination or subunit. The context-specific value could be highly variable, but archetypically a pound (*Pfund* – roughly half a kilogram, depending on the region) of any given coinage or precious metal consisted of 2 marks (*Mark*), 16 ounces (*Unze*), 32 lots (*Loth*), 512 pennies (*Pfennig*) and 1024 heller (*Heller*).
25 The *Heller* was the lowest-value coin in most German regions – usually, but not always, worth half of a penny. Other coinage values might be calculated or paid in *Heller*.

54. A land-ordinance for Thuringia issued by a duke of Saxony and the Thuringian nobility and towns (1446)

Müller (ed.), 'Die thüringische Landesordnung', pp. 9–35.

Following an approach that would be repeated in many fifteenth- and sixteenth-century land-ordinances, the legal provisions promulgated in Thuringia in 1446 touched upon a broad array of issues that the prince and the representatives of the regional elite jointly sought to regulate: the functioning of local courts, religious life, loose morals and excessive luxury, terms of employment and exchange in certain economic sectors and peace-keeping within jurisdictions under princely authority. Bound up with these regulatory provisions was the matter of taxation. The heavily indebted Duke Wilhelm was seeking revenues from his leading subjects, who sought both to constrain these demands and to obtain collective participation in regional governance in return for fiscal support. This extract contains examples of regulations in several of these areas, as well as the provisions for a new tax in return for oversight by a council of Thuringian nobles and towns.

We Wilhelm [III 'the Brave'], by the grace of God duke of Saxony, landgrave of Thuringia and margrave of Meissen [1425–82], make known to all with this document:

Per the providence and will of Almighty God, the principality of Thuringia (with certain additions) has come to us as our portion of our inheritance. From its beginnings, the same eminent principality has been very praiseworthily and estimably vested, endowed and traditionally furnished with a great many splendid counties, lordships, knighthoods and also towns. Additionally, as is well known from many legal documents, the towns have always adhered honestly, justly and without deviation to the princes, our late ancestors and relatives who previously possessed the named principality until our accession, which rightly pleases us.

So we now recognize clearly that, as a prince of Thuringia, there is no other way to remain in our princely power, honour and dignity, uphold our princely status, come out of the great indebtedness in which we found our principality, implement good counsel and a beneficent condition, bring our lands into righteous government and actually be able to put all of these things into effect than with the faithful support, assistance, counsel and obedience of our counts, lords, knights, towns and subjects. And these same can never be more effective and thorough in offering support, assistance, counsel and obedience in all the aforesaid, per our necessity, than by existing harmoniously and engaging faithfully with one another. From such harmony, that is truly to be hoped for, perfect and lasting peace may arise and persist in the lands. Thus, may all of God's service, honour and benefit be augmented and propagated through this peace. And may all estates, spiritual and temporal, be promoted, increased, improved and made greatly productive, and also clearly and greatly show and prove themselves and the whole common good in this regard, whereby towns and villages everywhere, which are currently in a truly dreadful and chaotic state, may be restored and rebuilt, and set up and established in a perfectly just condition.

To this end, as a prince who is unreservedly and entirely inclined towards peace and the prosperity and wellbeing of all of his principalities, lordships and subjects, we have taken to heart, deeply considered and weighed up all of the matters mentioned above, and thereupon earnestly entreated all of our counts, lords, knights and towns of the said principality of Thuringia collectively, via our request,[26] to counsel and assist us, so that – for the praise of Almighty God, the good of ourselves and our lordship and the benefit and prosperity of our lands, the counts, lords, knights and towns and our other subjects – pathways towards these goals written above may be initiated and established, resolved and brought to fruition in a righteous and appropriate form. For our counts, lords, knights and towns, named hereafter, have obeyed our lawful request and have, as faithful subjects, faithfully and diligently counselled their rightful hereditary lord.

Whereupon we, the aforenamed Wilhelm, duke of Saxony etc. and we, the counts, lords, knights and towns written below, namely Bodo, count of Stolberg etc., all counts and lords, and we the knights and towns named later in this document, have all unanimously established and enacted alongside our named gracious lord Duke Wilhelm – with timely counsel and well-deliberated

---

26 That is, the summons to the assembly at which the land-ordinance was promulgated.

consideration, and for ourselves and our heirs, inheritors and successors – the ruling, governing council[27] and ordinance written hereafter, and furthermore will ensure that it is upheld and adhered to in perpetuity, as behoves each of us, in the manner that follows:

[1] Item, since it is just that before all else Almighty God – who created us and all things, which are under His authority – should be contemplated and honoured by us above all other things, so – in order that He might cover our honest efforts all the more graciously with His divine grace, that they might be fruitful and praiseworthy – we will and establish first of all that the holy observance of holy Sundays should be sacredly upheld by all people, whatever their estate, in all of our lands, castles, towns, villages, jurisdictions, districts and everywhere else, and not violated by any work that qualifies as a breaking of the sabbath. However, any person who fails to uphold this every time should accordingly incur a fine of two pounds of wax, to be given to the administrators of the relevant parish church, for the use of the same church.

[...]

[3] Item, until now, the inhabitants of our lands have been frequenting many foreign courts, which is dishonourable, very injurious and extremely ruinous to these lands. In order to guard against that now and henceforth, we have established and instructed that no inhabitant of our lands, lordships and districts may cite or compel anyone to appear before any foreign courts any longer, be they spiritual or temporal, regarding any cases, whatever they may be.

For if a case is spiritual and lawfully pertains to a spiritual court, the plaintiff should bring them before relevant spiritual courts within our lands, and be satisfied with the justice they receive there, and also allow the case to proceed to its conclusion in the same court where it was initiated. And they should not appeal the case to foreign courts outside of our lands, for one can readily obtain doctors and educated people in these lands who can be employed for this purpose. Nothing may violate any of this, except where clerics

---

27 The last section of the land-ordinance (not included here) established a four-person governing council co-managed by the duke and nobility to oversee the implementation of the ordinance, similar in many respects to assemblies within alliances and at the level of the Empire as a whole.

get into a dispute about an ecclesiastical benefice, which they may have adjudicated in the appropriate judicial settings.

However, if the case is temporal, it should be brought before and summoned to the secular judicial officers and courts in whose jurisdiction the defendant is located and the case heard there. The plaintiff should see the claim they initiated through to its conclusion before this same court, as is appropriate, and be satisfied with the justice they receive there, and not appeal the case to any foreign court.

Thus, we should and wish to instruct all of our officials, judicial personnel, judges and assessors who preside over each of our courts earnestly, and always to have them state in their oaths, that they should not curtail anyone's access to our courts, but rather allow everyone to get assistance and proceed with rapid, righteous and readily granted justice, per the lawful traditions and customs of the courts, and as is fair and appropriate in the judicial process for every case brought before them in court. In this way, nobody should have their case or their rights curtailed, but everyone should proceed with their cases equitably, justly and without delay. And every foreigner who comes before the courts, whether they are representing themselves or through their lawyer, should be permitted to come and go freely and without impediment, and they should accordingly hold and conduct themselves benevolently and honestly in their words and actions. And should any judge discover that a foreigner is not conducting themselves appropriately in the courts or allowing justice to proceed in the ways set out above, whomever this applies to at a given time should be punished by us in their body and possessions.

[...]

[19] We also will and establish that henceforth, gambling with games of dice should be forbidden and entirely shunned in villages and taverns in these, our aforenamed lands, lordships and districts.

[...]

[26] Now, we the aforenamed Duke Wilhelm have especially greatly taken to heart the words of the holy gospel which read: 'Any kingdom divided against itself will fall' [Mark 3:24] etc. In light of this, we have fundamentally determined that nothing would be and become more beneficial for the accomplishment

of our stipulated ordinance in our principalities and lands – and more generally for the maintenance of lasting peace and the prosperity and preservation of every good estate of our principality, our lords, our heirs and all our people – than a unanimous treaty and, concomitantly, a permanent general tax and a commitment to mutual assistance and defence for ourselves and our subjects. We have entreated our aforenamed counts and lords and the knights and towns named hereafter earnestly about this, requesting that they reach agreement with us on this, which they have indeed willingly and obediently done. Thus, after extensive deliberation, we the named Duke Wilhelm and we his aforenamed gracious counts, lords, knights and towns have mutually reached a unanimous agreement, with complete resolve, to implement a lawful, lasting treaty and, concomitantly, a permanent tax and a commitment to mutual assistance and defence, to last for eternity, without end and without deviation.

[The remaining articles of the ordinance set out how the tax and mutual defence should be organised among the nobles and towns, under the oversight of a governing council of four people representing the ordinance's signatories. The tax would be gathered from all parties by the council's envoys and the proceeds delivered to the town of Greußen once per year on the Feast of the Purification of Mary, i.e., 2 February.]

55. An ordinance for the policing of prostitutes in Strasbourg (1471)

Brucker (ed.), *Strassburger Zunft- und Polizei-Verordnungen*, pp. 459–60.

Our lords the masters and council and the XXI[28] have proclaimed what is written below:

First, as was previously mandated, that all brothel-keepers, procuresses and those who publicly lead sexually dissolute lives or engage in prostitution, wherever they are based in the city, should move to Bicker Lane, Vincken Lane or Gröyben Lane, beneath the walls or other locations indicated to them, and it is proclaimed that they should remain there. And as some of them have since come back into the city and mingled with honourable people, and conducted their business as before, the same female persons should efficiently relocate to the aforementioned places within fourteen days, on pain of 5 shillings, and whoever disobeys this will incur the 5 shilling fine, and nevertheless be bound to relocate to the aforementioned places, as previously mandated and prescribed.

And so that the same prostitutes and immoral women can be distinguished from honourable women, it is proclaimed that the cloaks they wear should not have a hem, and should also hang at a three-finger distance above the ground. And under their cloaks they should wear neither colourful fur nor silk lining, nor should they wear any dress or shoes adorned with colourful fur or silk, nor attach fur trimming or gold buckles to their outer or inner garments. And whoever violates the points written above must pay a fine of 5 shillings as often as this occurs. And wherever the representatives of the council, the servitors of the *Ammeister*,[29] the tower guards and the guild journeymen come across one of the same prostitutes thusly attired, she should give a pledge for the 5 shillings.

---

28 Late medieval Strasbourg's government consisted of several *Meister*, forming a rotating magistrature at the apex of the regime, a 'large council' (*großer Rat*) and multiple privy councils. When the councils held session together, they issued documents in the name of 'the council and XXI' (the number referring to its notional membership tally).
29 The master representing the guilds on the council.

[The ordinance contains further detailed specifications about acceptable attire for prostitutes, including a prohibition on expensive jewellery and belts.]

No more of these sinful women should perch or sit on the steps in front of the altar in the cathedral, whether in the choir in front of the high altar or before the other altars lower down in the building. Anyone who contradicts this by doing so should be awaited outside of the cathedral, and as she exits her headscarf or cloak should be taken as a pledge and not returned until she has paid 2 shillings in compensation, each time this happens.

If it should happen that a married man should fornicate with a prostitute, whether on the night before a feast day or any other night, wherever the town guards come across this, both parties should be arrested and put into the tower-dungeon, and not allowed to leave for the next two days unless each pays 5 shillings. And if this arrest should take place on the night before a feast day, each should additionally pay a pound of wax and one shilling to the servitors of the *Ammeister*, per the ordinance.

The representatives of the council, the servitors of the *Ammeister*, the tower guards and the guild journeymen should also swear corporeal oaths to God and the saints to follow up earnestly on these things in the manner set out above, and not to ignore anybody involved in such things, and to that end every fourth penny [of unspecified urban revenues] should be made available for their use; and where they should fail to follow up on these things, or spare or ignore someone involved in such things, the masters and council should earnestly punish them for it, as is appropriate.

Proclaimed at the town hall on St Denis's Day [9 October] in the year 1471.

56. Nuremberg's *Reformation of Statutes and Laws* and the oath for the city's Jews (1484)

Beyerle et al. (eds), *Quellen zur Neueren Privatrechtsgeschichte*, vol. I/1, pp. 3, 92–94.

In late medieval and early modern judicial contexts, the German word *Reformation* implied a correction and improvement of ineffective or corrupted laws and regulations. The city of Nuremberg was the first of many political entities to embrace a wholesale legal 'reformation' of this kind, which partly reflects the growing prominence of magistrates educated in civil law. Much of the *Reformation* deals with the competences of and procedures to be followed in the city's courts, including the roles of litigants from many different social backgrounds. This extract offers a translation of the oath that Jews had to swear when participating in judicial proceedings. This is a late version of such a 'Jewish oath' – a demeaning formula that was imposed by many late medieval municipal courts.

This is the reformation of the statutes and laws which an honourable council of the city of Nuremberg has undertaken for the sake of the common good, necessity and certain causes, and to initiate and introduce the same statutes and laws, which are defined below. And since these laws have been created following the counsel of many highly educated doctors and in accordance with the written *ius commune*, insofar as they are compatible with the city of Nuremberg's status, traditions and circumstances, so, in order that this work may be publicised and made known to a large audience as cheaply as possible, an honourable council of Nuremberg has ordered, indicated and mandated in the name of the Almighty that the same reformation should be printed. Per this mandate, it was diligently printed and completed by Anton Koberger[30] on the eve of Pentecost [30 May] in the 1484th year after Christ's birth.

[...]

The form and order of the Jewish Oath, as employed in Nuremberg.

---

30 Also the printer of [2].

When a Jew has to take an oath, he should first – before taking the oath – have a book before him and to hand, containing the divine commandments written by God to Moses on Mount Sinai, and the following pronouncement and requirement should be made to the Jew using the words that follow.

> 'O Jew, by the one living and almighty God, creator of heaven and earth and all things, and by His Torah and commandments that He gave to His servant Moses on Mount Sinai, I require that you should truly state and affirm that this present book is the book on which a Jew can and should take and carry out a lawful, appropriate oath before a Christian or a Jew.'

Once, following the pronouncement of this requirement, the Jew has proclaimed and stated that it is indeed such a book, the Christian demanding the oath of him – or, instead, the person presenting the oath formula to the Jew – should lay out for and read out to him the following question and exhortation, namely:

> 'O Jew, I truthfully declare to you that we Christians pray to the one living and almighty God, who created heaven and earth and all things, and that outside of Him we do not have, honour or pray to any other gods. I am telling you this so and in order that you do not think that you are absolved before God of taking a false oath, in the sense that you might suppose and maintain that we Christians adhere to a false religion and pray to foreign gods (which is not the case). And since the *nesie*[31] or captains of the Israelites were obliged to uphold what they swore to the Gibeonites [Joshua 9:15–20], even though they served foreign gods, you are all the more obliged to swear and uphold a truthful and un-deceitful oath to us Christians, as ones who pray to a living and almighty God. Therefore I ask you, O Jew, if you believe that one who swears a false and deceitful oath thereby defiles and blasphemes Almighty God.'

The Jew should then say: 'Yes.'

And the Christian:

> 'O Jew, I further ask you if you are willing, with a well-considered disposition and without any malice or deceit, to invoke a living and almighty God as a witness to the truth that you do not wish to say or employ any untruth, falsehood or deceitfulness in any way in this matter concerning which an oath has been requested of you.'

---

31 *nasi* is more commonly translated as 'prince' in English, e.g. Numbers 34:18.

The Jew should then say: 'Yes.'

When all this has happened, the Jew should place his right hand all the way to the wrist inside the aforementioned book, and specifically on the words of the commandment and law of God which reads thus in Hebrew: *lo sissa etsche adonay eloecha laschaff ki lo ienaqqe adonay etascher issa etschemo laschaff*.[32] ('Do not take the name of the LORD your God in vain; for the LORD will not hold him guiltless or unpunished, who takes his name in vain' [Exodus 20:7; Deuteronomy 5:11].)

Immediately thereupon, and before the Jew has carried out the oath, he should repeat these words to the Christian to whom he should perform the oath, or instead to the person presenting the oath formula to him:

> 'Adonai, eternal, almighty God, lord over the angels, sole god of my forefathers, who gave us the Holy Torah, I invoke You and Your holy name, Adonai, and Your almightiness, that You would help me to carry out my oath that I must now take. And should I swear wrongfully or deceitfully, may I be robbed of all the grace of the eternal God, and may I be subjected to all the punishments and curses that God has imposed on the cursed Jews, and may my soul and body never have any part of the promise that God has made to us, and may I have no part in the Messiah nor in the promised territory of the blessed Holy Land. I also promise and witness by the eternal God Adonai that I do not want to request, ask for or take on any religious pronouncement or saying, absolution or forgiveness from any Jew or any other person whereby I would deceive anyone with this, my oath that I am now about to take. Amen.'

Thereafter the Jew should swear and speak to the Christian according to this oath:

> 'Adonai, creator of heaven and earth and all things, and of myself and the people standing here, I call on You through Your holy name for the truth at this time. And if N.[33] has promised me something about this or that business, I have no obligation or duty towards them in that regard, and I have not employed any falsehood or untruth in this matter, but only engaged with what has been publicly known, be it a matter of debt or something else, whatever it may be. This is therefore

---

32 This is how the Hebrew is rendered in the Latin alphabet in the source, not a modern transliteration.
33 A placeholder for the name of another party.

true, without any deceit, malice or concealment, and thus I beg God Adonai to help me and to confirm this truth. If, however, I have not upheld what is right or true in this matter, but rather employed any untruth, falsehood or deceitfulness therein, may I be *heram* and cursed for eternity. And furthermore, if I have not upheld what is right and true in the matter, may the fire that passed over Sodom and Gomorra pass over and consume me, as well as all the curses written in the Torah, and may the true God who created the leaves and the grass and all things never come to my help nor offer assistance in any of my causes or needs. If, however, I am indeed upholding what is right and true in this matter, may the true God Adonai help me, and nothing else.'

57. Compensating for sexual violence in a land-ordinance for Baden (1495)

Beyerle et al. (eds), *Quellen zur Neueren Privatrechtsgeschichte*, vol. II/1, p. 149.

Like other early *Landesordnungen*, Margrave Christoph of Baden's land-ordinance contains a miscellany of regulations, ranging from matters of public safety to property and inheritance law. It includes two regulations relating to sexual immorality and women's rights: one concerning adultery, and this one concerning rape.

Item, anyone who rapes a maiden or takes her virginity should – if he cannot or will not marry her – give her 30 florins in compensation for her maidenhood. However, we reserve for ourselves and our heirs the right to increase or decrease this according to what we may consider most appropriate and just in each case, depending on the circumstances of the matter and the people involved.

58. Sumptuary laws in an imperial recess (1500)
Senckenberg and Schmauß (eds), *Reichs-Abschiede*, pp. 78–79.

Concerning the excessive luxury of clothes or other things.

After all kinds of negotiations took place at previously held imperial diets regarding the excessive luxury of clothes and other extravagant things, and since especially at the imperial diet of Freiburg[34] certain ordinances and statutes were finally resolved but not actually promulgated, these same have now been renewed and adopted once again by all of us and the other aforementioned estates, and somewhat further clarified, added to and improved, as written hereafter.

We [Maximilian I] hereby ordain, intend, establish and will for all and every one of the electors, princes and other authorities, whatever their dignity, condition or estate – earnestly mandating for the avoidance of our disfavour and punishment – that they should order their respective subjects and associates to commence, firmly uphold and carry out this, our and the Holy Empire's ordinance and statute concerning excessive luxury and extravagance written hereafter, from the upcoming *Laetare* Sunday in Lent onwards, on pain of appropriate penalties. However, should any elector, prince or other authority be found delinquent or neglectful in the enforcement and punishment of these matters, our royal treasury should – after calling upon the elector, prince or other authority about this – have the power and authority to take in hand and punish the violators of this imperial ordinance, without any objection or hindrance on the part of the elector, prince or other authority to whom this violator is subject or with whom they are associated. As the forerunner, we also want to seriously put into effect the commencement and enforcement of this ordinance at our royal court and in our hereditary lands.

First of all, we intend, ordain, establish and will – in the manner discussed and ordained at the imperial diet of Freiburg – that the common peasants and working people in towns and the countryside should not put on or wear any fabric that costs more than a half-florin per cubit. Also, they should not wear any gold, silver,

---

34 Held in 1498 in Freiburg in the Breisgau.

pearl, velvet, silk or embroidered clothes, nor permit their wives or children to wear them. However, this article should not bind or affect the tradition of princes, prelates, counts, lords and the nobility, together with their officials and servitors, to annually clothe their servants in other ways.

Item, artisans and their journeymen, as well as unapprenticed journeymen, should not wear any fabric in their trousers or caps that costs more than three-quarters of a florin per cubit. As for tunics and cloaks, they should content themselves with domestic fabrics that do not cost more than a half-florin per cubit. Also, they should not wear any gold, silver, pearl, velvet, silk or embroidered clothes. Likewise, the artisans' wives, children and maidens should be made to understand that they need to adhere to this with their clothes.

Item, mercenaries should not wear any gold, silver or silk, nor any mantle or hood made of gold or silver. Also, they should not trim their clothes with silk.

Item, everyone should be forbidden from wearing folded shirts and mantles made of gold or silver, and also from wearing gold and silver hoods, with the exception of princes and people of princely rank. Counts, lords and the nobility should also not be encompassed by this, but each should hold and conduct themselves appropriately in this according to their estate, and avoid excess. And especially those of the nobility who are not knights or doctors should give up and avoid wearing pearls or gold in their shirts or mantles. Conversely, those of the nobility who are knights or doctors may wear two ounces of gold and no more, and those who are not knights or doctors two ounces of silver and no more, on their hoods.

Item, burghers in towns who are not nobles, knights or doctors should not wear any gold, pearls, velvet, scarlet, silk or sable or ermine lining. However, they may safely wear jackets made of velvet or silk, as well as camel hair. Likewise, their wives and children may edge, hem and colour their clothes appropriately with velvet or silk, but not with pieces of gold or silver. Also, their maiden daughters should not be forbidden from wearing pearl chaplets, though they should take care to put only an appropriate amount in them, and not engage in excess.

Item, those of the nobility who are not knights or doctors should not publicly wear gold or pearls, and if they want colours or embroidery added to their garments, they should have this done to an appropriate degree.

Item, those of the nobility who are knights or doctors should not wear any pieces of gold, though they should not be forbidden from wearing gold jackets.

Item, every short dress or tunic should be made to such a length that the front and back cover up a person appropriately.

Item, all archbishops, bishops and prelates should constrain and indicate to their clerics that they should clothe themselves in and adhere to honourable and spiritual garb, as well befits their estate, and give up unseemly extravagance.

59. The preamble to the first Empire-wide criminal code (1532)

Des ... heyligen Römischen Reichs peinlich gerichts ordnung, pp. IIr–IIv.

We Charles V, by the grace of God Roman emperor [etc.] publicly proclaim:

We have received substantial reports from our and the Holy Empire's electors, princes and other estates about how, in following the old customs and traditions, most criminal courts in the Roman Empire of the German nation have been staffed by people who lack education, experience and practice in our imperial law. And in many places, the same courts often act contrary to justice and common sense, such that either the innocent suffer corporal punishment or execution, or else the guilty are protected, sent to another court or acquitted through irregular, ill-intentioned and prolonged proceedings, to the great detriment of the plaintiffs who are victims of crime and the common good. And amid all this, because of the circumstances in the German lands, and following the old, long-running customs and traditions, the criminal courts in many places cannot be staffed with people who understand the law and are experienced and practiced in it.

Consequently, we have – together with the electors, princes and estates, and by our gracious, collective will – ordered certain educated, distinguished, experienced people to draw up a text about how and in what ways justice and equity might most appropriately be attained in criminal cases and judicial proceedings, and to put it together in a form that we can have issued in print, so that, considering the extent and dangers of what is set out in the same text that has just been revealed, all and every one of our and the Empire's subjects may henceforth conduct themselves in criminal matters in conformity with the *ius commune*, justice and praiseworthy, age-old customs, as everyone is doubtless keen to do on their own behalf, hoping thereby to receive their reward from the Almighty.

However, in issuing this gracious admonition, we have not taken anything away from the electors', princes' and estates' age-old and well transmitted, lawful and just customs.

60. Incorporating the imperial public peace into the *Bavarian Land-Ordinance* (1553)

Beyerle et al. (eds), *Quellen zur Neueren Privatrechtsgeschichte*, vol. II/1, p. 166.

Attempts to codify and rationalise law in Bavaria began with the reign of Emperor Ludwig IV (1314–47), who compiled a so-called *Landrecht* for Upper Bavaria. However, it was only in the sixteenth century that a single, unified Bavarian principality came into being, stimulating the creation of land-ordinances in print. This version is a comprehensive set of laws from 1553 consisting of six 'books'. The public peace constitutes the first, per the preface translated in this extract, while the topics covered in the second to sixth include judicial processes and fees in Bavarian courts; matters of guardianship, marriage and inheritance; sales and other financial transactions; rents and tithes; serfdom; regulations for schools, pharmacies and guilds; weights and measures; and disciplinary ordinances against vagrants, gamblers, minstrels, drunkards and blasphemers.

This book contains the Holy Roman Empire's public peace.

Since the first book of this land-ordinance is founded and established on the Holy Empire's public peace, in order that many in the principality of Bavaria should come to know what the public peace is and what it is established upon, a trustworthy transcription of the public peace is included here, specifically the version set up by his Roman imperial Majesty together with the electors, princes and other estates of the Empire at the diet held recently in Augsburg in the [15]48th year.

[The text of the 1548 *Landfrieden*-ordinance[35] is copied verbatim within the land-ordinance. Its provisions are very similar to public peace-ordinances of 1521 [**26**] and 1555 [**30**], minus the latter's clauses pertaining to religion.]

---

35 Edited in Kluckhohn et al. (eds), *Deutsche Reichstagsakten. Jüngere Reihe*, vol. XVIII, no. 75.

GLOSSARY

advocate: In the early to high Middle Ages, the word *advocatus* (German *Vogt*) primarily referred to a deputy with responsibility for – and a degree of control over – an ecclesiastical institution's temporal possessions. In the later medieval period, the definition expanded to indicate a range of local officials (sometimes called *Landvögte*) with authority to govern on behalf of a prince, lord or city. Additionally, the original Roman law meaning (*advocatus*, Germanised as *Advokat*) resurfaced in the fifteenth century to designate a lawyer tasked with defending a party in court.

aulic court: A judicial court of appeal attached to the court (*curia*, *Hof*) of the king or emperor of the Romans (hence *Hofgericht*) until the mid-fifteenth century. Local *Hofgerichte* with delegated imperial jurisdiction operated in some locations throughout this period, notably in Rottweil.

burgher: *see* citizen

burgrave: *see* official

cameral court: A new 'central' court of appeal (called the *Kammergericht*) set up under Emperor Frederick III at his court. A pan-imperial version, run by the imperial estates collectively, was mooted in the 1480s, established in 1495 and improved thereafter.

citizen: The word *civis* or *Bürger* designated a politically enfranchised member of a town or city. By no means all urban inhabitants enjoyed citizenship, which was typically reserved for men of middling and higher economic and social status.

council: *see* councillor

councillor: A term to designate a person who gave advice, or *Rat* (a word which meant 'counsel' – advice in the abstract; 'council' – an advisory meeting or institution; and 'councillor' – a giver of advice who sat on a council). Monarchs, princes and cities increasingly institutionalised the role of 'councillor', which became a governmental office staffed by noble clients and university-educated lawyers.

custodian: *see* official

diet: The German *Tag* (translated in some instances to *dieta* in Latin, whence the English 'diet') could refer to a dizzying array of meetings between two or more parties, for purposes such as dispute resolution, advice-seeking and joint policy- or law-making. Among its many other manifestations, this concept came to be applied to assemblies of the monarch and leading members of the Holy Roman Empire. By 1500 this specific type of diet was called a *Reichstag* ('imperial diet').

double ban: *see* imperial ban

elector: During the succession crises of the thirteenth century, the principle that each new king of the Romans should be elected not only became entrenched, but six German princes and the king of Bohemia successfully asserted their exclusive right to act as the 'electors'. This group's privileges were legally codified in the Golden Bull of 1356. While they were by no means always united, the late medieval electors developed a consciousness of themselves as co-leaders of the Holy Roman Empire, sometimes acting as a bloc in concert with or opposition to monarchs in imperial politics.

emperor: *see* king of the Romans

estate: The word 'estate' (*Stand*, plural *Stände*) had three related meanings: a status designation (e.g. 'of the knightly estate'); an entire group within the social order (e.g. 'the spiritual estate', meaning all clergy); or a cadre of high-ranking people who claimed to represent and embody an entire polity (e.g. a principality, or – by the late fifteenth century – the Holy Roman Empire) and to have the right to negotiate and make decisions on its behalf.

feudal: *see* fief

fief: The descendent of high medieval forms of tenure involving things called a *feudum* or *beneficium*, a fief (*Lehen* in German) was an item held in a form of 'feudal' tenure in which theoretical reciprocal obligations bound the recipient to the grantor. Princely lands and titles were held in fief from the king or emperor. Fiefs were typically heritable and some could even be sold or pledged. A range of people held fiefs, not just nobles.

GLOSSARY

florin: A gold coin (German plural *Gulden*), typically the most valuable of the currency denominations accepted in a given region. Florins/*Gulden* minted in a variety of places and with a variety of fluctuating values circulated in the late medieval and early modern German lands.

free cities: *see* imperial cities

imperial ban: Rooted deeply in the customs of early medieval societies, the basic idea of placing a malefactor in a 'ban' (*Acht* or *Bann*) involved excluding them from the community as a punitive and safety measure. Among other usages, this became a prerogative of the Romano-German king or emperor around the thirteenth century as a (poorly enforced) deterrent for peace-breakers, when it acquired two stages. First, the royal/imperial ban (*Acht*) was intended to compel a criminal to surrender to the judicial authorities. Failure to do so within a year and a day, or especially egregious crimes, merited the more serious 'double ban' (*Aberacht*): a person with this status was an outlaw who could be attacked with impunity. Delegated imperial courts and, from the late fifteenth century, the enforcers of the public peace could also apply the ban.

imperial circles: Regional groupings of princes, nobles and/or cities designated to assist in the operation of the new institutions created around 1500. Six circles were defined as recruitment pools for the staff of the short-lived imperial governing council (*Reichsregiment*), a number expanded to ten in 1512. All were then tasked with implementing the public peace on a regional level, which in practice meant that the members of the circles collaborated militarily as if in an alliance.

imperial cities: Urban communes under the sole and direct authority of the kings and emperors, who therefore conferred privileges and franchises directly upon these communities, were known as 'imperial cities' (*Reichsstädte*). Often they had been founded by monarchs in previous centuries. By the fourteenth century they had a very similar legal status to, and close affinity with, the 'free cities': urban communes formerly under the rule of bishops, which had become de facto independent after overthrowing their episcopal lords. This is underlined by the formula 'free and imperial cities' (*freie und Reichsstädte*).

imperial diet: *see* diet

GLOSSARY

imperially immediate: Entities described as 'imperially immediate' (*reichsunmittelbar* in modern German) had no lord except the monarch and the political community of the Empire. They were mostly princes and some nobles and free and imperial cities, as opposed to 'territorial' nobles, towns and common people under the intermediary lordship of another authority.

king of the Romans: Uniquely among European monarchs, the rulers of the late medieval Holy Roman Empire had a two-tiered title: upon election, they were considered 'king of the Romans' (*rex Romanorum, römischer König*) and could be crowned in Aachen. To become 'emperor' (*imperator, Kaiser*) they had to be crowned by the pope in Italy, which roughly half achieved in this period. In the first decade of the sixteenth century, Maximilian I began using the title 'king of Germany' (*könig in Germanien*) alongside 'Roman emperor-elect' (*erwählter römischer Kaiser*), a usage that continued under his successors.

land-peace: *see* public peace

official: The late medieval German lands saw the multiplication of locally delegated forms of authority within gradually intensifying lordships and principalities. A rich vocabulary developed to label the men who carried out these functions. The most frequent term was some variant of 'official' (*Amt[-mann]*), but a range of other specific and regional terms appear in the sources (e.g. *Pfleger, Vogt, Schultheiß, Burggraf*), designating officials with various jurisdictional and fiscal rights and duties in defined localities. Typically, these figures were local elites in their own right and derived 'private' benefit from their 'public' functions (which, indeed, relied on the officials' own networks of supporters and clients).

pledge: An item (*Pfand* or *Pfandschaft*) given as collateral in return for a loan or payment due. Applied to lands, offices and revenues, this form of transaction became the basis of a kind of tenure, alongside fiefs (which could themselves be held in pledge).

prince: From around 1200, the highest-ranking nobles and prelates in the German lands were called 'princes' (*principes, Fürsten*). This designation reflected a complex combination of title, rank, power, wealth and reputation among fellow elites, so it was not a stable group, and the 'princely' status of some marginal but still influential figures (e.g. the counts of Henneberg and the margraves of Baden) was a subjective assertion. The roles attributed to the princes collectively became more institutionalised as the Empire consolidated at the end of this period; e.g., through frequent 'colleges' or 'councils' of princes at imperial diets.

public peace: As in any pre-modern realm, normative political thought in the German lands of the Empire held that the king/emperor was responsible for preserving regional or public 'peace' (*pax [terrae, provincialis, generalis* or *publica]*, *[Land-]Frieden* – a concept open to interpretation, but generally indicating minimisation of illegitimate violence and indiscriminate feuding). Given limited monarchical resources and the size of the Empire, this duty was always deputised, whether to regional 'land-peace' alliances or, later on, the imperial estates collectively via mechanisms prescribed in pan-imperial ordinances, themselves sometimes called '[public] peaces'. The estates' assumption of this 'royal' duty reveals the explicit sense of collective governance in the Empire by the late fifteenth century.

recess: At any diet, including an imperial diet, the collective decision of those in attendance – in the form of an arbitrational judgement, an agreement to raise troops collectively, new legislation or a range of other outcomes, depending on the type of diet – was called an *Abschied*. This has traditionally been translated as 'recess' in English, especially for the imperial diets.

retainer: The word *Knecht* designated a vast array of positions and occupations in late medieval German society, and there is no perfect equivalent in English; 'retainer' probably comes closest. Depending on the context, it could refer to an unfree bondservant; an apprentice or journeyman in a workshop or guild; an assistant to a knight (such as a squire); a noble client of some kind; and a hired warrior or mercenary. These last three meanings are those that appear most frequently in this book. They overlap substantially with usages of the term 'servitor(s)' (*Diener/Dienstleute*), though this did not connote nobility to the same extent.

servitor: *see* retainer

BIBLIOGRAPHY

Published Primary Sources

Bader, Joseph (ed.), *Quellen und Erörtungen zur bayerischen und deutschen Geschichte. Achter Band. Erhard Schürstab's Beschreibung des Ersten Markgräflichen Krieges gegen Nürnberg* (Munich, 1860).
Berlichingen-Rossach, Friedrich Graf von (ed.), *Geschichte des Ritters Götz von Berlichingen mit der eisernen Hand und seiner Familie* (Leipzig, 1861).
Beyerle, Franz, Wolfgang Kunkel, Hans Thieme and Gustaf Klemens Schmelzeisen (eds), *Quellen zur Neueren Privatrechtsgeschichte Deutschlands*, 2 vols (Weimar, 1936–69).
Bock, Ernst, Heinz Angermeier, Heinz Gollwitzer et al. (eds), *Deutsche Reichstagsakten. Mittlere Reihe. Deutsche Reichstagsakten unter Maximilian I.*, 12 vols (Göttingen/Munich/Berlin, 1972–2022).
Brucker, Jean Charles (ed.), *Straßburger Zunft- und Polizei-verordnungen des 14. und 15. Jahrhunderts* (Strasbourg, 1889).
Brückner, Georg (ed.), *Hennebergisches Urkundenbuch. IV. Theil. Die Urkunden des gemeinschaftlichen Hennebergischen Archivs von MCCCLXXXV bis MCCCCXII* (Meiningen, 1861).
Buck, Thomas Martin (ed.), *Chronik des Konstanzer Konzils 1414–1418 von Ulrich Richental* (Ostfildern, 2010).
D. Martin Luthers Werke. Kritische Gesamtausgabe. 6. Band (Weimar, 1888).
Derschka, Harald (ed./trans.), *Der Schwabenspiegel. Übertragen in heutiges Deutsch mit Illustrationen aus alten Handschriften* (Munich, 2002).
Des allerdurchleuchtigsten großmechtigsten vnüberwindtlichsten Keyser Karls des fünfften: vnnd des heyligen Römischen Reichs peinlich gerichts ordnung / auff den Reichsztägen zuo Augspurgk vnd Regenspurgk / inn jaren dreissig / vnd zwey vnd dreissig gehalten / auffgericht vnd beschlossen (Mainz, 1533).
Die Chroniken der Schwäbischen Städte. Augsburg. Erster Band (Leipzig, 1865).
Dobozy, Maria (ed./trans.), *The Saxon Mirror: A Sachsenspiegel of the Fourteenth Century* (Philadelphia, 1999).
Fabian, Ekkehart (ed.), *Die Entstehung des schmalkaldischen Bundes und seiner Verfassung 1524/29–1531/35*, 2nd edn (Tübingen, 1962).
Fritz, Johannes (ed.), *Urkundenbuch der Stadt Strassburg. Sechster Band. Politische Urkunden von 1381–1400* (Strasbourg, 1899).

BIBLIOGRAPHY

Fritz, Wolfgang (ed.), *Monumenta Germaniae Historica. Constitutiones et acta publica imperatorum et regum. Elfter Band. Dokumente zur Geschichte des Deutschen Reiches und seiner Verfassung 1354–1356* (Weimar, 1978–92).

Henderson, Ernest Flagg (ed./trans.), *Select Historical Documents of the Middle Ages* (London, 1892).

Hohensee, Ulrike, Mathias Lawo, Michael Lindner and Olaf Rader (eds), *Monumenta Germaniae Historica. Constitutiones et acta publica imperatorum et regum. Dreizehnter Band. Teil 1. Dokumente zur Geschichte des Deutschen Reiches und seiner Verfassung 1360* (Wiesbaden, 2016).

Janicke, Karl (ed.), *Urkundenbuch der Stadt Quedlinburg. Erste Abtheilung* (Halle, 1873).

Jensen, De Lamar (ed./trans.), *Confrontation at Worms: Martin Luther at the Diet of Worms* (Provo, 1973).

Keyler, Regina (ed.), *Das älteste Urbar des Priorats Reichenbach von 1427* (Stuttgart, 1999).

Kluckhohn, August, Adolf Wrede, Johannes Kühn et al. (eds), *Deutsche Reichstagsakten. Jüngere Reihe. Deutsche Reichstagsakten unter Kaiser Karl V.*, 21 vols (Gotha/Göttingen/Munich/Berlin, 1893–2021).

Koller, Heinrich (ed.), *Reformation Kaiser Siegmunds* (Stuttgart, 1964).

Kollnig, Karl (ed.), *Die Weistümer der Zenten Eberbach und Mosbach* (Stuttgart, 1985).

Lauterbach, Klaus (ed.), *Der Oberrheinische Revolutionär. Das buchli der hundert capiteln mit xxxx statuten* (Hannover, 2009).

Liber sextus decretalium D. Bonifacii papae VIII. suae integritati una cum Clementinis & extravagantibus, earumque glossis restitutus (Rome, 1582).

Lünig, Johann Christian (ed.), *Des Teutschen Reichs-Archivs partis specialis continuatio I* (Leipzig, 1711).

Lyon, Jonathan (ed./trans.), *Noble Society: Five Lives from Twelfth-Century Germany* (Manchester, 2017).

Müller, Gerhard (ed.), 'Die thüringische Landesordnung vom 9. Januar 1446', *Zeitschrift des Vereins für Thüringische Geschichte* 50 (1996), pp. 9–35.

Müller, Johann Joachim (ed.), *Des Heiligen Römischen Reichs Teutscher Nation Reichs-Tags-Theatrum, wie selbiges unter Keyser Friedrichs V. allerhöchsten Regierung von anno 1440 bis 1493 gestanden*, 2 vols (Jena, 1713).

Müller, Rainer Albert (ed./trans.), *Peter von Andlau. Kaiser und Reich. Libellus de Cesarea monarchia* (Leipzig, 1998).

Priebatsch, Felix (ed.), *Politische Correspondenz des Kurfürsten Albrecht Achilles*, 3 vols (Leipzig, 1894–98).

Sachsse, Hugo (ed.), *Mecklenburgische Urkunden und Daten. Quellen vornehmlich für Staatsgeschichte und Staatsrecht Mecklenburgs* (Rostock, 1900).

Schedel, Hartmann, *Buch der Croniken und geschichten mit figure[n] und pildnussen von anbegin[n] der welt bis auf dise un[n]sere zeit* (Nuremberg, 1493).
Schneider, Eugen (ed.), *Ausgewählte Urkunden zur Württembergischen Geschichte* (Stuttgart, 1911).
Scott, Tom, and Bob Scribner (eds/trans.), *The German Peasants' War: A History in Documents* (Amherst, 1991).
Segesser, Philipp Anton (ed.), *Amtliche Sammlung der ältern Eidgenössischen Abschiede. Band 1. Die Eidgenössischen Abschiede aus dem Zeitraume von 1245 bis 1420*, 2nd edn (Lucerne, 1874).
Senckenberg, Heinrich Christian von, and Johann Jacob Schmauß (eds), *Neue und vollständigere Sammlung der Reichs-Abschiede ... Zweyter Theil derer Reichs-Abschiede von dem Jahr 1495 bis auf das Jahr 1551 inclusive* (Frankfurt, 1747).
Strauss, Gerald (ed./trans.), *Manifestations of Discontent in Germany on the Eve of the Reformation* (Bloomington, 1971).
Urkundenbuch der Stadt Lübeck. Achter Theil. 1440–1450 (Lübeck, 1889).
Warner, David (ed./trans.), *Ottonian Germany: The Chronicon of Thietmar of Merseburg* (Manchester, 2001).
Weinrich, Lorenz (ed.), *Quellen zur Reichsreform im Spätmittelalter* (Darmstadt, 2001).
Weizsäcker, Julius, Dietrich Kerler, Hermann Herre et al. (eds), *Deutsche Reichstagsakten: Ältere Reihe*, 22 vols (Gotha/Göttingen/Munich, 1867–2013).
Wilson, Peter (ed./trans.), *The Thirty Years War: A Sourcebook* (Basingstoke, 2010).
Wolkan, Rudolf (ed.), *Der Briefwechsel des Eneas Silvius Piccolomini*, 3 vols (Vienna, 1909–18).

Secondary Sources

Angermeier, Heinz, *Die Reichsreform 1410–1555. Die Staatsproblematik Deutschlands zwischen Mittelalter und Gegenwart* (Munich, 1984).
Annas, Gabriele, *Hoftag – Gemeiner Tag–Reichstag: Studien zur strukturellen Entwicklung deutscher Reichsversammlungen des späten Mittelalters (1349–1471)*, 2 vols (Göttingen, 2004).
Annas, Gabriele, 'Zum Begriff der "Gerechtigkeit" in Schriften zur Reichsreform des 15. Jahrhunderts', in Petra Schulte, Gabriele Annas and Michael Rothmann (eds), *Gerechtigkeit im gesellschaftlichen Diskurs des späteren Mittelalters* (Berlin, 2012), pp. 223–54.
Annas, Gabriele, 'Kaiser Friedrich III. und die Reichsversammlungen des 15. Jahrhunderts. Beobachtungen zu politischen Aushandlungs- und "Clearing"-Prozessen', in Günter Frank, Franz Fuchs and Matthias Herweg (eds), *Das 15. Jahrhundert* (Stuttgart, 2021), pp. 29–54.

BIBLIOGRAPHY

Annas, Gabriele, 'Die Geschichte der "Deutschen Reichstagsakten"', *Mittelalterliche Geschichte: Digitale Studieneinführung* (2021) https://mittelalterliche-geschichte.de/annas-gabriele-02/ [accessed 30 April 2025].

Arnold, Benjamin, *Princes and Territories in Medieval Germany* (Cambridge, 1991).

Bahlcke, Joachim, *Landesherrschaft, Territorien und Staat in der Frühen Neuzeit* (Munich, 2012).

Barraclough, Geoffrey, *The Origins of Modern Germany*, 2nd edn (London, 1984).

Baumbach, Hendrik, *Königliche Gerichtsbarkeit und Landfriedenssorge im deutschen Spätmittelalter. Eine Geschichte der Verfahren und Delegationsformen zur Konfliktbehandlung* (Vienna, 2017).

Begert, Alexander, *Die Entstehung und Entwicklung des Kurkollegs. Von den Anfängen bis zum frühen 15. Jahrhunderts* (Berlin, 2010).

Bennett, Judith, and Ruth Mazo Karras, 'Women, Gender, and Medieval Historians', in Judith Bennett and Ruth Mazo Karras (eds), *The Oxford Handbook of Women and Gender in Medieval Europe* (Oxford, 2013), pp. 1–20.

Blickle, Peter, *From the Communal Revolution to the Revolution of the Common Man*, trans. Beat Kümin (Leiden, 1998).

Boockmann, Hartmut, and Heinrich Dormeier, *Konzilien, Kirchen- und Reichsreform, 1410–1495* (Stuttgart, 2005).

Brady, Thomas, *German Histories in the Age of Reformations, 1400–1650* (Cambridge, 2009).

Brunner, Otto, *Land and Lordship: Structures of Governance in Medieval Austria*, trans. Howard Kaminsky and James Van Horn Melton (Philadelphia, 1992).

Buck, Lawrence, '"Anatomia Antichristi": Form and Content of the Papal Antichrist', *The Sixteenth Century Journal* 42.2 (2011), pp. 349–68.

Close, Christopher, *State Formation and Shared Sovereignty: The Holy Roman Empire and the Dutch Republic, 1488–1696* (Cambridge, 2021).

Daniels, Tobias, *Diplomatie, politische Rede und juristische Praxis im 15. Jahrhundert. Der gelehrte Rat Johannes Hofmann von Lieser* (Göttingen, 2013).

Freed, John, 'Reflections on the Medieval German Nobility', *American Historical Review* 91.3 (1986), pp. 553–75.

Fricke, Eberhard, 'Die Vemegerichtsbarkeit im kurkölnischen Herzogtum Westfalen', in Harm Kluetig (ed.), *Das Herzogtum Westfalen* (Münster, 2009), pp. 269–96.

Gotthard, Axel, *Säulen des Reiches*, 2 vols (Husum, 1999).

Graf, Klaus, 'Aspekte zum Regionalismus in Schwaben und am Oberrhein im Spätmittelalter', in Kurt Andermann (ed.), *Historiographie am Oberrhein im späten Mittelalter und in der frühen Neuzeit* (Sigmaringen, 1988), pp. 65–92.

Hardy, Duncan, *Associative Political Culture in the Holy Roman Empire: Upper Germany, 1346–1521* (Oxford, 2018).

Hardy, Duncan, '*Tage* (Courts, Councils, and Diets): Political and Judicial Nodal Points in the Holy Roman Empire, *c.* 1300–1550', *German History* 36.3 (2018), pp. 381–400.

Hardy, Duncan, 'Were There "Territories" in the German Lands of the Holy Roman Empire in the Fourteenth to Sixteenth Centuries?', in Mario Damen and Kim Overlaet (eds), *Constructing and Representing Territory in Late Medieval and Early Modern Europe* (Amsterdam, 2021), pp. 29–52.

Hardy, Duncan, 'Reform and Reformation', *Routledge Resources Online – Medieval Studies* (2023) https://doi.org/10.4324/9780415791182-RM EO206-1 [accessed 30 April 2025].

Hardy, Duncan, '"There Can Be No Agreement to Take up Arms against the Turks Unless We First Restore the Empire": The Fall of Constantinople and the Rise of a New Political Dynamic in the Holy Roman Empire, 1453–1467', *Austrian History Yearbook* 55 (2024), pp. 524–37.

Heckmann, Marie-Luise, 'Zeitnahe Wahrnehmung und internationale Ausstrahlung. Die Goldene Bulle Karls IV. im ausgehenden Mittelalter mit einem Ausblick auf die Frühe Neuzeit', in Ulrike Hohensee, Mathias Lawo, Michael Lindner, Michael Menzel and Olaf Rader (eds), *Die Goldene Bulle. Politik–Wahrnehmung–Rezeption*, 2 vols (Berlin, 2009), vol. I, pp. 933–1042.

Heinig, Paul-Joachim, *Kaiser Friedrich III. (1440–1493). Hof, Regierung und Politik*, 3 vols (Cologne, 1997).

Henderson, Ernest Flagg, *A History of Germany in the Middle Ages* (New York, 1894).

Hesse, Christian, *Synthese und Aufbruch, 1346–1410* (Stuttgart, 2017).

Hirschi, Caspar, *The Origins of Nationalism: An Alternative History from Ancient Rome to Early Modern Germany* (Cambridge, 2012).

Isenmann, Eberhard, 'König oder Monarch? Aspekte der Regierung und Verfassung des römisch-deutschen Reiches um die Mitte des 15. Jahrhunderts', in Rainer Schwinges, Christian Hesse and Peter Moraw (eds), *Europa im späten Mittlelalter: Politik–Gesellschaft–Kultur* (Munich, 2006), pp. 71–98.

Isenmann, Eberhard, *Die deutsche Stadt im Mittelalter 1150–1550* (Vienna, 2012).

Kintzinger, Martin, and Bernd Schneidmüller (eds), *Politische Öffentlichkeit im Spätmittelalter* (Ostfildern, 2011).

Kneupper, Frances Courtney, *The Empire at the End of Time: Identity and Reform in Late Medieval German Prophecy* (New York, 2016).

Kroeschell, Karl, Albrecht Cordes and Karin Nehlsen-von Stryk, *Deutsche Rechtsgeschichte. Band 2: 1250–1650*, 9th edn (Cologne, 2008).

Kümin, Beat, *The Communal Age in Western Europe, c. 1100–1800* (Basingstoke, 2013).

Lansing, Carol, 'Conflicts over Gender in Civic Courts', in Bennett and Karras (eds), *Oxford Handbook of Women and Gender*, pp. 133–47.

Lanzinner, Maximilian, 'Gemeiner Pfennig', in Albrecht Cordes (ed.),

BIBLIOGRAPHY

Handwörterbuch zur deutschen Rechtsgeschichte, 2nd edn, 4 vols (Berlin, 2005–2023), vol. 2, pp. 58–59.

Leukel, Patrick, *'all welt wil auf sein wider Burgundi': Das Reichsheer im Neusser Krieg 1474/75* (Paderborn, 2019).

Loud, Graham, and Jochen Schenk (eds), *The Origins of the German Principalities, 1100–1350: Essays by German Historians* (Abingdon, 2017).

Lyon, Jonathan, *Corruption, Protection and Justice in Medieval Europe: A Thousand Year History* (Cambridge, 2022).

Mertens, Dieter, 'Jakob Wimpfeling (1450–1528). Pädagogischer Humanismus', in Paul Gerhard Schmidt (ed.), *Humanismus im deutschen Südwesten. Biographische Profile* (Sigmaringen, 2000), pp. 35–57.

Miller, Ignaz, *Jakob von Sierck 1398/99–1456* (Mainz, 1983).

Monnet, Pierre, *Charles IV: un empereur en Europe* (Paris, 2020).

Moraw, Peter, *Von offener Verfassung zu gestalteter Verdichtung. Das Reich im späten Mittelalter, 1250 bis 1490* (Berlin, 1985).

Nonn, Ulrich, 'Heiliges Römisches Reich Deutscher Nation: Zum Nationen-Begriff im 15. Jahrhundert', *Zeitschrift für Historische Forschung*, 9.2 (1982), pp. 129–42.

Page, Jamie, *Prostitution and Subjectivity in Late Medieval Germany* (Oxford, 2021).

Paravicini, Werner, 'Das Schwert in der Krone', in Franz Felten Annette Kehnel and Stefan Weinfurter (eds), *Institution und Charisma. Festschrift für Gert Melville* (Cologne, 2009), pp. 279–304.

Patzold, Steffen, *Das Lehnswesen* (Munich, 2012).

Reinhard, Wolfgang, *Probleme deutscher Geschichte, 1495–1806: Reichsreform und Reformation, 1495–1555* (Stuttgart, 2001).

Reinle, Christine, *Bauernfehden. Studien zur Fehdeführung Nichtadeliger im spätmittelalterlichen römisch-deutschen Reich, besonders in den bayerischen Herzogtümern* (Stuttgart, 2003).

Reske, Christoph, 'Schedelsche Weltchronik', *Historisches Lexikon Bayerns* (2011) www.historisches-lexikon-bayerns.de/Lexikon/Schedelsche_Weltchronik [accessed 30 April 2025].

Robinson, Ian Stuart, 'Church and Papacy', in James Henderson Burns (ed.), *The Cambridge History of Medieval Political Thought c. 350–c. 1450* (Cambridge, 1988), pp. 252–305.

Roper, Lyndal, *Martin Luther: Renegade and Prophet* (London, 2016).

Rösener, Werner, 'Die Grundherrschaft als Forschungskonzept: Strukturen und Wandel der Grundherrschaft im deutschen Reich (10.–13. Jahrhundert)', *Zeitschrift der Savigny-Stiftung für Rechtsgeschichte: Germanische Abteilung* 129 (2012), pp. 41–75.

Rubin, Miri, *Cities of Strangers: Making Lives in Medieval Europe* (Cambridge, 2020).

Rückert, Peter, Anja Thaller and Klaus Oschema (eds), *Starke Frauen? Adelige Damen im Südwesten des spätmittelalterlichen Reiches* (Stuttgart, 2022).

Scales, Len, 'The Illuminated Reich: Memory, Crisis and the Visibility of Monarchy in Late Medieval Germany', in Jason Coy, Benjamin Marschke and David Sabean (eds), *The Holy Roman Empire, Reconsidered* (Oxford, 2010), pp. 73–92.

Scales, Len, *The Shaping of German Identity: Authority and Crisis, 1245–1414* (Cambridge, 2012).

Schlotheuber, Eva, and Maria Theisen, *Die Goldene Bulle von 1356. Das erste Grundgesetz des römisch-deutschen Reichs* (Darmstadt, 2023).

Schneider, Joachim, *Spätmittelalterlicher deutscher Niederadel. Ein landschaftlicher Vergleich* (Stuttgart, 2003).

Schubert, Ernst, *König und Reich. Studien zur spätmittelalterlichen deutschen Verfassungsgeschichte* (Göttingen, 1979).

Schubert, Ernst, *Fürstliche Herrschaft und Territorium im späten Mittelalter* 2nd edn (Munich, 2006).

Scott, Tom, *Society and Economy in Germany, 1300–1600* (Basingstoke, 2002).

Scott, Tom, 'The Early Reformation in Germany between Deconstruction and Reconstruction', in Tom Scott (ed.), *The Early Reformation in Germany: Between Secular Impact and Radical Vision* (Farnham, 2013), pp. 7–30.

Stieber, Joachim, *Pope Eugenius IV, the Council of Basel, and the Secular and Ecclesiastical Authorities in the Empire. The Conflict over Supreme Authority and Power in the Church* (Leiden, 1978).

Stollberg-Rilinger, Barbara, *The Emperor's Old Clothes: Constitutional History and the Symbolic Language of the Holy Roman Empire*, trans. Thomas Dunlap (New York, 2015).

Stollberg-Rilinger, Barbara, *The Holy Roman Empire: A Short History*, trans. Yair Mintzker (Princeton, 2018).

Sulovsky, Vedran, '*Sacrum imperium*: Lombard Influence and the "Sacralization of the State" in the Mid-Twelfth Century Holy Roman Empire', *German History* 39 (2021), pp. 1–26.

Teuscher, Simon, *Lords' Rights and Peasant Stories: Writing and the Formation of Tradition in the Later Middle Ages* (Philadelphia, 2012).

Toch, Michael, *Die Juden im mittelalterlichen Reich* (Munich, 2003).

Watts, John, *The Making of Polities: Europe, 1300–1500* (Cambridge, 2009).

Whalen, Brett Edward, *The Two Powers: The Papacy, the Empire, and the Struggle for Sovereignty in the Thirteenth Century* (Philadelphia, 2019).

Whaley, Joachim, *Germany and the Holy Roman Empire. Volume I: Maximilian I to the Peace of Westphalia 1493–1648* (Oxford, 2012).

Wilson, Peter, *The Holy Roman Empire: A Thousand Years of Europe's History* (London, 2016).

Zeilinger, Gabriel, *Lebensformen im Krieg. Eine Alltags- und Erfahrungsgeschichte des süddeutschen Städtekriegs 1449/50* (Stuttgart, 2007).

Zmora, Hillay, *The Feud in Early Modern Germany* (Cambridge, 2011).

INDEX

Aachen 6, 36, 93, 95, 115, 356
Albert II, king xv, 66
Albrecht I 'Achilles', margrave of
	Brandenburg-Ansbach 18,
	302, 308–12
Albrecht II 'Alcibiades', margrave of
	Brandenburg-Kulmbach 304,
	318–19
Alexander VI, Pope 253
alliances *see* associations
Alsace 13, 17, 48, 148, 226
Andlau, Peter of 24, 34–36
arbitration 4, 10, 19, 58, 150, 163,
	164, 168, 171, 174, 187,
	207, 208, 217, 237, 238,
	268, 278, 282, 283, 287,
	288, 289, 291, 294, 298,
	300–04, 305, 306, 308–12,
	313–15, 318–19, 357
assemblies *see* diets
associations 20, 24, 26, 56, 67,
	89, 103, 127, 150, 152,
	153, 170, 268–72, 273–76,
	277–80, 281–83, 284–87,
	288–92, 293–95, 296–99,
	300, 305, 331, 338, 357
	see also land-peace
Augsburg
	bishops 105, 108, 176, 177,
		185
	free city 23, 26, 37, 114, 129,
		130, 131, 139, 141, 173,
		174, 177, 185, 186, 189,
		193, 212, 213, 222, 273,
		304, 316, 318, 319, 325,
		352
	Peace of 129, 131, 212–22, 318
Augsburg Confession *see* Lutherans

Augsburg Interim 130
aulic council 128, 209
aulic court 87, 124, 128, 353
Austria 5, 17, 27, 48, 51, 52, 53, 55,
	66, 74, 115, 116, 126, 127,
	132, 148, 168, 176, 185,
	187, 189, 190, 193, 222,
	238, 279, 308
	see also Habsburgs
Avignon 38, 229, 248

Baden 108, 176, 177, 193, 263, 322,
	332, 347, 357
Bamberg
	bishops 37, 105, 108, 177, 316,
		318
	city 99, 194, 222, 302, 312
Basel
	bishops 108, 177
	free city 114, 237
	university 24, 34
	see also Council of Basel
Bavaria
	duchies/region 15, 104, 109, 326,
		352
	dukes 44, 46, 55, 105, 109, 135,
		176, 177, 178, 185, 222,
		263, 281, 306, 308, 309, 352
Berlichingen, Götz of 303, 316–17
Berlin 284, 286
Bern 113
Berthold of Henneberg, archbishop
	of Mainz 129, 132, 134, 136,
	137, 185
Bohemia
	kingdom 5, 12, 25, 37, 63, 66,
		72, 73, 86, 87, 92, 102, 106,
		107, 199, 281

Bohemia (*cont.*)
  kings 7, 35, 36, 38, 70, 71, 75, 76, 77, 82, 83, 84, 85, 86, 87, 92, 93, 94, 96, 98, 105, 246, 354
Boniface IX, Pope 42
Boniface VIII, Pope 257
Brabant 51, 55, 110, 148, 187, 190
Brandenburg
  electoral principality 17, 178
  margraves 7, 18, 35, 37, 44, 45, 47, 55, 72, 83, 84, 86, 91, 92, 94, 96, 107, 133, 134, 135, 176, 177, 185, 189, 193, 207, 281, 309
  margraves of Brandenburg-Ansbach 185, 206, 302, 318
  margraves of Brandenburg-Kulmbach 185, 263, 302, 304, 308, 318
  town 284, 286
  see also Albrecht I 'Achilles', margrave of Brandenburg-Ansbach; Albrecht II 'Alcibiades', margrave of Brandenburg-Kulmbach; Friedrich I, margrave of Brandenburg, burgrave of Nuremberg
Bremen
  archbishops 108, 178
  free city 207, 284, 285, 296
Bruges 52
Brunswick
  city 207, 284, 285
  dukes 108, 109, 178, 193, 206, 207, 263, 296, 313
Burgundy
  dukes 18, 48, 49, 51, 52, 53, 55, 127, 142, 148, 168, 187, 189, 190, 193
  region/territories 2, 5, 18, 26, 48, 239, 300
  see also Charles 'the Bold', duke of Burgundy; Habsburgs

cameral court 10, 20, 126, 128, 129, 143, 149, 151, 152, 155–67, 168, 170, 173, 174, 185, 187, 188, 189, 192, 196, 219, 220, 258, 319, 353
canon law *see* law
Carvajal, Juan 64, 68–69
Charlemagne 5, 23, 32, 121
Charles IV, king and emperor xv, 3, 15, 26, 28, 35, 37, 65, 66, 76, 82, 87, 92, 117, 269, 273, 276
Charles 'the Bold', duke of Burgundy 18, 26, 48
Charles V, king and emperor xvi, 3, 25, 54, 55–61, 127, 129, 130, 190, 193, 199, 207, 209, 210, 212, 213, 218, 264, 318, 325, 351
Chur 108, 177
cities *see* imperial cities
civil law *see* law
Cleves 109, 178
coinage 7, 59, 87, 123, 125, 220, 224, 250, 251, 329, 333, 335, 355
Cologne
  archbishops 7, 35, 36, 48, 55, 72, 82, 83, 84, 107, 121, 132, 281
  archdiocese and archiepiscopal principality 48, 83
  free city 85, 115, 129, 177, 187, 188
Common Penny 129, 169, 170
conciliarism *see* Council of Basel; Council of Constance
confessions, confessionalisation 3, 126, 130, 193, 215, 271, 318, 320
Constance
  bishops 108, 177
  free city 28, 44, 51, 54, 113, 207, 230, 273, 296

INDEX

Lake 115
see also Council of Constance
Council of Basel 3, 12, 18, 64, 68, 223, 225, 226, 231, 232, 233, 237, 241
Council of Constance 3, 12, 28, 44, 223, 225, 226, 229, 230, 233, 242, 248
councillors 62, 64, 68, 71, 102, 116, 125, 126, 128, 148, 155, 164, 165, 166, 190, 213, 214, 215, 218, 220, 221, 222, 226, 242, 245, 246, 262, 277, 279, 282, 284, 289, 291, 295, 296, 298, 305, 308, 316, 353
Counts Palatine 7, 25, 35, 43, 45, 46, 51, 55, 56, 59, 72, 83, 84, 85, 86, 92, 94, 96, 105, 107, 109, 112, 132, 134, 148, 187, 207, 208, 222, 281, 306, 308, 309, 334
see also Friedrich I 'the Victorious', Count Palatine
courtly assembly (*Hoftag*)
see courts
courts 39, 41, 63, 84, 87, 100, 101, 103, 104, 118, 119, 121, 124, 128, 144, 145, 149, 150, 159, 160, 165, 171, 196, 215, 224, 236, 237, 245, 246, 258, 266, 268, 278, 279, 289, 309, 325, 330, 333, 334, 336, 338, 339, 351, 352, 353, 355
arbitrational courts *see* arbitration
courtly assembly (*Hoftag*) 59, 63, 65, 82, 83, 84, 85, 88, 92, 93, 94, 95, 96, 102
feudal courts 322
imperial court (*curia, Hof*) 5, 27, 57, 60, 63, 77, 83, 85, 88, 95, 230, 246, 348, 353
princely courts 17, 112, 320

regional courts (*Landgerichte*) 237, 320
spiritual (ecclesiastical) courts 278, 290, 314, 338
urban courts (*Stadtgerichte*) 237, 343
Vehmic courts 66, 121–23, 290
see also aulic court; cameral court
Curia 58, 68, 226, 231, 245, 246, 253, 259, 263
customary law *see* law
Czechs *see* Bohemia

Danube, river 2
diets
arbitrational/judicial diets 62, 98–99, 150, 164, 165, 166, 207, 208, 274, 275, 278, 282, 283, 289, 301, 305, 309, 354, 357
Hanseatic diets 284–87
imperial assemblies (pre-1490s) 3, 4, 12, 15, 16, 24, 25, 28, 40, 41, 62, 63, 64, 65, 67, 68, 69, 70–71, 72–73, 74–75, 98, 107, 116, 125, 127, 132–38, 142–47, 225, 229
imperial diets (1490s onwards) 1, 3, 27, 51–54, 57, 59, 63, 125–126, 127, 129, 130, 131, 139–41, 148, 151, 155, 156, 167, 168, 169, 170, 171, 173–74, 176, 177, 182, 184, 186, 187, 188, 189, 190, 191, 192, 193, 194, 195, 198, 199–200, 202, 203, 204, 206, 207, 208, 209, 210, 212–13, 215, 220–23, 228, 262, 264, 304, 316, 318, 319, 325, 348, 352, 354, 357
regional assembly (*Landtag*) 323, 337, 354
see also arbitration; courtly assembly (*Hoftag*)

INDEX

economic history *see* coinage
ecumenical/ecclesiastical council *see* Council of Basel; Council of Constance
Eichstätt 37, 108, 176, 177, 185
electors *see* Bohemia; Brandenburg; Cologne; Counts Palatine; Mainz; Saxony; Trier
emperor *see* Romano-German kings and emperors
Empire *see* Holy Roman Empire
England 25, 287
Esslingen 114, 207, 273, 276, 302, 306–07
Eugenius IV, Pope 64, 223, 225, 233, 248

Ferdinand I, king xvi, 54, 127, 130, 193, 195, 199, 212, 213, 218, 222, 264, 318
feudal law *see* law
feudal tenure *see* law
fief *see* feudal law
Flanders, Flemings 52, 53, 55, 110, 148, 190, 193
France 2, 6, 18, 25, 51, 52, 53, 92, 126, 127, 139
Franconia 8, 11, 15, 26, 37, 84, 99, 104, 302, 304, 308, 318, 319
Frankfurt on the Main 34, 35, 79, 80, 95, 115, 116, 124, 127, 142, 143, 146, 169, 170, 177, 229, 282, 283
Frederick I 'Barbarossa', king and emperor 5
Frederick II, king and emperor 6
Frederick III, king and emperor xvi, 18, 26, 27, 33, 48–50, 52, 63, 64, 66, 67, 68, 74–75, 116, 126, 127, 128, 132, 142–47, 148, 241, 288, 308, 309, 353
free cities *see* imperial cities
Freiburg in the Breisgau 114, 115, 192, 348

Friedrich I, margrave of Brandenburg, burgrave of Nuremberg 43, 45, 47, 72, 281
Friedrich I 'the Victorious', Count Palatine 308
Friedrich III 'the Wise', duke of Saxony 55, 185
Fulda 112, 172, 177, 183

Gemeiner Pfennig see Common Penny
gender history *see* masculinity; women's roles
general council *see* Council of Basel; Council of Constance
Germany, Germans
 earlier medieval origins 5, 11–12, 23, 32–33
 geographic features 2, 8–9
 'German nation' 1, 12, 15, 31, 48, 49, 51, 52, 53, 54, 55, 56, 57, 58, 60, 62, 140, 144, 147, 148, 149, 151, 155, 171, 173, 174, 175, 188, 191, 194, 195, 207, 208, 212, 213, 215, 227, 228, 241, 244, 256, 262, 263, 264, 265, 266, 297, 298, 351
 Germania 11, 13, 68
 identity 12–13, 23
 language 11–12, 17–19, 23
 see also Holy Roman Empire; Romano-German kings and emperors
Golden Bull 7, 9, 24, 34, 35, 56, 59, 60, 65, 66, 76–97, 117, 226, 269, 311, 354
Goslar 177, 207, 284, 285
Grievances (*gravamina*) of the German nation 58, 202, 226, 227, 228, 262–67
Guelders 110, 148, 178

INDEX

Habsburgs 2, 6, 14, 26, 27, 55, 115, 127, 129, 130, 132, 139, 148, 190, 193, 222, 270
  see also Romano-German kings and emperors
Hainault 110, 148
Halberstadt
  bishops 108, 178, 303, 313, 314, 315
  city 115, 284, 285
Hamburg 115, 207, 284, 285, 287
Hanse, Hanseatic League 271, 284–87
Hedwig of Saxony, abbess of Quedlinburg 10, 303, 313–15
Helen of Troy 76
Henneberg, counts of 110, 183, 308, 323, 324, 331, 356
Henry I 'the Fowler, king 33
Henry VII, king and emperor xv
heresy, heretics 36, 72, 107, 233, 243, 264, 270, 281, 282
Hessen
  landgraves 105, 108, 176, 206, 210, 296
  region 104, 178
Hildesheim
  bishops 108, 178
  city 284, 286
Hofgericht see aulic court
Hohenstaufen *see* Staufer
Holy Roman Empire
  internal configuration 6–14, 268–72, 320–26
  laws *see* diets; peace-ordinances; public peace
  origins 1, 5–6, 23, 29–30, 31–33
  'reform' plans 3, 14, 17, 56, 66, 127, 132, 223–28, 229–30, 231–40, 241–49, 250–55, 303
  rulers *see* Romano-German kings and emperors

see also cameral court; diets; imperial circles; imperial governing council; 'imperial reform'; public peace
Hungary 2, 48, 51, 52, 53, 63, 72, 75, 127, 132, 133, 142, 148, 154, 167, 187, 190, 199, 229
Hus, Jan 229
Hussites 2, 25, 36, 63, 67, 72, 107, 233, 270, 281–82

imperial cameral court *see* cameral court
imperial circles 10, 126, 129, 176, 177–78, 187–89, 219, 220, 270, 355
imperial cities 7, 8, 15, 26, 37, 48, 88, 102, 103, 115, 177, 178, 182, 185, 186, 206, 211, 218, 221, 222, 225, 232, 234, 235, 239, 245, 265, 269, 273, 324, 355, 356
imperial court *see* courts
imperial diets *see* diets
imperial governing council 53, 56, 129, 173–86, 190, 191, 199, 355
'imperial reform' 14, 17, 66, 127, 223–28, 234
Italy 2, 5, 12, 13, 23, 36, 39, 53, 55, 63, 74, 79, 83, 93, 96, 127, 129, 139, 141, 225, 247, 281, 356

Jakob of Sierck, archbishop of Trier 69, 226, 241–49
Jerusalem 55, 190
Jews 87, 183, 259, 321, 324, 343–46
Johann Friedrich I, duke of Saxony 207, 211, 296, 299
Johann 'the Constant', duke of Saxony 206, 207, 296, 299

INDEX

Julius Caesar 32, 76
Julius II, Pope 139

Kammergericht see cameral court
king of the Romans *see* Romano-German kings and emperors
Kurfürsten see electors

land-ordinances 323, 325, 326, 336–40, 347, 352
land-peace 20, 26, 37, 67, 89, 98–106, 127, 152, 174, 269, 270, 273–76, 356, 357
   see also peace-ordinances; public peace
Landfrieden see land-peace; peace-ordinances; public peace
law
   canon/spiritual 24, 34, 36, 64, 159, 227, 250, 257, 258
   civil/Roman 128, 142, 159, 161, 162, 227, 236, 250, 251, 258, 325, 343, 353
   criminal 7, 99, 161, 171, 286, 289, 309, 317, 323, 325, 326, 351, 355
   customary 4, 6, 9, 19, 34, 36, 56, 77, 81, 84, 85, 87, 89, 96, 105, 117, 118, 122, 128, 135, 153, 157, 164, 165, 177, 181, 184, 187, 212, 215, 221, 227, 234, 251, 258, 266, 290, 293, 300, 321, 323, 325, 330, 334–35, 339, 351, 355
   feudal 7, 10, 18, 23, 29, 47, 57, 150, 235, 236, 322, 327–30, 354
   imperial/'constitutional' law 3, 65, 66–67, 128, 129, 130, 351
   ius commune 64, 216, 258, 343, 351

   see also Holy Roman Empire; land-ordinances; land-peace; peace-ordinances; public peace; recesses (*Abschiede*)
leagues *see* associations
Leipzig 316
Liège 36, 110, 178
lordship 2, 4, 7, 8, 14, 17, 42, 93, 105, 152, 153, 157, 165, 168, 181, 186, 187, 198, 211, 216, 217, 221, 243, 247, 268, 300, 321, 322, 323, 327, 331, 336, 337, 338, 339, 356
Lorraine 12, 108, 148, 178
Lübeck 85, 115, 177, 178, 207, 284, 285, 286, 287, 296
Lucerne 113, 271, 277, 278, 279, 280
Ludwig IV, king and emperor xv, 6, 352
Luther, Martin 3, 19, 126, 202, 227, 228, 256–61
   To the Christian Nobility of the German Nation 227, 256–61
Lutherans 126, 129, 130, 131, 215, 217, 264
Luxemburgs 2, 26
   see also Romano-German kings and emperors

Magdeburg
   archbishops 55, 108, 176, 178, 185, 314
   city 85, 207, 284, 285, 287, 296
Main, river 79
Mainz
   archbishops 7, 34, 35, 38, 42, 55, 72, 78, 79, 80, 82, 83, 84, 91, 92, 107, 128, 129, 132, 134, 136, 137, 180, 185, 189, 195, 207, 208, 222, 281, 282, 283

INDEX

archdiocese and archiepiscopal principality 34, 79, 92, 198, 222
free city 115, 325
see also Berthold of Henneberg, archbishop of Mainz
Martin V, Pope 233, 248
masculinity 9, 301–02
Matthias 'Corvinus', king of Hungary 53, 127, 132, 133
Maximilian I, king and emperor xvi, 25, 27, 33, 48, 51–54, 126, 127, 128, 129, 132, 139–41, 147, 148, 155, 168, 171, 173, 187, 190, 271, 316, 348, 356
Mecklenburg 109, 178, 185, 272, 293–95
Mehmed II, Sultan 74
Memmingen 114, 207, 273, 296
Metz
 bishops 108
 free city 65, 88, 92, 115
Milan 39, 51, 53, 93, 239
military history see warfare
money see coinage
Munich 44, 109, 135, 185, 308, 309
Münster 108, 176, 178

Nicholas V, Pope 74, 242, 248
nobles, nobility 2, 4, 5, 6, 7, 8, 9, 10, 12, 16, 17, 19, 23, 24, 27, 30, 53, 56, 57, 62, 67, 71, 77, 78, 120, 125, 155, 163, 173, 183, 190, 192, 199, 230, 235, 236, 240, 243, 260, 265, 268, 270, 289, 290, 295, 302, 303, 305, 309, 316, 322, 323, 331, 336, 338, 340, 349, 350, 354, 355, 356, 357
Nuremberg 37, 52, 59, 64, 65, 69, 70, 72–73, 77, 88, 95, 99, 105, 107, 115, 125, 127, 129, 132, 133, 137, 142, 144, 174, 177, 202, 207, 208, 209, 211, 266, 302, 308, 309, 310, 311, 312, 316, 318, 324, 343
burgraves see Friedrich I, margrave of Brandenburg, burgrave of Nuremberg

ordinances see land-ordinances; peace-ordinances
Otto I 'the Great', king and emperor 31, 33
Ottomans, Ottoman Empire 52, 64, 74, 126, 127, 130, 139, 142, 148, 258
see also Turks
Ottonians 5, 23

Palatinate of the Rhine see Counts Palatine
papacy 5, 6, 22, 29, 32, 36, 38, 43, 49, 53, 54, 58, 64, 65, 72, 74, 75, 139, 143, 144, 145, 223, 225, 227, 228, 229, 231, 232, 233, 241, 242, 243, 245, 247, 248, 249, 250, 251, 252, 253, 256, 257, 259, 260, 261, 263, 356
Papal Schism see schism
Peace of Augsburg see Augsburg
peace-ordinances 3, 10, 11, 15, 16, 20, 56, 60, 66, 67, 116–24, 125, 127, 128, 129, 142–47, 148–54, 168, 187–89, 190–92, 208, 209, 212–22, 224, 238, 269, 270, 290, 300, 316–17, 326, 352, 357
see also land-peace; public peace
peasants 8–9, 39, 102, 120, 197, 265, 286, 289, 301, 321, 327, 334–35, 348

INDEX

Peasants' War 9, 130, 193, 194, 197, 228, 262, 265, 271
'Perpetual Public Peace' *see* public peace
Pfalzgrafen see Counts Palatine
Piccolomini, Aeneas Silvius 64, 65, 68–69
Pius II, Pope *see* Piccolomini, Aeneas Silvius
Poland 2
Pomerania 55, 109, 178, 193
popes *see* papacy
prince-electors *see* electors
princes
    estate or group within the Empire 2–14, 263–65, 321–23, 356
    principalities 2, 4, 8, 14, 15, 19, 26, 31, 32, 85, 86, 87, 91, 93, 96, 105, 146, 153, 157, 165, 177, 178, 186, 187, 198, 216, 217, 229, 243, 247, 272, 293, 296, 297, 322, 326, 336, 337, 340, 352, 354
    spiritual and temporal 24, 77, 81, 82, 98, 116, 117, 120, 142, 143, 144, 145, 148, 149, 155, 163, 171, 173, 175, 176, 190, 191, 222, 282
    see also Baden; Bavaria; Bohemia; Brandenburg; Burgundy; Cologne; Counts Palatine; Hessen; Mainz; Mecklenburg; Pomerania; Saxony; Trier; Württemberg
Protestants, Protestantism *see* confessions, confessionalisation; Lutherans; Reformation
Protestation at Speyer 130, 199–206
public peace 20, 56, 66, 126–30, 148–54, 155, 166, 171, 174, 187, 188, 190–92, 193, 195, 196, 205, 212–22, 270, 288, 290, 303, 316, 317, 326, 352, 355, 356, 357
    see also land-peace; peace-ordinances

queens and empresses 9, 93, 94

Rapperswil 11
recesses (*Abschiede*) 125, 129, 130, 176, 177, 182, 184, 186, 187, 193, 194, 198, 199, 200, 202, 203, 204, 205, 206, 207, 209, 210, 212, 218, 221, 222, 263, 302, 325, 348, 357
Reformation
    Catholic 126
    ecclesiastical 17, 19, 223–28, 229–30, 231–33, 256, 259, 262–67
    judicial 66, 88, 121, 324, 343–46
    Protestant 3, 11, 14, 16, 126, 130, 224, 320
    see also confessions, confessionalisation; 'imperial reform'; Lutherans; Royal Reformation
Reformation of Emperor Sigismund (*Reformatio Sigismundi*) 18, 225–27, 231–40
Regensburg
    bishops 105, 108, 177
    free city 64, 74, 75, 105, 115, 127, 131, 142, 144, 209, 221
Reich see Holy Roman Empire
Reichshofrat see aulic council
Reichskammergericht see cameral court
Reichskreise see imperial circles
Reichsreform see 'imperial reform'
Reichsregiment see imperial governing council
Reichstag see diets

INDEX

Rhine Palatinate *see* Counts Palatine
Rhine, river 2, 7, 35, 40, 42, 48, 49, 55, 72, 83, 84, 86, 96, 104, 105, 112, 189, 222, 227, 271, 278, 281, 305, 306, 308, 309, 334
Rhineland 13, 15, 26
Richental, Ulrich 28, 44–47
Roman law *see* law
Romano-German kings and emperors
  constitutional role 5–7, 22–28, 29–30
  election 6–7, 24, 34–36, 76–97, 55–61
  see also electors
  list xv–xvi
  origins and title 5–6
  summonses to imperial assemblies 70–71, 74–75, 139–40
  see also Albert II, king; Charles IV, king and emperor; Charles V, king and emperor; Ferdinand I, king; Frederick III, king and emperor; Ludwig IV, king and emperor; Maximilian I, king and emperor; Rudolf I, king; Rupert, king; Sigismund, king and emperor; Wenceslas, king
Rome 5, 6, 32, 38, 40, 41, 51, 55, 70, 145, 222, 223, 246, 248, 249, 259, 260, 265, 273, 276
Rottweil 114, 128, 273, 274, 276, 353
Royal Reformation 66, 116–24, 142, 143, 153, 291, 311
Rudolf I, king xv, 6
Rupert, king xv, 25, 43

Sachsenspiegel see Saxon Mirror
Salians 5, 223
Salzburg 177, 222, 308
Savoy 108, 239
Saxon Mirror 17, 23, 85

Saxony
  dukes 7, 35, 44, 46, 47, 55, 56, 59, 72, 83, 84, 85, 86, 92, 93, 94, 95, 96, 107, 109, 132, 135, 176, 178, 185, 189, 206, 207, 209, 210, 211, 281, 296, 299, 303, 313, 314, 315, 323, 336–40
  electoral principality 15, 303, 323
  law 85
  region 5, 11, 13, 23, 296
  see also Friedrich III 'the Wise', duke of Saxony; Johann Friedrich I, duke of Saxony; Johann 'the Constant', duke of Saxony
Schedel, Hartmann 23, 31
  Nuremberg (World) Chronicle 23, 31–33
schism 3, 25, 38, 64, 70, 220, 223, 229, 248, 282
Schmalkalden 324, 331
Schmalkaldic League 2, 130, 272, 296–99, 318
Schwabenspiegel see Swabian Mirror
Sigismund, king and emperor xv, 26, 28, 44–47, 63, 66, 72, 107, 115, 121, 122, 128, 225, 226, 229–30, 231, 233, 234, 237, 239, 242, 248, 270
Spain 32, 55, 61, 139, 190, 193, 259
Speyer
  bishops 108, 177
  free city 115, 130, 193, 195, 199, 202, 204, 205, 206, 228, 262, 296
Staufer 5, 6, 7, 11, 223
Strasbourg
  bishops 108, 177
  free city 63, 70, 72, 114, 125, 132, 177, 185, 194, 207, 296, 301, 305, 324, 341–42
Stuttgart 302, 306, 307

373

INDEX

Swabia 11, 13, 15, 37, 67, 84, 103, 104, 177, 207, 269, 273–76, 302, 306
Swabian League 197, 270, 271, 288–92, 303, 306, 308
Swabian Mirror 22, 23, 29–30, 235, 237, 251, 258, 322, 327–30
Switzerland, Swiss 2, 5, 17, 48, 53, 113, 271, 277–80

Teutonic Knights/Order 172, 182, 183, 308
Thuringia 13, 55, 104, 178, 296, 313, 323, 336–40
towns *see* imperial cities
Trier
   archbishops 7, 35, 55, 69, 72, 82, 83, 84, 91, 92, 93, 107, 132, 226, 241, 281
   archdiocese 42
   city 115, 129, 187, 188, 316
   see also Jakob of Sierck, archbishop of Trier
Tübingen 353
Turks 53, 64, 74, 126, 143, 144, 145, 146, 173, 180, 207, 208, 209, 253, 258
   see also Ottomans, Ottoman Empire
Tyrol 55, 115, 116, 148, 189, 190, 193

Ulm 85, 114, 177, 207, 212, 273, 276, 296, 306, 316
universities 8, 12, 19, 24, 155, 227, 233, 256, 257, 354
'Upper Rhine Revolutionary' 227
urban society *see* imperial cities

Vehmic courts *see* courts

Vemegerichte see courts
Venice 139, 259
Vienna 14, 15, 69, 77, 130, 241, 248

warfare 10, 213, 300–04, 308–12
   Burgundian Wars *see* Burgundy
   Hussite Wars *see* Hussites
   Italian Wars *see* Italy
   Schmalkaldic War *see* Schmalkaldic League
Wenceslas, king xv, 25, 38–43, 63, 67, 70–71, 98, 99, 105, 106, 270
Wesel 73
Westphalian courts *see* courts
Wiener Neustadt 75, 132, 133
Wittelsbachs 53, 109, 270, 326
Wittenberg 44, 256
women's roles 4, 9–10, 39, 120, 181, 182, 253, 302–03, 313, 321, 322, 324–25, 327, 341–42, 347
   see also queens and empresses
Worms
   bishops 176, 177
   free city 108, 115, 127, 129, 130, 139, 148, 154, 155, 167, 168, 170, 172, 174, 190, 191, 195, 200, 208, 220, 228, 262, 263, 266
Württemberg 105, 110, 135, 177, 302, 306–07, 322, 332
Würzburg
   bishops 37, 105, 108, 176, 177, 185, 308, 318
   city 99

Zurich 113, 271, 277, 278, 279
Zwingli, Ulrich 126

EU authorised representative for GPSR:
Easy Access System Europe, Mustamäe tee 50,
10621 Tallinn, Estonia
gpsr.requests@easproject.com

www.ingramcontent.com/pod-product-compliance
Lightning Source LLC
Chambersburg PA
CBHW050159240426
43671CB00013B/2176